With an impressive combination of sound scholarship and cogent interpretation, the author has woven a rich and revealing tapestry of Western Europe in the Central Middle Ages.

The primary focus is Western Christendom—economic life, society, government, and religion. Byzantium, Moorish Spain and North Africa, Scandinavia, and Russia are treated as frontiers and discussed to the extent that they affect the mainstream of Western Europe.

The enormous importance of the Church in the middle ages is acknowledged with extensive coverage of monasticism, Papal reform, the Papal conflict, new monastic orders, popular religion, and the crusades.

Professor Brooke's authoritative work makes an invaluable supplementary text for upper-level courses dealing with medieval history.

A bibliographical note following each chapter lists important secondary works as well as medieval sources.

A GENERAL HISTORY OF EUROPE

EDITED BY DENYS HAY

EUROPE IN THE
CENTRAL MIDDLE AGES
962-1154

CHRISTOPHER BROOKE

HOLT, RINEHART AND WINSTON, INC.
NEW YORK

Published throughout the world, except the United States
by Longmans, Green and Co. Ltd

940.1
B79E

TO MY MOTHER

IN MEMORY OF MY FATHER

Contents

in the early eleventh century, p. 253 – inspiration and programme of the reformers, p. 253 – the work of Leo IX, p. 257
– his councils, p. 258 – Peter Damian, p. 260 – Frederick of
Lorraine, Cardinal Humbert, p. 260 – papal elections and the
decree of 1059, p. 262 – the cardinals, p. 263 – Hildebrand
(Gregory VII), p. 265.

CONTENTS

Maps

Genealogical Charts

Acknowledgements

We are grateful to the following for permission to include copyright material:

Burns & Oates Ltd and Henry Regnery Company for extracts from *The Letters of St Bernard of Clairvaux* translated by B. S. James, Copyright 1953, Henry Regnery Company, Chicago; Professor Dom David Knowles and Cambridge University Press for extracts from *The Monastic Order in England* and *The Historian and Character* by Dom David Knowles; Chapman & Hall Ltd and the Executor of the late C. Scott-Moncrieff for extracts from his translation of *The Song of Roland*; Chatto & Windus Ltd for extracts from *The Rule of St Benedict* translated by F. A. Gasquet; Columbia University Press for extracts from *The Letters of Gerbert* translated by H. P. Lattin, in the Columbia Records of Civilisation series, 1961; Thomas Nelson & Sons Ltd for an extract from *Walter Daniel's Life of Ailred of Rievaulx* edited and translated by Sir Maurice Powicke in Nelson's Medieval Texts, 1950; Miss R. Hill for extracts from the *Gesta Francorum* in the same series, 1962; Dr Joan Evans and Oxford University Press for an extract from *Monastic Life at Cluny* by Joan Evans, and Routledge and Kegan Paul Ltd for extracts from *The Alexiad* translated by E. A. Dawes, *Guibert de Nogent's Autobiography* translated by C. C. Swinton Bland and *The Works of Liudprand of Cremona* translated by F. A. Wright.

Preface

I first made the acquaintance of the subject of this book when, at the age of ten, I helped my father with the proofs and index of his *History of Europe, 911–1198*. Over the years which followed I learned much from him, but not enough to have written another book like his. Those who wish to read a full and coherent narrative of these centuries will find it in his book. Although I have tried to sketch the political history of my period, the main design of this book is to sketch the life of the age under every aspect which can now be viewed. I have tried to make it wide-ranging, but not complete. There is no more false idea about the study of history than that a period may be grasped from a single book. To those who wish to make these centuries their own, I commend first of all the sources listed in chapter II, next the books which have especially guided me, those by my father, Professor Knowles and Professor Southern, and finally all the good books which I have listed and many more which I have by ignorance or oversight or shortage of space omitted.

The first and greatest of my debts has already been indicated; and there are many more. Since I began to write the book I have had invaluable help from Professor Denys Hay, Dr R. A. Markus and my wife, who read all of it in manuscript and the two former in proof as well; and I am also very grateful to Professor P. T. Bauer and Mr Philip Grierson, who read parts of it, to Dom Aelred Watkin, Headmaster of Downside School, to Dr G. M. Richards and to other friends and colleagues for help on many particular points, and to the publishers. All these have helped to eradicate many errors and infelicities, as have generations of students whose sceptical eyes or well-timed enquiries have revealed to me that I was expounding nonsense to them.

Since this book was set up in proof, the books listed on p. 35 have been supplemented by the new edition of *Cambridge Medieval History*, vol. IV (ed. J. M. Hussey, 2 parts); those on p. 209 by R. W.

Southern's British Academy Lecture 'The place of Henry I in English history', and those on p. 294 by the section on Cistercian origins in D. Knowles, *Great Historical Enterprises and Problems in Monastic History* (London, 1963).

LIVERPOOL, 1963   CHRISTOPHER BROOKE

I

Introduction

Between the tenth and the twelfth centuries great changes took place in western Europe. Everywhere population grew; new lands were brought under cultivation, new techniques of agriculture devised to save the increasing numbers from starvation. Some of the peasantry looked out for new lands away from their old villages; many of the younger sons of knightly and baronial families had to find land hundreds of miles from their homes. Economic life revived in a variety of ways: towns sprang up, and markets; industry grew—a small affair by modern standards, but gargantuan by those of the early Middle Ages; merchants in ever greater numbers plied the Mediterranean and the trade routes of northern Europe. Western Europe expanded its frontiers, and the initiative in warfare, in trade and in the things of the mind, passed from Islam and Byzantium to western Christendom. A popular religious revival flowed through many different channels, in reforms and massacres, in orthodoxy and heresy, in the quest for the earthly Jeru- salem by crusades and pilgrimages, and the quest of the heavenly Jerusalem in monasteries and hermitages nearer home. The papacy was transformed and the papal monarchy was established as the head- quarters of a wide and deep movement for reform. Closely allied with the papal reform was the intellectual revival of the eleventh and twelfth centuries, and all the many scholarly, literary, and artistic movements comprised under the label 'the twelfth-century renaissance'.

The changes were dramatic; and it is only too easy for the historian, now that he is gradually becoming aware of their extent, to over- dramatize them. To those who lived through them, little of this was known. They were aware of some dramatic events—an eclipse, a flood, or a crusade; but most of the movements of the time only impinged on them in fragments. The few men who had the feeling of living through a revolution attributed it to the advent of Anti-Christ,[1] and presumed

[1] Not, however, particularly associated with the year 1000, as the common legend has it (but see H. J. Focillon, *L'an mil*, Paris, 1952).

that they were witnessing, not the end of the 'Dark Ages', as the modern historian assumes, but the first signs of the end of the world. If we had the chance to explain our attitude—our interest, even our excitement—at this vision of new ideas and new forces at work, our conception of a 'renaissance' as both a rebirth and a new birth, even the most alert of contemporaries would have been horrified. To them the word 'new' was synonymous with the word 'bad'; 'novelty' was a term of abuse. It is true that they were not merely reactionary or wholly conservative in their outlook. But progress (in their view) was only possible in a very limited degree, and only possible at all if one based oneself securely on the models of the past. The most radical proposals were put forward as attempts to enforce existing law, to live up to well-known ideals, to re-establish ancient customs. Perhaps they were a little aware of what they were doing; but they were not at all aware that they were living through an era of change such as Europe had not seen since the fall of the Roman Empire.

The historian of this period is thus faced with a dilemma and a paradox. Of the larger movements he knows far more than contemporaries knew; of the details of daily life, of the ordinary ideas and assumptions of men—even, for instance, of the religious beliefs of the enormous majority of western Europeans—he knows extremely little. He is thus compelled to portray the world in very different colours from those in which it appeared to contemporaries; and it would be disingenuous of him not to confess as much. The areas of our ignorance are almost infinitely great. To understand this, it is peculiarly necessary for us to start by considering, however briefly, the sources of our knowledge. We also have to consider with great care what is included in the Europe of this period; for its boundaries and its local varieties, social, economic, cultural and political, profoundly affected its history. From this we pass on to an analysis of its economic, social and constitutional organization, which are essential to an understanding of its history as story, and of the ecclesiastical reform, the investiture contests, and the crusades, which must fill a substantial part of any book on this period.[1]

Our period, then, was one of rapid change. But to the men who lived through it, change came as a thief in the night. They saw too little of it; we are in danger perhaps of seeing too much.

---

[1] Readers with no previous knowledge of the events of these centuries may find it easier to read some of the narrative chapters before they embark on Chapters IV to VI.

II

Sources

I have always thought that history was more profitably and pleasantly studied from sources than from secondary works, and that a slight acquaintance with contemporary writers makes a period more intelligible and gives us a fuller insight into it than hours of patient plodding through the best modern authorities. But we cannot study history by reading sources alone. We need experts to comment on them and often to translate them for us; and there is much material that is not in a readable form and much more which does not reveal its message until a great deal of criticism and analysis has taken place. It is very often true, none the less, that modern historians have tried to put themselves between us and the sources in an unwarrantable way; to convince us that they know more than the sources can tell us, or that what they can tell us is in some way more significant than what we can learn from contemporaries.

BIBLIOGRAPHY. C. P. Farrar and A. P. Evans, *Bibliography of English translations from medieval sources* (Columbia Records of Civilization, New York, 1946), gives a full catalogue of what is available in translation (to 1946). The standard bibliographies of medieval sources are: A. Potthast, *Bibliotheca historica medii aevi* (2nd edn., 1896; in process of being replaced by the new *Repertorium fontium historiae medii aevi*, Rome, 1962–   ); U. Chevalier, *Répertoire des sources historiques du moyen âge* (3 vols., Montbélard, 1894–1907); ENGLAND: C. Gross, *The sources and literature of English history from the earliest times to about 1485* (2nd edn., London, 1915: a new edition is in preparation); FRANCE: A. Molinier, *Les sources de l'histoire de la France des origines aux guerres d'Italie*, vol. II (Paris, 1902); GERMANY: W. Wattenbach and R. Holtzmann, *Deutsche Geschichtsquellen im Mittelalter*, II, Heft 1–4 (900–1125) (1938–43).

A large selection from the sources of English history, which gives a cross-section of the sort of material available for this period, is contained in *English Historical Documents*, ed. D. C. Douglas: vol. I, *c.* 500–1042, ed. D. Whitelock (London, 1955); vol. II, 1042–1189, ed. D. C. Douglas and G. W. Greenaway (London, 1953). Of the sources referred to specifically below, the following translations are available: Liudprand of Cremona, *Works*, trans. F. A. Wright

3

In modern history the vast quantity of the surviving material makes it necessary for most of us to be highly selective in our reading of the sources, and to rely on the selections which scholars have made for us. For much of the Middle Ages this is not so. There is nothing to prevent a student of the period from reading a high proportion of the literary

(London, 1930); Richer, *Histoire de France*, ed. and French trans. R. Latouche (2 vols., Paris, 1930–7); Gerbert, *Letters*, trans. H. P. Lattin (Columbia Records, 1961); Orderic Vitalis, *Ecclesiastical History*, trans. F. Forester (London, 1853–6: the translation below is my own; a new ed. and trans. by Mrs Marjorie Chibnall is in preparation); William of Malmesbury, *History of the kings . . .*, trans. J. A. Giles (London, 1847); *Historia novella*, ed. and trans. K. Potter (Nelson's Medieval Texts, 1955); *Life of St Wulfstan*, trans. J. H. F. Peile (Oxford, 1934) (new versions of the *History of the kings* and of the *Gesta Pontificum* are in preparation); Otto of Freising, *The two cities*, trans. A. P. Evans and P. Knapp (Columbia Records, 1928); John of Salisbury, *Historia Pontificalis*, ed. and trans. M. Chibnall (Nelson's Medieval Texts, 1956) and other works, especially *Metalogicon*, trans. D. D. McGarry (Berkeley and Los Angeles, 1955), Michael Psellus, *Chronographia*, trans. E. R. A. Sewter (London, 1953); Anna Comnena, *Alexiad*, trans. E. A. S. Dawes (London, 1928); *Anglo-Saxon Chronicle*, trans. G. N. Garmonsway (rev. ed., Everyman's Library, 1960) *or* D. Whitelock *et al.* (London, 1961); the *Gesta Francorum*, ed. and trans. R. Hill (Nelson's Medieval Texts, 1962); Adam of Bremen, *History of the Archbishops of Hamburg–Bremen*, trans. F. J. Tschan (Columbia Records, 1959); Eadmer, *Vita Anselmi*, ed. and trans. R. W. Southern (Nelson's Medieval Texts, 1963); Abelard and Heloise, *Letters*, trans. C. K. Scott-Moncrieff (London, 1925: includes *Hist. Calamitatum*); Guibert, abbot of Nogent-sous-Coucy, *Autobiography*, trans. C. C. Swinton Bland (London, 1925); H. E. Butler, *The Autobiography of Giraldus Cambrensis* (London, 1937); Suger's account of his work at Saint-Denis is ed. and trans. E. Panofsky, *Abbot Suger on the abbey church of Saint-Denis* (Princeton, 1946: slightly abridged); Suger, *Vie de Louis VI le Gros*, ed. and French trans. H. Waquet (Paris, 1929); Gregory VII, *A selection of the letters . . .*, trans. E. Emerton (Columbia Records, 1932); Henry IV's letters, with Wipo's Life of Conrad II and the anonymous Life of Henry IV, trans. T. E. Mommsen and K. F. Morrison, *Imperial Lives and Letters of the eleventh century* (Columbia Records, 1962); St Bernard of Clairvaux, *Letters*, trans. B. S. James (London, 1953); *Anglo-Saxon Writs*, ed. and trans. F. Harmer (Manchester, 1952); most of Domesday Book is translated, shire by shire, in the relevant sections of the *Victoria County Histories*; Geoffrey of Monmouth, *History of the Kings of Britain*, is in *Six Old English Chronicles*, trans. J. A. Giles (London, 1848), also trans. S. Evans (Everyman's Library, 1904); the *Song of Roland* has been frequently translated, e.g. by C. K. Scott-Moncrieff (London, 1919).

Lampert of Hersfeld, *Annales* (ed. O. Holder-Egger, Hanover and Leipzig, 1894) has not been translated into English. For the Bayeux Tapestry, see the Phaidon Press edition, with commentary by Sir Frank Stenton and others (1957). On art and architecture, see Chapter XVI; on coins, Chapter IV.

evidence for a topic which particularly interests him. In this way the period covered by this book is particularly well served. The sources are not only comparatively few; many of them are also exceedingly readable. It was the golden age of the narrative source. Its history can only to a very limited extent be reconstructed from documents; to a great extent the historian relies on chronicles and histories meant to be read as literature. Their purpose was to entertain and to edify: almost all of them have a preface in which they lay stress on the value of learning from the experience of the past, and of seeing God's purposes at work. Their form was in part traditional when the period opened; but the idea of writing literary history received a great fillip from the intellectual revival of the eleventh and twelfth centuries. This was a period when men were becoming increasingly interested in expressing their thoughts on paper, and in revealing their learning, their literary skill, and their emotions and feelings. The age of medieval humanism passed fairly soon: by the thirteenth century Latin had become desiccated once again as a vehicle for human expression. But in the interval a wide variety of books had been written, including historical works, biographies, auto-biographies and letters, which provide direct evidence to the historian in a highly readable form.

Chronicle and history

1. *Liudprand to Lampert.* By contrast, the late tenth century had been a bad period for the writing of history. The few men in that century who took the trouble to note the events of their own times, or to compile a record of the past, did so in one of three ways. They might use an Easter Table. These tables were in the first place tables of the elaborate arithmetic connected with the computation of the date of Easter, laid out for each year of grace. The year of grace, the year A.D., is so essential a part of our mental equipment that it is difficult for us to imagine a world in which it was unknown. Yet even in the tenth century its general acceptance as the method of computing years was in some countries comparatively recent, in others not yet complete; and everywhere it still had older rivals. The use of the year of grace had been perfected and popularized by the Venerable Bede in the eighth century, and he had also used his mathematical skill in popularizing the technique for determining the date of Easter. The result of both these endeavours was summarized in the Easter Tables, which were kept in numerous monasteries in later centuries. Such a table established the dates of the feast and related the year of grace to other cycles, and so it performed

one of the functions of the modern diary; and, as in a diary, space could be found in it to note important events. Thus in a manuscript still preserved in the Swiss abbey of Einsiedeln, a monk of the same abbey noted on an Easter Table in the tenth century, among other things, where Otto the Great spent Christmas each year between 963 and 966. In another manuscript written at Einsiedeln about the same time the computistic material has been simplified, and space left for a note on the events of the year—space which allowed, with a good deal of crowding, for up to thirty words for a single year, and occasionally a little more.[1]

These brief, jejune annals, which tell sometimes in almost telegraphic style of the deaths of kings, of the accessions of bishops, of earthquakes and eclipses, were glosses on Easter Tables. They were also decadent descendants of the noble chronicle of St Jerome, the basis of a great deal of medieval historical writing, which had been written before the year of grace was invented, but had managed to lay out a great deal of information year by year—the years being distinguished by the Greek Olympiads (the four-year cycle of the Olympic games), the Roman consuls, the regnal years of kings, and other criteria. From Jerome and his immediate successors the men of the early Middle Ages inherited the idea of arranging history as a series of chronological events, year by year; and chronicles considerably more substantial than the annals of Einsiedeln were written throughout our period; they were rather rare in the mid tenth century, very common in the twelfth.

The Easter Table had been made possible by the work of the Venerable Bede; and, if he may therefore be called the stepfather of the most jejune form of historical literature of the tenth century, he was certainly the father of history in the best sense in the period of this book. The idea of history as the reconstruction of the past in literary form, not confined by the boundary of annals, was never quite forgotten: Bede himself owed much to the classical and post-classical historians whose works he knew; and historians of the eleventh and twelfth centuries were also inspired by Bede's models and by Bede himself. Literary history was very rarely attempted in the tenth century: to this the outstanding exception was Liudprand of Cremona, who seems to have owed nothing directly to Bede, but much to the classical historians and to Roman literature in general. Liudprand reminds us that the tradition of cultivated Latin was far from dead in tenth-century Italy, and gives us

[1] See R. L. Poole, *Chronicles and Annals* (Oxford, 1926), Chapter I; facing pp. 5 and 6 are facsimiles of the Einsiedeln manuscripts.

a hint of one of the sources to which we may look for the origin of the intellectual revival of a century later.

Liudprand, bishop of Cremona in north Italy, lived from *c.* 920 to 972. He was brought up in the court of one of the Lombard princelings, fell foul of his successor, and so entered the service of the Emperor Otto the Great. He was a descendant of the Lombard invaders, and so in origin a German; but he was also a thoroughly well educated Christian bishop, and he wrote some of the best Latin of the Dark Ages; he was lively and sophisticated as a writer, yet shows no sign of profound reflection on any topic save his own misfortunes. He wrote three books: the *Antapodosis* ('Tit-for-tat'), an account of recent history leading up to the victories of Otto the Great; a short chronicle of Otto's visit to Italy in 962–3; and a letter to Otto describing Liudprand's second visit to Constantinople in 968–9. The *Antapodosis* is a shapely book, carefully planned, yet full of entertainment. Everything Liudprand wrote was informed with the observant eye of a comic artist, but with a violence of prejudice and fancy which he would and could do nothing to control. He is our chief, indeed almost our only evidence for large stretches of tenth-century history, in particular for the Italian affairs of Otto the Great and the internal history of the papacy. Some historians have lamented that so important a source should contain so much that is trivial, should be so impervious to dates and so free with lively and fanciful opinions. It is true that some of his prejudices are unattractive: both the papacy and the Italian ladies of the period have suffered from his attitude to women. But this apart, Liudprand was a shrewd and lively witness. If our knowledge of Victorian England was reduced to a single writer, we could do worse than be left with Dickens.[1]

Perhaps his greatest interest, however, lies in his accounts of his visits to Constantinople. He went in 949 as an envoy of a Lombard prince, and again in 968–9 on a mission for Otto the Great. On the first visit he was well received, and was enchanted by the Byzantine capital and the Byzantine court. On the second visit he was old and ill, and badly treated, and he could find nothing good to say of Byzantium. Thus the two descriptions complement one another, and show us two sides of the great city: on the one hand the splendour and magnificence of the court, the elaborate ceremonial, the fantastic mechanical devices of the imperial audience chambers, the survival of Roman traditions of banqueting on couches; on the other the foreigner's difficulty in

---

[1] The analogy, of course, must not be pressed: e.g. each of Dickens's major novels is many times the length of Liudprand's collected works.

accommodating himself to a new country, with draughty houses, appalling food, and undrinkable wine, the squalor of a large city, the less elegant aspect of the court ceremonial—bad discipline, ill-fitting costumes. His disgust on the second visit was summed up in his account of the Emperor Nicephorus Phocas:

> He is a monstrosity of a man, a dwarf, fat-headed and with tiny mole's eyes; disfigured by a short, broad, thick beard half going grey; disgraced by a neck scarcely an inch long; pig-like by reason of the big close bristles on his head; in colour an Ethiopian, and as the poet [Juvenal] says: 'You would not like to meet him in the dark.' . . . The king of the Greeks has long hair and wears a tunic with long sleeves and a bonnet; he is lying, crafty, merciless, foxy, proud, falsely humble, miserly and greedy; he eats garlic, onions and leeks, and he drinks bath water. The king of the Franks [Otto], on the other hand, is beautifully shorn, and wears a garment quite different from a woman's dress and a hat; he is truthful, guileless, merciful when right, severe when necessary, always truly humble, never miserly; he does not live on garlic, onions and leeks. . . .[1]

Thus the blinding effect of Liudprand's eccentric temperament has revealed to us both the grandeur and something of the squalor of Byzantine life: we see an ancient and glorious civilization rejoicing in the maintenance of the Roman heritage, and a court where delight in mechanical contrivances blends with elaborate ritual; we see also an ordinary city where there is poverty and wretchedness as well as wealth, and the ordinary variety of human life, whereby some men are well-dressed, some are threadbare, and the foreigner is alternately delighted by the novelty of the scene and repelled by the strange food which turns his stomach. But we also see why East and West were drifting apart in this age, and when Liudprand and Nicephorus became really heated, their diplomatic exchanges revealed the roots of this growing cleavage: the survival of the old antagonism of Roman and barbarian. 'You are not Romans but Lombards' was the emperor's taunt.

> He even then was anxious to say more and waved his hand to secure my silence, but I was worked up and cried: 'History tells us that Romulus, from whom the Romans get their name, was a fratricide born in adultery. He made a place of refuge for himself and received into it insolvent debtors, runaway slaves, murderers and men who

[1] Trans. F. A. Wright, pp. 236, 259. 'Bath water' may mean 'mineral water'.

deserved death for their crimes. This was the sort of crowd whom he enrolled as citizens and gave them the name of Romans. From this nobility are descended those men whom you style "rulers of the world". But we Lombards, Saxons, Franks, Lotharingians, Bavarians, Swabians and Burgundians so despise these fellows that when we are angry with an enemy we can find nothing more insulting to say than —"You Roman!" For us in the word Roman is comprehended every form of lowness, timidity, avarice, luxury, falsehood and vice.'[1]

The society of the West was no longer tribal. Barbarism (in a social rather than a literary sense) was definitely on the way out, although the great revolution in manners of the eleventh and twelfth centuries was still to come. The man who spoke the words quoted above was a thoroughly cultivated Italian bishop, an expert Latinist, a master of Roman literature. But scratch the surface, and one may still find the heroic German underneath; this roll call of the tribes reminds us of some earlier Germanic lays; this magnificent outburst shows that for all his culture, Liudprand was something of a barbarian at heart—the divergence between East and West was profound.

In the generation following Liudprand's one can only find a writer of comparable verve and skill in the famous scholar Gerbert (Pope Sylvester II), whose letters were the outstanding literary achievement of the late tenth century, and whose influence as a teacher is described in precise detail in the chronicle of Richer. He tells us how Gerbert prepared his pupils in dialectic and rhetoric, and put them in the hands of a sophist to sharpen their powers of argument; he goes to some length to tell us of his instruction in arithmetic, geometry and astronomy. 'He was ardent in his studies, and the number of his pupils grew from day to day. The great teacher's name was carried not only over Gaul but through the peoples of Germany, across the Alps into Italy to the Adriatic.'[2]

Gerbert was one of the founders of the revival of learning, which only became a widespread revival in the middle of the eleventh century. At that date one may find scholars in many parts of Europe, especially in the north of France, in Germany and Italy, reflecting the new fashions:

[1] *Ibid.*, pp. 242–3. The word Roman had a variety of meanings: as applied to the old Roman empire, which Liudprand's master Otto I was engaged in reviving, even Liudprand would have accepted it as an honourable term; it was as applied to the folk of Rome itself in his own day, or (as here) to the contemporary Greeks, that it could be regarded as a term of abuse.

[2] Richer, vol. I, pp. 54 ff., esp. pp. 64–5.

interest in literature, especially classical literature, in rhetoric and logic; interest, too, in human affairs, and notably in history. The period from about 1050 until about 1150 was the golden age of medieval historical writing. Brief, factual annals were still composed, and every variety of chronicle; but there was a greater concentration of effort in writing history in a broader sense than at any other time in the Middle Ages.

What did they mean by history? They meant, first of all, the story of God's work among mankind. The larger histories were either histories of the world, starting with the Creation; or histories of the Church, starting with the Incarnation. Divine interventions, to help the good, to deter the wicked, were of special concern; and men were held up to praise or blame, as they furthered God's work and walked in his ways, or did evil in the sight of the Lord and provoked God's anger by their vanities. So far, the Books of Kings were the chief inspiration and model of medieval historians; and it is notable that their morality was that of the historical books of the Old Testament. The good are commonly rewarded, the wicked punished; disaster reveals hidden sin. But there is much more to the historians of this period than that. Most of them were more concerned with the present than the past: wrote at much greater length about events of their own lifetime than about those of earlier ages. Partly this was because they lacked materials to write the sort of history they enjoyed about the past, and they lacked, too, historical imagination. But the events of their own world filled them with wonder and curiosity. Most of them were monks, tied to their cloister, eagerly enquiring of visitors what they could learn of the world, sometimes travelling and able to learn for themselves, constantly passing information to fellow-workers in other houses. They knew some of their medieval predecessors; they sometimes attached their own chronicles to them as appendixes, to save themselves having to write ancient history as well as modern. But their models, for the most part, lay in the past. They wrote to entertain; they aimed to be as vivid as a historical novel. Sallust was one of their chief models; like him they filled their pages with imaginary speeches, meant either to provide suitable comment on events, or to represent what the characters ought to have said or might have said—or even, occasionally, the sort of thing they actually had said. If we read these books without preconception, we shall hardly believe that they are sober history; they are too good, very often, as novels. Yet the speeches and other trappings can deceive us. The anonymous chronicler of the First Crusade has a fantastic notion of the sort of thing a Moslem Emir ought to say, and has no scruple in providing us with his intimate conversations. The German Lampert of Hersfeld, living (to his sorrow) in a house always faithful to the Emperor Henry IV, pretended to know the inmost secrets of the Saxon rebels. Yet the anonymous chronicler was usually severely factual; and Lampert, though never quite that, has survived the storms which raged over his reputation a hundred years ago, and is accepted today as basically truthful.

Lampert is an excellent illustration of what the new learning could produce so early as the mid eleventh century, and of the humanism of Germany in that period. He became a monk at Hersfeld in 1058, when he was already a deacon and, no doubt, a scholar; and it is noticeable that his chief work, his *Annales*, was as brief and perfunctory as it could be down to the 1050s. From then on it grows in length and elaboration, until it reaches the climax of Henry IV's meeting with Gregory VII at Canossa (see pp. 279–83), and the election of the anti-king Rudolf. Then Lampert laid down his pen; and although he lived on to be abbot of Hasungen for some years after 1081,[1] he tells us no more.

Lampert, then, wrote mainly contemporary history; but he modelled himself so closely on Livy and Sallust that his pages sometimes have an antique flavour: echoes of Livy, an author curiously little known in the Middle Ages, have been found on almost every page. He gives colour, drama, urgency, to every crisis; and his personal views—though not so deeply prejudiced as some historians have asserted—are constantly apparent. No historian of this period attempted to be 'objective'. Objectivity in the modern sense would have been contrary to their notions of revealing the divine pattern; and it was commonly a passionate interest in events which inspired them to write. Lampert's famous account of Henry IV's winter march to Canossa and of how he waited three days between the second and third circle of walls of the castle, was often in the past disbelieved. He was supposed even to have invented the plan of the castle. But in this detail he has been vindicated by the spade; and in general he has been proved reasonably accurate— not in every particular, not in his imaginary speeches, in his dramatic flourishes, in his baroque elaborations, but in the broad lines of his splendid narrative.

[1] See E. E. Stengel, in *Aus Verfassungs- und Landesgeschichte, Festschrift zum 70. Geburtstage von T. Mayer*, II (1955), pp. 245–58; W. Heinemeyer, *Archiv für Diplomatik*, vol. IV (1958), pp. 226 ff. The influence of Livy on Lampert is the subject of a monograph by G. Billanovich, *Lamperto di Hersfeld e Tito Livio* (Padua, 1945).

2. *Orderic to John of Salisbury.* Two years before the close of Lampert's *Annales* a man was born who was to be an even more prolific historian. Orderic was the son of a French father; born in Shropshire, baptized with an English name, and very conscious of his English origin, he spent his life as a monk at St Évroul in Normandy, and in his later years compiled a massive chronicle of Norman and European history. The bulk of it, once again, tells of events in his own lifetime; and at its heart lies his narrative of events of special interest to him: the history of Norman monasteries, especially his own; of their patrons, the Norman barons; of the stirring events of his day, especially the First Crusade. He too indulges in speeches and in drama; yet his sense of veracity was stronger than Lampert's, and though he sometimes confuses, he rarely invents. There is a rich, disorderly profusion about his book; and its special value lies in his love of detail, and in his portraits of men, lay and clerical, whom he had known: from these we gain a rare knowledge of the Anglo-Norman upper classes of his day.

When Ernald bishop of Le Mans died, King William [I] said to his chaplain Samson of Bayeux [later bishop of Worcester]: 'The see of Le Mans is deprived of its bishop; God willing, I will put you in his place. Le Mans (*Cenomannis*) gets its name from canine frenzy (*a canina rabie*); it is an ancient city, and its people are insolent and offensive to their neighbours, and stubborn with their lords and eager to rebel. I decree that you shall take the episcopal reins—you, whom I have brought up from childhood with constant affection, and now wish to raise among the magnates of my realm.'

Samson replied: 'According to the tradition of the apostles a bishop should be beyond reproach. But my whole life has been thoroughly reprehensible, and I am stained with sin, both of mind and body, in the eyes of God; nor can I attain to such glory, despicable wretch that I am owing to my sins.'

Said the king: 'You are a man of cunning, and see clearly that you ought to confess yourself a sinner. But I have decreed a judgement unshakeable, nor will I alter it, that you are to undertake the office of bishop, or present another, who can be made bishop instead of you.'

Samson was delighted to hear this, and said: 'Now, my lord king, you have spoken very well, and you will find me, with God's support, swift to do this. See, you have in your chapel a clerk who is poor, but noble and of good character. Grant him the bishopric in the fear of

God, since he is worthy, I think, of such honour. . . . Hoel is his name and he is a Breton by race; but he is a humble man and good none the less.'[1]

The king had Hoel summoned, but still required some convincing that this insignificant young man was the right choice. Eventually, however, he appointed him; the people rejoiced in 'so pure and simple an election' —Orderic was not at all bothered by Gregorian notions that elections should be free of lay intervention—and Hoel became bishop of Le Mans, which he served in holiness for fifteen years.

The conversation is doubtless apocryphal, though there may have been some kernel of truth in the story. But Hoel was undoubtedly appointed by William, and Orderic's purpose is not to deceive—he would not expect his audience to accept reported speech literally—but to vary the form of his narrative, and to enable him to make lively and pointed comments on Hoel, on Samson and on the king. Orderic was a shrewd observer, with an eye for drama and for detail; kindly on the whole, sharp on occasion, delighting to reveal both the piety and the worldliness of his contemporaries. He travelled a little and drank in avidly what he saw; but he always rejoiced in the security of the cloister, and contrasted it with the vicissitudes of life in the world.

Behold, I am worn out by age and illness [he wrote in 1141] and I wish to finish this book. . . . I am now passing my sixty-seventh year in the worship of my Lord Jesus Christ, and I rejoice in the security of obedience and poverty, while I see the princes of this world oppressed by heavy misfortunes. . . . Behold, Stephen, king of the English is held sighing in prison; Louis, king of the French, campaigning against Goths and Gascons [i.e. in the south of France], is troubled by many anxieties; the bishop of Lisieux is dead, and his see lacks a bishop: when they will receive a bishop, and of what kind, I know not. What more should I say? Amid these events, I turn my speech to thee, Almighty God, and beg twice over that your kindness have mercy on me. I thank you, most high king, who freely made me, and disposed my life according to your good pleasure. You are my king and my God, and I am your slave, the son of your handmaid, who have served you as best I could from the first days of my life. On Easter eve I was baptized at Attingham, a village in England lying on the mighty river Severn. There you gave me rebirth by

---

[1] Orderic, ed. A. Le Prevost and L. Delisle, vol. II, pp. 248 ff. (Paris, 1840).

water and the Holy Spirit, by the ministering of Orderic the priest, and gave me too the name of that same priest, my godfather. When I was five I went to school at Shrewsbury, and dedicated my first lessons to you in the church of St Peter and St Paul. Sigward the well-known priest taught me the elements of letters, . . . and introduced me to psalms and hymns and other necessary learning. . . . It did not please you that I should lead my life there longer . . . in case I ran the danger of failing to follow your law owing to the human affection of my parents. And so, O God of glory, who ordered Abraham to leave his country, his father's house and kindred, you inspired my father Odeler to give me up and surrender me wholly to you. Weeping, he gave a weeping child to Rainald the monk, and sent me into exile for your love—nor ever after saw me. A small boy did not presume to contradict his father, but I obeyed him in all things, since he promised me that I should possess paradise with the innocent. . . . I left my country, my parents, all my kindred and my friends, who wept bitterly as they commended me with kind prayers to you, most high God. Receive their prayers, and of your mercy grant their request, O merciful God of Sabaoth.

At ten years old I crossed the Channel, and came, an exile, to Normandy, knowing no one, known to none. Like Joseph in Egypt, I heard a tongue I knew not. Yet by your grace I found among strangers every kindness and friendship. I was received to the monastic life in the monastery of St Évroul by the venerable Mainer [the abbot] in the eleventh year of my life, on the eleventh before the Kalends of October, a Sunday [21 September 1085] and tonsured in clerkly manner. I was given in place of my English name, which seemed ugly to the Normans, the name Vitalis, a name borrowed from one of the companions of St Maurice the martyr, whose martyrdom was then being celebrated [22 September]. I have lived 56 years in this abbey, by thy favour, loved and honoured by all the monks and all who live here much more than I deserved. I have suffered heat and cold and the burden of the day labouring among your children in the vineyard of Soreth,[1] and I have awaited my penny wage with confidence, since you are faithful. Six abbots have I revered as your vicars, and so my fathers and masters—Mainer and Serlo, Roger and Warin, Richard and Rannulf. They were lawfully the heads of the monastery of St Évroul; for me and the others they kept watch, since

---

[1] The old Latin version of Isaiah 5: 1–2 (known to Orderic from its use in the liturgy) reads: '. . . et plantavit vineam Soreth'.

they had to give account of us . . . and with thy company and aid, provided all things necessary for us.

Then, with a historian's precision—perhaps even more with an old man's vivid memory of the events of long ago—he gives the dates and circumstances of his ordination as subdeacon, deacon and priest; 'and now for thirty-four years I have faithfully performed your mysteries with an eager mind'.

Thus, thus, O Lord God, who made me and gave me life, you have freely made your gifts to me in these diverse orders, and justly set apart my years for your service. . . . I thank you for all your kindly gifts, kind father, with all my heart I praise and bless you, and with tears I beg your pardon for all my countless faults. . . . Give me the will to persevere in your service, unfailing strength against Satan's crafty malice, until I may receive, by thy gift, the inheritance of eternal salvation. And what I ask for myself, here and to come, I desire too, merciful God, for my friends and benefactors, and for all your faithful children according to your providence. Our own merits do not suffice to obtain things everlasting, for which the perfect ever ardently long; and so, O Lord God, maker and ruler of the angels, the true hope and eternal blessing of the just, may the glorious intercession of the holy Virgin mother Mary and of all the saints help us in your sight, by the aid of our Lord Jesus Christ, redeemer of all, who liveth and reigneth with you in the unity of the Holy Spirit, God for ever and ever. Amen.[1]

In this moving confession we come very close to this attractive Anglo-Norman—lively, devoted, a little complacent, perhaps, yet without guile; and very near the heart of the Benedictine monasticism which produced so many of the best of our sources. We can feel in his pages the spiritual comfort and the physical discomfort of his cloister, well stocked with monks and books, and opportunities for quiet reflection and prayer, but open to the heat of summer and the cold draughts of winter.

The most eminent historian of Orderic's generation was another Anglo-Norman, sharper in mind, with a stronger sense of form and relevance; and an interest in the past and a capacity to elicit history from obscure documents which gives him kinship with scholars of more recent times. William, monk of Malmesbury in Wiltshire, wrote a

[1] Orderic, *loc. cit.*, vol. v, pp. 133 ff. (my own translation, but partly based on R. W. Church's, in *St Anselm* (1888 edn.), pp. 134 ff.).

variety of works of history and hagiography, and also biblical commentaries. He wrote histories of the English kings and of the English bishops; lives of the saints of Malmesbury and Glastonbury; a life of the saintly bishop Wulfstan of Worcester; a history of Glastonbury abbey in which he showed unusual skill in arranging early charters in order and deducing the succession of abbots and the history of the monastery from them. Like Orderic, William wrote to entertain: he liked to break off his narrative to tell a story, lest the reader weary of 'straight history'. He sharpened his wits by inventing an elaborate speech defending the primacy of Canterbury over York, which he put into the mouth of Archbishop Lanfranc. Characteristic of his combination of wit and drama is his account of the burial of William Rufus.

> A few of the peasants carried his corpse to the cathedral at Winchester on a horse-drawn wagon, with blood dripping from it the whole way. There in the cathedral crossing, under the tower, he was interred, in the presence of many great men, mourned by few. Next year there followed the collapse of the tower. I forbear to tell the opinions which were held on this event, lest I seem to believe in trifles—especially since it could have collapsed in any case, even if he had not been buried there, because it was badly built.[1]

William was not, however, a sceptic: he has much to tell us in almost all his works of portents and wonders and miracles. Nor was he solely guided by the love of truth. 'What are the qualities that make a historian?' said Lytton Strachey. 'Obviously these three—a capacity for absorbing facts, a capacity for stating them, and a point of view.' When writing contemporary history, William makes no effort to hide his point of view.

The intellectual revival is apparent in the development of historical studies in the late eleventh and early twelfth centuries. Orderic was learned and on occasion rhetorical; to literary learning and rhetoric William can add some knowledge of dialectic (though he claimed to know little), and a mind trained to critical thought. In Otto of Freising, theologian and bishop, and John of Salisbury, scholar and humanist, we meet the twelfth-century renaissance at its finest. Both had sat at the feet of Abelard. Otto looked on history as St Augustine had looked on history, as a part of God's grand design; and he characteristically called his major work *The Two Cities*, after the model of Augustine's

[1] *Gesta Regum*, ed. W. Stubbs (Rolls Series), vol. II, pp. 378–9 (my own translation).

City of God. It combines the conception of Augustine (so far as it was understood in the twelfth century) with the theme of universal history, as conceived, for instance, by Augustine's pupil Orosius; Otto's sources were many, but these two were his main foundations. His book was a singularly complete history. It opens with the Creation, and closes, not with contemporary events (though these have their place), but with the Last Judgement, the resurrection of the dead, and the life of the world to come.

John of Salisbury's effort at history was more modest. His one historical work was a continuation of a well-known continental chronicle of the eleventh century; this saved him from troubling with the Creation, or any earlier history, indeed, since he used a version which had already been continued down to 1148. What he wrote were simply reminiscences. He took care to specify his solemn purpose—all chroniclers, he says, have a common purpose—to reveal God's works, to teach by example, and to provide soundly based precedents for customs and privileges; but the book is confined to a brief narrative of events seen from the point of view of the papal curia in the years 1148–51, when John was a frequent visitor there. It gives a brilliant and not uncritical picture of St Bernard's activities at the council of Rheims in 1148; it is famous for its vignettes of figures of the time. John mocks at the princely Bishop Henry of Winchester, and makes Pope Eugenius III take him humorously to task, with a preposterous little fable; and in one of his most moving passages he describes how a divorce suit came before the same pope. The pope rebuked the witnesses; and then, in tears, slipped suddenly from his throne and threw himself at the husband's feet, so 'that his mitre, slipping from his head and rolling in the dust, was found after the bishops and cardinals had raised him [from] under the feet of the dumbfounded count'—the husband. And the pope begged the count to take his wife back; and gave him as a 'dowry' absolution from his sins. 'And taking a ring from his own finger he placed it on the count's, adding: "Let this ring, a token of faith and contract, be a witness before God between thee and me, that I have given thee a wife in the sight of the church, and that thou hast received her into thy protection" '—and John goes on to tell us that he himself was present on this occasion.[1] The vivid description belonged to the century, and was a special gift of John's; the drama, the symbolism, the tears belonged to the Middle Ages as a whole.

[1] *Historia Pontificalis*, trans. M. Chibnall, pp. 81–2 (cf. p. 79 for the bishop of Winchester and the pope's fable).

Byzantine historians

The convention of western chroniclers, and authors in general, was to express in their writings a humility and sense of inadequacy which they did not always feel. Strangely enough, in Byzantium, where the tradition of historical writing was more ancient and continuous, though in this period less fruitful than in the west, the opposite convention ruled. Michael Psellus, the liveliest of eleventh-century historians in Constantinople, was pathologically vain as well as being wholly unscrupulous. 'The fact to which I am about to refer will undoubtedly win for me high approval among men of learning. . . . Philosophy, when I first studied it, was moribund so far as its professors were concerned, and I alone revived it. . . .' Later he describes how, for a brief time, he became a monk: 'Many persons had claims on my friendship, but two men in particular. . . . They were both much older than I, and lest I should be accused of perverting the truth'—one always knows with Psellus that when he speaks of truth his modesty is about to be overcome—'. . . I was more advanced in my studies. . . . Just as my studies were more advanced, so, if I may be allowed to say it, was my spiritual progress. My position at court, moreover, was higher than theirs. . . .' The three decided to enter a monastery. One of them feigned sick, and then discovered that the monastic life made him marvellously better. Psellus decided to imitate him. The Emperor Constantine was very fond of Psellus, and was very reluctant to let him leave court; hence this little deception. 'He loved my conversation immensely. There is no reason, surely, why I should not admit it'; and Psellus launches into a panegyric of his method of delighting the emperor, and of how he instructed him above all in rhetoric, which he describes as an 'exact science'.[1] The enthusiasm of Psellus for rhetoric could have been paralleled in the West at this time; but in most respects he helps us to get an insight into the differences between East and West. His vanity was absurd; yet in part it was the convention of the society in which he lived; and the other most readable Byzantine historian of the eleventh and twelfth centuries, the Princess Anna Comnena, also reveals that Byzantine authors were expected to boast if they wished their books to be read. But Anna, one feels, had something to boast about: she was one of the few ladies of the age who was sufficiently educated to be an authoress in her own right; and the theme of her *Alexiad*, the life of her father the Emperor Alexius Comnenus (1081–1118), was considerably

---

[1] Psellus, pp. 127, 191–4. On Psellus, see also below, pp. 351–3.

more inspiring than the decadent emperors of the mid eleventh century who stirred the muse of Michael Psellus.

Exceptional narratives

For all their variety, the western chroniclers whom we have so far considered all had much in common. A special interest attaches to a small class of 'sports' among the sources of this period: narratives with special qualities which make them, each in its own way, unique. Thus England produced the *Anglo-Saxon Chronicle*, or rather chronicles—the one major set of vernacular annals. The idea of collecting and dis-seminating earlier materials in English, and keeping them up to date from year to year, belonged to the age of King Alfred (871–99); and although it is commonly held that Alfred was not himself responsible for the *Chronicle*, his own translations into English must have inspired it. Various copies were continued well into the eleventh century; one even to 1154. But the *Chronicle* remained a monument to the vernacular revival which began in Alfred's reign; and such a work could not long survive the Norman Conquest, when monks and canons became increasingly French-speaking, and Latin became for a time the only language common to all the literate people in the kingdom, as well as the language of learning.

The Norman Conquest itself was recorded in the famous Bayeux Tapestry, now thought to have been woven in England for Bishop Odo of Bayeux, the Conqueror's half-brother. The Tapestry is a very early source for the events it describes. It is by no means an objective source. Its purpose was to portray Harold, not as a villain, but as the tragic hero of an epic: the man of courage and nobility who made one fatal blunder, who swore an oath (on the Bayeux relics) and broke it; and so came to his doom. But the special value of the Tapestry lies in the precise image it gives us of all those things which the chroniclers ignore: houses, costume, boat-building, the baggage trains, horses and armour.

Whoever designed the Bayeux Tapestry, it was inspired by church-men and intended to hang in a cathedral. Narratives written by laymen for laymen are extremely rare; but one of the earliest, most vivid and useful chronicles of the First Crusade, the anonymous *Gesta Francorum*, was actually written by a crusading soldier. He was a Norman from south Italy—in Italy the literate layman was by no means so exceptional as north of the Alps—who went on Crusade in the contingent of the Norman Bohemond, but carried on to Jerusalem after Bohemond had made himself lord of Antioch. In his company we can travel with the

Crusaders, share their hardships and their delights, and taste a little of their ferocious zeal for the destruction of the infidel and the recapture of the Holy City.

Biography

The anonymous crusader wrote of what he saw; what he did not see, he invented—and his accounts of Moslem politics are delightfully absurd. The mixture of fact and fiction was characteristic of historians of this period; but the more learned could defend their practice (if they had ever troubled to do so) by referring to the learned models on which their practices were based. Many of them knew Sallust; one or two knew Livy; all knew a few of the earlier chroniclers of the Middle Ages; most knew Bede, a few had read Suetonius; all had read some saints' lives. From these last two traditions stemmed the biographies, which were a popular form of historical record in these centuries. The saints' lives were not always historical records. In the eleventh and twelfth centuries in particular every monastery and every church wished to have a life of its patron saint, or of any saint whose relics it possessed. If the patron were an apostle, or a well-known figure like St Martin, this presented no great difficulty. But of many saints only the names were known. Thus the lives of the Welsh saints were written in the late eleventh and early twelfth centuries, mainly from topographical legends, guesswork, invention—and the common hagiographical practice of appropriating good stories from one saint to another. By a rather more serious process of research William of Malmesbury provided lives for several obscure saints in western England. A generation earlier, a wandering Flemish monk called Goscelin had provided many English churches with lives of their founders. Goscelin embroidered, as did all hagiographers; but he made a serious attempt to find out what he could, to use early documents and earlier lives and legends where he could lay hands on them. He wrote of men and women long since dead. But it was also a well-established practice to write of men recently dead—whether lives of saints, like the first five abbots of Cluny, or the great English bishops of the tenth century, or simply men of eminence, like the archbishops of Bremen who were the theme of Adam of Bremen's *History* (written in the 1070s), a fascinating account of ecclesiastical affairs on and beyond the shores of the Baltic.

At the turn of the eleventh and twelfth centuries a new fashion arose in the writing of biography. It first appears in the life of St Anselm by the English monk Eadmer, who had been Anselm's close friend and companion in his later years. In a sense it was not a saint's life, since Anselm had not been formally canonized; yet it was written in the evident hope and expectation that he would be. Nor is it a saint's life in form: he does not try to make Anselm superhuman or remote, or to fill his pages with miracles; he tries to portray Anselm just as he was—attractive, inspiring and exasperating.

Eadmer's *Life* was a remarkable achievement; even the team who wrote the life of St Bernard of Clairvaux, with elaborate care and from first-hand information, did not succeed in portraying his humanity so clearly. To find anything so vivid one must turn to the autobiographies of the age; and it is in the *Historia Calamitatum* of Peter Abelard that one finds the clue to this fashion for intimate biography. Abelard was an egoist and had suffered many misfortunes. In an earlier age he would have grumbled, no doubt, but kept the vicissitudes of his life to himself. But he was one of the small group of humanists of this period who believed in self-expression (see p. 319); believed that a man could and should lay his sufferings and emotions bare, as Augustine had laid his in the *Confessions*, or St Jerome in his letters. Even more clearly were the difficulties and splendour of Abelard's life revealed in his letters to Heloise; and her replies—the spirited answers of a respected abbess to a man whom she still regarded as her husband—plumb the paradoxes of twelfth-century humanism in a unique way. With Abelard and John of Salisbury there is never any doubt that humane emotions and humanist interests can live wholly within a Christian context. The Abbess Heloise used the language of the Roman Stoics as if their thought were her own.

Less searing, but even more characteristic of the age, is the *Autobiography* of Guibert de Nogent, a French Benedictine abbot, who tells us in a vivid and simple way what the life of a churchman of noble family and ordinary attainments was like. Guibert had certain characteristics which lend his book a special interest—characteristics common enough in themselves, but rarely so vividly revealed. His devotion to his mother has given us a splendid portrait of a pious lady of great strength of character and capacity, 'beautiful, indeed, I should in a worldly and foolish fashion have called her, had I not austerely declared beauty to be but an empty show', as he observes before embarking on the theme at considerable length. 'Who can stop when he once begins a tale?' he frankly observes on another occasion; and his book is packed with stories, relevant and irrelevant, of folk-lore and miracle and all sorts, revealing the furniture of a devout and curious mind. His prejudices were wholly conventional, whether commenting on how to get the ear of the papal curia, 'for it is the way of the world to become pleasant on the mention of gold', or in accepting the notions of the papal reformers on the wickedness of lay-folk owning churches. The last appears in a passage which is a nice summary of Guibert's interests.

We are not unaware that the martyr Leodegarius [St Leger] was an eminent miracle-worker and a ready helper in need. For I, when still very little, but clearly remembering this, was living with my mother when at Easter I was violently ill of a quotidian fever. Now close to the town there was a church dedicated to Sts Leodegarius and Machutus, where my mother in humble faith supplied an oil lamp continually burning. When, therefore, I turned against almost every kind of food, summoning two clerics, her chaplain and my school-master, she ordered that I should be taken thither in their care. In accordance with the bad practice of ancient custom that church came under her control. The clerics coming there begged that a bed should be made for them and me before the altar. And lo, in the middle of the night the ground inside the church began to be beaten as it were with hammers and at times the locks of the chests to be torn off with a loud noise and sometimes the cracking of sticks to be heard above the chests. Now the clerics awaking through the sound, began to be afraid that the fright would make me worse. To be brief, although they muttered low, yet I caught the words, but was only moderately afraid because of their companionship and the comfort of the shining lamp. Thus passing through the night I returned safely to my mother as if I had suffered no inconvenience, and I who had turned from the most delicious dishes, now was eager for ordinary food and just as ready for a game of ball.[1]

The final touch reminds one of the autobiography of Gerald of Wales, born at the very close of our period (c. 1145), who describes how as a boy his brothers built sand castles and palaces, but he designed churches and monasteries in sand and dust; and so his father, a baron of the Welsh march, nicknamed him 'my bishop' and set him to letters.

Guibert was approximately a contemporary of the great abbot of Saint-Denis, Suger, monk, author, builder, and royal minister to Kings Louis VI and VII. Saint-Denis still retains much evidence of his work; and this has a special interest, because it marks the first serious step in the transition from 'Romanesque' to 'Gothic' fashions in architecture,

[1] Guibert, pp. 9, 127, 138, 222–3 (slightly adapted).

and because Suger left no less than three accounts of the motives, methods and results of his work. Suger's 'autobiography' is a rich quarry for the historian of art and architecture, and we shall have occasion to pillage it later on (see pages 73–4, 338–9). But it was not the only literary product of his fondness for reminiscence. We are told that he used to keep his monks up far into the night describing events he had seen or heard of; and his *Life of King Louis VI* is a monument to his shrewd, observant eye as well as to the able, kindly, conscientious king who inspired it.

In an age without newspapers contemporary affairs became a kind of history, and the modern divorce between 'contemporary' and other sorts of history was unknown. But the wealth of historical writing, of histories, secular biographies, ecclesiastical biographies, and historical sketches,[1] is a striking witness to growing interest in the affairs of the world, and growing capacity to express that interest.

Letters

The humanism of Heloise and Abelard expressed itself, among other things, in the writing, and preservation, of letters. This was nothing new: throughout the early Middle Ages men occasionally appeared who followed the example of Cicero and St Jerome in preserving their letters. Strange legends circulated round the great scholar Gerbert, Pope Sylvester II (999–1003), of his skill as a magician, his pact with the devil, the vagaries of his life. It comes as a shock to turn from these to the vivacity of his own letters, of which a number survive, on points of friendship, scholarship and administration and political and clerical intrigue (see pp. 167–70). These were to be the subjects of the letter collections throughout our period. As time passes they become more numerous: the papal reform and the contest of Gregory VII and Henry IV are illuminated at every turn by Gregory's letters—formal, yet reflecting the electric personality of the pope—and the small number of letters which survive written in Henry's name are almost equally illuminating for the attitudes and principles of Gregory's opponent.

Supreme among the letter writers of the twelfth century was St Bernard of Clairvaux. The ascetic who repudiated secular learning, anyway for himself, and refused to be bound by the laws of metre when writing verse, none the less practised the most polished rhetoric in his letters, and allowed his secretaries to assist him in revising them for

[1] For example, the vivid account of the murder of the count of Flanders written by Galbert of Bruges (trans. J. B. Ross, Columbia Records, 1960).

publication. But in his case literary grace was no cover for insincerity: the charm, the exaltation, the prophetic fervour which exhorts and denounces were all genuine parts of the complex make-up of the great Cistercian (see pp. 310–15).

Other literary sources

Famous as Bernard's letters justly are, they form only a small proportion of his total output. In addition he wrote many sermons, much other devotional and theological literature. Many of the Latin sources of our period are gathered in some sixty volumes of the Abbé Migne's *Patrologia*. If one extracted from these all the chronicles, saints' lives, biographies, and letters, the greater part of these lengthy volumes would still be left. Sermons, theological books, biblical glosses and commentaries would account for a great proportion; much controversial literature survives, such as the products of the great pamphlet war which accompanied the contest of empire and papacy; and in and out of Migne one finds the ever-widening scope of learned writing produced by the intellectual revival of the eleventh and twelfth centuries—the work of grammarians, poets, rhetoricians, astronomers, musicians and the rest. These categories will be discussed in later chapters, when we consider the intellectual life of medieval churchmen; they are listed now to indicate the range of material which the historian has at his disposal.

The range of material must to a fair degree dictate the historian's interests and the manner of his approach. He cannot hope to reconstruct a detailed political narrative from memoirs and annals written at least a few months, and often many years, after the event. He cannot hope to understand the secrets of the royal council chambers of Europe by reading the speeches put into the mouths of great men by monks who had never met them. The literary sources introduce him directly, and often vividly, to the educated churchmen of the day; rarely to the rank and file of the church; to the ordinary layman very rarely indeed. Yet the historian of this period is exceedingly lucky to be presented with so many vivid portraits, so many commentaries on events, so much insight into the attitudes, aspirations and assumptions of the churchmen of the day. Above all, he is never in danger of being bored. Nor is he entirely dependent on the literary sources.

Documents

In the tenth century, government was mainly conducted by word of mouth; kings and noblemen were illiterate. In the twelfth century

members of the lay upper classes were still, by and large, illiterate—
though not all; and some kings were well educated even by the best
clerical standards. But whether literate or not, kings and princes had
staffs of clerics who conducted an increasing amount of business in
writing. They issued instructions in writing; they kept written accounts.
So many of the things which we consider most characteristic of government depend on its literacy that we easily forget how recently and slowly
this evolved. The switch from illiterate to literate government is one of
the striking features of this period. Otto the Great issued charters: large
and imposing pieces of parchment, authenticated by the impress of his
seal, which usually describe how he gave or confirmed a grant of land
or a legal immunity or some other privilege to a bishop or an abbey.
They are splendid documents. But they are rare when compared with
those of Frederick Barbarossa, and although this might be partly
explained by the ravages of time, it is clear that the chancery, or writing
office, of Barbarossa was far more prolific than Otto's. Long before and
long after the period of this book the official letters of the popes were
sent out with the small but impressive leaden seals attached—the
bullae, from which the letters themselves came to be called 'bulls'.
The practice of keeping copies in registers of the more important
of these was also established before the tenth century, although the
only register to survive between the tenth and the late twelfth centuries
is that of Gregory VII. But even in the papal chancery there was
a world of difference between the small output of the tenth-century
popes, written in the traditional Roman cursive hand, which hardly
anyone could read outside the boundaries of Italy, and the profusion of bulls which circulated in every corner of Europe in the mid
twelfth century written in papal minuscule, a fine and clear version
of the common handwriting of western Europe of the time, the
descendant of the Carolingian minuscule. Every monastery of any
pretension sought in the twelfth century to have its properties and
privileges confirmed by papal bull; innumerable litigants took their
pleas to Rome and returned with bulls directing judges in their own
countries to handle their cases, and informing them what the law was
on the issues in dispute. The former types of bull were called privileges, the latter decretals. Neither were new inventions; but they were
issued after the papal reform of the eleventh century in unprecedented
numbers: the scale and the precision of the papal chancery's activities
were new.

The Anglo-Saxon monarchy provides a remarkable example of the growth of literacy. Its special invention (whose date is quite uncertain) was the 'writ', the letter converted into an instrument of formal government. But only slightly over 100 genuine royal writs survive from the period before 1066.[1] From between 1066 and 1100 we have 500; from between 1100 and 1135, 1,500. These figures are not merely a measure of Norman energy; they reflect what was happening all over Europe.

The Germanic peoples, under the influence of Christianity, had committed selections from their laws to writing from time to time. The Church's law was theoretically written. But the Church's law was confused, and the greater part of the secular laws of peoples and kingdoms was unwritten before the twelfth century. The revival of Roman law and canon law in the eleventh and twelfth centuries inspired the lawyers concerned with the customary laws of kingdoms likewise to see their laws as coherent systems; and although the systematic treatises on secular law belong to a subsequent age, the trend had already begun which was to lead in the later Middle Ages to the reception of Roman Law in many continental countries.

Increasing use of charters meant that title to land came increasingly to depend on written testimony. For centuries cathedrals and monasteries had reckoned to fortify their privileges and properties with written evidence; the extent to which other folk did the same depended on the legal arrangements of different countries. The assumption of written evidence, however, did not come in (except in Spain, where under Muslim influence law and government were exceptionally literate) until the eleventh and twelfth centuries, and was rarely complete before the thirteenth. In England it was made possible by the imaginative energy of William the Conqueror. In Domesday Book (1086) he and his advisers set out to describe systematically the tenurial pattern of the whole of England and what we should call its economic basis. The result is a fascinating wilderness of statistics: full of errors, omissions, inequalities, full too of invaluable information, unique for its period in attempting to be systematic. Only the combined efforts of the most highly organized royal government in Europe of its day and the immense energy of the king could have produced it.

The Norman Conquest of England had involved a major revolution

[1] They are no doubt the survivors of a much larger number, and these crude statistics may give a misleading impression; but there are strong grounds for thinking that the ratio between the numbers of pre- and post-conquest writs does not give an entirely false picture of their growth in this period.

in land tenure: the bulk of the land held by secular lords changed hands, often more than once, between 1066 and 1086. This process led to numerous disputes, and although the Domesday inquest itself provided an opportunity for resolving a number still outstanding, the chaos in land tenure of this period provided a powerful stimulus to speed the transfer from oral to written testimony of men's right to land. This circumstance encouraged one of the more curious features of the age: the tendency of landowners, especially ecclesiastical landowners, to forge their title deeds.

Forgery

The Norman Conquest gave a special urgency to the work of forgers in England, but their activities were part of a general movement which made the eleventh and twelfth centuries the golden age of medieval forgery. This is a bold claim: the eighth century had produced the Donation of Constantine, the ninth the Forged Decretals; every age has contributed to the stock of spurious literature in European libraries. But no student of charters can doubt that the period from 1000 to 1150 saw more activity in forging charters than any other. It coincided with the intellectual revival, which provided the means and the skill to forge: it coincided with the switch from oral to written testimony, which provided the incentive to support and improve older instruments, oral, or less precise. It coincided with the papal reform, which made papal bulls more valuable and useful, and so encouraged men to forge them. Forgery, too, was comparatively safe. It was not that it was condoned by society at large: in the late twelfth century Pope Lucius III had specifically to insist that unfrocking, degradation, branding and exile were more suitable punishments for clerks convicted of forgery than physical mutilation; and forgers of coins were commonly mutilated. But it is clear that many forgers, when convicted, had nothing worse to fear than degradation. The ecclesiastical muniments of this period have survived in far greater bulk than the lay, and it may be that laymen forged more often than we know. But if it is true that the more sensational forgeries were committed in the interests of ecclesiastical communities, we may recall the immensely powerful effect of group loyalty, which would tend to excuse irregularities and protect those who perpetrated them; and we can rarely be sure how widespread was the knowledge that forgery was being committed. We do well to remember, too, that most forgery was in the interests of rights which really existed, or which the authors had tolerably good reason to think existed;

many forgeries added nothing of substance to genuine documents, some were written only to replace originals damaged by fire, mice or water.

In 1131 an attempt was made to settle an old dispute between the archbishop of Rouen and the abbot of St Ouen at Rouen as to whether the abbey was exempt from the archbishop's control—a common source of litigation in this period. The case came before the pope, and was decided by the intervention of the bishop of Châlons, who had formerly been abbot of the great house of St Medard at Soissons. He said that while he was abbot, 'one of his monks called Guerno, in his last confession, had confessed that he had been a forger, and among other things which he had concocted for various churches, he asserted —with tearful repentance—that he had protected the church of St Ouen, and the church of St Augustine, Canterbury, with spurious papal privileges; and as a reward for his iniquity he confessed he had received some precious ornaments and carried them off to St Medard's.'[1] The late Professor Levison was able to identify a substantial group of documents forged by Guerno for St Augustine's, and to show that his hand could be traced at Peterborough, St Medard, Soissons (his own home) and St Ouen at Rouen; and one could add that he also probably had a hand in at least one forgery for Canterbury cathedral. At about the same date a monk of Reichenau was providing a number of Rhineland monasteries with valuable documents, and Peter the Deacon was busily rewriting the muniments, and in effect the history, of Monte Cassino. In the mid twelfth century Westminster abbey became the centre of a factory, whose work can be detected among the muniments of various English communities—Coventry, Gloucester, Ramsey and Battle—and perhaps on the Continent too. It is evident that much work was done by experts, as we should expect in an age of growing specialization. How much we cannot tell; some forgery was clearly the product of local self-help. But the master forger is a figure of this age, and when our period closed he was still at work. His work, however, was nearly done: by then muniment rooms were mostly well provided, and it was becoming commoner for forgery to be detected. Forgery was still not uncommon in the late twelfth century; by the late thirteenth it had resumed its normal place among the crimes and follies of mankind.

In its golden age forgery had not been confined to charters. We have

[1] Cited in W. Levison, *England and the Continent in the Eighth Century* (Oxford, 1946), pp. 207–8, in the appendix on the St Augustine's forgeries, on which this passage is based.

mentioned the activity of the itinerant hagiographer; when he was making bricks without straw—compiling saints' lives from air, which once written would none the less serve as evidence of the rights and privileges of the saints' churches—he was engaged in an activity not so very different from that of the forger of charters. In the *Book of Llandaff* (c. 1135) lives of the supposed founders of the see are combined with a multitude of supposed charters to the supposed founders and their successors. Less serious in intention, but no less sensational, was the *History of the Kings of Britain* by Geoffrey of Monmouth (c. 1138), which traces the predecessors of Cadwallader, a seventh-century Welsh king, as kings of Wales and Britain, far back into the mists of time. The authors of these books had access to a great deal of tradition, legend and even to historical documents now lost; and there is an authentic element in both. But they also have their share of Celtic fancy, which perhaps helps to explain the imaginative flavour of these works; in honesty or dishonesty they can be paralleled from many parts of Europe at this time.

Vernacular literature

Geoffrey's book was written in Latin, and his fictions were widely accepted and found their way into many serious chronicles. But his real achievement lay elsewhere. He solemnly asserted that his book was a translation of one written in Breton which was brought out of Brittany by his friend Walter, archdeacon of Oxford; and his fondness for imaginary translations appears also in the passage in which he described the laws of Dunuallo Molmutius—Dunuallo and his laws were the purest fiction—composed in the British tongue, translated into Latin by Gildas, into English by King Alfred, and still, so he tells us, in force. The motif of translation had a great vogue among the writers of vernacular romance in French and German in the late twelfth and thirteenth centuries; it became common form for the poet to indulge in polite mystification by pretending that someone else was the true author of his poem—which has probably confused modern critics more than it did the original hearers. But this was not the extent of their debt to Geoffrey, who was chiefly notable for having floated King Arthur, the central figure of his history. Arthur was beginning to be a popular figure of legend in the late eleventh and early twelfth centuries; Geoffrey put him on the map; in the late twelfth century his court became the centre of innumerable romances, in English, German, and above all in French.

The subject of the courtly romance was the solitary quest of a knight in pursuit of adventure, to do honour to a lady. Solitary adventure, an atmosphere of fantasy, courtly love and a growing emphasis on the code of chivalry—or, in many cases, a growing criticism of current notions of chivalry—were its leading themes. The romance, however, belonged to the second half of the twelfth century; its predecessor in our period was the *Chanson de Geste*. The *Chanson* was an epic of military prowess; but its knightly hero was no solitary, his adventures were more worldly than in later romances, chivalry was only slowly evolving, and courtly love was a thing of the future. The *Chanson de Geste*, indeed, provides us with our best evidence of the changes in the ideals and aspirations of feudal society in the early twelfth century; and brings us in direct contact with laymen, for whom they were written, and, often, by whom they were written. The greatest of them, the earliest version of the *Song of Roland*, is a remarkable work of literature. It was written by a cleric, but reflects lay society, for the most part, well enough; and, above all, it reflects the ideals of lay society on the eve of the Crusades.[1] The centre of the romances was the court of Arthur or the court of Alexander the Great; the centre of the *Chansons de Geste* the court of Charlemagne. We know that the courts of kings and barons were entertained by minstrels throughout the Middle Ages; and that the heroic lay and the heroic epic played a crucial part in the education of the lay upper classes of Europe. We have examples of early Germanic lays and epics, mostly from Icelandic and Anglo-Saxon sources; but how the court of Otto the Great or Edward the Confessor was entertained we cannot tell. The *Song of Roland* as we know it belongs to the late eleventh century; the legend had grown up slowly over the centuries; but none of its immediate predecessors has been recorded.

The change of outlook which was to usher in the romance was being formed in the south of France at the turn of the eleventh and twelfth centuries, in the Provençal lyrics of the early troubadours. Already they betoken a wide variety of emotions: they portray and they criticize romantic love in lyrics whose sophisticated artificiality suggests a mature rather than a wholly new tradition. Romantic love, anyway as a theme of literature, was a novelty in Europe at this time; and its origin has been the subject of heated controversy. Perhaps it was the product of a special creation; but it is a striking coincidence that a similar range of

---

[1] On the *Song of Roland* and its date, see below, pp. 358ff., esp. 359n.

themes, expressed in similarly sophisticated lyrics, had flourished for several generations in a civilization whose frontiers marched with those of Provence in this age: in Moslem Spain.

Architecture, art and archaeology

Vernacular literature has introduced us to one very valuable historical source of a kind of which historians have traditionally tended to be shy, because the material is the province of the literary historian, and requires delicate criticism before it can be made to deliver its message. Roland and Lancelot did not belong to the actual world of the twelfth century but they have much to tell us of it none the less. In a similar way, it is only recently that historians have begun to take adequate note of the findings of the archaeologist, and of the historians of art and architecture. Geoffrey of Monmouth was inspired by the ruins of Roman Caerleon to people the city with the court of King Arthur; and since the romantic revival historians and antiquaries have wandered in cathedrals and churches and the ruins of castles and abbeys, and peopled them with their medieval inhabitants. This is, indeed, a powerful incitement to historical imagination, and it is being increasingly conducted in liaison with the archaeologist. The days when a historian could boast, with Lady Bracknell's Gwendolen, that he had never seen a spade, are rapidly passing. Castles, churches and abbeys remain the most spectacular of medieval sites, because ordinary houses in this period were rarely built of stone or of any durable material; and because medieval settlements have usually been occupied continuously from that day to this, which makes excavation difficult. Even now that we realize how many deserted villages there are to be uncovered, the simplicity of medieval houses, the poverty of peasant furniture, and the long periods over which the same site was occupied, make historical reconstruction difficult. But the spade and the air photograph have done much to reveal the pattern of medieval settlement and the environment of medieval life, and will do more.

The study of medieval building, sculpture and painting provides evidence of the material environment, and also of the cultural achievement of the age. To put the matter briefly, this was a great age in the history of book illustration, of illuminated manuscripts, and of European architecture—the age of high Romanesque and of the conversion to Gothic (see pp. 338–40). These topics will find their place elsewhere; here we must only observe that no collection of medieval sources would be adequate which was not copiously provided with photographs of buildings, sculptures, paintings, and with aerial photographs of towns, castles, monasteries, villages and fields.

Coins

Physical remains have much to tell us of the material basis of society; and they are all the more valuable because sources for economic history are so scarce. We have no statistics; almost no means of measuring quantity in economic matters. All we can do is to analyse the factors of change, and observe to some degree the direction of change. One type of material evidence does, however, yield us some quantitative notions, and that is coins. The discovery of coins is in large measure a haphazard affair; but not entirely so. The distribution of finds, the nature of hoards, the quality of coins—monetary history of every kind has many lessons to teach, and may even on occasion give us some idea of the quantity of trade in particular areas. From inscriptions on the coins of later Anglo-Saxon England have been deduced the technique by which the government organized the numerous mints and minters; and so the complexity and efficiency (for its day) of English government have been revealed in a new light. In recent years, to take quite a different example, there has been much controversy on the effects of the Battle of Manzikert (1071), in which the Turks defeated the Byzantine Empire. Traditionally it was supposed to have led to disaster and decline, including economic decline and debasement of the coinage. Not long ago it was questioned whether this debasement had taken place, and if so, whether it could be associated with Manzikert. By analysing the fineness (i.e. the proportion of precious metal) in a group of coins of the period, Mr Philip Grierson has been able to show that the Byzantine currency retained its quality down to *c.* 1035; it then declined a little, in the troubled years of the mid eleventh century; then, quite suddenly, dropped to half its former level in the years immediately following Manzikert.[1] Clearly Manzikert was every bit the disaster to the Byzantine economy it has commonly been portrayed.

Impressive as the Anglo-Saxon currency was, its weight was variable; that is to say, its weight was periodically altered by royal edict—why, we do not know—and one of the few innovations of the Norman kings in this respect was to make it more stable. It was this stability which gave English currency the name 'sterling' which it has had ever since;

[1] *Byzantinische Zeitschrift*, vol. XLVII (1954), pp. 379–94 (cf. *ibid.*, vol. LIV (1961), pp. 91–7); summarized in *Congrès International de Numismatique*, Paris, 1953, vol. II (Paris, 1957), pp. 297–8.

and the proof is based on a nice mingling of numismatic and philological evidence.[1] This may remind us of the value of language as historical evidence: its history reveals the mingling of races, as in England, the formation of stable frontiers, as between France and Germany. The development of dialects is often connected with political movements; the history of the dialects of Spanish in this and later centuries follows the fortunes of the various kingdoms which spread from north to south in the process of reconquest.

Other materials

We have ranged widely over the materials for our history; and we can sum up by saying that nothing in the past is alien to the historian; every survival is grist to his mill. And this will remind us that the most remarkable survival of all has yet to be mentioned. Man's knowledge of himself, of human nature, remains, whether he likes it or not, one of his most powerful weapons in reconstructing the past. It is a dangerous weapon, since it constantly invites us to anachronism, to reading our own thoughts and emotions into the past. But used imaginatively and discreetly, it is useful, indeed essential, and many historians have failed to notice how freely they use it. There is indeed an ambiguity in our use of it. Part of the time we use it directly, as evidence of what people do; most of the time we use it analogically, to provide comparisons of what they do under comparable circumstances. This is but one instance of many in which the comparative method can help us. Men of this age had inherited many semi-barbaric customs, which were breaking down under the force of growing civilization. This is a situation which can be paralleled time and time again in the societies studied by the modern social anthropologist. The European economy of this period was what modern economists would call 'underdeveloped'; which is not to say that it was primitive or stagnant: it was developing rapidly. Again, modern analogies can be most helpful in suggesting lines of enquiry, and, perhaps most particularly, in directing our attention away from the false analogies offered by that kind of economic theory which is based on the experience of modern, advanced, industrial economies. These comparative methods provide stimulus, direct our thoughts. They are not substitutes for evidence. This must be emphasized, since the evidence for economic history in our period is so scanty that we could easily paint a picture derived from modern studies of

[1] P. Grierson, 'Sterling', *Anglo-Saxon Coins*, ed. R. H. M. Dolley (London, 1961), pp. 266–83.

underdeveloped countries which the evidence might not contradict, and yet which might also be quite imaginary.

For in the end we must admit that the area of our ignorance is very great. The large majority of the population of Europe at this time were peasants; of their history we know exceedingly little. Of the things which men saw fit to put in books, and the buildings they built, we can know much; what books and stone will not reveal remains largely hidden from us. It was the age, above all, of the church, the castle and the manuscript; and whoever studies it must first become acquainted with these things.

III

The Shape of Europe

The main subject of this book is western Europe, or, to use a term more in accordance with medieval notions, western Christendom. The area of western Christendom was very much smaller than that of modern Europe; and at first sight there seems to be something tiresomely parochial about pushing eastern Europe and Spain to the periphery. Yet to write the history of Europe as a whole in this period is not feasible: the subject has no unity, and one cannot do adequate justice to all the members at once. Western Christendom owed a common allegiance to the pope; most of it had once formed part of the empire of Charlemagne. Its social institutions, legal traditions and governments had many similarities one with another. Part of it had lain within, part without the Roman empire; but the distant memory of Rome, the inheritance of Germanic barbarism and allegiance to the Holy Roman Church were common to all its peoples.

BIBLIOGRAPHY. Essential for this, as for all chapters, is a good historical atlas: e.g. Westermann's *Atlas zur Weltgeschichte*, II (Berlin, etc., 1956), *Muir's*, ed. R. F. Treharne and H. Fullard (London, 1962), W. R. Shepherd's (8th edn., Pikesville, 1956), F. W. Putzger, *Historischer Schulatlas* (1958 edn.: small, but useful); or the older, larger *Hand-Atlas* of Spruner-Menke (3rd edn., 1880). The *Historical Atlas of Modern Europe*, ed. R. L. Poole (Oxford, 1902) and the volume of maps of the *Cambridge Medieval History* are also valuable. It is essential to study a good physical map, such as may be found in many atlases.

On Islam, see R. A. Nicholson, *A Literary History of the Arabs* (2nd edn., Cambridge, 1930); B. Lewis, *Arabs in History* (4th edn., London, 1958); P. K. Hitti, *History of the Arabs* (6th edn., London, 1958); G. E. von Grunebaum, *Medieval Islam* (2nd edn., Chicago, 1953); E. Lévi-Provençal, *Histoire de l'Espagne musulmane* (3 vols., Paris, 1944–53); R. W. Southern, *Western views of Islam in the Middle Ages* (Cambridge, Mass., 1962).

On Byzantium, see J. M. Hussey, *The Byzantine World* (London, 1957) and *Church and Learning in the Byzantine Empire* (Oxford, 1937); N. H. Baynes and H. St J. L. B. Moss, *Byzantium* (Oxford, 1948); L. Bréhier, *Le monde byzantin* (3 vols., Paris, 1947–50); G. Ostrogorsky, *History of the Byzantine State* (English trans. by J. M. Hussey, Oxford, 1956), with elaborate bibliographical

This must be our excuse for concentrating on the West; but it would be foolish to make it an argument for ignoring what lay on the frontiers. Western Europe was in constant touch, throughout our period, with Islam, the Byzantine Empire, the Magyars, Poles and Scandinavian peoples; and aware of more distant Slav and Asiatic races, above all of the kingdom of Rus, or Russia. Without these contacts our central theme, in many ways, would be unintelligible.

Islam

To the Romans the Mediterranean had been *mare nostrum*, the centre of the empire's communications, surrounded on every side by her provinces. From the early eighth century onwards, its western and southern shores had lain in Islam; its eastern shores had been disputed between Islam and Byzantium since the seventh century; its northern shores were divided between Byzantium and the West, its islands (with few exceptions) between Byzantium and Islam. By the tenth century Western Christendom was accustomed to being the poor neighbour of great empires and higher civilizations. Far and away the greatest cities of Europe, throughout our period, were Cordoba, the capital of Muslim Spain, and Constantinople, the capital of the Byzantine Empire. To both came ambassadors of the Emperor Otto I (936–73); to both he was a northern barbarian chieftain of powerful pretensions—a parvenu, but a man to be reckoned with. But they can have had little idea at that time that within two centuries the northern barbarians would have gone over to the offensive, and would be in a position to challenge both empires, not only in the battlefield, but in wealth, in enterprise, and in culture.

Islam, indeed, was no longer an empire in the tenth century. The unity which Mohammed had created and his successors fostered was made possible by the extreme simplicity of Islam's basic organization; but its simplicity, in the long run, failed to give it cohesion; its success spread it from the gates of China to the Atlantic coast; and by the tenth

notes, and *Pour la féodalité byzantine* (Brussels, 1954). On Russia, G. Vernadsky, *Kievan Russia* (New Haven, 1948); N. K. Chadwick, *The Beginnings of Russian History* (Cambridge, 1946); for recent Russian studies see summaries in *XIe Congrès International des Sciences Historiques*, Stockholm, 1960, esp. *Resumés des Communications*, pp. 90–1 (B. A. Rybakov).

On the Viking world, see E. O. G. Turville-Petre, *The Heroic Age of Scandinavia* (London, 1951); Sir Thomas Kendrick, *History of the Vikings* (London, 1930); P. H. Sawyer, *The Age of the Vikings* (London, 1962).

On the other countries of western Europe, see below.

century it was falling rapidly into pieces. Yet the fragmentation can easily be exaggerated: more than one of the pieces was larger than the empire of Charlemagne.

The unity of Islam had been based on a book, the Koran, the religion it inspired, and the language in which it was written. Wherever the Muslims conquered, they spread the Koran and the use of Arabic; and they accepted to full citizenship whoever would join their religion. In early days the incentive was stronger: Muslims were exempt from taxation; there was some proselytizing. But it was above all the simplicity of the union between Islam the faith and Islam the empire which was the secret of its success. Islam had many heresies; but in the first centuries of its existence it was never troubled by race or nationalism. It included different cultures—it absorbed ancient cultures in many of its conquests—but these did not make for rigid frontiers. It had almost no political institutions, save allegiance to its pope-emperor, the successor of the Prophet, the caliph. The caliphs could be tyrannical, and many savage acts were committed in their name; but compared with any other imperial rulers of the medieval world, their policies towards subject peoples, even those of different faith from theirs, were astonishingly liberal.

In this tolerance of diversity lay the strength and weakness of early Islam. The religious zeal of the faithful helped to convert them into splendid warriors; the lightness of their yoke made submission easy to Christians, Jews and 'infidels'. But the diversity remained; assimilation was slow and was never anything like complete; and the unity of Islam, being based on religion, was extremely sensitive to the breath of heresy.

The most important of the heresies was that of the Shiites. The heresy was political as well as religious, and its adherents claimed that the true line of caliphs should descend from the Prophet's daughter Fatima or her husband Ali. When the self-styled successors of Fatima, the 'Fatimites', established a Shiite empire in north Africa (910)—and eventually set themselves up as caliphs in Cairo (969)—their state formed a barrier between the orthodox Muslim worlds of east and west. To the east lay the Abbasid Caliphate, with its capital in Baghdad, weakened by division, and even within itself by religious schism, since the Shiites were strong in Persia, and Persia was dominant in the Caliphate. For the time being, this weakness gave Byzantium the opportunity to revive its power in Syria and Palestine. But in the eleventh century the divisions and the weakness were overcome by the conquests of the Seljuk Turks. The Turks were orthodox, and retained the Caliph as a figurehead; nor did they attempt to persecute the cultural life of Persia. Under their patronage flourished the famous poet and astronomer Omar Khayyam; and, although the greatest age of Persian Muslim culture was passing, there was no noticeable decadence in the eleventh or twelfth centuries. The Turks, meanwhile, restored political and military vigour to that slice of Islam in their charge; and in 1071 they finally cancelled all Byzantium's gains and conquered a large stretch of Asia Minor at the battle of Manzikert.

Muslim Spain

If Persia was passing its zenith when our period opened, Muslim Spain was still clearly waxing. The Caliphate of Cordoba was established by Abd-ar-Rahman III in 929; under his forceful and enlightened control (929–61), and under the equally forceful rule of the vizier Almanzor (died 1002), Cordoba was the centre of the most highly organized and militant state in what we call Europe, and of a literary and artistic culture of great magnificence and sophistication. To this day the mosque at Cordoba is one of the finest monuments of medieval Europe. A Christian church needed a substantial sanctuary in which the Eucharist could be celebrated with full solemnity, and (in the western fashion of this age) in view of a large congregation. The mosque at Cordoba has a tiny, richly decorated 'chapel', the Mihrab, which the caliph entered on special occasions. But the mosque as a whole is a vast square covered space, whose roof is supported by row upon row of exquisite arches; originally the vista ran from end to end, from side to side, but it is now broken by the choir of a Christian cathedral in the Renaissance taste. A mosque was essentially a shelter, in which the folk of Cordoba could gather to pray at regular intervals each day; and the size of the mosque at Cordoba is eloquent testimony to the growth of its population. Approximately one quarter of the present arcading was built at the end of the eighth century, largely out of Roman and Visigothic remains. In the following two centuries it spread gradually farther and farther in the direction of Mecca, until finally, under the patronage of Almanzor, an immense addition was made alongside the earlier portions, so that the area is now very nearly square. The modern visitor is given a vivid impression of the size and wealth of Cordoba in its heyday. Its population is not precisely known, though it is said to have contained about 200,000 houses and 700 public baths. Few cities still convey so much of the atmosphere of medieval Europe. In the mosque one may recall how much medieval Europe owed to Islam, in the influence of its art, architecture and literature. In its transmission of the philosophy and technology of the ancient world, the technical achievements and the spices of the Far East, Cordoba in particular was the symbol of Muslim splendour north of the straits of Gibraltar, and the home of many great Muslims, including the twelfth-century philosopher Averroes. One can also visit the tiny synagogue, the fourteenth-century successor to that in which the Jewish philosopher Maimonides worshipped in the twelfth, and reflect how great a part the Jews played, in spite of their small numbers, in the transmission of goods and of knowledge between the old and the new civilizations of the Mediterranean world. One may also reflect on the contrast between the stability of Jewish life in Muslim Cordoba, and its insecurity in Christendom, especially after the outbreak of the crusades. In Islam the Jews and Christians formed an accepted minority—the 'peoples of the book' as Mohammed had called them, to whom he acknowledged a considerable debt; in Christendom the Jews had come to be a solitary minority of non-Christians, fertilizing the economy by their ability as traders and money-lenders, an ability made possible by their faith, made necessary to the Christians on account of the Church's prohibition of usury and interest; but they were unpopular as alien minorities invariably are, who enrich themselves as well as the communities among whom they live.

In Cordoba Muslims, Jews and Christians lived side by side. Even at the height of the Caliphate, Spain was richly varied. Neither in religion nor in geography was it a united country. In the north lay the Christian kingdoms and principalities, occupying nearly a third of the peninsula; and the population of these was, nominally at least, entirely Christian. In the south the population contained three main elements: the Muslims, descendants of all the races who had inhabited Spain in earlier centuries, as well as of the Arabs and of the races of Islam, but definitely Arab speaking; the Mozarabs, the Christians under Muslim rule, racially indistinguishable from the bulk of the Muslims, bilingual, speaking Arabic and dialects derived from Latin, the chief ancestors of modern Spanish; and the 'Slavs'.[1] Muslims had scruples about enslaving Muslims, and so recruited their considerable population of slaves by capturing Christian prisoners and by purchase in Christian markets. The Christians, similarly, had scruples about making, and even sometimes about keeping Christian slaves, and so tended to export

[1] Also some Berbers, at least in the time of the Almoravides, when they were numerous in southern Spain.

the considerable number of slaves they collected, from their own peoples, from the periphery of Europe, and above all from the 'Slav' countries. The Christian slaves, and their emancipated descendants, formed a substantial part of the population of Muslim Spain.

For centuries Christian and Muslim had lived together in Spain, and there had been plenty of give-and-take over Muslim and Christian frontiers. It was only in the course of the eleventh century that the Christian peoples of the north discovered a fervour—a partly religious fervour—to reconquer the rest of Spain (see pp. 376–80). The *reconquista* was a crusade, but in so far as it was waged by native Spanish warriors, a somewhat more gentlemanly crusade than those in the east; and the conquerors could always count on the friendly interest, if not the open support, of the native Christians in the Muslim lands they overran. It was only when the reconquest came to draw recruits from north of the Alps that the spirit of fanaticism entered into the Spanish crusades, a spirit which was to reappear in the later history of the peninsula, above all in the expulsion of Jews and Muslims by Ferdinand and Isabella in the late fifteenth century.

The *reconquista* had many vicissitudes. Its beginning was made possible by the collapse of the caliphate after the death of Almanzor in 1002; it was made easier by political revival in the north of Spain, especially in the old county, now the kingdom of Castile, which could recruit great leaders like the famous Cid in its service. Spain is surrounded on three sides by the sea, on the fourth by the Pyrenees, one of the most impenetrable mountain barriers in Europe. Its geography has often cut it off from other countries, but has never given it unity. Down the centre runs a succession of mountain chains and plateaux, and its great rivers run into the Bay of Biscay, the Atlantic and the Mediterranean. The north has links with France; the west is isolated, the east is a part of the world of the Mediterranean, the south of Africa. Cordoba had owed its greatness to its command of the best bridge over the Guadalquivir. This bridge, like London Bridge, has existed since Roman times; like London in Roman and Norman times Cordoba formed a good centre for a ruler whose power lay also farther south. For a time a strong ruler in Cordoba could hold Muslim Spain together; but its natural tendency was to fall into little fragments. So it was for most of the eleventh century. But by the end of the century, it had been reunited. The fragments of the old caliphate had been crushed between two 'barbarian' conquerors. The new Christian powers of the north had come south, united under the emperor of León-Castile; a new power had come out of Africa, and had formed a large, new Muslim empire of fervent orthodoxy, that of the Almoravides, stretching from the area of modern Ghana to the Tagus, almost to the gates of Toledo. The twelfth century saw some shifting of the frontier this way and that; the next crucial stage in the Christian reconquest did not come until the thirteenth, when Cordoba itself became a Christian city; then only the kingdom of Granada remained in Muslim hands, surviving until the fifteenth century.

The Byzantine Empire

In the Mediterranean plied Muslim trading ships and pirates, Byzantine naval forces and merchants, Christian pirates and merchants. From the eighth to the tenth century the Muslim fleets were dominant; in the tenth Byzantium had a great recovery; in the eleventh both began to give way before the rise of the mercantile and naval fleets of the Italian cities. In the ninth century the Muslims had established themselves in Sicily and south Italy, had frequently raided the French and Italian coasts and even penetrated some distance inland. In the tenth century they were still strong enough to add Sardinia to their conquests. Early in the eleventh century the fleets of Pisa and Genoa reconquered Sardinia; later in the century the Normans conquered Sicily; in the twelfth century Islam even lost the Balearics. Byzantium, meanwhile, still held Crete and Cyprus and the Aegean islands, and her fleets (with some vicissitudes) were strong. But more and more of her western commerce was passing into the hands of her western ally, Venice. She suffered much from the Normans as conquerors (in south Italy) and as raiders (in Greece) in the late eleventh century; she suffered too from the trail of destruction left by the First Crusade; and when our period closed the time was not far distant when a western adventurer, King Richard I of England, would conquer Cyprus, and sell it to the Knights Templars, who rapidly passed it on to Guy de Lusignan, ex-king of Jerusalem (1191–2), and when Venice would conquer Constantinople itself (1204).

Meanwhile, in the late tenth century, Byzantium was the most considerable of the Mediterranean empires; Constantinople was a larger city than Cordoba. Under the most successful, and least attractive, of the emperors of the Macedonian dynasty, Basil II (963–1025), the empire was extended to wider limits than it had enjoyed since the rise of Islam; Syria and Palestine were reconquered; the Balkans became largely Byzantine, the empire of the Bulgars submitted; the kingdom of

Rus, after a sensational effort to capture Constantinople itself, became tributary, and, after many vicissitudes, accepted the Christianity of Constantinople. The revival was short-lived; it was followed by the decadence of the Macedonians, the rule of Basil's nieces, Zoe and Theodora, and their various husbands; and then by the collapse of the dynasty and the disaster of Manzikert (1071) (see pp. 351-3). Though Byzantium recovered quite substantially under the intelligent rule of Alexius Comnenus (1081-1118), the loss of half its territory made it permanently weaker than it had been under Basil II; and the weakness of the later Comneni and the debacle of 1204 have led many historians, looking at Byzantium with western eyes, to view its decadence and collapse as inevitable. We do well to recall, however, that the Eastern Roman Empire survived the Western by a thousand years—considerably longer than the Roman Empire had existed in the West, far longer than the life of any other human empire save the Chinese and the Egyptian. Byzantium was comparatively strong in the year 1000; comparatively weak in 1150.

The Emperor Constantine, in choosing the site for his new imperial city, his second Rome, had looked for a centre both strategically and tactically strong. Constantinople was many times besieged, but only twice taken by external enemies in over 1100 years. Its strategic position was also one of great and permanent economic significance. It lay where nature had dictated that routes should run both north to south and east to west; and historical circumstances provided the material of trade in these four quarters and merchants to keep the markets of the city active during most of its life. And throughout our period Constantinople was peopled by a large population, which included a considerable proletariat similar to that of ancient Rome itself, but also a considerable body of active, intelligent and wealthy men in whose direction the city's prosperity mainly lay. A modern traveller would feel more at home in medieval Constantinople than anywhere else in Europe, at least before the fourteenth century. It was a world in which many men were moderately well educated, knew their Bible and their Greek classics, could talk sensibly about God and earthquakes and rising prices; a world in which money consisted in small change and large, with shops and commercial houses and factories—the nearest thing one could meet in Europe to an industrial city; a world in which the gentlemen banded together in guilds and clubs.

Politically the empire was still the Roman Empire, and very conscious of its elements of continuity. In one of the palaces of Constantine VII,

Liudprand of Cremona was treated to a feast in the Roman fashion, at which the guests reclined on couches. In more serious matters, too, Rome was remembered. Her law was still in force, though much modified. Two traditions had moulded the authority of the Roman emperor in earlier days. According to Roman law, the prince was the people's representative; and the monarchy was still, in theory, elective. But Roman law also laid down that 'the prince's will is law'; and an emperor, once elected, was answerable to no man. He might be (and frequently was) deposed; but Byzantine law had, strictly speaking, no theory either of consent or of the right of resistance such as those which modified the divinely ordained authority of Western kings. The tradition of East Rome, in fact, set the prince's will firmly in a religious context. The divine aura surrounding the old Persian monarchy had been imported by Diocletian as early as the late third century into the ceremonial and atmosphere of the Roman imperial court. Constantine and his successors had been compelled to usher out the worship of the emperor, since it was clearly incompatible with Christianity; but this only meant that the emperor became God's representative, instead of being a god himself, and so far as earthly activity was concerned this was not a serious limitation.

The Roman emperors were elected, but they had always had the right of adopting heirs and arranging for their nomination and election as their successors. King-making in the west and emperor-making in Byzantium differed little in this period. The old emperor designated; the people acclaimed; the patriarch crowned the new emperor. There were, however, three notable peculiarities in the emperor's position. It was not necessary for him to rule alone. He could have colleagues. An empress was not a mere consort, she was an empress regnant. And an emperor had often had his successor crowned long before his death. This practice was common under the Macedonians, who used it—or were compelled to tolerate it—in co-opting successful generals and empress's husbands, and in avoiding disputed successions; it may be that they also consciously used it to make autocracy less lonely. The emperor's great difficulty was to perform his many functions without dividing his authority. Above all, he had to go through an endless succession of parades, to rule the wide provinces of his empire, and to lead his armies. These labours could often be conveniently divided. The hereditary ruler from 912 to 959 was Constantine VII Porphyrogenitus, whose tastes were academic: he wrote treatises both on the organization of the empire and on the ritual of the imperial ceremonies. To some extent no doubt he engaged in the ritual and the administration himself; but between 919 and 944 control of the empire, and especially the leadership in the army, lay with the successful general, Romanus Lecapenus, who had nominally been co-opted, but in fact had usurped the throne. Constantine remained in the background, ready to be produced and made effective emperor when Romanus was overthrown. Between 963 and 976 there were (in theory) three emperors, and at least one empress; between 976 and 1025 there were two emperors. In none of these periods was there any doubt, except in moments of crisis, who was in control.

The imperial palace lay between Sancta Sophia, the patriarch's cathedral, and the hippodrome, the race-course. The latter was the centre of political intrigue as well as of some of the emperor's most elaborate ceremonial; and a day at the races was nearly the undoing of more than one Byzantine emperor. The patriarch stood in much the same relation to the emperor as the pope had stood to Charlemagne or Otto the Great: that is to say he was normally under the effective control of the emperor, but commonly doubted if he should be. The difference between the two offices was, however, profound. By a tradition already ancient, the popes claimed independence of all secular control. They might deem it politic to forget the claim; they might allow it to lie fallow for a generation; but their claims were higher than the patriarch's, and were never wholly forgotten. Western historians would have reckoned the papal reform and the erection of the papal monarchy inconceivable if they had not happened; yet we must recognize that even before them there were major differences between the positions of pope and patriarch. Above all, the patriarch was constantly under the emperor's eye; in the West during our period, only Otto III tried to live in Rome itself. In the councils of the Eastern Church, the emperor frequently, and decisively, intervened. But he was not a theocrat; he had no power to perform sacraments; and if he was hedged by divinity, he was also hedged by mortality—the tradition of the patriarchs, of orthodoxy, usually outlived the private heresies of any individual emperor. Nor did the emperors of our period attempt to dictate theology to their patriarchs.

Communication between the Eastern and Western Churches was rare and growing rarer. There never was a formal schism. From the ninth century onwards, attempts were made from time to time to settle the differences in theology and practice between what most people imagined to be two branches of the Catholic Church; after the breakdown of negotiations in 1054 (see p. 257), relations became tenuous in the extreme. When serious efforts were made to heal the breach thereafter, it was generally assumed that two divided churches were negotiating for reconciliation. The change in emphasis was profound and significant; but one cannot say precisely when the change took place. Already in Liudprand's time the divergences were profound; but the theological differences and differences in eucharistic and other practices which were their outward and visible signs were not (in the view of most of the leaders of the two churches) of major substance; the final breach came on the question of authority: new Rome could not accept the supremacy of old.

We have spoken so far as if the history of the Byzantine Empire was the history of Constantinople; and, although Byzantine historians constantly object to this point of view, it has something to commend it. In the security of the capital, and its wealth, lay a part of the secret of the empire's long survival. Most of the provinces changed hands from time to time. The Serbs and Bulgars in the late tenth and early eleventh centuries were semi-barbarian tribes which owed a very uncertain allegiance to Constantinople; her suzerainty farther north, or on her south-eastern frontier, was equally uncertain. But Greece, Macedonia and Asia Minor formed a permanent core to the empire, and in the provinces, or themes as they were called, in these countries lay much of the empire's strength. These were her main recruiting ground, even after the growing independence of the war-lords of Asia Minor in the tenth and early eleventh centuries had created a kind of feudalism there, half-independent of imperial control. These provinces also provided the bulk of the imperial taxes; and in them—as well as in the markets of Constantinople—lay the source of the empire's wealth. Small wonder that after the battle of Manzikert and the loss of a great part of Asia Minor to the Turks, the empire suffered a major economic crisis; and the emperor felt himself compelled, as we have seen, to authorize a debasement of the coinage to half its former fineness.

The Viking world

Constantinople, then, was not the whole of the Byzantine Empire; and the political influence of the emperor, and the religious influence of the Church, spread far outside his borders. His armies mainly consisted of mercenaries, and were recruited from a wide area of eastern Europe and the Near East; not the least important source was Scandinavia. The presence of the Varangians in Constantinople reminds us that in the tenth century we are still in the heyday of Viking influence and expansion. In the eleventh century one Viking, King Cnut, ruled in Denmark and England, and even for a time in Norway and parts of Sweden; in 1027 he visited Rome and was treated with the highest respect both by pope and emperor. At about the same time Harold Hardrada was serving his apprenticeship in the Varangian guard in Constantinople; he fought in Byzantium and Russia; he came north again and ruled Norway; and he died on the battlefield of Stamford Bridge near York in 1066, a victim to his own ambition to be king of the English. The Vikings were almost as active in the East as in the West; and it was only at the end of the tenth century that their conversion to Christianity began.

It was a great age of missionary endeavour. The outcome was that Hungary, Poland and Scandinavia were converted by missions under Western auspices, Russia from Byzantium. More than the chance of a missionary's loyalty was involved in this: the missions were not accomplished in a moment, and the political orientation of the countries played a large part in a successful medieval mission. But it might well have happened, none the less, that Scandinavia was converted from Byzantium, or Russia from the West, and in either event the history of Europe would have been profoundly affected.

In the tenth and eleventh centuries Christianity was preached in the English Danelaw and in Scandinavia by English and German missionaries. The headquarters of the Scandinavian churches were set in the province of Hamburg-Bremen; and so it is to Adam of Bremen (died c. 1081) that we are chiefly indebted for our knowledge of the growth of Christianity in these countries; a gradual growth, with many vicissitudes, which was by no means complete when Adam died. The English Danelaw had ceased to be a missionary church by the time of the Norman Conquest: even Lincolnshire and Yorkshire were effectively rechristened, and the Normans firmly planted at Lincoln the bishop whose predecessor had peered timorously across his immense diocese from safe Saxon ground at Dorchester in the west of Oxfordshire, and at York the archbishop whose predecessors had frequently preferred the safety and wealth of Worcester. In Iceland, about the year 1000, Christianity came to rule; and the leading figures in the island's history for several generations were a remarkable line of cultivated warrior bishops, who passed their authority from father to son. About the same time Norway was in the hands of its first two Christian kings, Olaf Tryggvason and St Olaf; Denmark had already been converted, and Christianity was beginning to make headway among the Swedes. 'If ever they are in difficulties on the battlefield', wrote Adam of Bremen of the Swedes, 'they invoke the aid of one of the multitude of gods whom they worship; after a victory they show him great devotion and give him precedence over the others. Now, however, by general consent, the God of the Christians is proclaimed stronger than all.'[1] So, little by little, Thor and Woden (Odin) were driven from their last strongholds.

Adam had a special interest in the geography of the Baltic countries, and much that he says is highly illuminating; save that the farther east he went, the foggier was his information, and he peopled the eastern Baltic, not only with Russians, but with Amazons and 'Cynocephali', 'Men who have their heads on their chests. They are often seen as prisoners in Russia, and they utter words by barking.' Of the other Baltic lands he knew more, and attempted to distinguish them by geography and race.

> Norway's craggy mountains and excessive cold make it the least fertile of lands, suitable only for flocks. . . . On these they live, using their milk for food, their wool for clothing. And so, in no way softened by luxurious food, the boldest soldiers are produced. . . . Compelled by poverty at home, they circle the whole world and bring back from their pirate raids the wealth of every land.

In contrast:

> Sweden is a most fertile country; the land is rich in produce and in honey, excelling in the rearing of flocks, excellently provided with rivers and woods, everywhere stocked with foreign merchandise. And so you may say that the Swedes are deficient in no form of wealth, save pride. . . . For they think nothing of all the instruments of vainglory—gold, silver, royal horses, beaver and marten skins, which make us mad in admiring them.[2]

But he knows most of the Danes, and underlines what he clearly regarded as their two most notable characteristics, piety and piracy.

Adam knew how different the Scandinavian countries were geographically, and how varied were their political arrangements and their religious institutions in his day. But we can discern through the variety some basic similarities: the rough and ready process by which the Vikings came to accept Christianity; their common dependence on the sea; their political instability; their immense capacity for travel, adventure and experiment. Nature forced adventure on them. Norway is

[1] Adam of Bremen, book IV, Chapter 22 (my own translation).
[2] *Ibid.*, Chapters 19, 30, 21.

mountainous, Denmark so flat that its highest peak scarcely reaches 500 feet above sea-level. But both have this in common, that communication is, and always has been, first and foremost by sea. Norway was divided into small communities round the heads of its numerous fjords; a large part of Denmark consists of a group of islands. These divisions made for political divergence; made also for an unstable population, since a slight rise rapidly spilled over the narrow resources of a Norwegian valley or of a Danish island. From Scandinavia had come many Germanic tribes in prehistoric times; and the wealth of Roman and of Byzantine gold in the Baltic islands shows that the Scandinavians had profited, partly no doubt as mercenaries, partly as pirates, from the chaos of the barbarian invasions. In the Viking era, from the eighth to the twelfth centuries, they again spread over the world, both the known world, and even—if the tradition strongly entrenched in the sagas can be credited—to the coast of America. By the late tenth century their period of most extensive emigration was over: they had settled in Scotland and Ireland, in Iceland and Greenland, in the English Danelaw, in Normandy and in Russia; but their most sensational adventures were still to come—the conquest of England by Swein and Cnut, and of England, south Italy and Sicily by the Normans. The conditions of life in Scandinavia at the turn of the tenth and eleventh centuries are clearly reflected in the careers of the two Olafs.

Olaf Tryggvason was a Viking serving in the Danish armies in England, who in 995 returned to his native Norway to claim the throne. He was a vigorous and brilliant figure; for a short time he won the support of the chieftains. But he overreached himself, and was killed in battle in the year 1000. Soon after he was succeeded by Olaf the saint, who also began his career as a Viking in England, in the invasions which led up to Cnut's conquest of the island in 1015–16. In the later stages of these campaigns, Norway was denuded of its leaders, and in 1015 Olaf seized his chance of invading Norway. He held his own there more or less, with some difficulty, and with diminishing support, until he was ousted in 1028 by Cnut himself. Two years later he died in an attempt to recover his kingdom; and his last battle became famous in saga, and was somewhat strangely thought to be a kind of martyrdom.

The Olafs were both heroic, swashbuckling Vikings. St Olaf, like the great Cnut, had more than one wife; but his affairs were a marked advance on pagan conditions, reflected in contemporary Sweden, where 'each man has two or three wives or more according to his means; rich men and princes have wives past counting'.[1] Their Christianity, indeed, set them apart from their predecessors; just as it was his Christianity which enabled Cnut to step into the shoes of the Old English kings. But the Olafs wore their Christianity with a difference. Olaf Tryggvason believed in baptism by force or fraud: he is said to have maimed or burnt or exiled the stauncher pagans, and picturesque stories were told of his treatment of them. That he could succeed at all shows that paganism was a dying force in his day; his methods help to explain why he was unpopular. The saint was more conventional in his techniques of conversion, but his attitude was essentially the same: the Christian God had proved Himself more powerful than Thor or Odin, and so he nailed his colours to the Christian mast.

The tone and the tastes of this heroic world were recorded in that part of the Viking world where Christian learning and pagan valour were united in a single dynasty, in Iceland. There the old poetic Edda, the lays of pagan gods and the legends of the age of the barbarian invasions, were first recorded in writing. There the vernacular prose saga reached its greatest heights in the twelfth and thirteenth centuries. The heroes were partly Icelandic, partly Norwegian, partly from else-where in the Viking world; and as time passed strangers from other worlds joined them, including King Arthur and Thomas Becket. It is curious that in this small island on the very edge of Europe the history of European vernacular literature down to the thirteenth century should have found its epitome, and significant too, of the way in which the Scandinavian peoples collected plunder in so many parts of Europe. But before the mid twelfth century the Vikings had shown signs of settling down; the monarchies were becoming slightly more stable; the people were becoming slowly more Christianized; piracy, which had made the Vikings wealthy, had been converted into trade, which enabled them to keep their wealth.

Immense quantities of silver coins have been excavated in Scandinavia and the Baltic islands. The largest quantities came from England—largely, no doubt, the remnant of the famous Danegeld, the tribute paid by the English king to the Danes at the turn of the tenth and eleventh centuries—and from Islam. The history of the silver from Islam, found on the shores and islands of the Baltic, has been the subject of much controversy. Did it come by trade or by loot? Why was it silver which came, and not gold? Why did it cease in the mid eleventh century? The answer to both the last two questions lies in the source

[1] Adam of Bremen, book IV, Chapter 21.

49

of the silver; it came from the Muslim emirates north-east and east of the Black Sea, whose currency at this time was almost entirely of silver; and it ceased in the mid eleventh century, when these emirates ceased to coin money. But the fact that it came so far north, and in such quantities, established the part which the Vikings played in the life of the peoples lying between them and Islam, especially in the kingdom of Russia. The Scandinavians in Russia were partly traders, maybe, but mainly mercenaries and condottieri; and the silver came to them in payment for their services, and by loot.

Russia

From the ninth century to the thirteenth the Russian kings of the dynasty of the 'Rus' ruled from Kiev and Novgorod a great empire covering most of Russia-in-Europe, with its centre in the Ukraine. About its end there are no doubts: it was reduced to insignificance by the Mongols, who conquered a great part of it in the mid thirteenth century. But its beginning is still the subject of dispute. According to legend the empire of Novgorod and Kiev was founded by Rurik, who settled in Novgorod and died between 870 and 879, and his successor Oleg, who moved on to Kiev; and Rurik and Oleg were members of a group of Vikings, the 'Rus', who gave their name to Russia. This has led some historians to look upon Russia as a Viking colony, and the empire of Kiev as a Viking creation; and on the mixture of loot and trade and military adventure on which its greatness was founded as another expression of the Viking spirit. No-one doubts that the bulk of the population, their language and customs, were Slav; and recent Russian historians have tried to minimize the Viking influence. The literary evidence, however confused, leaves little doubt that the dynasty was Viking in origin; and it may well be that the 'Rus' came first as a band of mercenaries. It is also clear, both from the chronicles and from the Baltic finds of silver, that Vikings plied in Russia and farther south as mercenaries, and often returned to their homeland. But this apart, excavation has shown no trace of Scandinavian influence in Russia in these centuries; and it is clear that the Rus, like the Normans, absorbed the civilization of the people over whom they ruled.

Russia, in these centuries, was never effectively united for any length of time; frequently Novgorod and Kiev were ruled by different members of the dynasty; the vast area of the kingdom, its diverse character and comparatively sparse population prevented the establishment of a highly organized monarchy. But it was strong enough to threaten the

Balkans from time to time, and just strong enough to act as a buffer between the tribes and empires farther east, and eastern Europe. Not unnaturally, Russia was drawn into the sphere of Byzantine politics by the great warrior Basil II, whose career was at its height in the time of Vladimir I of Kiev (980–1015). In 988 Basil gave Vladimir the princess Anna (probably his own sister) in marriage; in return Vladimir seems to have promised fealty to Basil, and certainly accepted Christianity. Various attempts had been made to convert the Russians before; they knew something of both Western and Eastern Christianity, and Vladimir himself had investigated the claims of Islam. The conversion of the Russians was not accomplished in a moment, but the establishment of the church in Kiev in 988 was the vital step. It ensured that the cross should rule in Russia, not the crescent, and it helped to ensure that her relations should be with Byzantium, not with the West. In her relations with Byzantium there were many vicissitudes; she did not accept the emperor's suzerainty for long. But she was a barrier against Asiatic incursions on the Empire's northern frontier—and, incidentally, sealed Europe from Asia—until the coming of the Mongols.

Eastern and central Europe

Between Russia and Germany lay the Baltic peoples, still pagan and comparatively independent of German or Christian influence in the late tenth century; and also the Poles, Bohemians and Magyars. The Baltic peoples who bordered on Germany, were akin to the Slavs:[1] in language and tradition, as well as in mode of life, their links lay farther east, with Russia and the Balkan peoples; the southern Slavs had already felt the influence of Byzantine Christianity in the ninth century, in the work of St Cyril and St Methodius. But the Magyar invasions, at the turn of the ninth and tenth centuries, had divided the northern Slavs from Byzantium, and the tendency in the period of this book was for the countries bordering on Germany to fall more and more under Western influence. The tenth and eleventh centuries saw the final crystallization of the frontiers of France and Germany; they saw the other chief linguistic frontier, that between Teuton and Slav, progressively smudged. This frontier has remained both fundamental and dangerously confused ever since.

The frontier of the Germany of Otto the Great was drawn, very roughly, along the Elbe. His Saxon margraves fought and plundered and pillaged east of the Elbe, much as the Norman marchers were to do

[1] See below, p. 63.

in Wales from the late eleventh century on; and, as in Wales, the frontier moved this way and that according to the play of political circumstances. The definitive settlement of the lands east of the Elbe only came in the great age of colonization, in the twelfth century. Meanwhile their conversion went on apace.

In Poland, Hungary and Bohemia, the tenth and early eleventh centuries saw a remarkable transformation. Early in the tenth century Duke Wenceslas—the 'good king' of the Christmas carol—had German suzerainty imposed upon him, and accepted with more readiness the Christian faith, together with German relics and clergy. In 935 he was murdered, and German control and the Christian faith were not re-established for some years. In the long run Bohemia became a Christian country under the rule of its duke; subject to the emperor when the emperor was powerful enough to be feared; subject too to frequent civil war. The link with Germany persisted throughout our period, even though for a time in the eleventh century the dukes were made kings.

Less consistent was the relation between Germany and Poland. Poland, like Bohemia, had accepted the overlordship and the religion of the Ottos. The visit of Otto III, as emperor and apostle, to the shrine of St Adalbert at Gnesen, where he established the first Polish archbishopric, marked the coming of age of Poland as a duchy under Western influence. But the duke, Boleslav the Mighty (992–1025), was by no means inclined to continued dependence; after Otto's death he proceeded to conquer the borderlands between his own and the Saxon frontier; and in a series of campaigns he kept the Emperor Henry II at bay. They made peace in 1018, which left Boleslav free to attack the kingdom of Rus, which he did with some success, and to call himself king. From then on Poland remained Catholic and Western in religion, eclectic in politics and culture, a principality only rarely owing more than a perfunctory allegiance to the Western emperor.

In the same year that Otto III established the archbishopric of Gnesen, he also provided Hungary with an archbishopric, at Gran, and its ruler, St Stephen, with a crown. The famous royal crown of Hungary is not the one worn by St Stephen, though the royal mantle, used in coronations as late as 1917, is a genuine relic of the founder of the Hungarian monarchy. After the defeat on the Lechfeld (955), the Magyars or Hungarians could no longer hope to live by pillaging their neighbours; they made the dangerous and difficult decision to be civilized. The details of this process are hidden from us. But the chief architect of the Hungarian monarchy in our period was St Stephen, who made the Church his ally not only in the conversion of Hungary to a country of Western type, but also, like the emperors of his day, the instrument of government. As in Bohemia and Poland, the government was patriarchal, but weakened by frequent civil war due to the uncertainty of the rules of succession. The kings of Hungary had, however, two particular advantages: they were, at this date, proprietors of most of the land in their kingdom, and in due course they drew great profit from the mineral resources of the country, tapped largely by German settlers in the thirteenth century. The fact that two of their eleventh-century kings, Stephen and Ladislas I, were venerated as saints underlines the close liaison with the Church; it also reminds us of the close relations with the papacy. When empire and papacy came to blows, and the power of the German monarchy was weakened, the kings of Hungary could be relied on to give the papacy moral support at least, and so help to win for themselves virtual independence of the empire.

Thus by the early twelfth century the countries of central Europe had grown to maturity under the wings of empire and papacy; had come to value their relation to the Roman Church, though they often sat lightly to it; and to take lightly, without valuing, their relation to the emperor. But in northern Europe, in the no-man's-land between Germany and Poland, and along the Baltic coast, lay a group of peoples whose position was still undefined. In the tenth century Germany had driven east and conquered them; in the late tenth century they had recovered their independence. In the twelfth century, at the very end of our period, the *Drang nach Osten* began again. Once again Church and king worked hand-in-hand; and conversion went ahead of the soldiers and the settlers. Humble preachers went barefoot to preach to the Pomeranians, who viewed their ragged habits, and despised the God whose poverty was reflected in them. A little later, in 1124, came Bishop Otto of Bamberg, also a man of eloquence and fervour, but clothed in full pontificals, with a splendid retinue. The Pomeranians were duly impressed, and with their baptism the Catholic faith had conquered the whole Baltic littoral to the boundaries of Russia. Along it, and in all the lands between Elbe and Oder, the Germans began to settle.

Western Europe

1. *Internal physical boundaries.* Encircled by the sea, the empires of Islam and Byzantium, and the pirate kingdoms of Russia and the

Vikings, the shape of Europe between the tenth and the twelfth centuries was defined. In Spain its border was ill-defined and fluctuating;
the Slav and Magyar peoples of eastern Europe lived under its shadow,
increasingly assuming its manner of life; the Vikings in the north
gradually settled down to be semi-Christian. Within this outer circle
lay the peoples of Germany, Italy, northern Spain, France and the
British Isles; all securely Christian—save where the Vikings had a
strong hold—for centuries before the tenth; all owing traditional

I. EUROPE: PHYSICAL

allegiance to the pope; most speaking a Teutonic or a Romance language; most under the sway of a lay, military aristocracy more or less imbued with 'feudal' institutions. To illustrate the unity and diversity of western Europe, let us look in turn at three maps: at the physical map scored by nature and early man on the European peninsula, at the political map as it was drawn in the year 962, and at the map of European languages. The first was the most lasting; the second the most superficial; but a clear understanding of all three is necessary if the story told in this book is to be understood.

In these regions, mankind lived by bread, beer and wine, and moved, where possible, by water. We shall have plenty of opportunity to modify this statement in due course; for the moment it will help us to give a first interpretation to the physical map of Europe. Over the middle of Europe, from northern France, through north Germany to Poland and Russia, spreads an immense plain, in which nature had planted immense, rich forests of deciduous trees. Since Neolithic times mankind had hewn and burned clearings in these forests, and had grown wheat for his bread and barley for his beer. There was still plenty of forest to provide pasture for pigs, timber for builders and for firewood, hunting grounds for the sport of kings and nobles; above all, land which the growing populations of all these countries could reclaim. In Frisia and the Low Countries, the cultivator had to compete, not with forest, but with water; and expanding population led him to reclaim marsh and fen. The lowland plain extends over northern France and south-eastern England; in England forest and marsh, as in the neighbouring continental territories, offered a challenge to the colonizer. The Baltic, the North Sea and the English Channel had been, and still were, the highways of the Viking peoples. The Baltic was also a frontier between lowland Germany and Denmark and mountainous Norway. In this sense the English Channel was not a frontier. The plain and the hills met in the north and west of Britain, and the boundary between them represented very roughly the frontier of England with Wales and Scotland. South-east Britain, the lowland zone, had many links with the Continent; these grew as the eleventh century wore on. The highland zone of Britain was part of the Celtic lands, which included Ireland and Brittany, were united by tradition, and (in a measure) by language, and by the sea highway which ran down from the western isles of Scotland to the Bay of Biscay; but united in no other way.

The centre and south-east of France forms a borderland, in character and situation, between northern Europe and the world of the

Mediterranean, the Massif Central acting as a physical indication of the division. In climate and outlook the Mediterranean world is in strong contrast with that we have just described. It is not wholly cut off from northern Europe. The Pyrenees are a formidable barrier, but they can be outflanked by land or water, and crossed in two or three places in the summer months. The Alps can be more easily outflanked and also more easily crossed. But there were only four important routes through the central Alps in our period, a fact of great political importance to Germans with an ambition to rule in Italy. These came through Bavaria, by the long mountain road over the Brenner Pass; or through Swabia and the kingdom of Burgundy, over the Septimer, the Great St Bernard or the Mont Cenis. The last, though farthest from the centre of Germany, was probably the most important. Over it, for instance, came Henry IV, through the winter snow, on the road to Canossa; and Lampert of Hersfeld's account of his journey, checked by modern scholars on the ground, has done much to restore the historian's credit. Opposite its foot, in the late twelfth century, the Lombard cities in revolt against Frederick Barbarossa—king of Germany, duke of Swabia, and king of Burgundy—planted the fortress of Alessandria, named after Pope Alexander III, the fortress which Napoleon mastered in 1796 in order to secure his communications with France and Switzerland before marching to the foot of the Brenner to intercept the armies coming from Austria to attack him.

Italy and Spain are the countries of the vine and the olive, of Roman crops, of the Romance languages, of the distant survival of Roman civic life. But there the resemblance ended. For central and northern Italy, including the rich lands of the Po valley, lay in western Christendom; whereas the most fertile parts of Spain were in Muslim hands. Barcelona, it is true, lay in the Mediterranean world; but the emperor of León-Castile lived in a world of his own, bordering on the Atlantic and on the Caliphate of Cordoba; and if ever he lifted his eyes beyond Cordoba, it was to Africa.

2. *Political frontiers.* The empire of Charlemagne had broken up in the course of the ninth century into three large fragments; the western corresponded roughly to what it is convenient to call France, although the frontiers were very different from those of today; the eastern fragment, with similar convenience and inaccuracy, we shall call Germany. The 'Middle Kingdom' contained Lorraine, Provence, Burgundy and much of Italy; but this area remained a kingdom only very briefly. By the late tenth century it was a collection of kingdoms

and principalities; the more southerly subject to anarchy, the more northerly disputed between Germany and France (see pp. 166 ff.).

Politically, Europe was overshadowed in 962 by the imperial figure of Otto the Great.

> By his many victories [writes the Saxon chronicler Widukind after describing Otto's crushing victory over the Hungarians on the Lechfeld in 955] . . . he won the fear and respect of many kings and many nations. Many ambassadors he received, from Rome and Greece and the Saracens; and from them gifts of diverse kinds, gold and silver bowls, and copper bowls, wrought in a strange variety of fashions; glassware and ivories; coverlets of every shape and size; balsam and scents of every kind; animals such as the Saxons had never seen before —lions and camels, monkeys and ostriches. Thus was Otto the hope and resource of the whole of Western Christendom.[1]

He was king of the Franks and of Italy (i.e. Lombardy), overlord of the dukes of Poland, Hungary and Bohemia and of the king of Burgundy; he was Roman emperor. He was, in name, all and slightly more than all Charlemagne had been. It is true that, as with Charlemagne, there was another Roman emperor; but however much Otto and his successors might concern themselves about their relations with Byzantium, there was little danger of political competition, save in south Italy. There was also another king of the Franks, lord of what we call France, but a much weaker monarch than Otto; and one who might have admitted Otto's suzerainty, as his predecessor had admitted that of Otto's father. We are accustomed to think of Germany as the core of Otto's empire, as a closely knit country owing undoubted allegiance to him. There is some truth in this; but it is well to remember that the frontiers of Germany were not clearly defined in his day; that the idea of a kingdom of 'Germany' was a novel one, and very little spoken about by contemporaries; and that each of the duchies of which Germany was composed had close links with some outside power. Otto was a Saxon, and his first wife an Anglo-Saxon princess; this reminds us of the link of old Saxony and England in language and tradition. The Old Saxons, furthermore, had not forgotten that they had been independent of the Franks until the time of Charlemagne. Otto's kingdom was still the kingdom of the Franks. The centre of his domain as king lay in the old Frankish homeland, of which his share was Franconia and Lotharingia or Lorraine. The Frankish homeland sprawled across the linguistic

---

[1] Widukind, *Rerum gestarum Saxonicarum libri tres*, Book III, Chapter 56.

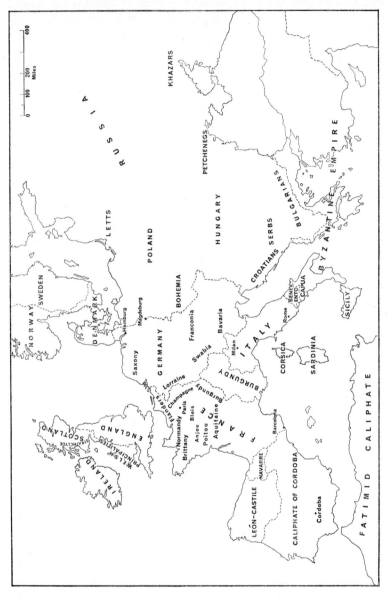

2. EUROPE IN 962

frontier between German- and French-speaking territory. Lorraine herself was border country; politically she was 'German' throughout our period; there were still strong links between Franconia, Lorraine and northern France; but they were weakening as the linguistic frontier reasserted itself, and Lorraine looked both ways, as it has done in every century since. South of Lorraine lay the duchies of Burgundy and Swabia, whose peoples had memories (like those of the Saxons) of the days when they had been independent of the Franks. Bavaria and Swabia, too, had linguistic and other links with the Lombards beyond the Alps, and the Saxon emperors had constantly to guard against the Italian ambitions of the southern dukes. In recent years historians have emphasized that the German dukes were not independent princes, but royal officers; that the 'tribal' duchies were new and artificial creations. But the fact remains that the frontiers approximately conformed to the ancient frontiers of the German kingdoms and tribes; that their peoples remembered these ancient divisions; that the centrifugal tendencies were profound.

Even more profound were the divisions of western Francia, of what we call France. Geography and history had combined to divide France into the northern plain and the southern uplands. The south, deriving its name from the old Roman province, was called 'Aquitaine'. But the unity of Aquitaine was very precarious; the title 'duke' was held from time to time by one of the leading counts, most commonly the count of Poitou, whose overlordship was rarely recognized by more than a proportion of his neighbours. In the north the fragments were smaller and more precise. Northern France was a model of the decay of Carolingian power. In the west the count of the Breton march had absorbed the Celtic enclave of Brittany, and made himself duke of Brittany. To the north-east of Brittany lay the Viking state of Normandy, legitimized in the early tenth century, still a prey to civil war and faction, but slowly emerging as one of the principal powers of north-western Europe. Farther north-east again lay the county of Flanders, covering the area from which the Vikings had been cleared by the adventurous Count Baldwin II (879–918). On the eastern frontier lay the duchy of Burgundy, another aggregation of Carolingian counties, representing that fragment of the old Burgundian kingdom still on French territory (see Map 2). Poised within this circle of powerful counties lay the French royal domain, steadily diminishing as the last of the French Carolingians struggled to win support by granting away the last of the imperial domains. Soon the duke of the Franks, Hugh Capet, was to replace the Carolingians (987), but he was only able to bequeath to his heirs a fragment of the northern plain of France as the royal domain, the Île de France. Round him were growing up the counties of Blois and Champagne and many others; and to his west the county of Anjou, soon to rival Normandy as the home of violent, ambitious lords; eventually to be united with Normandy as the nucleus of the enormous French domains of King Henry II of England. The authority of the king of France over these many principalities was precarious in the extreme.

South-east of France lay the fragments of the old Middle Kingdom, Provence and Arles, Savoy and the other counties of the kingdom of Burgundy; and across the Alps the Lombard kingdom, the various fragments of Lombard authority in Italy, and the states owing temporal allegiance to the pope. Otto I gathered all these under one ruler; and although he confirmed the grants of his Frankish predecessors to the papacy, he treated the whole of Italy, save what was held by the Byzantine Empire and by the Muslims, as his own territory. This, however, was no more than a temporary rationalization. During most of our period the hold of the emperors in Italy was erratic and precarious. Power became diffused through two channels; first through the great nobles, like the counts of Tuscany, and the leading bishops; second through the Italian cities, such as Venice, Pisa and Genoa, encouraged by their growing wealth to assume or to struggle for independence. The power of the cities emphasized the dependence of Italy on the Mediterranean. In politics it looked both north and south, was conscious of its Roman and German past, and its Greek and Muslim, and Italian, present. Italy also contained the papal patrimony, dependent, in 962, either on local faction or on imperial protection; but capable of reviving its ancient glory and traditional authority, and, before our period closed, of becoming the centre of a state more sophisticated in its organization and widespread in power than any emperor of the period could hope to have.

West and south of the old Carolingian Empire lay two independent empires, those of Spain and England, and two areas of semi-independent peoples, the Celtic lands and the Basque. It is now established that the king of León had called himself emperor at least since the opening of the tenth century. In practice, he was one of a number of counts and kings who held semi-independent sway along the northern borders of Spain, in what was left to them by the Muslim conquests: the Atlantic principalities of Galicia, León and Castile, the Pyrenean kingdoms of Navarre and Aragon, and the Mediterranean county of Barcelona or Catalonia. Geography and to some extent language held them apart;

opposition to the Moors held them together; a strong 'emperor' joined them in union; but when he died his sons divided his inheritance.

The unity of England was apparently much more secure. The lowland zone of Britain formed the most compact geographical area in Europe. King Edgar (959–75) was heir to a line of kings who had united England under the sway of the old kingdom of Wessex and subdued the Danes and Norse over most of the country; Edgar himself was a ruler after the pattern of Otto the Great, strong and pious, suffering little opposition from his lay subordinates (far less than Otto suffered) and none from the Church. Like Otto he had suzerainty over the neighbouring princes; like León, his kingdom was sometimes called an empire. But its hold over the Celtic tribes on its borders was very precarious, and it still lay exposed to Viking attacks. Within a few years of Edgar's death Danish attacks were renewed, and the country was eventually conquered and subdued by Swein and Cnut. None the less, the foundations of a strong monarchy had been firmly laid; and England survived into the eleventh century, the most highly organized monarchy in western Europe.

In marked contrast were the principalities of Scotland, Wales and Ireland, still as anarchic as Viking kingdoms, as some of them partly were. Ireland and Wales had the memory of an age when they had been more civilized than England, and as time passed they came more and more under English influence; but Scotland was the only country of the three which was strongly influenced by her English neighbour before the mid twelfth century. The success of the Normans in conquering England, and their failure to conquer Britain were two of the most striking features of the history of our period.

The other minority had no sort of political independence: the Basque peoples, lying where France and Spain meet at the western end of the Pyrenees, were divided politically between the princes of southwestern Aquitaine (Gascony), Navarre and Castile, and divided geographically by the barrier of the Pyrenees. In culture and language they retained, and still retain, a remarkable degree of independence.

The languages of Europe

A study of the linguistic frontiers of Europe and of their shifts and changes over the centuries is a profoundly illuminating exercise, so long as we are prepared to learn lessons and not to draw precise deductions from it. Men are acutely sensitive to linguistic differences: they notice at once if even fellow-countrymen speak their own language in a different way. Differences of dialect and tongue reflect, and sometimes cause, the innumerable emotions which have tied men to their homes and separated them from their neighbours. The modern Englishman, in particular, is inclined to forget that any man can be at home in two or three languages; but he is only too much aware that a single, international language may make communications possible among peoples of very different backgrounds.

3. THE LANGUAGES OF EUROPE, 10th–11th CENTURIES

Europe was dominated, then as now, by three large linguistic groups: the Romance languages, children of Latin, the Germanic languages, and the Slavonic; and united by the common language of the western Church, Latin. But this simplicity is misleading. All these languages come ultimately from one family, the Indo-European, yet that does not make it much easier for a Frenchman and a Russian to understand one another today. Already by the tenth century there were many distinct tongues within each of these groups, and innumerable dialects. It is indeed extremely difficult for us to know which languages and dialects were mutually intelligible. But we do well to be warned by the example of modern Basque. 'Millennia of isolation without literary or cultural control have split Basque into numerous dialects, which are not mutually intelligible . . .; with at least 25 subdialects, and local differences for each village and even for each generation of speakers.'[1] Basque is exceptional, for three reasons: it is one of the very few languages spoken in Europe which is not Indo-European—it is, indeed, a family of its own; it is very ancient, and has therefore had far longer to develop its schisms than have its neighbours; and its isolation has enabled it to be as eccentric as it wished. But dialects and languages were always more isolated in medieval than in modern Europe, and new linguistic boundaries and frontiers were constantly in process of formation.

To find another language not of Indo-European origin, we have to travel into eastern Europe, which is a fascinating palimpsest, revealing the history of Europe with devastating clarity. Its languages, with one exception, are those of the numerous peoples deposited in these regions by the invasions of Europe between the second millennium B.C. and the tenth century A.D.: Greek, Latin (in the form of Roumanian), Slavonic (of various kinds), Baltic, Esthonian and Magyar. Of these the last two alone are non-Indo-European. In addition to these languages, the modern linguistic map shows innumerable islands, large and small, of German-speaking folk stretching as far east as south Russia. It is true that the German peoples occupied parts of this area long before the Slavs; but these pockets of German speech are more recent. They are due to the *Drang nach Osten*. In the tenth and eleventh centuries the frontier of Slav and German lay, roughly and uneasily, on the Elbe. In the twelfth century it finally began to move eastwards; since then there has been no frontier, in any useful sense of the term, at all, but an immense area of coexistence. Throughout our period, however, there must have been growing numbers of folk of Slavonic or Baltic tongue who spoke German with their German overlords, the emperors, and of Christian clergy who spoke Latin in the lands of Roman allegiance and Greek in those which had received their baptism from Byzantium.

Compared with the boundary of German and Slav, that between Romance and German was comparatively tidy. Then as now, it was a belt, not a frontier; it spread over most of what we call Belgium,

[1] W. J. Entwistle, *The Spanish Language* (London, 1936), p. 15.

Lorraine, Alsace and parts of Switzerland and the Tirol. The most remarkable breach lay in north Italy, which we still call Lombardy after the German tribe which conquered it in the sixth century; nor was the German language forgotten there in the tenth. At both ends, indeed, of the frontier between French and German the greatest confusion reigned. Various dialects of Romance, predecessors of modern Italian, were spoken throughout the Italian peninsula; but in Sicily the ruling class spoke Arabic; in south Italy Greek; north-eastern Italy lay in an area where Greek and Italian and German met and mingled. At the other end of the frontier lay the British Isles, divided between the area dominated by the various dialects of Old English, or Anglo-Saxon, and the Celtic lands, where the dialects of the two main branches of the Celtic family were spoken, roughly corresponding to what we call Welsh ('Brittonic', in Wales, Cornwall and Brittany) and Gaelic (in Scotland and Ireland). Nor was the British pattern simplified by the Norman invasion, which added a dialect of French to the languages spoken in England and other parts of the island; a dialect which remained the language of its court for three centuries and modified the English language more profoundly than any other Germanic tongue has been modified by a Romance influence.

In France, apart from the Celtic enclave in Brittany and the half-Germanic frontier lands, the dialects fell naturally into two groups: the *langue d'oil* and the *langue d'oc*.[1] The *langue d'oc* ruled over an area roughly equivalent to the duchy of Aquitaine; nor was Aquitaine finally subdued to the royal allegiance until the *langue d'oc* had submitted to its northern sister, many centuries after the twelfth. The *langue d'oc*, commonly known as Provençal, was close to Catalan; the two were more like one another than was either to the dominant dialects of France or Spain. In Christian Spain Catalan ruled on the eastern seaboard, whose natural links were with Provence, and whose ruling class looked east and north rather than west or south. The other Christian principalities each had its own dialect, and their growth in later centuries followed closely the political history of the *reconquista*, while as each pushed south it absorbed more and more influence from Arabic. Galician pressed south into Portugal, and so became the ancestor of modern Portuguese. Castilian, from being the dialect only of old Castile, spread through the centuries all over central Spain, and so became by the end of the Middle Ages the dominant dialect which it still remains. But it has not

[1] i.e. French and Provençal; called (from the thirteenth century) the tongues of '*oil*' and '*oc*' from the words in each for 'yes' ('*oil*'=modern '*oui*').

destroyed its rivals. Galician and Portuguese are still independent; Catalan is as distinct as ever; the dialects of the south gave their language to Spanish America. There is no country whose history is more reflected in its language than Spain.

In a world in which political frontiers were constantly shifting and great dynasts very rarely had any idea of 'nationality', the sense of belonging to a people, to a coherent group, to a nation, could never have the force it has commonly had in the last two centuries. Where it existed, it depended above all on language, usually allied to a notion of common history. It was language above all which enabled Frenchmen to talk of 'la douce France', and enabled the linguistic frontier between French and German to become fossilized, though never clarified. But this was the only linguistic frontier in Europe which corresponded to political fact and national feeling in any useful sense of the word, save perhaps those in the Celtic lands.

We are here involved in a question of great difficulty and delicacy. We can prove that it meant much to the French that they did not speak German. But in the same period England was conquered by a French dynasty who had no need to learn English, so far as one can tell. The Scottish kingdom was transformed under the influence of the wife of King Malcolm (the Malcolm of *Macbeth*), an English princess brought up in Hungary, who was at home in Latin but spoke no Gaelic (see p. 348); the English Church throve under the primacy of two Italians— and the English biographer of Anselm gives no hint of any linguistic difficulty or resentment—who doubtless depended mainly on Latin for communication. It is clear that in one sense linguistic frontiers counted for more than now; but that in another they scarcely existed. The upper clergy spoke Latin; the lower clergy had a smattering of it; most folk who travelled at all picked up two or three languages; interpreters were easy to find. Although the West Saxon dialect of Old English played a considerable part in English government before the Conquest, it was very rare for there to be an official language in this period apart from Latin. The days when one dialect became the literary or the ruling language of a people lay in the future. Otto the Great was a good linguist: we are told that he could speak French and Slav, though the observation that he did not often do so may be a polite way of saying that he was not very good at them. Mostly he spoke German, that is, his native Saxon dialect, which no doubt sounded as strange in Bavaria as pidgin in Oxford. The linguistic map is full of fascinating details and strange perplexities.

IV

Economic Life

The basis of life in tenth-, eleventh- and twelfth-century Europe lay in agriculture: in the growing of corn, the rearing of sheep and cattle and of other essential sources of food and drink. In the tenth century a large majority of the population lived near the subsistence level. That is to say, they grew their own food and provided by their own labour the bulk of life's necessities. Subsistence in this sense has little in common with the life of the modern Englishman who grows his own vegetables in his garden. The good gardener, with the aid of modern fertilizers and scientific knowledge, can usually be sure of a tolerable crop; if his garden fails him, he can turn to the greengrocer. The worst he has to fear is a temporary rise in the cost of living. A man who lives at the subsistence level has no greengrocer to turn to and no money to buy food if his crop fails. He is not alone: he is normally a member of a community which will care for him in need. But a serious famine will put the whole community in straits, and against famine the subsistence

BIBLIOGRAPHY. In general: H. Pirenne, *Economic and Social History of Medieval Europe* (London, 1937); *Cambridge Economic History* (vols. I–III, Cambridge, 1942–63, so far published; a revised edition of vol. I is in the press), which has full bibliographies; H. Sée, *Histoire économique de la France*, vol. I (Paris, 1939); R. Latouche, *The Birth of Western Economy* (Eng. trans., London, 1961). For sources, R. S. Lopez and I. W. Raymond, *Medieval Trade in the Mediterranean World* (New York, 1955), J. H. Mundy and P. Riesenberg, *The Medieval Town* (Princeton, 1958). On building, see Chapter XVI. On coins, A. Engel and R. Serrure, *Traité de numismatique du moyen âge* (vol. II, Paris, 1894) is the only general account; for bibliography, see P. Grierson, 'Report on Medieval Numismatics', *Congrès International de Numismatique*, Paris, 1953, vol. I, pp. 55–101, and *Coins and Medals: A select bibliography* (Historical Association, 1954); on German coins, A. Suhle, *Deutsche Münz- und Geldgeschichte von den Anfängen bis zum 15. Jahrhundert* (2nd edn., Berlin, 1955). On technological change, L. White, *Medieval Technology and Social Change* (Oxford, 1962) (fascinating, but to be used with caution); on trade see *Cambridge Economic History*, vol. II; J. N. L. Baker, *Medieval Trade Routes* (Historical Association, 1938); E. E. Power, *The Wool Trade in English Medieval*

AGRICULTURAL SOCIETY

farmer has no defence. In tenth-century Europe many folk were at the mercy of famine, but happily very few were entirely dependent on what they could grow; and in the two centuries covered by this book a remarkable economic development took place which carried the peoples of Europe quite substantially above the subsistence level. This change, which established trade, markets, industry on a new level—primitive by our standards, but advanced compared with what had gone before— and saw many changes in agriculture itself, is the theme of the present chapter.

A mainly agricultural society needs many hands at time of harvest; but at other times of year cannot provide all of them with full employment. It is a matter of observation that a high proportion of the population are under-employed in a subsistence economy. 'In a purely subsistence economy', writes Professor Bauer, 'idleness tends to be regarded as part of the nature of things.'[1] As the economy develops, more diversity of employment will be found; but it may be many centuries before full employment is a possibility; meanwhile, idleness is no longer part of the order of things; the Church distinguishes between

[1] P. T. Bauer, *West African Trade* (Cambridge, 1954), p. 19n. For comparative purposes, with all the qualifications which have to be attached to the comparative method, medievalists can derive much stimulus from the study of underdeveloped countries in the modern world; for an introduction, see P. T. Bauer and B. S. Yamey, *The Economics of Underdeveloped Countries* (London, 1957).

History (Oxford, 1941); A. R. Lewis, *Naval Power and Trade in the Mediterranean, A.D. 500–1100* (Princeton, 1951); Y. Renouard, *Les hommes d'affaires italiens du moyen âge* (Paris, 1949). On slavery, C. Verlinden, *L'esclavage dans l'Europe médiévale* (vol. I only so far, Bruges, 1955); M. Bloch, 'Liberté et servitude personnelles au moyen âge, particulièrement en France', *Anuario de historia del derecho español*, vol. x (1933), and *Cambridge Economic History*, vol. I, Chapter VI. On towns, see H. Pirenne, *Mediaeval Cities* (Princeton, 1925); M. V. Clarke, *The Medieval City State* (London, 1926); A. B. Hibbert, 'The origins of the medieval town patriciate', *Past and Present*, vol. III (1953), pp. 15–27; *Cambridge Economic History*, vol. III.

On agriculture, *Cambridge Economic History*, vol. I and Marc Bloch's classic *Les caractères originaux de l'histoire rurale française* (2nd edn., 2 vols., Paris, 1952–6); G. Duby, *L'économic rurale et la vie des campagnes dans l'occident médiéval* (2 vols., Paris, 1962).

H. R. Loyn, *Anglo-Saxon England and the Norman Conquest* (Longmans' Social and Economic History of England, 1962) gives a clear idea of the nature of the evidence in this period, and how it may be used to reconstruct the economic history of England.

67

deserving and undeserving poor, between the voluntarily and involuntarily idle; the government grows anxious about 'sturdy vagabonds'. These trends were operating during our period; their full working out lies far beyond it.

The analogy of modern underdeveloped societies will suggest to us that the profit motive and ordinary economic forces are likely to be very influential in the economy we are studying. No doubt external forces—beliefs, social customs and taboos—may seriously upset purely economic calculations; but this is equally true of our own society. In the tenth century a lord valued the land he held as the source of warriors, as property which could be used to reward and support his knights. By the twelfth century he valued it increasingly as the source of money: money, it is true, which could be used to hire knights; but the difference was profound none the less. A twelfth-century lord used his money for other things, for supporting a grander standard of living, for instance; but above all he used it to pay for his wars and to pay for his buildings. These buildings might include a castle or two for himself; they very frequently included a church and a monastery where monks might pray for his soul. The generosity of laymen to the Church was sensational throughout our period; most conspicuously in the twelfth century. A brief inspection of the 'economics' of medieval building will help to make clear much in what follows.

The economics of building

It is sometimes suggested that the great sums invested in building in the Middle Ages retarded economic development, since they concentrated resources in unfruitful projects. This is the kind of argument which in the nature of the evidence can neither be proved nor disproved. Our evidence will never tell us whether there was at certain times a great surplus of labour; but all analogy and all the hints we have—of mobs in town and country, of throngs of pilgrims, of great armies of attendants on princes and lords—suggest that much of the population was normally under-employed. Under-employment helps to explain the grandiose schemes which so many early societies engaged in: the Egyptians built pyramids; the Romans built roads and walls; King Offa built his splendid dyke; King Alfred of Wessex and King Henry I of Germany built great ramparts round their town-like fortresses; and the men of our period built cathedrals, monasteries and castles. It may well be, then, that in doing so they were employing labour which would not otherwise have been occupied; and labour must certainly have been cheap. A second point is that the expense of these building projects was a powerful incentive to the lords to earn the means to pay for them; and we can find all sorts of evidence of the way in which the need of the lords for money spurred them to economic activity in this age. They helped towns and trade to flourish so that the surpluses of their fields could be sold for a good price; and if they often undid their good work by engaging in warfare and disrupting this trade, war itself had to be paid for, and fewer and fewer lords as the centuries passed reckoned to pay for war out of loot as their predecessors had done. The gravamen of the charge against medieval building is that it wastefully diverted money which could have been used in building up capital, or more productively invested. The argument is purely economic; and few will now regret the money which was spent on building the abbeys and cathedrals and churches of this period. But it reminds us that all economic arguments have their limitations; and the benefactors of medieval monasteries, if they had understood the jargon of modern economics, would have replied that their investment was in salvation, and that they were laying up capital in heaven.

Especially striking in this context is the paradox of the Cistercians. As the leading monastic reformers of the early twelfth century, they repudiated all ostentation of wealth; they refused to have any land they could not till themselves; they rejected the rising living standards of the age. To all appearance they represent, from a purely economic point of view, a return to subsistence agriculture. Yet notoriously they were in the forefront of economic development. They made strenuous efforts to be efficient farmers; where their lands were especially suited to sheep-farming, as in Wales or northern England, they reared large flocks whose wool they had to market; and although they did not become merchants themselves, they early formed an alliance with merchants who could sell their wool in distant markets; they acquired the reputation of being shrewd in business; their refusal to have costly ornaments prevented them accumulating useless 'capital' in the form of treasure, gold and silver and precious stones of which many older monasteries had large supplies which they could sometimes pawn but never sell; their austerity of life inhibited them from conspicuous consumption. The explanation of this paradox has never been made entirely clear, although it is evident that in later generations the Cistercians acquired the reputation of wealth—which meant that kings and princes mulcted them, and so forced them to save—and that in due course they became less austere both in life and in ornaments. Perhaps the explanation lies partly in the immense buildings, which they put up so swiftly and efficiently, and which must have been largely paid for out of the monks' resources. Certainly there seems to be some link between the quiet (yet deeply spiritual) efficiency of the *Carta Caritatis*, the precise way in which the monasteries were designed—to a single plan all over Europe —to be solid, sober expressions of devotion and to perform their function with the minimum of waste, and the economic efficiency of their management. As builders the Cistercians were in the forefront of technical improvement: no one who has explored the conduits and drains of a Cistercian abbey, and reflected that nothing comparable had been built since the time of the Romans, can fail to be impressed by their concern that material things should be decently (though not luxuriously) ordered. It is interesting to reflect that what the Cistercians did as pioneers of water supply and drainage in large establishments out in the country, the friars were later to do for water supply and drainage within the towns of Europe. Cleanliness went hand in hand with godliness.

To achieve their aims the Cistercians needed a site very precisely suited to their needs. This explains why they so often moved their abbeys in early days; and to this Clairvaux itself was no exception. The original site, well up a narrow valley, was splendidly wild but too small. The little city of the Cistercian abbey might number five or six times the regular inhabitants of houses of most other orders, and Clairvaux at its height housed seven hundred souls. This was exceptional: many Cistercian houses were built for about twenty choir monks and two or three times the number of lay brothers; but the size of Clairvaux was not unparalleled, since Rievaulx under St Ailred, with 140 choir monks and 500 lay brothers, ran it close. The growth of Clairvaux rapidly made its first home too crowded, and it was moved downstream to a place where the valley widened, where the water still had some pressure in it, but there was considerably more space. And so, in the 1130s and 1140s, in St Bernard's later years, Clairvaux II rose on the banks of the Aube. 'The most noble Count Theobald of holy memory [King Stephen's elder brother] heard this and gave much towards the cost, and promised further contributions.' So the first biography of Bernard describes the logistics of this large operation.

The bishops of the region, noblemen and merchants of the land heard of it, and joyfully offered rich aid in God's work. Supplies were abundant, workmen quickly hired, the brothers themselves joined in the work in every way: some cut timbers, others shaped stones, others built walls, others divided the river, set it in new channels and lifted the leaping waters to the mill-wheels; fullers and bakers and tanners and smiths and other artificers prepared suitable machines for their tasks, that the river might flow fast and do good wherever it was needed in every building, flowing freely in underground conduits; the streams performed suitable tasks in every office and cleansed the abbey and at length returned to the main course and restored to the river what it had lost. The walls which gave the abbey a spacious enclosure were finished with unlooked-for speed. The abbey rose; the new-born church, as if it had a living soul that moveth, quickly developed and grew.[1]

A later visitor to the abbey was captivated by the adventures of the river Aube, and paid his tribute to the technical achievements of Bernard and his colleagues—for although much water had flowed through the channels since Bernard's death, the system described is in essentials still that of the twelfth century.

[The water] is let into the abbey by the south wall, which acts as porter, and so far as the wall permits, the river plunges with vigour into the mill, where it is very busy and active so that the corn is ground under the weight of the mill-wheels and the fan shaken which winnows the wheat from the chaff. Now the river is in the next building: it fills the boiler and submits to the fire which heats it to make the monks' drink [ale], if perchance the vine has given a barren answer to the vinedresser's labour. . . .

But the river is not off duty yet. The fulling mills near the flour-mill call it to them. In the flour-mill the river worked to prepare the brothers' food; it is only right to insist that it next thinks of their clothing. It does not refuse the request. It raises and lowers alternately the heavy hammers [and so fulls the cloth for making habits]. . . . When it has turned so many wheels faster than ever it comes out foaming; one would say that it had milled itself. Then it goes into the tannery and works both hard and carefully to help make the brothers' shoes; then it breaks up into a crowd of little branches and goes its busy course visiting the various offices, looking diligently everywhere for work to do, whatever its aim: be it to cook, to strain, to turn, to grind, to bathe, to wash, offering its assistance, never refusing. Finally, since there is nothing for which we do not owe it thanks, it carries away the rubbish and leaves all clean behind it. The branch

[1] *Vita prima*, Book II, Chapter 5 (*Patrologia Latina*, vol. CLXXXV, col. 285).

of the river which is diverted through the abbey has thus rigorously completed all it set out to do; with a rapid current it goes to rejoin the Aube . . . and casts into its lap the waters which the Aube had furnished for us: the main river, impoverished and idle in its original bed, regains the vigour it had momentarily lost.[1]

The Cistercians worked in an age when the vast majority of men lived according to a traditional formula of toil in return for a small material reward. But it was also an age which had discovered powerful incentives to economic progress, and in this progress the Cistercians, for all their repudiation of the world, were pioneers. To the student of economic history, this is one of the most important and interesting facts about our period. But our subject is economic life in general, in which economic progress played a small part, and we must look at the Cistercian achievement in a much wider context before we can try to understand its meaning.

The effort put into building is conspicuous in most parts of Europe between the tenth and twelfth centuries: in Germany especially in the tenth and early eleventh centuries; in the Norman kingdoms especially in the late eleventh and twelfth centuries; in France especially in the twelfth—but in all these countries at other times too. The style and function of these buildings will be studied in another context (pp. 331 ff.); we are concerned now with their cost. Between 1066 and 1154 the number of religious houses in England alone rose from sixty to nearly five hundred. Many were small affairs, with churches on the scale of parish churches; many more were big—they included new cathedrals, new abbeys on the grandest scale; and all the old cathedrals and abbeys were rebuilt. The Cistercians had fifty-one houses in England by 1154. Many were only partly built, but the scale of their foundations was in most cases already planned, and a serious start had been made with many of them. This is to say nothing of parish churches and castles, which were built in large numbers at this time.

How was it done? How did the Normans organize the loads of timber needed for scaffolding, for frames for arch and vault, for permanent roofing? How did they organize the even larger supplies of stone, which had mainly to be transported by water, either across the Channel from the neighbourhood of Caen, or down the Welland or Nene from the Barnack quarries, or from whatever other sources they used; how did

[1] *Patrologia Latina*, vol. CLXXXV, cols. 570–1 (cf. E. Vacandard, *Vie de S. Bernard*, vol. I (4th edn., Paris, 1910), pp. 421 ff.).

they collect and organize the armies of masons needed for the work, and in particular the skilled craftsmen in stone and wood and paint and glass; above all, how did they pay for these things?

On all these points we are imperfectly informed. We may note in passing that the Normans showed their capacity as energetic organizers in many other ways, and that the crudity of early Norman masonry (even in a country with so rich an artistic tradition as England) strongly suggests that skilled masons were very scarce for a generation or so. But to find any answer to these questions, we do well to turn to France in the early twelfth century, and see what Abbot Suger has to tell us of his work at Saint-Denis. He paid for the new work partly out of endowment, partly out of offerings. He assigned 200 livres per annum to the building fund. Of this sum a quarter came from the revenue of a landed property, three-quarters from pilgrims' offerings. One may fancy that Suger was particularly skilful and perhaps particularly lucky in attracting pilgrims, and he had the advantage of being near Paris, the capital of the French kingdom, and one of the hubs of European life of the day.

Even in Paris it was not easy to collect stone and wood or find masons. Suger tells vivid stories of his difficulties: of how the workers in the quarry at Pontoise—where in good weather the local nobles and crafts-men freely lent a hand in hauling blocks up from a deep chasm and working them in preparation for transport to Paris—of how the workers went off on account of heavy rain one day, and of how the ox-drivers complained that they had nothing to do, nothing in their carts; but a small number of boys and disabled folk, hearing their complaints, were filled with great zeal and prayed for assistance to St Denis, who lent a hand so that seventeen of them were able to haul up blocks from the bottom of the chasm, which would normally have taken 140, or at least 100, men. Then the carpenters of Saint-Denis and of Paris said it was impossible to find timber of sufficient size for some of the work, nearer than Auxerre. Suger was much distressed, 'but on a certain night, when I had returned from celebrating Mattins [the midnight office as it then was], I began to think in bed that I myself should go through all the forests of these parts, look around everywhere' and solve the troubles if they could be solved. 'Quickly disposing of other duties and hurrying up in the early morning, we hastened with our carpenters, and with the measurement of the beams, to the forest called Iveline.' The foresters smiled at him, and said he ought to know that there were no timbers of this size in those parts; and if there had been, the castellan of Chevreuse had taken them all to build palisades and defensive works for his private wars. Suger, however, had the courage of his convictions, and went to look for himself. 'Toward the first hour we found one timber adequate to the measure. . . . By the ninth hour or sooner we had, through the thickets, the depths of the forests and the dense, thorny tangles, marked down twelve timbers . . . to the astonishment of all. . . .' And so the new roof was built.[1]

Suger was a man of exceptional capacity and enterprise; but the story he tells must have been repeated time and time again all over Europe. If one multiplies the quarrymen, the ox-drivers, the boatmen, the foresters, tree-cutters, carpenters, masons, by the number of cathedrals and larger monasteries being built in Europe in this period, one gets some idea of the magnitude of the effort involved. Perhaps it was unproductive; yet it clearly revealed many new ways in which resources could be used, and compelled men to save and to improve the resources they had, above all to improve communications.

Transport

A visitor from modern Europe to the Europe of the tenth or eleventh century would be struck very forcibly by the cost and difficulty of transport; by the cumbersome nature of the currency and absence of credit; by the instability of economic conditions—the weakness of law and order, the insecurity of markets. He might well be deceived by these contrasts into thinking the economy more primitive than it was. Roads were few, and unbelievably bad by our standards. Transport by water was cheaper and swifter; and heavy goods were taken by water whenever possible. Straight roads rarely existed except where the Romans had made them; local roads twisted and turned round the boundaries of fields or estates: the field counted for more than the road. Yet all these things had been equally true in the time of the Roman Empire. The main roads, the great military roads of the Roman legions, were better kept and had harder surfaces in the time of the Empire. But they were built straight up hill and down dale; heavy carts could often not be pulled along them; rivers were commonly forded not bridged, which again made difficulties for a cart. The Romans transported, by and large, by pack horse and mule. By the twelfth century at the latest ideas of land transport had considerably advanced. Wherever possible, goods went by water, by sea, by canal and by river, where the tolls had

[1] Panofsky, *Abbot Suger* (see above, p. 4), pp. 92–7.

not driven the merchants to abandon them, as the tolls levied by the multitudinous lords of the Rhineland tended to do. But there is striking evidence that carts and wagons had been much improved, and that bridges were being built in many parts to make it possible for them to go longer distances. A soft, padded horse-collar was widely used by the twelfth century; this enabled horses to pull a variety of lighter and heavier carts, faster and over greater distances than had been possible before. Hitherto the older waist-band had tended to slip on to the horse's neck and either throttle him or prevent him from pulling hard; hence the slower and less efficient ox had been generally used. Technical advance of this kind shows that the cart was being seriously used; bridge-building that roads were not entirely neglected. Sometimes, it is true, they must have been little more than what Marc Bloch described as 'l'endroit où on passe'; but one may presume that efforts were made to drain long-distance roads and keep them clear of obstruction; and kings and princes in several countries regarded the main roads as their roads. In England any road leading to a port or a market was a royal road, and this indicates that royal interest was not confined to providing roads for the movement and provision of royal armies, but was concerned with trade and markets. Yet one may also assume that royal interest was more constantly engaged in collecting fines for damage to the king's highway than in ensuring that the damage was repaired.

Currency

Whatever view we take of the vicissitudes of European currency in earlier centuries, most of western Europe had a substantial silver currency from the eighth century onwards. There can be no question that Europe was on the silver standard throughout our period, and all men of any substance, and many of little, were fully accustomed to handling money; and that their wives also knew the uses of gold coins —bezants as they were called, whether they actually came from Byzantium or not—as ornaments and for occasional barter. Most countries had only one denomination of coin; and by our standards its use was exceedingly cumbersome. But its use, none the less, meant that the money economy had entered every corner of European life. In England the currency consisted of the silver penny, and remained so, effectively, until the fourteenth century. In the tenth and eleventh centuries an elaborate system of royal control ensured that the coins were comparatively uniform throughout the country: every few years—in the mid eleventh century every three years—the dies were called in and new ones issued by agents of the royal government; thus, although the minting was done in a large number of different local centres, the coins were controlled by the government. There were still, however, fluctuations in weight; but after the Norman conquest the weight became more stable, and it was from this, so it appears, that the English penny acquired its familiar name of 'sterling', from an Old English word *stere* or *stiere*, meaning 'strong' or 'fixed'.[1] In other respects it altered little through these centuries: on one side the king's head was shown, on the other a cross; and it remained a remarkably stable currency, in spite of the delinquent moneyers (to whom savage punishments were meted out from time to time), and in spite of the irregular issues occasioned by political vagaries such as the anarchy of Stephen's reign (1135–54).

In King Stephen's time the royal grip over the mints rapidly slipped; some fell into the hands of his rival, the Empress Matilda, and several bishops and barons minted coins in their own names. For a brief space England relapsed into the numismatic anarchy normal in most parts of the Continent at this time. But this anarchy, though it reflects political conditions (sometimes, it must be said, with remarkable infidelity), must not be used as a guide to the economic health of Europe. With few exceptions, the countries of western Europe had a large and expanding silver currency, based on the silver denarius or penny, which was sufficiently copious and sufficiently stable to meet the needs of the day. But many pennies of this period were of extremely base silver (known as *billon*), and canny governments and merchants would insist on payment in currency of a fixed weight and fineness, where feasible, rather than in a mere counting of coins of very variable nature.

The currencies of France were in appearance imitations of those of the Carolingian age; but time and neglect had led to strange alterations in the images upon them. The Capetian kings only kept control over the mints in the royal domain. These mints were increased in number by Philip I and in efficiency by Louis VI; in appearance, however, they remained, by and large, decadent followers of their Carolingian predecessors. All the leading French princes had their own mints, some more active than others; once again, most of them followed old designs with increasing disregard for their original significance. A common type, used among others by the counts of Blois, started as a royal head and ended as a senseless pattern. The duke of Brittany in the early eleventh century celebrated his political importance by putting 'Alen

---

[1] See above, p. 33n.

rix' ('King Alan') on his coins. Fulk Nerra of Anjou (987–1040) appears as 'Fulk count by God's grace', a view which might have been challenged by the victims of his ferocity; but these signs of interest in the coin as a vehicle of propaganda were short-lived. Later minters put the names of counts of Anjou on the coins; but they called them Fulk or Geoffrey according to taste, not according to the name of the reigning count. The dukes of Normandy inherited in England the currency which, politically and economically, one might call the most advanced in Europe. But they lost all interest in the coinage of Normandy itself, which finally disappeared altogether in the mid twelfth century. The counts of Poitou might claim to be dukes of Aquitaine, but they were content, from the ninth century to the late twelfth, with issuing without alteration a coin of Charles the Bald. The coinage of France reflects, then, though imprecisely, the political divisions of the country. It is noticeable that no major reforms of the currency were organized until after the middle of the twelfth century; and that one of the strongest currencies was that of Tours, whose strength seems to reflect economic circumstances, not political control. Tours had been a royal mint in the tenth century; the city was under Angevin dominion in the late eleventh and twelfth centuries, but the coins never bore an Angevin title, and the mint was under monastic control.

The currency of Germany reflects the political organization of the kingdom even more clearly than that of France. Until the reign of Henry IV (1056–1106) a high measure of royal control over the mints inherited from Carolingian times was preserved. But the right of minting was frequently granted away, especially, in accordance with the policy of the Saxon and early Salian emperors, to bishops and abbots. The number of secular princes with minting rights remained comparatively small, though slowly increasing, until the late eleventh century. From then on royal control collapsed: the princes became more interested in minting rights and the currency came to reflect the new diversity in German political and social power: the princely families issued their own coinage, and the Hohenstaufen made no consistent effort to recover the ancient imperial monopoly.

Germany, France and north Italy were the world of the silver penny, the descendant of the Carolingian penny. South Italy was in the Byzantine world, Sicily and Spain were largely Muslim. In these regions Byzantine and Muslim coins had been for centuries the currencies chiefly used; and when they developed, on any serious scale, their own coinages, the coins reflected those which they replaced or with which they would still have to live. The chief coins of the Mediterranean world were the gold dinar and the silver dirhem of the Muslims. Their chief rival, the Byzantine nomisma, though debased, was still powerful; and any gold coin north of the Alps was called a bezant. The counts of Barcelona in the early eleventh century began to issue gold coins with a nonsensical Arabic inscription accompanied by the count's name and title in Latin. The Normans in south Italy, at much the same time, were starting to issue the *tarini*, gold coins likewise based on Arabic currency: on what were known as *tari*, quarter-dinars. In 1140 Roger II started a silver currency in imitation of the Byzantine for the duchy of Apulia, hence called the ducat. The Norman currencies were to be of considerable importance in the future; not till the late thirteenth century were they overshadowed by the currencies of the north Italian cities, the Florentine florin and the Venetian ducat, which came to rule the Mediterranean world in the later Middle Ages.

This was still well in the future when our period closes; but already, in a humbler way, the rise of new currencies was reflecting the economic and political growth of the lesser states of Europe. Thus the Scandinavian countries received, with Christianity, the idea of minting their own coins, though some generations passed before the mint replaced tribute and plunder as the chief source of silver coins in the Viking world. Scotland first produced a native currency in the age of Norman infiltration, the early twelfth century; León-Castile in the days of Alfonso VI and the climax of the first period in the *reconquista*.

Markets and the growth of towns

The rough and ready currencies of the eleventh and early twelfth centuries supplied the growing markets in the European towns. Most towns, by our standards, were small affairs even in the twelfth and thirteenth centuries; but their rise or revival between the tenth century and the twelfth marks a vital turning-point in European economic and municipal history. Towns and markets cannot be distinguished. In medieval Latin *castrum* means a fortress or a castle or a town. In many contexts it is impossible to tell which is the correct translation; it is clear that the ideas were inextricably interwoven in the medieval mind. It has, indeed, been much disputed whether towns arose in the tenth century as local centres of refuge in which merchants as well as peasants found security, and so became the homes of permanent markets; or whether the ramparts were built round places which already housed such markets. This dispute is now seen to be unreal. In the tenth and eleven centuries, and even, often enough, in the twelfth, a market needed to be protected by force; no market would be acceptable for long if it was not associated with a city wall; but equally, a wall alone does not make a city, and there are countless examples of well-walled towns which are now untenanted. The walls of Chester and the walls of Porchester are built on Roman foundations. The Roman walls of both stood empty and derelict at the end of the ninth century. The walls of Porchester were rebuilt by King Edward the Elder and those of Chester by his sister, the Lady of the Mercians, at the opening of the tenth century. Chester rapidly became once again the leading port of north-western England, which it remained until the silt of the Dee turned the ships away from it in the later Middle Ages. Porchester flourished somewhat less, but was the town and fortress of south-eastern Hampshire until King Richard I founded Portsmouth in the late twelfth century. Then it rapidly ceased to be a town.

In both these cases the walls and the market worked together to mark the destiny of the town. Both Chester and Porchester were the result of conscious creation, though both were founded on an existing Roman site. Many cities had an older, some a continuous history going back to Roman times; others grew more gradually where a bridge or a monastery or the natural centre of a region of the capital of a prince or the presence of natural resources of some kind suggested or dictated that a town should be. In some cases we can see the reasons of growth very clearly, in others they are mysterious.

The growth of towns was not governed by purely economic factors. In this period Rome grew once more, largely because of the development of the papal Curia and the increase in the pilgrim traffic. Even larger were Palermo, London and Paris; great commercial centres but also capitals of kingdoms and, in the case of Paris and Palermo, leading centres for scholars and artists. A large royal court was increasingly the centre of a flourishing social and mercantile life, a place where money was to be won and lost; and the royal courts were ceasing to be constantly peripatetic by the twelfth century; the idea of a 'capital' came for the first time for many centuries to have some meaning. Chester and Bristol were the chief ports for the Irish trade; perhaps even more, they carried much coastal traffic, were the bases for supplies for armies invading Wales. But their rapid rise in the tenth and eleventh centuries still remains a little mysterious. The only solid information about Bristol's traffic in the eleventh century is the famous story of how St Wulfstan, bishop of Worcester, went to Bristol to preach against the slave trade. He is said to have been successful in preventing the merchants of Bristol selling English slaves into Ireland. It is clear that this had been a profitable business, and we may doubt if the slave trade had been all in one direction; we may wonder too whether his success at Bristol may not have diverted some of the traffic to Chester. But this can only be matter for guesswork, because there is no positive evidence of a slave market in Chester at all. The growth of towns reflects the growth of trade in every corner of Europe at this time; but the nature of that trade and its local varieties is in great measure hidden from us.

The slave trade

The slave trade reveals a further difficulty in reconstructing the economic history of this period. So far as the evidence goes (which is not very far) the slave trade would appear to have been the most substantial long-distance trade in northern Europe in the early Middle Ages. It is clear that it was still very active in our period. Particularly active were the slave routes which led from the countries of the 'Slavs', who provided us, in common with almost all European languages, with the word 'slave', to Muslim Spain, and the Mediterranean world in general. This, at least, is the slave trade we know about, because it was (in the eyes of contemporaries) entirely respectable. The Church forbade the enslavement of Christians, and preached that their manumission was a good work. It did not compel slave owners to free their slaves; still less did it forbid a Christian to sell one pagan to another pagan. It is, however, clear that the slave trade was not confined to pagans. It had been traditional for centuries for fathers in some parts of Europe to sell their surplus children; and even commoner had been the enslavement of prisoners of war who were not ransomed: the very idea of ransom, so powerful throughout the Middle Ages, reveals the fundamental, ineradicable notion that a prisoner of war was his captor's property. The Church pleaded for charity and mercy; but it did not cut at the root of slavery altogether: that was left for the Evangelicals to accomplish.

None the less, in many parts of Europe, the population of slaves was markedly declining; had indeed declined in some countries almost to vanishing point before our period opens (see pp. 106–8). England was not one of these: in England and the Mediterranean countries slavery was a recognized institution and slaves were numerous in the late eleventh century; in the Mediterranean countries they remained so throughout the Middle Ages. The Norman Conquest led to the rapid extinction of slavery in England. This is not to say that the Normans were more humanitarian than their English predecessors, or that the lot of the English peasantry improved after the Conquest. In 1066 there were thousands of slaves; in 1150 there were none—but there were hundreds of thousands of villeins, tied to the soil, suffering most of the disabilities of slaves. Some of the ancestors of the villeins had been slaves; most had been comparatively free in 1066. The slave had become assimilated in England to the serf, as elsewhere in Europe some centuries before.

If the lot of the villein was often much the same as that of the slave, his status was none the less different. He could not be bought and sold, anyway without his land; he could not be sent to a distant market. The disappearance of slaves in many parts of Europe would seem to mean that the slave markets were less active in the eleventh and twelfth centuries than they had been earlier. This reveals a basic difficulty: we can be sure that trade in general was rapidly increasing in these centuries; but the best documented commodity of the early Middle Ages was actually, so it seems, in decline. It may well be that long-distance trade in slaves was not declining, that they passed in ever greater numbers from the German frontier to the Mediterranean countries. But this is only a 'maybe': we can only with assurance describe the commodities of trade, we cannot tell in detail which were rising and which falling. Our picture of medieval commerce is woefully incomplete.

Trade in general

In general we can say that the most sensational developments lay in the markets and the ships of the Italian cities, especially of Genoa, Pisa, Florence and Venice: by the late twelfth century Venice and Florence were the richest cities of the Mediterranean, which is as much as to say, of Europe. Venice lived above all on the inheritance of Byzantium: she had largely captured the Byzantine carrying trade in the eleventh century; and all the Italian cities profited by the decline of the Byzantine and Muslim fleets in this period. Through the markets of Venice, in this direction and that, passed 'leather goods, furs, salt, grain, oil, iron, copper, tin, mercury, timber, fruit, soap, animals and slaughtering meat and slaves as well as expensive textiles and "spices"'.[1]

Spices of all kinds, especially pepper and ginger, had for centuries come from the Far East via Islam; from the eleventh century on they came in quantities which made them more than the occasional fancy of

[1] *Cambridge Economic History*, vol. II, p. 332 (R. S. Lopez).

the very rich. 'The growth of Mediterranean trade . . . meant that the pervading flavour of pepper, cinnamon and ginger could cover a multitude of shortcomings in the kitchen; it meant that great men on their deaths could be embalmed in spice instead of being rudely preserved in salt; it brought a host of private luxuries for the rich—clothes and ornaments for the person, hangings and rugs for the house.'[1] It was in this period that oranges, raisins, figs and almonds made their debut on the tables of northern princes and merchants. And these northern merchants were building up their own, more local trade, as well: in ever increasing quantity, grain, wool and cloth were shipped around their world; and timber, sometimes from far away in northern and northeastern Europe, and stone for building. Piety and war were the chief expenses of the upper classes of northern Europe, and not the least of the expenses of their southern cousins too. War involved supplies for armies as well as money to pay mercenaries and ransoms; it also meant the manufacture of armaments, and the mining of metal ores to make weapons. Piety was even more profitable to the metal-worker: the wonderful artefacts described in the *De diversis artibus* of Theophilus were in ever increasing demand (see p. 340); and to meet it, larger supplies of precious metals had to be found. The silver mines of Saxony flourished in the eleventh century; so did those of other parts of Europe; and the humbler metals, such as lead and tin, the particular products of parts of Germany and England, were also much in demand. Churches were lit by wicks floating in oil, but also by candles of pure beeswax; and the growing size and splendour of the churches was a great incentive to the beekeepers, especially in north-eastern Europe, later to become Europe's chief source both of bees and of grain; and the bee also, of course, produced honey, which was the chief equivalent of sugar in this period.

Specialization was not confined to products, like silver and tin, which can only be found in widely scattered parts of Europe. Clothes can be made in any home, and salt found wherever there is sea; but in this period an increasing quantity of cloth was made in a few flourishing centres of industry, of which north Italy and Flanders came from the eleventh century to be the chief, and a proportion of the enormous quantities of salt used in preserving meat and fish, as well as great men, came from the area of Venice and Stavanger, from the salt-pans of the Bay of Bourgneuf in south-west France and from the mines of Worcestershire and Cheshire.

[1] Southern, *Making of the Middle Ages*, pp. 41–2.

Technological advance

Industrial development is as difficult to define with precision as commercial. It was reflected, for instance, in improved machinery; but when we ask the question, at what time did the spinning wheel or the fulling mill, which revolutionized Europe's cloth industry, come into common use?—it is very difficult to give any precise answer. To say when they were invented is more difficult still. It is, however, clear, that the idea of technological improvement was not unfashionable in the early twelfth century; and to this century may belong the spinning wheel and the fulling mill.[1] The latter was invented before the twelfth century; for grinding grain the watermill had been common for some hundreds of years. But the multiplicity of mills at Clairvaux was unusual, and the fulling mill only came into normal use in many parts of Europe, such as England, in the late twelfth and thirteen centuries. In much the same period there were substantial improvements in building, notably in the technique of building high vaults, for which the architects of Durham Cathedral provided the technical skills later developed by the 'Gothic' builders in the Île de France, and in warfare, in which this period saw an advance not only in the design of castles, but also of siege-engines, especially in the introduction of the trebuchet, a kind of catapult of great striking power (see p. 130).

The improving landlords of this period also enjoyed a variety of devices not known to the Romans: an efficient horse-collar which enabled the horse to be used extensively as a draught animal as well as the slower ox; rotation of crops according to the three field system, by which each of three open fields in a village was planted in turn with wheat or rye, sown in autumn, oats, barley, peas or the like, sown in the spring, and the third year left fallow—thus providing the villagers with a varied diet and improving the yield from the land; and the watermill for grinding corn. All these seem to have been known, perhaps well known, in tenth-century Europe. But their diffusion proceeded steadily, in terrains suited to them, throughout the eleventh and twelfth centuries; we can hardly map their progress, we can only state a general proposition. Those historians of technology who like to date such developments have tended to associate the spread of these inventions with the documentary evidence. This seems quite arbitrary; and the watermill gives a dire warning of the consequences of trusting in positive documentary

[1] Loyn, *op. cit.*, p. 113, cites what may be evidence of a spinning wheel in the eleventh century; specific evidence does not come before the late thirteenth (L. White, p. 119).

evidence. The invention is very old, but it was not in common use in Roman times. There are scattered references to mills which reveal that it was becoming more widely used in the early Middle Ages; but nothing to prepare us for the shattering revelations of Domesday Book, in which no less than 5,624 have been counted, a figure indeed which may be too low for those actually recorded, and is certain to be too low for those which actually existed.[1]

The watermill seems to have become popular at about the same time that the payment of tithes to churches came to be enforced, that is to say in the eighth, ninth and tenth centuries. In early days tithes were often popular with landlords, who took a substantial commission on a nominally spiritual tax; in a similar way the watermill brought a large income to its owner, who was usually the lord of the manor, which would not otherwise have been his. The mill was a symbol of seignorial domination throughout the Middle Ages, since the lords attempted to enforce a monopoly of grinding; and we may be sure that countless villagers had surreptitious querns in their cottages which many of them would prefer to use to the expensive, if labour saving, services of the local mill. But this can hardly be the whole story of the rise of the water-mill, because Domesday Book reveals that they were as prolific in parts of England where lords were scarce or their yoke was light as in counties where strong manorial control was common. We may be sure that the Cistercians were not the only folk to rejoice in the mill as a labour-saving device; even though we must also not forget that in a society in which, by and large, labour is cheap and under-employment common, labour-saving devices may not infrequently be, or appear to be, instruments of torment.

Agriculture and colonization

The vast majority of the population of Europe, in the twelfth century as in the tenth, or the fifth, lived by what they grew; and enjoyed remarkably little of the luxuries of life which were increasingly at the command of the more fortunate. Bread of wheat or rye; meat and fish; a little fruit; ale and water, or in happier countries wine: such was the fare of the peasantry throughout the Middle Ages. They lived in houses in which windows, if they existed, were simply holes, with one room which the animals shared with the whole human family. They had mighty little furniture. Life was hard; and even in the relatively

[1] The count was made by Miss M. Hodgen, *Antiquity*, 1939, pp. 261ff.; cf. Loyn, *op. cit.*, pp. 356ff.

prosperous thirteenth century a bad harvest or a flood meant starvation for some, as is revealed in the striking fluctuations in the death-rate on apparently well-to-do English episcopal manors.

Yet we should do wrong to deduce that the changes of these centuries brought no improvement to the lot of peasants. If our criterion of improvement is in terms of income per head, then we should have to admit that we cannot tell whether the rise in overall wealth had proceeded faster than the rise in population or slower, whether average real income had risen or not. But if we take the more meaningful criterion preferred by some modern economists that economic progress is to be measured in terms of the choices and opportunities open to men, then we may say, with confidence, that there was progress between 962 and 1154: the choices open to men became considerably wider. The English peasant, tied to the soil, liable to be forcibly returned if he migrated to improve his lot, might well have expressed astonishment if this point had been put to him; yet even he had opportunities to prosper, to buy his freedom, or, if he escaped to a town for sufficiently long, to claim his freedom, which had scarcely existed in the tenth century.

None the less, the level of living was still very low. Population was growing almost everywhere, and as it grew the land became overburdened. This could be solved by more intensive cultivation, by the reclamation of waste land, or by emigration. All these methods were frequently tried in the twelfth century, and although the immense efforts made to colonize new land gave hope and opportunity to the enterprising, they involved a tremendous upheaval, comparable in its way to the colonization of the American frontier in the nineteenth century. The work of colonization was organized by improving landlords, even sometimes by speculators in land; and by princes and their agents on the grand scale in the newly won lands of eastern Germany. But the heyday of the *Drang nach Osten* lay in the future in 1154.

The pioneers in the work of reclamation were often monks or secular clergy—though we are liable to exaggerate their initiative, since they have left us more memorial of their doings than laymen. A vivid example of the need and the technique of reclamation within an area already well settled comes from the chronicle of Morigny, near Étampes, in the diocese of Sens. In the early years after its foundation about 1095, this abbey had to struggle to build up its domains and earn its living.

We obtained the village or rather the wilderness of Maison-en-Beauce [near Chartres] in this manner. It was the property of the nuns of

Saint-Éloi, but a multitude of raiders and frequent invasion by robbers had reduced it to a wilderness. So we gave the abbess and the nuns a suitable sum of money and fixed an annual rent, granted them everything which they could reasonably ask, and took over this land, so long untilled, to cultivate it [1102]. We looked in our community for someone suitable for this great task, but without success, until Baldwin . . . who had already worked so hard on building the cloister and the dormitory, now, unperturbed by the immensity of the task, volunteered for the job . . . [and the chronicler enlarges on the intolerable burden that the capable Baldwin undertook]. He brought into cultivation the place so long untilled; he uprooted briars and thistles, ferns and brambles, and other weeds and rubbish, with ploughs and mattocks and other farmers' tools. He collected about eighty peasant settlers (*hospites oblatiarios*) there. Some wicked men, seeing the place flourish, began to chafe and to raise claims on it. Some with threats demanded a bran tax for their hounds, others a chicken tax, others a tax for 'protection'; 'the jurisdiction there is mine', said one. Some asked for this, others for that, and they belaboured our Baldwin—very truly ours—with constant tribulation. He was one, they many; yet he resisted their attacks so far as he could, now by going to law, now by paying money. This compelled him to go all over the district of Beauce at the time of harvest, demanding corn with great persistence; this he sold, and with the money softened the hearts of the insurgents, and freed the land from its customary burdens. One harvest time he had such pain in legs and feet that he could travel neither on foot nor on horseback; but he put a bold face on it and was not ashamed to tour Beauce in a two-wheeled farm cart —or rather preferred this shame to leaving the work undone. Such was the devotion of Baldwin to this place: his good, honest, faithful work may God reward.[1]

Morigny was a small, struggling community. Abbot Suger, the improving landlord of Saint-Denis in the next generation, did not travel in farm carts. But his own writings tell us his delight in land 'richly fertile in corn and wine, wonderfully fruitful'; and of how he freed it from burdens, royal exactions, being wasted by raiders, or merely from being untilled. At Beaune-la-Rolande he replanted vineyards, given over to the plough for twenty years; restored others almost dead; bought others from a tenant; 'and made the villages almost

[1] Ed. L. Mirot (Paris, 1909), pp. 5–6.

depopulated by plunder to be peopled again by settlers [*rehospitari*]'.
He tells too of another place entirely deserted, or only visited by peasants
from the next village, where he established three ploughs in a new
manor-house and farm buildings. 'We set there too sheep and cows and
fodder for them, on account of the richness of the pastures and for the
restoration of the arable' (i.e. to provide manure).[1] The estates of Saint-
Denis were run as a large business, to which each property contributed
according to its capacities: corn or wine or meat or wool for the table,
the chalice, the clothing of the monks and for sale, to provide for the
abbey's many expenses, especially for the cost of Suger's building
operations.

The *hospes*, the settler, was a familiar figure in many parts of Europe:
in land newly reclaimed from waste, fen, or the sea, in the parts of
western Europe already heavily settled; or in the great forests of central
Europe, which were once more attacked with fire and axe. To attract
them, the landowners and their agents offered favourable terms; new
kinds of settlement were devised to suit the conditions of the time, and
many of the settlers found not only economic benefits, but unwonted
freedom in their new lands. The rise of serfdom in eastern Europe,
which was to have so many consequences in modern centuries, lay far
in the future.

In the early 1140s, just before our period closes, the people of Holstein, under Count Adolf, had by violent warfare conquered the
territory immediately to their east, what is now eastern Holstein, to the
south-east of Kiel. In 1143 the Count celebrated the conclusion of his
conquest by rebuilding and fortifying the town (*castrum*) of Lübeck.

Because the land had been deserted [says the chronicler Helmold, no
doubt with a touch of exaggeration], he sent messengers to every
country, to Flanders and Holland, Utrecht, Westphalia, Friesland, to
invite anyone who was suffering from land-hunger to come with his
family to receive a very 'good land and a large',[2] fertile, well-stocked
with fish and flesh and good pasture for cattle. He said to the folk
of Holstein, 'Have you not conquered the land of the Slavs and paid
for it with the deaths of your brothers and other relations? Why are
you the slowest to come and possess it? Be the first: cross to the
pleasant land and dwell there and enjoy its delights—the best of it is
your due, since you took it from the hand of the enemy.' At his words

[1] *Œuvres complètes de Suger*, ed. A. Lecoy de la Marche (Paris, 1867), pp.
174–6, 181.
[2] Cf. Exodus 3: 8.

a vast multitude of various peoples rose up, and taking their households and their possessions with them came to the land of the Wagrians to Count Adolf, to possess 'the land which he had promised them'.[1]

This was the first act in the real *Drang nach Osten*. But what Adolf did on the grand scale had already been done, less grandiosely, by hundreds of landlords elsewhere in Europe.

It is significant that Adolf inaugurated his movement by rebuilding Lübeck. In the first place, he was providing his new territory with a strong fortress; but he was also providing it with what was shortly to become one of the great ports and trading centres of the Baltic. The surplus produce of his new lands could be marketed in Lübeck, and other smaller centres, and carried by ship to more distant markets; and in return its ships brought the goods which the folk of Lübeck and its hinterland did not provide for themselves, supplied the necessities and luxuries which were the reward of their toil. The relation of town and countryside is vital to the economic life of this period: the markets gave the peasants the incentive to prosper, even when the landlord was not compelling them to earn silver by extracting a large rent.

It is also significant that Helmold goes on from describing the peasant migration organized by Adolf to mention the monasteries founded by his associate, Vicelin of Neumünster; for monastic communities were frequently established as pioneers in the new lands. The order most popular among the princes of eastern Germany was the Cistercian. Nor is this coincidence. It has already been noted as a paradox that the Cistercian order, which had the special aim of creating islands cut off from the world, after the precise pattern of the monasteries of St Benedict's day, should have become so closely associated with the world and its wealth. We can now attempt a fuller explanation of the paradox.

The conditions of economic progress

Historians have long been puzzled as to why the landlords of the Middle Ages proved so much more enterprising than the landlords of the Roman Empire, although the latter, by and large, were much better educated, had much better opportunities for making technical and scientific discoveries if they had wished to do so. It would be absurd

[1] Helmold, *Cronica Slavorum*, ed. J. M. Lappenberg and B. Schmeidler (*Monumenta Germaniae Historica*, Scriptores Rerum Germanicarum, 1909), pp. 111–12. The closing words echo Deuteronomy 9: 28 and 19: 8.

to look for a single cause to explain so large and complex a contrast. But it serves to underline the remarkable enterprise which is a characteristic of economic life in the late eleventh and early twelfth centuries, and to set one aspect of it in high relief. Between the Roman senator and the men who tilled the soil a great gulf was fixed. Even the bailiff, the farm manager, was commonly, if not normally, a slave, without a direct incentive to improve the yield of the land under his care. Virgil might make a heroic effort to render agriculture a suitable subject for cultivated society; but the *Georgics* were read for Virgil's sake, not for his views on farming, and their doctrine was often ignored. Of necessity the medieval landlord was nearer to the land, more dependent on its produce. There was indeed a bond of common interest between him and his peasantry, though this often seems hard for us to believe when we observe how they treated one another. This bond of common interest—which extended, as we shall see, to the *bourgeoisie* as well (see pp. 114-17)—and this close liaison between the landlord and his land was artificially enhanced to a point approximating to perfect efficiency by the Cistercians. Their insistence on manual labour meant that even the choir monks had some taste of toil; they were perhaps the only people in the Middle Ages seriously to believe the modern notion that toil is a fine and dignified thing. The heavy physical work was no doubt done mainly by the lay brothers; but these too were monks, as much under the spiritual care of the abbot as the choir monks. Cîteaux was noted for its egalitarianism in a society which was anything but egalitarian. At the same time, there was a minimum of waste. The Cistercians had to earn their living: their communities had many mouths to feed, and in early days enormous buildings to pay for. The economic motive, the incentive to earn and to save, remained strong. At the same time the extreme frugality of their life, their rigid asceticism, kept to a minimum the conspicuous consumption on which so much of the growing resources of the age was spent. We must not exaggerate: the whole world was not Cîteaux. But the mill-wheels and the conduits of the Cistercian abbeys never cease to remind us that technical change and economic progress—however slow they may appear to modern eyes—were a marked feature of the age. And behind these changes lay a society which, for all its violence and rapacity, was in some measure attuned to economic advance.

V

Society

Population

The society of ancient Rome had been strongly, though not rigidly, hierarchical: the senators at the summit were immensely rich, and their status depended, in theory at least, on birth. The king and kinglets of barbarian Europe commonly knew their pedigrees back to Woden; and any lapse of memory—or the promotion of a man unprovided with ancestors—was quickly remedied by pious invention. If we look forward again to the great lords of the later Middle Ages, heralds could proclaim their ancient, or moderately ancient lineage, and they carried the crest of their family, or families, on their coat of arms. But in the period covered by this book society was not quite so hierarchical as before or after; nor did a man's place in the sun depend on the number and dignity of his ancestors.[1] Many of the great men of tenth- and eleventh-century Europe, indeed, had little idea who their ancestors were.

This is not to say that society was classless. It was indeed hierarchical: both in theory and practice it made a great difference where a man was

---

[1] There has been much discussion recently about the history of the European nobility, which has perhaps tended to make the families of the eleventh and twelfth centuries appear somewhat less fluid and the nobility of the late Middle Ages less rigid than used to be thought (see e.g. G. Duby in *Revue historique*, vol. CCXXVI (1961); L. Genicot, *Annales*, vol. XVII (1962)).

BIBLIOGRAPHY. Marc Bloch's *Feudal Society* (English trans. by L. A. Manyon, London, 1961) and F.-L. Ganshof, *Feudalism* (trans. P. Grierson, London, 1952) are the classics on feudal society; Bloch's book ranges more widely. See also R. Bezzola, *Les origines et la formation de la littérature courtoise en occident*, Part II (2 vols., Paris 1960); S. Painter, *Mediaeval Society* (Ithaca, 1951), *William Marshall* (Baltimore, 1933) and *French Chivalry* (Baltimore, 1940). Of local studies G. Duby, *La société aux XIe et XIIe siècles dans la region mâconnaise* (Paris, 1958) is of particular interest. On the clergy, see Chapters XII–XV; for merchants, artisans and slaves, Chapter IV (and on slaves and wage labourers in England, M. M. Postan, *The Famulus* (*Econ. Hist. Rev. Supplements*, 2)). On population, Duby (see p. 67 n.), vol. I, pp. 211 ff.; L. Genicot in *Cahiers d'hist. mondiale*, vol. I (1953); J. C. Russell, in *Transactions of the American Philosophical* born. But the hierarchy was far from rigid, and it was possible to move a certain distance up and down the ladder; possible, and common. This fluidity was partly made necessary by a rapid growth in population, and it combined with the growth in population to make the period of this book one of social and economic change such as Europe had not seen since the fall of the Roman Empire in the West.

In one sense it is paradoxical to talk of fluidity in tenth- or eleventh-century society. The occupations open to a man were, by our standards, exceedingly few, and those open to a woman narrower still. King Alfred had expressed a traditional division in society when he said that a kingdom must have those who pray, those who fight and those who work. Even in the twelfth century the majority of the population of any country in western Europe, except perhaps in Flanders and north Italy, were clerics, knights or peasants. Yet a change had taken place. These classes had grown and become more diverse; merchants and artisans were more numerous, and their place in economic life far more effective, than in the tenth century. Increasing numbers, increasing opportunities, and new ideas proved solvents of the old hierarchy; and it is only towards the end of our period that a new type of hierarchy, with ideals and aspirations of a novel sophistication, was beginning once again to build walls round the classes of society. The rise of 'chivalry' meant a stricter code of manners; but it also meant a new snobbery. These changes will be the themes of this chapter.

Great emphasis has already been laid on the rise in population which took place in these centuries. Modern historians have for long assumed this rise, and stressed its importance; and yet its nature and the evidence for it have never been properly analysed. If we wish to map trends in population in the modern world, we can use the statistics provided by a modern census. We can measure the population precisely; we can tell whether its rise was due to the birth of more children or to men and women living longer, that is, to a rise in the birth-rate or a fall in the death-rate. If the birth-rate is rising, we can discover whether this is due to women bearing more children or having them younger, so that the generations succeed one another more rapidly. Before 1801 there were no censuses; and the farther back one goes the more difficult it is to find any precise evidence for population. It has been established that a great rise took place in the English population in the eighteenth

Society, New Series, vol. xlviii (1958) and *British Medieval Population* (Albuquerque, 1948). On the care of the poor, B. Tierney, *Medieval Poor Law* (Berkeley and Los Angeles, 1959).

century; but whether it was due to a rising birth-rate or a falling death-rate is still controversial. What hope have we of assessing movements in population in the tenth, eleventh and twelfth centuries?

The only national survey of the period, the English Domesday Book, does indeed give figures from which the total population has been deduced. But Domesday was concerned with tenants and householders, not with heads; it has many omissions; and its arithmetic is often baffling. What is inferred from it is based almost as much on guesswork as on evidence. Lacking overall figures for population, we cannot hope to settle problems in detail. Nor will our evidence tell us anything satisfactory about whether birth-rates and death-rates were rising or falling, still less about whether the age of marriage was shifting. It is very rarely that we know the age of a bride. Matilda, daughter of King Henry I of England, was eleven when she married the Emperor Henry V; twenty-six when she married Geoffrey, count of Anjou; sixty-five when she died (see pp. 233–4). It is hard enough to tell how characteristic these figures were in the twelfth century; impossible to tell how they compared with earlier centuries. Matilda was the first English princess since the seventh century whose year of birth is precisely known; as for her youthful marriage, this appears to have been becoming commoner as marriage alliances were sought with ever more reckless haste by the great dynasts of the twelfth century. Henry, count of Champagne and king of Jerusalem at the end of the twelfth century, had been twice betrothed before he won the heiress of Jerusalem: once, when he was five or six, to a lady of two, later on to her younger sister. The marriage game was played for the highest stakes by kings and emperors and counts; there is no reason to suppose it reached these proportions elsewhere in the social scale. Among the landed classes men expected to marry young (by our standards) in the Middle Ages and women younger; and probably had done so for centuries before our period opens. Yet even on this issue we must be cautious: marriage was an irrevocable step; though death more often and more rapidly parted married couples in the twelfth century than it does in the twentieth, a prince might well take careful thought before he threw the dice, just as, even then, a prudent man might spend many years looking for the woman of his choice. Matilda's uncle, William Rufus (who was far from prudent), never married; her father waited till he had acquired the English throne, and then, at the age of thirty-two, instantly sought the hand of a Scots princess descended from the Old English line. His comparatively late marriage did not, however, seriously affect the birth-rate; for apart from his three legitimate children, Henry acknowledged over twenty bastards. In this story we see reasons why a great man might marry early or late, and some of the artificiality surrounding royal marriages. Similar stories could be told of many European kings, princes and nobles in our period; it is possible to get some notion of the variety that existed among the upper classes. But we know far too little to generalize the effect of their habits on the population at large, and of marriage among the lower classes we know next to nothing.

Henry I's eldest legitimate child died in infancy: his second, Matilda, died aged sixty-five; his third, William, died aged seventeen in the wreck of the *White Ship* in 1120 (see p. 233). From evidence such as this we can build up a picture of a society in which child mortality was common; in which many of the children who survived their first year none the less died before they were twenty, as was still the case down to the early nineteenth century; in which a serious famine or an outbreak of disease might rapidly depopulate a whole region—and yet in which the expectation of life of those who passed twenty was probably not sensationally lower than it is today. The lay upper classes were warriors and faced the hazards of war; the women of all classes faced the only slightly lesser hazard of childbirth. Kings rarely died fighting. One or two English kings were murdered and one died in battle in this period; no French or German king died a violent death. Most of the clergy and the peasants were not subjected to the hazards of battle, and the higher clergy seem to have been good risks for the actuary. We know the approximate age of eight English bishops who were in possession of their sees in 1153: all of them seem to have lived to be over seventy.[1] Many men and women lived into their sixties, and a few lived to be eighty or more. A few, indeed, were alleged to have lived beyond a hundred, and it is possible that some of the cases were authentic. But some were certainly not: anyone of very advanced age could be called a centenarian; precise calculations were rare, or rarely accurate.

It is thus possible to analyse factors in the situation, but not to make general statements about many aspects of the movement in population at this time. Yet to deny that population rose, over most of Europe throughout these centuries, would be excessively sceptical. The evidence is elusive and often circumstantial; in sum it is conclusive.

The staple food of mankind in the Middle Ages was bread, and his staple drink ale or water. In most countries north of the Alps wine was

---

[1] Cf. David Knowles, *Episcopal Colleagues of Archbishop Thomas Becket* (Cambridge, 1951), p. 157.

the luxury of the rich, even though all the wine drunk at this time was what we should call 'vin ordinaire'; and even communion wine (which had done so much to foster the growth of the northern vineyards) was drunk less and less by the laity in these centuries, until communion in one kind became the rule. Milk was valued for butter and cheese; fruit juices were the ascetic refreshment of monks and hermits. The English were already noted for their addiction to beer—a luxury perhaps to the peasant, but a luxury very widely consumed. While it is true that men's consumption of bread and beer can vary, the quantity of these basic foodstuffs remains a tolerable, rough criterion of the size of a population. Flour for bread was ground mainly out of wheat and rye; beer was brewed from barley. Other crops were grown, mainly for cattle fodder; fertility of soil varies; but in general one can say that the area producing corn (and in wine-growing areas, especially south of the Alps, wine) is a rough test of population. There is abundant evidence to show that in almost every corner of Europe the area under the plough was expanding: villages were growing; new lands were being colonized; marshes were being reclaimed, forests felled; in the eleventh and twelfth centuries the frontiers of Europe were being pressed outwards, and on Germany's eastern frontier, and to a lesser extent elsewhere, new land was being settled by peasants as well as by lords.

The nature of this colonization has already been discussed; what concerns us now is the over-all impression of growth. The criterion of land under cultivation is crude, and resists refinement: it is exceedingly difficult to say whether in a particular country in a particular decade or generation the rate of growth was steady; in some places at some times there may well have been local and temporary declines. Such evidence only helps us to see the long-term trend over two or three centuries. Whatever had happened before or was to happen after, it is clear that the population of western Europe at large was growing between the tenth century and the thirteenth. How much did it grow? We cannot tell.

There is another way in which we can inspect the growth of population, and that is by seeing it at work in all the various classes of society. If we look at the Church we find the numbers of monks and secular clergy growing, especially in the eleventh and twelfth centuries; we also find that more and more of them lived a life of celibacy after the papal reform. Were they draining manpower from the classes from whom they were recruited? At the same time towns were growing, and steadily becoming centres of commerce and industry. Were merchants and artisans increasing in numbers at the expense of other classes? The answer to both these questions must be no, since wherever we look we find the same signs of growth. A closer look at this growth will reveal how European society was divided, and how its groups were changing in this period.

Society was arranged in a dual hierarchy, of laymen and clergy. In many ways the division was the most fundamental in Europe. The upper clergy were Latin speaking, celibate (at least in principle, after the papal reform), conscious of being members of an international class, owing an allegiance to Church and papacy as powerful as their allegiance to their local lords and kings. They were educated, in later centuries often highly educated, while most layfolk were illiterate. The barrier was not, however, absolute: local feeling and local loyalties could be immensely powerful too; and all Churchmen had secular relations and friends.

In the lay hierarchy one can distinguish three main grades: kings, princes, great nobles; knights or landed warriors; and peasants. Within these were many divisions; and the second and third, in particular, obscure one of the great barriers, that between freedom and unfreedom, to which we must return. Outside this hierarchy lay another, that of commerce, industry and domestic service, at whose foot, in southern Europe at least, lay a multitude of slaves. The clergy can be more simply divided, between upper clergy—pope, cardinals, bishops and all those groups from whom popes and bishops were recruited, monks, canons regular and secular, archdeacons, scholars, royal and episcopal clerks—and lower clergy, the parish clergy, the rank and file. Here too the distinction was not absolute, and hides many other differences; but the bulk of the lower clergy were half educated at best, and led quite a different life from their superiors.

Barons and knights

These centuries were the age of what is commonly called the feudal society. Few historical labels are more ambiguous than 'feudal', and for that reason I shall use it as little as possible. Traditionally it has two main uses: by the Marxists to describe the type of society which pre-ceded 'capitalist' society; by legal historians to describe a particular kind of legal relationship. In Marc Bloch's great book, *Feudal Society*, the word is used to describe the whole range of social customs and organization of the upper classes of society, among whom the feudal bond, in the narrow sense, was powerful.

The feudal bond established in the first place a special relationship between the lord and a man whom we should call a cavalry officer, whom they called a vassal. It enabled the lord both to recruit a knight and to reward him. The vassal knelt before his lord, and placed his hands between his: and so became his man. This was the act of homage. Then he rose and swore a solemn oath to keep faith, to be true to his lord. By this act he performed fealty. These oaths, and the bond they established, had their origin in the relation of lord and follower in the courts of the barbarian chieftains and they had a powerful religious aura, though this did not always prevent them being broken. 'They are faithful to their lords', wrote William of Malmesbury of the Normans, 'but swift to break faith for a slight occasion. A breath of ill-fortune and they are plotting treachery, a bag of money and their mind is changed.' Yet treachery was the greatest crime in the feudal code: loyalty and generosity its supreme virtues. The lord gave his vassal protection, and rewarded him; the vassal swore to serve his lord. The special feature of feudalism was that the reward took mainly the form of endowment with land. Knights were often maintained in their lord's household; but the 'domestic knight' was either a young apprentice hoping to receive his reward in due course, or an anomaly, if a rather common anomaly. Feudal conceptions reckoned that a plot of land should be the normal basis of the feudal contract, and this notion was never lost sight of, however common the domestic knight and the vassal who held a money fief might become (see p. 132).

It may seem at first sight that the plot of land, the fief, as it was called, was a reward for service, something granted in exchange for service, which would fall in when the vassal died and be regranted to a new vassal. It may seem also that each vassal could only have one lord: otherwise the bond would be less personal than it purported to be, and the vassal might be involved in a serious conflict of loyalty. And the solemnity of the oath may seem to imply that the contract between lord and vassal was irrevocable. None of these propositions was in fact true. None the less, they are worth considering, because they help us to understand both the origin and the artificiality of feudalism. Originally the fief had not been hereditary. The lord could grant it to whom he would. But very soon pressure from the vassals—and also, it may be, the simple fact that a good vassal's children were likely to be good vassals themselves—made it common, then normal, and finally an inherent part of the feudal contract that the grant was heritable. Vestiges of the original life-lease remained. When the vassal died, the heir paid a 'relief', a large sum of money as a kind of entry-fine, before he was allowed to enter his inheritance. If the heir was a child, he was in wardship to the lord: the lord was his legal guardian and had control of the estates and of the person of the ward until he came of age. If a vassal died leaving daughters only, or if an heir who was a minor had sisters, they were also the lord's wards, and he could freely dispose of their hands in marriage—freely, but with two provisos. If they were children, they could be betrothed, but the Church insisted that they retained the right of refusing their consent to the marriage when they grew up. Social custom made this proviso almost nugatory. But it strongly defended the girl from being 'disparaged', that is to say, from being married to her social inferior. It was the complaint of the Empress Matilda that her father had married her, an empress, to a count. This was disparagement indeed. Matilda was a widow, not a minor; Henry I, being a king, could dispose of his daughter's hand when her husband died. But the widow of a vassal was commonly at the disposal of the vassal's lord: so long as her consent was obtained (by whatever means) and so long as she was not disparaged, she could be married to whom the lord chose. At different times and in different places these matters were regulated by somewhat variable customs. But on the whole it seems true to say that the minors and the ladies were at their lord's disposal, and that they had little chance of resisting what he did; but that none the less the lords were limited by custom, and even a king would be expected to consult his counsellors when he disposed of an heiress, as Henry I promised to do in his coronation charter.

While the heir or the heiress was in wardship, the lord enjoyed the profits of the fief, and from the marriage of a desirable heiress he might also hope to reap a substantial benefit. In the ninth and tenth centuries the financial aspect of feudalism was on the whole less important than the military. The lord valued his land first and foremost as the source of knights. By the twelfth century he valued it as much as the source of money; and in many cases knight service was commuted in practice for a money payment—for what in England was called scutage. The need for money made the lord increasingly concerned to turn the fiefs of his vassals to his own financial advantage when he could. Thus wardship and the control over wards' and widows' marriages became increasingly important. So likewise did the relief: a strong lord might flout tradition and levy an enormous relief from his vassals. He was also able to exact other taxes from them, notably the 'aids'; these were originally considered to be 'free-will' offerings to help the lord in difficult situations, but like so many voluntary contributions, they rapidly became customary taxes in many parts of Europe. In Germany and north Italy it seems that this never happened. But in France and England, by the early twelfth century, it was generally expected that the vassal would pay an 'aid' when the lord was captured in war and had to be ransomed, when his eldest son was knighted, and when his eldest daughter was married.

Some lords were fortunate enough to gather aids on other occasions; many lords had great difficulty in gathering aids at all. This was especially the case when the relationship between lord and vassal was somewhat remote, either because the vassal was virtually independent of his lord, as were most of the vassals of the king of France, or because the vassal had many different lords. Even so early as the late ninth century it was recognized that in practice a man might be a vassal of more than one lord, and thus the second of our presumptions was breached. By the eleventh and twelfth centuries this was no longer an exceptional case. In 1124 Louis VI, king of France, took a banner from the altar of the abbey church of Saint-Denis to be his standard in the defence of France against a German invasion (see pp. 205–6). As king, he was the overlord of the abbey; but the standard (the celebrated *Oriflamme*, which figures in the *Song of Roland*) was that of the count of the Vexin, and in this capacity Louis was the vassal of the abbey and the saint. It symbolized that he was putting himself under the protection of the saint, the patron of his kingdom; but it also revealed the sort of anomaly which had entered the feudal hierarchy. A king could be the vassal of his own vassal. Similarly, a knight or baron could hold of several lords. This naturally reduced the effectiveness and strength of the feudal oath and the feudal bond. It also raised serious practical difficulties. If one of his lords was at war with another, which should the vassal support? To this a variety of solutions were given at different times. It was commonly held that the first lord to whom he had sworn fealty had the first call on his service; but in some cases it was held that the richest fief gave the vassal his strongest obligation; or again, that it depended on the circumstances, on which lord had the greatest need—a lord must be helped if he was fighting in self-defence, but his claim was less if he was fighting in someone else's defence; or the vassal might be expected to fight on both sides, that is to say, to provide troops for both armies. Thus it was possible for him to find his own men in the army which he was attacking. There was much diversity of opinion and of custom. All were agreed that multiple homage was an aberration, displeasing to God; but we may assume that it was rare for a man to refuse a good gift or a bargain on this account.

The problem was naturally most acute in the lands where feudalism was most highly developed: in northern France and the Low Countries, in England and south Italy after the Norman conquests, and in Syria after the First Crusade. It was in these countries, and also in Catalonia, that the most radical solution to the problem of multiple homage was attempted. A distinction was drawn in the eleventh and twelfth centuries between ordinary homage and 'liege' homage. Liege homage was absolute, or, as the Catalans said, 'solid' (*soliu*); it overrode other obligations. In England the king claimed that all his subjects owed fealty to him in some degree, and in due course this came to conflict with the possibility of any of his vassals owing liege homage to any but the king. In the later Middle Ages, both in England and France the idea of liege homage tended to be overruled by the idea of allegiance to the king. But in the second half of the eleventh century and in the early twelfth, liege homage was still a new and growing force in France and England: an experiment which was proving widely acceptable as a solution to the intolerable problem of divided loyalties.

Multiple homage might compel a man to break his contract with one or another of his lords. In other cases a major breach of the contract by the lord would justify the vassal in abandoning his lord. The right to break fealty, of *diffidatio*, had ancient roots and was everywhere prized. Yet the customs surrounding it were never clearly defined. In the nature of things it could not be regulated by any court. The court which would normally have taken cognizance was that over which the lord presided; and although it was in the lord's court that the vassal made his defiance, it was usually done, not in person, but by messenger or herald, and the vassal could not at that stage accept any ruling of the court. Thus when a man's vassals rebelled against him, it is possible to say that they were exerting, in due form, the ancient right of resistance, of *diffidatio*, or, with William of Malmesbury, that they had proved swift to break faith. In fact it is far from clear how regular was the solemn act of *diffidatio*. The feudal oath was sacred; yet rebellion, justified or not, was very common.

Thus practice and theory were often far apart, in this and in other ways, even in the classical feudalism, feudalism as it was known in the north of France between the ninth and the twelfth century. The farther one went east from the Rhine, or the farther south from the Loire, the more diverse social custom and land tenure became: and above all, the commoner became 'allodial' land, land not held of any lord. Only in the Norman and the crusading states, colonized in great measure from the homeland of French feudalism, did one find any attempt to live up to a conception of feudalism as coherent as that of northern France.

Everywhere the upper class were warriors; everywhere land was the symbol of status, and, in these centuries, the main basis of wealth. What one found in the stricter forms of feudalism was an attempt to organize landed wealth more directly and coherently for the recruitment of knights. In principle a given plot of land produced one knight for a specified length of time each year; to ensure that the service was regular and the responsibility clear, attempts were made—never very successfully, except for a time in England—to keep the holdings intact, to prevent their being divided between younger sons. Strict feudalism was a highly artificial way of making land produce knights, and it is doubtful whether it ever existed outside the imaginations of historians. Yet in northern France and England, and to a lesser extent throughout western Europe, feudal and quasi-feudal institutions can be found during these centuries.

In its origin feudalism provided for the recruitment of vitally needed cavalry troops in a society which lacked the liquid money to pay troops in cash. The knights were never more than one arm of any fighting force; and it is hardly likely that any force of knights was ever recruited entirely by 'feudal' means. At least by the eleventh century every king expected to recruit a part of his army by paying mercenaries, or from knights who received a fee not in land, but in cash; though he did his best to make his great nobles provide contingents for which he did not have to pay, or (at least in the twelfth century) pay him in cash if they did not serve him in person. As so often, one sees the survival of a social custom long after its original purpose has been wholly or partly superseded. Freer use of money for recruitment made it easier for kings to recruit armies when and how they wished; and for knights and nobles to lead their lives according to their own inclinations. But as the men of the upper class were bred for war, as they enjoyed fighting and felt that in war their intimate bond of loyalty to their chief was most fully expressed, the connexion between fief and military service was an unconscionable time in dying. It was very much alive in England and the French principalities in the mid twelfth century, and if anything on the increase in Germany. And even in the fourteenth and fifteenth centuries, when feudal tenure was no longer the key to social organization or, in the main, to recruitment, kings like Edward III and Henry V of England were popular precisely because they led their noble colleagues on warlike adventures.

Yet even in the eleventh century there was something artificial in William the Conqueror's notion of dividing England into about 6,000 knights' fees. No Norman king in England recruited his knights entirely by feudal service; his army always had a substantial mercenary element in it. There never were 6,000 knights in England; and it was rare in the twelfth century for more than a thousand knights to gather in answer to a feudal summons. But the Conqueror's scheme of knight service was the nearest to a comprehensive feudal hierarchy that any European king or prince attempted.

Thus, in course of time, the artificiality of feudal organization was more and more broken down by the use of money, until in twelfth-century England, feudal service was commonly replaced by the payment of a tax, scutage, 'shield-money'. This gave both parties greater flexibility, while increasing their dependence on money.

For a variety of reasons the European nobility of the eleventh and twelfth centuries were coming increasingly to need money: to indulge their taste in war, to meet a higher standard of living, to pay for their ever more costly gifts to their friends, their superiors and inferiors, and above all to the Church, to indulge their taste for extravagant building, and to give dowries to their daughters and patrimonies to their younger sons.

War was the traditional occupation of this class. As young men the members of it were apprenticed to practised warriors, taught the profession of arms; even as children they learned to follow the chase, to hunt boar and stag and wolf, not to mention all the lesser game of the forest; they learned how to handle and appraise a hawk; and in the evenings, in their father's halls, or in the halls of other great lords to whom they had been sent to learn their profession, they listened to the minstrels singing songs of knightly prowess. The heroic lay had been the fare of royal and princely halls in earlier centuries; and traces of these, as they survived in Iceland in later times, can still be found in the poetic Edda. Of early Germanic epics the only substantial survivor is the English Beowulf, probably of the eighth century, whose text pre-supposes the existence of a large repertoire of lost epics. Of the minstrel songs of the tenth and eleventh centuries we know exceedingly little. There is evidence, however, of a steady development in oral tradition between the death of Count Roland in a Basque ambush in 778 and the song about Roland which inspired the Normans as they went into battle in 1066. Not long after Hastings was written the version of the *Song of Roland* which is the earliest *Chanson de Geste* to survive (see p. 359).

From the *Chansons* and from the Provençal lays of the troubadours, we learn a great deal about the aspirations of society of this age. John of Salisbury tells us that a new custom had arisen in his time that on the day on which a young man was to be girded with the belt of knighthood he went solemnly to church, laid his sword on the altar, and offered himself and his service to God. The religion of this age was a house with many mansions. There was a real bond of friendship and understanding between many of the great churchmen of this age and leading warriors; it would be a nice point to decide whether the happiness of St Margaret's marriage to King Malcolm of Scotland (see p. 155) was more or less remarkable than the depth of St Anselm's friendship with Hugh of Avranches, the first earl of Chester, the savage hammer of the Welsh. Knights who made contact with men of this kind could not but be touched by their qualities. But one cannot help feeling that the description by the author of the *Gesta Francorum*, himself a knight, of the capture of Jerusalem in 1099, is a more characteristic specimen of the 'religion' of twelfth-century knights.

> After this our men rushed round the whole city, seizing gold and silver, horses and mules, and houses full of all sorts of goods, and they all came rejoicing and weeping from excess of gladness to worship at the Sepulchre of our Saviour Jesus, and there they acknowledged themselves his serfs. Next morning they went cautiously up on to the Temple roof and attacked the Saracens, both men and women, cutting off their heads with drawn swords.[1]

This curious mingling of piety, enthusiasm and sadistic cruelty is recorded time and again in the vernacular literature of the age—sometimes naïvely, sometimes satirically, for there were evidently plenty of reflective men who saw the paradox, and pondered on it. Yet for all their brutality, the *Chansons de geste* lay more emphasis on courage, generosity and loyalty as the virtues of the warrior. Early in the thirteenth century the aspirations of the knightly class were summed up in the *Life of William the Marshal*, a great man who, had he lived in the twentieth century, might have made his choice between being a high civil servant and a champion professional boxer. In his own day the two

---

[1] *Gesta Francorum*, trans. Rosalind Hill (Nelson's Medieval Texts, 1962), p. 92 (slightly adapted: cf. R. W. Southern, *Making of the Middle Ages*, London, 1953, p. 105n.).

kinds of profession were by no means incompatible. By his athletic skill William became rich and acquired land, an heiress, an earldom; and in the end his wisdom in the council chamber made him regent of England. His career was exceptional, but it shows what could be done.

William the Marshal was a knight-errant in the first age of chivalry, a great tournament man when tournaments were beginning to be civilized. Both these developments lie, in the main, outside our period. The tournament in the early twelfth century was a mock battle little different from the real thing; the highly organized jousting which we usually associate with such an event was only beginning to develop. The courtly romances of the late twelfth and early thirteenth centuries were considerably more civilized and sophisticated than the *Chansons de geste* of the early twelfth century. There is a profound contrast between the role of Roland's betrothed in the *Song of Roland*, which is trivial, and of the ladies in the romances of Chrétien de Troyes, who control the action. Equally striking is the difference between the German *Rolandslied* of the mid twelfth century and Wolfram von Eschenbach's *Willehalm* in the early thirteenth: in the former, the heathen are cattle for the slaughter; in the latter their destiny, their value in God's eyes, are the central theme of the poem. Wolfram's humanity was exceptional even in his own day (see p. 330); and there was no doubt much that was fanciful and artificial in the cult of courtly love. But enough has been said to show that the world of vernacular literature in 1200 was a much larger, more diverse, more interesting world than in 1100. And this must in part have reflected a greater diversity among its patrons. Loyalty and glory were the themes of the *Song of Roland*. Neither was forgotten: loyalty is still the central theme of Wolfram's *Parzival*. But Wolfram's idea of loyalty is extremely complex and subtle; the range of human emotions deployed in his poem is astonishingly wide and deep. Once again, Wolfram was exceptional; but he was an illiterate knight, and he shows what was possible. Roland had been a warrior at war; the knights of the Round Table found themselves in every possible, and impossible, situation. The code of military behaviour had come to permeate the whole world of knightly behaviour, not just the field of battle. Fashion and artistic imagination spread a thick veil of Celtic fancy over the romances; but through the veil we can discern the real human problems of Wolfram and his like; in this respect they follow in the footsteps of the twelfth-century humanists, Abelard, Heloise and Ailred. The layman of the tenth, eleventh and early twelfth centuries was more remote from our experience and has left no comparable memorial.

The social fluidity of this age is difficult for us to gauge with any precision. Anglo-Saxon law recognized that a peasant who prospered became a thegn and the thegns were a wide class including folk who would be called knights and folk who would be leading barons after the Conquest. But it would be difficult to find from the surviving evidence a single case history of this kind. Our ignorance is profound. Within the military classes, we can sometimes reconstruct family trees which reveal how wide a range of status was held by men within a single family group. The letters of Gilbert Foliot, successively abbot of Gloucester, bishop of Hereford and London in the twelfth century, are singularly revealing, because they show us not only the range of a large family circle, but the strength of feeling which could exist between distant relatives. Gilbert was a good family man; though conscientious as a bishop according to his lights, he felt bound to help the host of nephews and cousins, who clamoured for patronage, to whatever he could provide. His father was probably steward of the king of Scotland as earl of Northampton, and so a baron of some standing, but not a tenant-in-chief; Gilbert's brother or nephew rose by marriage into this rank. His uncles included a bishop, an abbot and one of the barons who was a profiteer from the anarchy of Stephen's reign. His more distant relations included Miles of Gloucester, a marcher baron who was responsible for Gilbert becoming abbot of Gloucester, and was subsequently earl of Hereford. His relations also included men of every stratum of the knightly classes; one of them was a domestic knight of a great baron, with no property save his armour. The whole spectrum of the Anglo-Norman upper classes is included in this single family group. The barons were comparatively few in number; the Church normally forbade them to marry their sixth cousins or any nearer relatives, and seriously attempted to enforce the prohibition on third cousins; and even though they did not always accept this limitation, it meant that they looked far and wide in their own class for marriage alliances. This gave the baronage a strong sense of cohesion; but the large families which many of them had, and the opportunities for enrichment and impoverishment which growing population and growing wealth provided, meant that any great man had a large number of poor relations, and that the rungs on the ladder between the poor knights and the great princes were thronged with men moving up and down, sometimes at breakneck speed.

Service to a king or a great lord was often the key to patronage and status. In England a man who had served as a royal official might end as an earl, as did Henry I's trusted adviser Aubrey de Vere. This road to promotion was even more conspicuous in Germany and the Low Countries, where the feudal hierarchy was less organized than in England, and where a king depended on his domain servants for administrative and judicial services, and military aid, far more than in England or France. These men were the *ministeriales*, originally unfree tenants; as the nobility became increasingly independent, the *ministeriales* were promoted to fill their place in the royal service, and they received increasingly valuable patronage and endowment; abbots of imperial monasteries were even forbidden to distribute fiefs to free tenants—they were to be reserved for the unfree, the *ministeriales*. In due course many of these became great barons in their own right; but their origin was not quickly forgotten, and served as a constant reminder that royal patronage and service to the great counted for as much as blood and status.

Freedom, serfdom and slavery

Just as there were classes of free and unfree warriors, so there were, in every European country, free and unfree peasants. These formed far and away the largest group in the population of Europe, and it is the evidence that their numbers were expanding rapidly which offers the most substantial proof that the population of western Christendom as a whole was rising at this time. We have already looked at some of the indications that the area under cultivation was expanding: within the frontiers of old villages, in land formerly waste, in forest and marsh, and on the frontiers of Christendom. In old villages, the greater bargaining power tended to be with the lord and the larger landowners; the peasantry lost status as they had to sacrifice more and more to find enough land to feed themselves. In new lands, lords were prepared to offer special advantages to recruits, including a greater measure of freedom. These factors alone would have made for a rapid shift between free and unfree populations; but in many parts of Europe the relation between them was complicated by local custom and legal variety. In some the dominance of the lords was strong, in others the tradition of freedom much stronger. Here and there villages under strict seignorial control sat side by side with communities of free peasants.

Unfreedom varied in its nature: it depended on a wide variety of relationships between lord and man. The medieval warrior was what some today would call a drone: however necessary his protection might be or might seem to his peasant tenants and neighbours, and however much the enterprise of individual warriors may have fertilized the economy, he was not personally engaged in making a livelihood for himself and his family. He had to be supported, and supported in some style, by the labour of the peasants. In northern France this had been traditionally organized by the institution known as the *villa*, a country estate of variable size, often more or less the equivalent of a village, where all the land was the lord's; some part of it he let out to tenants, some part of it he farmed directly; but even his own domain was in large measure tilled by the peasant tenants, who held their land in return for services in money, services in kind, and above all labour-services, for a defined amount of work for the lord. The economy of the *villa* had undergone so many transformations over the centuries that its nature and workings were subject to every kind of variation. But in the eleventh and twelfth centuries a village society dominated by the lord, to whom the majority of peasants owed varying degrees of allegiance, of service and of rent, was characteristic of wide areas of western Europe. These are the institutions which we call the manor or the *seigneurie*. In the old *villa* the labour force had consisted mainly of serfs, or villeins, who were personally free but were tied to the plot of land on which they lived, and to the services it traditionally rendered to the lord, and of slaves, who had no freedom and no land.

By the tenth century slaves were rarely to be found in France or Germany; they were a minority, though still a substantial minority, in England; they were still common in southern Europe (see pp. 80–1). No satisfactory explanation of their decline in northern Europe has been produced. It has been suggested that the supply of slaves dried up and that slaves are by their nature infertile, so that a slave population dies out if not constantly recruited; but neither proposition can be defended. It has been suggested that the pressure of the Christian Church, which always encouraged manumission and discouraged the slave trade, had its effects in the end. This is not wholly untrue, but it is difficult to accept the view that the French and Germans were decisively more humane in the Dark Ages than Italians, Spaniards or Englishmen. The voices of churchmen were heard from time to time, perhaps frequently, complaining of the enslavement of Christians, or of the treatment of slaves; but there was no radical attack on the institution as such. The Church no doubt helped to speed up the decline of slavery; it did not cause it in the first place.

Slavery in the Mediterranean world was continuous from Caesar to Columbus. As Professor Verlinden has shown, the negro slave was much in evidence at the end of the Middle Ages in Portugal and Spain long before he was exported to the Americas. Shylock's argument, that just as the Christians claimed slaves to be their property, so:

> The pound of flesh which I demand of him,
> Is dearly bought; 'tis mine and I will have it—

would have been equally appropriate in the Venice of the central Middle Ages. In the ancient world slaves had been most commonly used as domestic servants and artisans, and this may well have continued to be true in the Middle Ages. The evidence has not yet been fully sifted; but one may guess that the use of slaves as agricultural labourers was not common even in the Mediterranean world in the Middle Ages. And it is fairly clear that the slaves of northern Europe died out between the eighth and the twelfth centuries by absorption into the larger class of serfs or villeins, personally free, but tied to the soil, retaining certain symbols of unfreedom.

'Retaining' is perhaps a misleading word. Marc Bloch showed that on two estates in the heart of northern France there were already in the early ninth century only twenty-five slaves out of 278 householders; whereas at the end of the twelfth century all but a handful of the population of these villages were serfs; none slaves. The village community at the earlier date had been diverse—mostly free, but with varying degrees of subjection to the lord, who was the abbot of Saint-Germain-des-Prés. At the later date, even though the ultimate degradation of slavery had been removed, a majority of the community had lost status.

The serfs had swallowed the slaves, a process made hopelessly obscure by the fact that the same word, *servus*, often did service for both. The servitude of the slave and of the serf was hereditary. No doubt by 1200 all or virtually all the inhabitants of these two villages were descended from the twenty-five slaves of 400 years previously. This could be explained by saying that the lords had exacted their full rights: had insisted that the children of the bond remained bondmen. Or it could be argued that the abbots had been merciful: that they had allowed the slaves to become serfs. Very likely there is an element of truth in both suggestions. We can conjecture that some of the slaves had bought themselves to serfdom; that penury had compelled the free to sell their freedom for bread. We can guess that both the lords and the village community found a uniform system, in which all the tenants had land of their own, and all worked to till the lord's domain, had its advantages; in particular, that the lords preferred the service of serfs, whose lives they did not have to organize in detail, to that of slaves, who were dependent on them for food and clothing and a roof over their heads. The documents sometimes distinguish between a slave living in his master's house and a slave with a cottage of his own, but not very often. We may well wonder whether the ambiguity in the word *servus* does not hide a fundamental ambiguity running right through the period; we may wonder just how much difference there was between slaves and serfs in the early Middle Ages. And if we had asked the abbot of Saint-Germain, he might have answered that the servitude of serf and slave alike was a small matter compared with man's servitude, since the Fall, to the devil; and that all men were slaves.

But there is more to it than this. In conditions of rising population, such as we may assume for most of this period over most of Europe, land is scarce and labour plentiful, and the lords may commonly compel land-hungry peasants to accept their terms. But there may well have been situations in which the boot was on the other leg; and in the centuries before the tenth, the centuries in which slavery was steadily declining, there is no reason to suppose that land was scarce, or that the landlords normally had the whip-hand. One answer to this problem may be found in the documents which record the surrender of their freedom by substantial small landholders in the eleventh century: the landlords bought their subjection for a substantial grant of land; in return, by becoming serfs, the peasants agreed never to leave their plot of land. The lord's labour problem was solved, in theory, for ever. Transactions of this kind must make us pause before we condemn all landlords as gradgrinds, or make too large assumptions about the nature of medieval serfdom.[1]

The landlords of this period often had a bond of sympathy with their tenants in that they too had to struggle for a living, and that their living conditions, especially in the tenth and early eleventh centuries, were not widely different. There is no ground, however, to cover the lot of the medieval peasant with a romantic haze. It was commonly, perhaps normally, hard. Of the incidence of poverty and famine we know comparatively little, but we know enough to be sure that both were common. The parishes disposed (in theory at least) of quite substantial sums intended for charitable uses, and these were supplemented by the

[1] See Southern, pp. 98ff., esp. p. 101.

monasteries. How large they were, and how they were used, we do not know. In the twelfth century the canon lawyers devised an elaborate, and comparatively humane, legal framework for poor relief. The Church accepted the responsibility (up to a point) which our own generation has laid on the welfare state. No doubt its administration was haphazard; no doubt there were many abuses. But some efforts were made to cope with the problem of poverty. These efforts would seem pitifully inadequate to a modern social reformer. But in an affluent society the problem of poverty is fundamentally different from what it is in an underdeveloped economy.

The peasantry on a manor or *seigneurie* paid rent to the lords in money and in service. The balance between the two varied according to economic circumstances, and it is very difficult for us to reconstruct the nature of these services in detail over a wide area before the thirteenth century. But there are copious indications that already in the eleventh century, and perhaps long before, money played a part at least as important as labour. And one aspect of the decline of slavery is the rise of a class of wage-earning agricultural labourers. The records tell us continually who holds the land; they very rarely tell us who tills it. Thus the wage-labourer is a mysterious figure: but there are plenty of indications that he was no stranger in the eleventh century, still less in the twelfth. He was not necessarily landless: he seems often to have been a smallholder, with land insufficient of itself to support him. The records tell us a little about the labourers employed by the lords. They tell us almost nothing about the labourers employed by the more prosperous peasants. Yet they often make it clear that such folk existed. Thus all the peasantry needed money to pay rents, and many needed money to pay for labour by the end of this period. This is a striking indication of the role of money in European society as a whole; it reveals that even the peasantry must have reckoned, under good conditions, to produce, and to sell in the local market, a substantial surplus. Since a great proportion of them were engaged in growing corn and other basic needs of life, there must already have been a considerable proportion of the European population who needed to be fed by the labour of others.

Merchants and artisans

We can list the types of people who depended on peasant labour for their bread, but grew it not themselves; but we can never hope to have any clear appreciation of the numerical strength of each class. It is clear that in the period between the tenth century and the thirteenth all the categories were tending to grow. There had long been some specialists, like vine-dressers or fishermen or cowherds or shepherds, who were producing food, but depended on others for their staple diet. Medieval society also contained a large and growing number of professional warriors and churchmen, 'those who fought and those who prayed', who did not till the soil, or engage in any normal form of economic activity. It also contained an immense number of domestic servants and other members of royal, baronial and ecclesiastical households. There were artisans, especially in the cloth industry; miners, metal-workers, makers of weapons, shipbuilders; carpenters and stone-masons. If much land transport was undertaken by peasants as part of their multifarious labour services or to earn a little money on the side, much too, by land and sea, must have been undertaken by professionals. Finally, there were merchants, the men who organized the markets that enabled the corn or flour or bread to find its way to the hungry, the wool to the weaver, fuller and dyer, the cloth to the man who needed a new costume, timber to the shipbuilder, timber and stone to the church.

We have already emphasized the value of coins as evidence; among other things they sometimes reveal the number of minters at work in a city, and so give us a hazy but valuable indication of the relative size of the towns of a kingdom. This is especially true in England. 'In the last generation of Anglo-Saxon England', writes Mr H. R. Loyn, 'there were twenty known moneyers at work simultaneously in London; more than ten at York; at least nine in Lincoln and Winchester; eight at least at Chester; seven at least at Canterbury and Oxford; and at least six at Gloucester, Thetford and Worcester.'[1] It is clear that money was to be made honestly at this profession; even clearer that forgery and other types of fraud were frequently used by moneyers as short-cuts to wealth. Many no doubt became substantial citizens; theirs was an important industry. But of their social status and origin, and their place in the community we know little, and Mr Loyn suggests that the term moneyer (in English *mynetere*) may have covered both 'the gentleman, who farmed the office, and the craftsman working in the mint'.[2] Savage penalties were meted out broadcast to the craftsmen, which suggests both a low status in the eyes of the king and a low standard of honesty.

Ambiguities of this kind constantly disturb our attempts to describe the social organization of Europe at this time; and behind them all lies a more fundamental uncertainty. In a great number of cases we do not

[1] Loyn, *op. cit.*, pp. 126–7.
[2] *Ibid.*, p. 125.

know how specialized particular occupations were, how many different jobs a single man might hold. Official statistics in modern Nigeria show a large majority of the population engaged in agriculture; observation, I understand, shows that virtually the whole population is engaged in trade. In developing economies these two propositions are not incompatible. It is clear that among the more prosperous merchants in the twelfth and thirteenth centuries there was the first beginning of a tendency towards specialization, in types of goods carried and markets exploited; but growing trade, freer movements of peoples, no doubt enhanced the number of folk who could earn a few pennies peddling or carting. We know hardly anything of the details of this; once again, our ignorance is fundamental.

As for the great merchants, there has been much argument among modern historians about how they were recruited. Investigation of town plans reveals that many cities were growing at this time; the records reveal increasing long-distance trade; in the Mediterranean there was a growth of the commerce of the Italian cities so striking that Professor Lopez has labelled it 'the commercial revolution'. Towns south of the Alps threw up new aristocracies of wealth, the patriciates; north of the Alps many communities of merchants and artisans tried to form 'communes', to win their freedom from feudal or royal control and feudal taxes. How had the new city fathers acquired the wealth and prestige to embark on these schemes? Were they, as has been asserted, in large measure recruited from chapmen who had made their pile— new men in the full sense of the phrase; or were they, as some more recent historians have emphasized, more often recruited from the younger sons of local landed families who had taken to trade?

About 1180 the British Walter Map told the story of:

Sceva and Ollo, alike in age, not in character, boys of low birth, [who] acquired at the same time a small capital, and in our days became first hawkers of small commodities, and then by continued success of large ones. From packmen they rose to be carriers, from being carriers to be masters of many waggoners, and always remained trusty partners. With the growth of their trade, as another author [Juvenal] says, the love of money grew as great as grew the wealth. The bond of partnership and the joint union of stock now became irksome, and separate ownership was agreed upon.[1]

[1] *De nugis curialium*, trans. M. R. James (Cymmrodorion Record Series, 1923), p. 218.

This tale is fiction, but it shows the kind of success story which a twelfth-century Englishman could expect his audience to swallow; and it is probably significant that he set the story in Italy, the land of merchants and wealth. The rise of Sceva and Ollo is reminiscent of a purely English story of the same century, a true one, of the rise of Godric of Finchale. He acquired a small capital by scavenging and became a pedlar; then he became a partner in a ship; and his skill as a sailor and his fondness for travel took him to Scotland and Italy, to Denmark and Flanders. As his biographer develops the theme of his travels, it becomes difficult to tell whether Godric is more of a merchant or a pilgrim: we find him at Jerusalem, at Compostella and at Rome. Eventually we find him established as a hermit at Finchale, having abandoned the pursuit of earthly treasure.

The story of St Godric was one of the foundations of Henri Pirenne's notions about the recruitment of merchants in this age. His critics have pointed out that Godric's is an isolated story, whereas we know of a number of instances in which leading city magnates were recruited from local landed families, in Italy, in England and elsewhere. It may well be that the sons of barons and knights jostled with Sceva and Ollo in the markets of the twelfth century; and it is likely enough that there were more rich men's sons than poor men's sons wearing the alderman's robes. It is clear that mercantile capital was often provided by men of means, whether they themselves were active or sleeping partners in the business. All we know for certain is that there was much variety of origin in the merchant class, then as now; and this is what we should expect. A merchant needed enterprise and capital. The story of Godric, and all that we know of medieval commerce and transport, suggest that a merchant needed to enjoy adventure and risk for its own sake. The European economy was being developed and fertilized in this age by men who regularly undertook journeys of great difficulty, risks of unknown dimensions. Children of parents with means were more likely than the children of the poor to have capital; but enterprise was even more essential, and there is no reason to suppose that this was the prerogative of any group or class in the Europe of the day. The term 'merchant' covers a wide variety: from Sceva and Ollo as hawkers to Sceva and Ollo as men of substance. In all probability the social origin of the merchants was as varied as their status and wealth. It was an age in which all classes of society were expanding, in which men from every walk of life who enjoyed adventure and travel could find new opportunities as merchants to invest their talents at a large rate of interest.

Yet whatever they did with their talents, the one thing, notoriously, which wealthy men in the Middle Ages were not permitted to do was to lend their money at interest. The Church utterly forbade the levying of interest on a loan as usury. In the later Middle Ages canonists and theologians came to see with increasing clarity some of the objections to this view; and throughout the Middle Ages Christian money-lenders had their ways of evading it. The commonest evasions, certainly well known in the twelfth century, were the pretence that the original loan was greater than in fact it was, or the securing of a loan by a temporary grant of land; in the former case the difference between the actual loan and the repayment in fact constituted interest; and in the latter the rent on the land might do the same. But the prejudice against money-lending was a serious bar to the development of credit and of the money economy in general; and it was singularly fortunate for the Europe of the eleventh and twelfth centuries that there was a substantial group of active and intelligent people to whom usury was not forbidden. Like the Indians and Levantines in modern Africa, the Jews played a vital part in fertilizing the economy of medieval Europe. As the economy developed, the Jews became wealthier; and although everyone benefited from their presence, few realized the benefit, whereas many felt the pressure of the interest the Jews demanded. In some parts of Africa, the Indian and the Levantine are the victim of a nationalist and racial prejudice, at whose root lies, among other things, the same fundamental misunderstanding of their economic role. In the Middle Ages the Jew was hated because he was a Jew, a representative of the people who crucified Jesus, and also because he was thought to be a Shylock. The citizens of the rising towns of the eleventh and twelfth centuries hardly realized what they owed to the Jews, and entirely forgot that Mary and Jesus (humanly speaking) were the kin of their victims; and they took fearful vengeance on the crucifixion of their pockets and their Master. For the first time in European history the Jews were not only persecuted, they were massacred. But they still received some protection from folk like the English kings who found profit in them, and especially from William Rufus, who seems quite sincerely to have disliked the Church's intolerance; and the Church itself strongly condemned violent persecution.

By necessity and by choice the Jews were a race apart, the only class entirely segregated from the rest of the community. From almost every other walk of life a way could be found to the city patriciate; and even the Jew could come there if he would submit to conversion. A Roman

Jew of the mid eleventh century was inspired to baptism by Pope Leo IX, and took the Christian name of Leo. His son, Peter, was a leading supporter of Gregory VII; and the 'Pierleoni' became a substantial Roman family. One of them became a cardinal, and, in 1130, pope—or, as he came to be reckoned, an anti-pope.

A number of indications that merchants and artisans were increasing in numbers and significance have been considered; and in the last chapter the rise of towns was seen in its economic context (see pp. 78–80). In the late eleventh and early twelfth centuries the growing populations and growing wealth of the towns led to a struggle for emancipation: the attempt on the part of towns all over Europe to free themselves from the shackles of secular control, to win a measure of self-government, so that their affairs could be regulated to suit the interests of the citizens, not of whoever happened to be lord of the land on which the town was built. This struggle passed through many phases between the eleventh and the fifteenth centuries, but in the beginning the struggle was most bitter in parts of Europe where municipal life was oldest established, especially in Italy; in northern Europe, where towns sprang up, so to speak, as foreign intrusions in a feudal country-side, it was easier for the feudal and royal authorities to come to terms with the pretensions of the towns. Surprisingly enough, a bond of common interest often united the town and the ruler. Within the town wealth and power was in the hands of a body of merchants with a certain degree of cohesion, a comparatively homogeneous group. In Italy merchants and petty nobles lived side by side within the walls of the town, and feudal strife and mercantile peace were unhappy bed-fellows.

Even in the north there were many difficulties, and much prejudice against the rising towns. Louis VI of France granted a large number of charters to towns on the royal domain, or on ecclesiastical territories or fiefs of vassals. Occasionally, he felt compelled to withdraw a charter, as when the people of Laon fell out with their bishop in 1112. Some of them were involved in his murder later in the same year. From the account of this episode in Guibert de Nogent's *Autobiography*, one can sense the resistance of conservative opinion to new-fangled municipal institutions; and the horror with which a churchman regarded burghers who were not content to be subjected to their bishop, especially when they plotted to kill him. A generation earlier many Rhineland cities had taken advantage of the conflict between Henry IV and the Church to rebel against their episcopal overlords. Even before the outbreak of conflict, the people of Worms had expelled the bishop, and in 1074 the son of a leading burgher in Cologne, incensed by the way the archbishop's servants had commandeered one of his father's boats for his domestic purposes, stirred his fellow-citizens to action by telling them how disgraceful it was that they should be less venturesome than the smaller and poorer city of Worms.

These Rhineland cities were not viewed with suspicion by all the leaders of Church and State. Henry IV himself gave them encouragement. In the same period the counts of Flanders and other great nobles of the Low Countries were learning the benefits of good relations with merchant communities. In exchange for favour, protection and freedom to administer their own commercial affairs without serious interference, the counts found that their lands prospered and their pockets were lined as never before. Enlightened self-interest led many kings, dukes and counts to grant privileges of partial self-government. In the mid twelfth century the leaders of the *Drang nach Osten* were learning the value of towns: the foundation of Lübeck by Count Adolf (see pp. 87–8) was a precedent which kings and princes were to follow in many parts of Europe in the following 150 years.

In Italy the story was more complicated. There many towns had a continuous tradition of civic life far older than in the north; and some of the Italian cities were far richer and more powerful than any northern competitor. The eleventh century saw the rise of cities like Pisa, Genoa, Florence and Venice to heights undreamed of hitherto. It also saw the decline of the old forms of political authority in the peninsula. In the south, the rule of the Greeks was replaced by the far stronger rule of the Normans, and city development, under the friendly control of the Norman dukes and kings, followed a pattern not so different from that in northern Europe. In the rest of Italy the power of the emperors declined, or became a sporadic and confusing influence in a situation rendered anarchic by the gradual disappearance of the great nobles. When the Countess Matilda of Tuscany died in 1115, for instance, she had no effective successor, and great cities like Florence achieved a new measure of independence. But the cities were compelled to make alliance with the petty nobles of their neighbourhood to protect them against outside enemies. In many cases the petty nobles were directly interested in the town's affairs; more and more these men, the *grandi* as they were called on account of their noble birth, came to live in lofty towers within the walls of the cities. The towers might be used for defence against foreign attack; they were frequently used for the game of domestic warfare. With a characteristic burst of wild exaggeration—which throws a flood of light, none the less, on twelfth-century Italy—Benjamin of Tudela asserted that when he visited Pisa in 1154 he saw ten thousand towers. In Siena and San Gimignano one may still recapture the atmosphere of these fantastically turreted cities.

While the *grandi* were defending the cities and fighting among themselves, and the *popolo grasso*, the substantial merchants, were making the cities rich, the direction of affairs in many cities had fallen into the hands of the local bishops. As in the north, the Church was the chief sufferer from the communal movement; or rather, the Church under one aspect, since in Milan, whose archbishop was the greatest prelate of north Italy, the *popolo* formed an alliance with the papal reformers, and were supported by the papacy in their struggle for ecclesiastical reform and some measure of independence (see pp. 274 ff.). In Florence the first attack on the bishop came in the 1060s, where it was accompanied, as in Milan, by accusations of simony; Florence, however, admitted its more distant allegiance to the Tuscan counts until 1115. In Pisa, the archbishop held out until the mid twelfth century. In the mid twelfth century, in most Italian cities, there was considerable uncertainty whether the local bishop, or a revived imperial authority, or the rising mercantile patriciate, would hold sway in the future. The solution of these conflicts lies beyond our horizon, but it is worth dwelling for a moment on the history of one Italian city, because its story was interesting and important in its own right, and a striking contrast to what normally happened elsewhere.

Of all the cities of medieval Italy, Venice in the early twelfth century was the one which bore most resemblance to Athens in the age of Pericles. The hinterland was important to her, but her strength and wealth lay in her ships, and in her immunity from attack from the Italian mainland: as Athens had been protected by her walls, so Venice was protected by her marshes and lagoons. In this great city lived the merchants and other freemen, governed nominally by a democratic constitution, in practice by the chief citizen, the doge (or duke): it was only in the late twelfth century that the growing concentration of mercantile wealth led to the formation of the oligarchy which ruled Venice throughout the later centuries of her glory and decline. The citizens were assisted by a large body of slaves, and their wealth depended on their increasing hold over the trade of the eastern Mediterranean, where they had trading posts and colonies in much the same area that Athens had had her empire. The culture of twelfth-century

Venice is not to be compared with that of fifth-century Athens, nor indeed with the Venice of the Bellini and Titian. But the foundations of a prosperous intercourse with the east in art and architecture as well as in merchandise were already well laid. Venice could dispense with the *grandi* and their towers; its duke could hold all rival authorities at arm's length. Nominally a part of Western Christendom, the city could act as go-between among eastern and western Christians, and Christians and Muslims; could ignore the storms and interpret the ideals of the age in its own way. In the early thirteenth century it conquered the Byzantine Empire.

Already by the mid twelfth century Venice and Florence were the commercial capitals of Europe. Whether they were the most populous cities of the time one cannot say: Palermo and Paris may have been as large. But Venice stood out from all rivals in the homogeneity of its citizens and of their activities. This cohesion was not due to their origins. Venice was formed out of the amalgamation in the period between the seventh and the ninth centuries of a group of island fortresses, which had become the homes of refugees from all over northern Italy; and by the twelfth century, with settlers from other parts of Europe, and with the influx of a cosmopolitan slave population which no doubt mingled with the citizens in some degree, the Venetians were ethnically very mixed. But the races had lived together and inter-married for many generations, and achieved a genuine cohesion—of common social organization and common interests and culture. Venice, by the standards of the day, was an old city; her patriciate was comparatively well established.

If we could pay a visit to a meeting of the city fathers of almost any other great town in this period, I fancy that we should be surprised by the variety of their origin and of their personal histories. In a few cities, especially in Italy, where the information is relatively copious, some kind of pattern emerges. Thus the great names in Genoa in the eleventh and early twelfth centuries included the scions of a number of local landowning families, who were evidently concerned in the trade as well as the politics of the city. In the mid twelfth century new names appear in increasing numbers. The *popolo grasso* were catching up the *grandi*. Before 1150 indeed it is clearly a mistake to draw too sharp a distinction between *grandi* and *popolo*. In northern Europe the information is usually very sparse in this period. What we do know offers some surprising associations. One of the leading London aldermen of the early twelfth century was a canon of St Paul's; not only so, but it is likely that his father had been a canon before him, and certain that one of his sons succeeded to his canonry. Ralph, son of Algod, was a member of a dying class, the married upper clergy of the days before celibacy was enforced. But the clergyman-financier remained a familiar figure throughout the Middle Ages.

The clergy

Like the world of commerce, the clerical profession offered increasingly varied opportunities to young men with the means, the talents or the vocation to seize them. It is very likely that a high proportion of the clergy in the tenth and eleventh centuries were hereditary clergymen. Once again, our ignorance is very great; but wherever we go in Europe, we find traces of what seems to have been a widespread and quite accepted practice, before the papal reform and the insistence on celibacy. Iceland, with its hereditary bishopric, was exceptional. But in no part of Europe was it wholly exceptional for an eleventh-century bishop to have children. Most of these were born, no doubt, before the fathers obtained high office. But there are plenty of instances of priests living openly with their wives. We very rarely know the names of parish priests or cathedral canons in this period. Lists survive from a group of churches on the Welsh border in the mid and late eleventh century; most passed by hereditary succession. Lists survive of the canons of St Paul's from the turn of the eleventh and twelfth centuries onwards. At least a quarter of the first generation were married, and several passed on their canonries to their children. The founder of Tiron, preaching celibacy in Normandy about 1100, was nearly lynched by the clergy's wives, as had been the archbishop of Rouen in person, when promulgating a decree against them in 1072. Professor Southern has made famous the extraordinary story of how the twelve great-great-grandchildren of a tenth-century priest divided a substantial part of the income of Arezzo cathedral among themselves in the late eleventh century. The tale could go on. It is striking that much of the evidence belongs to the two or three generations after the papal reform. But in the second quarter of the twelfth century, among the upper clergy, comes a change; bishops with children and hereditary canons become an extreme rarity. The lower, parochial clergy seem often to have had wives and children; but the ladies and children of the close, of whom Heloise herself had been one, become a thing of the past.[1]

[1] Heloise is said to have been the niece, not the daughter, of Canon Fulbert: but she was certainly brought up by her uncle.

Celibate clergy there had always been. The increasing numbers of monks in the tenth and eleventh centuries show that even before the papal reform the life of celibacy had a large number of devotees. The anxiety of the papal reformers to put all clergy under a rule shows that experience suggested to them that celibacy could only be enforced on monks or folk living a quasi-monastic life. The monks of the tenth and eleventh centuries, furthermore, had included many of the most intelligent and talented men of the age. But they had been few in number. The new orders of the late eleventh and twelfth centuries attracted ever increasing numbers of recruits. It is interesting to observe that just at the point when the old sources of clerical recruitment, the married clergy, were taking to celibacy, the supply of clergy did not dry up, it multiplied exceedingly. In England alone—the only country for which even approximate figures have been worked out—the number of monks rose from about 850 to well over 5,000 between 1066 and 1154.

Much lies hidden behind this sensational growth. We do not know in detail whence the monks were recruited; but on the whole they seem mainly to have come from the upper classes, and perhaps from the families of substantial town-dwellers. Peasants' sons could become lay brothers in Cistercian houses, but it was probably not common for them to take the habit as choir monks. It was possible for a man to achieve social promotion in the Church: if a few bishops were sons and brothers of kings or great lords, many more owed their position to talent and service, not to birth. The bishops of Norman Sicily were as much parvenus as their Norman masters. The Conqueror's bishops in Normandy included his half-brother, Odo of Bayeux, and several of high baronial rank. There was a tendency for the highly born to be preferred to the prince bishoprics of Germany; and in the tenth and early eleventh centuries training to knightly pursuits had been almost a necessary qualification for a successful German bishop. But in the twelfth century, by and large, whoever could enter the ranks of the privileged clergy could hope for a bishopric; and the ranks of the privileged clergy were open to all who could find patronage, whether because of birth or talent or good luck. Thus the Church offered opportunities to the ambitious as well as to the devout, although it would be a mistake to regard it as an egalitarian institution. None the less, the rapid rise in the numbers of monks does have a social implication. Since we know from other evidence that the warrior and mercantile classes of Europe were not being depleted in this period—on the contrary, were steadily rising—we can see here further evidence of the rise in population of this age, a rise all the more striking since it could continue and grow in strength even though so many men and women were following a life of celibacy.

A rise in numbers would by itself help to explain why the upper classes were looking for new and wider choice of occupation; it does not go far towards explaining the popularity of Cîteaux. This problem will be discussed later (pp. 303–4); but it is worth dwelling a moment on the evidence that a life of spiritual adventure, or of intellectual adventure in the rapidly growing schools, was a rival in appeal to the traditional life of hunting and fighting of the European ruling classes, or to the life of mercantile enterprise or travel. The horizons were opening in every direction.

The man who entered a monastery did so, in principle, for life; there were of course apostates; there were also a number who moved on to a stricter way of life; and a few who were promoted to abbeys elsewhere, or to bishoprics, or even to the papacy. But most monks stayed, like Orderic Vitalis (p. 14), where their parents or their vocation had placed them. It was commonly a life of great stability. In contrast, the secular clerk, the clergyman who was not under a rule or monastic discipline, was often an inveterate wanderer. Early in life he went from school to school, sometimes half across Europe; then he looked for patronage to give him a livelihood. This he might find in the service of a bishop; for many bishops in the late eleventh and twelfth centuries were coming to have large staffs of young clerks, who learned the business of ecclesiastical administration and rose to be canons or archdeacons, or were seconded or translated to the royal service. Through the royal *capella* of the German kings, or the royal chapel of the Anglo-Saxons lay the path to bishoprics (see pp. 139–40). The monk-bishop was not a rarity in this period; many of the greatest bishops had been monks. But they were usually in a minority. Bishoprics were most commonly the reward for service to one or other important secular potentate.

Bishops, archdeacons, canons, civil servants, monks: these are the men whose lives we may study in the sources, whom we can meet face to face in their own writings, the educated, privileged clergy. But of the clergy as a whole, they were a minority, probably always a small minority. On the same occasion on which Orderic was ordained priest by the archbishop of Rouen, there were ordained 244 deacons and 120 priests. The majority of these manned the parish churches and chapels of the diocese, or acted as chaplains to great laymen. Many of them, perhaps, were children of the ladies who had lynched the archbishop's predecessor thirty years before. Their manner of life and lack of learning were denounced by reformers; but they lived according to their own customs and traditions, and there is little evidence that they were more commonly celibate, or less ignorant, in 1200 than in 1000. In truth, we know little of them. In social status they varied considerably. The better off, or more fortunate, merged into the ranks of the privileged clergy; the poorer were sons of serfs. They lived the lives of the folk among whom they worked; and this may have helped many of them to make real contact with their parishioners. In many cases, perhaps, it simply meant that clergy and people were equally barbarous. The papal reform tended to drive a wedge between the educated, celibate higher clergy, and the rank and file. But there is every reason to suppose that there already existed that division which makes the Church of the later Middle Ages so strangely resemble a military hierarchy, with the upper clergy as commissioned officers, the rural deans and archpriests as N.C.O.s, and the parish clergy as privates. The letters written by bishops to their subordinates in the twelfth century rarely give the impression of personal contact with anyone below an archdeacon or a canon. Thus the Church, for all the opportunities which it gave to men to find new lives and lofty ideals, to transcend the limitations of the age, still, in its main structure, reflected the social organization of the world. And to women it gave virtually no opportunity at all.

The place of women

It was a man's world. The opportunities open to women in this period scarcely expanded, may even have contracted. In 1066 the number of English nuns was a quarter of the number of monks; the number rose rapidly, but even so, in 1154 they were probably less than a fifth the number of monks. And yet religion seems to have been the only respectable profession open to a woman other than marriage and child-bearing. In the upper classes, the girls were at the mercy of their father's dynastic ambitions; they were pawns in the marriage game. Many women died in childbirth, but it was not so dangerous as the warlike pursuits of the men-folk. It is very difficult to give any precise figures to illustrate or establish this; but a rough count of the twelfth-century marriages noted in three volumes of the *Complete Peerage* reveals that among the English upper classes of the twelfth century it was much commoner for a lady to have two or more husbands than for a man to have two or more wives; in the cases noted, almost twice as common

(36 to 19).[1] There are far more cases in which each party is only known to have married once, but the evidence is so fragmentary that it is likely that the figures seriously underestimate the number of second, third and fourth marriages. The improvement in medical knowledge and other changes of recent times have made marriage a far more stable institution than it was in the Middle Ages; nor have the divorce rates in European countries yet reached proportions to suggest a serious qualification to this statement.

A small proportion of the ladies of the upper classes entered convents; the remainder were married off, where possible, shortly after puberty; in the very highest society they had commonly been betrothed, sometimes more than once, in babyhood. The lot of a spinster or a widow in such a society was not enviable. Although the monastic reformers of the twelfth century frowned on the practice of placing children in monasteries, and the Cistercians forbade it, we may be sure that throughout the Middle Ages many nuns were dedicated to religion by the same procedure as they would have been dedicated to husbands—by parental fiat. There was no lack of enterprise in founding monasteries or endowing them; it seems likely that if spinsters had been a serious problem to the fathers of the age, more convents of nuns would have appeared.

Of the place of women among the artisans and peasants we know almost nothing. So far as we can tell, the men-folk ruled in every sphere; but it may be that the further one got from the world of high feudalism the less of a slave the woman became; it is certainly true, in a rather different way, that the Norman Conquest brought both a more complete feudalism and a fall in the status of women. It may be too that in the lower regions of society women were freer to find at least part-time employment: the distaff provided occupation for almost all, and even if the invention of the spinning wheel may have reduced the opportunities for some, it enormously increased those of others. There is copious evidence that less reputable professions attracted many women to them; and in the tenth century monogamy was not yet the established practice in parts of eastern and northern Europe; nor, of course, among the Muslims. But the majority of women in all walks of life looked to make their career as housewives. For all the subjection, the limitation of opportunity, many no doubt ruled their husbands as well as their households in that as in all ages; great ladies may often have run the estate when the lord was away on campaign. In a similar way the recluse

[1] Vols. x–xii; cf. Brooke in *Studies in Ecclesiastical History*, vol. i (forthcoming). It may be that ladies commonly married much younger than men.

Christina of Markyate (see pp. 304–5) succeeded in dominating her circle of acquaintance, which included the abbot of St Albans, from her cell. We would give much for a few case histories, like that of the fourteenth-century merchant of Prato, of how a medieval household actually worked. The ladies of our period of whom we know more than the name were almost always ladies of exceptional character or talent, who force themselves on our notice partly at least for this reason. Yet when all allowance is made for this bias in the evidence, one cannot help being struck by the conspicuous part in our story which was played by the Empress Theophanu, the Empress Agnes, the Countess Matilda, St Margaret, the Empress Matilda, Queen Eleanor—great ladies who rose above the limitations of their sex, as commonly understood, as rulers, as saints or as viragoes; and the twelfth century would have been greatly the poorer without the life and work of the English Christina, the Hertfordshire anchoress, or of the French Heloise, the Stoic of the Paraclete, or of the German Hildegarde, the mystic of Bingen.

VI

Kingship and Government

Kingship

Medieval kingship was a strenuous occupation. If he played strictly according to the rules, the king had to combine some of the qualities of general, prize fighter, judge and monk. He was expected to defend his people and to keep the peace, and yet also to provide his warrior barons with suitable exercise. He was expected to set an example in knightly exercises, and to show a personal example of prowess in war, although he and his enemies were sufficiently prudent to value him more highly alive than dead, so that a crowned king was rarely killed in battle. He was expected to keep good order; that is to say, to see that offenders were punished, that evil-doers went in fear of him, that disputes over land were settled in an orderly manner; and personally to supervise his royal court. He was the protector of the Church in his land, and the Church required him to take a keen and personal interest in its affairs. Daily mass was a minimum for any conscientious nobleman; many kings attended a considerable part of the daily office as well. And this

BIBLIOGRAPHY. F. Kern, *Kingship, Law and the Constitution in the Middle Ages* (trans. S. B. Chrimes, Oxford, 1939) and the later chapters of Bloch's *Feudal Society* give the best general accounts. On English law, see F. Pollock and F. W. Maitland, *The History of English Law* (2 vols., 2nd edn., Cambridge, 1898). Also important are H. Mitteis, *Lehnrecht und Staatsgewalt* (reprinted Darmstadt, 1958) and *Der Staat des hohen Mittelalters* (3rd edn., Weimar, 1948); F. Lot and R. Fawtier (eds.), *Histoire des institutions françaises au moyen âge*, vols. I, II (Paris, 1957–8: the chapter on Flanders in vol. I, by F.-L. Ganshof, is especially useful for the relations of the king and the great feudatories in France). On French administration see also W. M. Newman, *Le domaine royal sous les premiers Capétiens* (Paris, 1937); for German, H. Bresslau, *Handbuch der Urkundenlehre* (3rd edn., vol. I, Berlin, 1958), Chapter 7; H.-W. Klewitz in *Archiv für Urkundenforschung*, vol. XVI (1939), pp. 102 ff.; for English, *Dialogus de scaccario*, ed. and trans. C. Johnson (Nelson's Medieval Texts, 1950), which includes a text of the document describing Henry I's household, the *Constitutio domus regis*; V. H. Galbraith, *Studies in the Public Records* (Edinburgh, 1958); H. M. Cam, 'The evolution of the mediaeval English Franchise', *Speculum*, was only a part of the ceremonial which surrounded the office with glamour and reminded the king's subjects that he was God's anointed —a notion which inspired them with great awe, when they were not actually engaged in rebellion against him.

Some took their duties more seriously than others. The biographer of Edward the Confessor shows us (in what is meant to be a panegyric) the picture of a thoroughly idle king, who spent much of his time 'in the glades and woods in the pleasures of hunting'. This was the normal relaxation of a king's leisure: Henry I of Germany was so keen a huntsman that he 'would take forty or more wild beasts in a day'; the Norman kings turned a substantial proportion of their kingdom into game preserves; hunting was the natural sport of a militant aristocracy, venting on animals the energy and spleen left over from fighting their own kind. It is clear that the Confessor retained his native energy to the end of his life, since Earl Harold built a hunting lodge for him in Wales as late as 1065. But apart from hunting, he seems to have left the business of government to his earls, although he continued to enjoy the society of churchmen, especially of foreign churchmen, gave his heart to the building of Westminster Abbey, engaged in the royal works of mercy, stood meekly through divine office and mass, and—a special note of conscientiousness—'at these times, unless he was addressed, he rarely spoke to anyone.'[1] The biographer says nothing of a king's other chief relaxation, the evening carouse. It was noted of Henry I of Germany that he was merry in his cups, but never to the detriment of royal dignity; and of William I of England that he was so abstemious that he never took more than three cups of wine after dinner. Such banquets are portrayed for us on the Bayeux Tapestry, or at least the early stages of them.

---

[1] *Life of King Edward the Confessor*, ed. and trans. F. Barlow (Nelson's Medieval Texts, 1962), pp. 40–1.

---

vol. XXXII (1957), pp. 427–42 reprinted in *Law-Finders and Law-Makers* (London, 1962) (and see Chapter X). On the *fief-rente*, see B. Lyon, *From fief to indenture* (Harvard, 1957); on Anglo-Norman mercenaries, J. O. Prestwich in *Transactions of the Royal Historical Society*, 5th Series, vol. IV (1954); on the art of war, R. C. Smail, *Crusading Warfare* (Cambridge, 1956); R. A. Brown, *English Medieval Castles* (London, 1954); on the imperial idea see R. Folz, *L'idée d'empire en occident* (Paris, 1953) and *Le souvenir et la légende de Charlemagne dans l'empire germanique médiéval* (Paris, 1950); on king-making, H. Mitteis, *Die deutsche Königswahl* (2nd edn., Brünn, 1944); P. E. Schramm, *A History of the English coronation* (Oxford, 1937). See further books listed in bibliographies to Chapters VII–X.

As leader of the Church Edward the Confessor played his part, though not perhaps very adequately, since he left on his death an archbishop of Canterbury who was not recognized as such by the pope. Whether or not he fulfilled his part as judge and lawgiver, it is very hard to say: later generations spoke of the good laws of King Edward, but we cannot tell if he deserved the compliment. The two other functions of a king he shirked: he did not lead his armies to war, anyway in his later years, and he did not provide an heir. The latter was very likely his misfortune, or his wife's. In that ascetic age he earned a strange renown for his childlessness; it was attributed, rightly or wrongly, to celibacy, and this was regarded as a sign of virtue. This interpretation was kind to Edward, because it was more normal even then to demand of a king that he produce an heir, and Edward's childlessness unloosed on his luckless kingdom the horrors of 1066.

A king reigned 'by grace of God'; his monarchy was surrounded by a divine aura. Yet his subjects had a right of resistance, of rebellion against him, if he failed to rule them justly and to give them due protection. In practice, therefore, he ruled, if he ruled effectively, by force and fear. Medieval kingship was an extraordinary mixture of harsh reality and lofty ideals. They cannot be understood apart. Edward was fortunate to be able to do only half his job and escape condemnation. More characteristic was the active Louis VI of France, who succeeded on the whole in being a successful king, but only by the most strenuous activity. The ideal of medieval kingship is clearly revealed in Suger's *Life*. Louis was never free from wars and rumours of wars; time and again Suger notes his constant activity (anyway in the campaigning season) in spite of his immense girth. With particular pride he notes how in the crisis of 1124, when the king of England and the emperor were allied against him, and Henry V planned an attack on Rheims, Louis put himself dramatically under the protection of St Denis, 'the special patron and singular protector after God of the kingdom'; how he came to the saint and begged him to defend his kingdom, preserve his person and resist his enemies, as the saint was accustomed to do. It was the custom when a foreign invader stepped on French soil for the relics of Denis and his companions to be set on the altar, from which they personally conducted the defence of the realm. And so Louis took a standard from Denis as symbol that he was the saint's vassal (see p. 98), summoned the feudatories of France, and set off to defend Rheims. It is a nice point to decide whether it was the impression made by this tremendous scene staged by Suger in his abbey church, or the memory (usually rather rusty) of their solemn feudal oath, which rallied the feudatories of France, even the count of Blois, who was at war with him, to help Louis against the German.

However we interpret the process of causation, Henry V was baffled, not by the bones, but by the big battalions. So let us start with them.

War and marriage

Warfare was the means by which the upper classes provided themselves with exercise and occupation, and justified their existence. In earlier days they had actually earned their living by war and become rich from the plunder they could collect on their annual expeditions. In the slightly more settled conditions of the tenth century most soldiers were provided with a regular livelihood, and the practical uses of war had diminished. Some of the shrewder politicians of the period realized this; they saw how inconclusive wars generally were, and attempted to attain their ends by more sensible means. The history of the English monarchy well illustrates both the importance and the unimportance of war. It was by conquest that Alfred and his successors created a single English kingdom out of the ruins caused by the Danish invasions of the ninth century. It was by conquest that the Danish King Cnut made himself the first king of a truly united England in the early eleventh century. The significance of the battles of Stamford Bridge and Hastings in 1066 hardly needs emphasis; though we do well to recall that it was not so much William's victory, as the fact that the two battles had removed his two most serious rivals for the throne, which made the year so decisive in English and Norman history. William II, Henry I and Stephen all won the throne by holding rivals at bay, and in each case warfare played its part; in Henry's case the battle of Tinchebrai (1106) enabled him to imprison his elder brother for life and made him secure in Normandy as well as in England (see pp. 231 ff.).

Decisive battles, the death of kings in battle or the life imprisonment of great men were rare events; and against the very exceptional, decisive outcome of the battles of 1066 and 1106 we must set the endless, indecisive campaigns of William I and Henry I on the borders of their French domains; the indecisive warfare of Stephen's reign which led to anarchy in England. Henry I shored up his doubtful claim by marrying a princess of the English royal line; what Stephen had lost in warfare, Henry II recaptured owing to a series of successful marriages—those of his parents, which united a claim to all the territory of Henry I with Anjou, and his own, which added to these Aquitaine, that is to say, some title to most of southern France. Henry II spent a large part of a long career campaigning in France; but his wars added very little to what he had gained by marriage. Nor was the lesson lost on him. The hectic marriage alliances which he, in common with most twelfth-century potentates, engaged in showed a recognition that marriage was a more reliable weapon than warfare in realizing large ambitions.

It is natural to consider the dynastic marriage policies of this period in the same context as warfare, since both were engaged in by the kings and great nobles for very much the same reasons. Both were a regular part of the customs of European high society: however little women might be regarded, the queen and the duchess were essential figures in the palace and the castle. They minded the hearth and provided the heir. The laws of the Church made a man look outside his kindred for a wife, and the dynasts made virtue of necessity and constructed elaborate alliances by their marriages. These alliances were similar to the games of dice much favoured at the time: the marriages might or might not be successful; they might or might not have political consequences. Henry II's inheritance was won by a series of marriages which were politically successful but domestically disastrous. It is observed elsewhere how his unfortunate mother had been used by Henry I in his immensely grandiose designs. The designs were brilliantly successful in the long run, but his daughter suffered for them. Many marriages were more satisfactory than Matilda's alliance with the count of Anjou. It was universally accepted that no man married merely for love, and many men and women no doubt made the best of the circumstances, and fell in love with their partners. More often, perhaps, some kind of friendship not closely akin to modern ideas of marriage subsisted between husband and wife, and many men (in particular) were unfaithful. The political consequences of marriage were frequently cancelled out by other counter-alliances. On several occasions in the centuries of this book, a single family group ruled over most of Europe. Their relationships and marriage alliances did not conduce to peace, but they commonly gave the warfare of the period the appearance of civil war, even though the rank and file of the soldiers can hardly have felt the bond which united the leaders on both sides.

Though warfare came increasingly to be in competition with marriage marketing as the chief business of kings, it lost none of its importance in the eyes of contemporaries: the more indecisive it became, the more attached they were to it. It is remarkable indeed how little under-standing we have of warfare in this period; and we shall never know in detail how medieval kings acquired and held their power unless we can find out more precisely how they recruited their armies and led them.

Weapons and recruitment

The most powerful weapon in twelfth-century warfare was the castle; and the chief development in military technology in our period was in the architecture of castles and the technique of their destruction, and in siegecraft in general. Nicephorus Phocas had mocked Liudprand of Cremona in the tenth century because western armies consisted solely of knights and knew nothing of siegecraft. At this time fortifications consisted mainly of earth banks and wooden palisades. The stone castle was only developed at all widely in the eleventh century, when the large keep, fort and dwelling-house in one, of which the Tower of London is a particularly fine example, came into fashion among men of exceptional wealth. Even then, most great men had to be content with 'motte and bailey', with a mound having a wooden lookout tower on top as a central defensive position, and a large enclosure surrounded by an earth rampart in which living quarters could be sited. Continued experience of stone fortresses, and contact with Muslim and Byzantine forts on the crusades, provided new ideas of defence. If a castle acted as one of a related group it could provide defence in depth: an army could be inhibited from penetrating behind a group of castles by the threat to its communications which they provided, and the danger of attack from the rear. This was a real benefit, and helps to explain why so many medieval campaigns rapidly declined into a series of fruitless sieges and failed to lead to any deep penetration of enemy territory.

The effectiveness of the castle for the defence of a country was, however, qualified by two circumstances. First of all, medieval armies were sometimes not dependent on lines of communication: they did not, often could not, live on their own supplies, and reckoned to feed themselves on the land they passed through. It has been observed that Christian fortresses in Syria on numerous occasions failed to act as any sort of check on the movement of Muslim armies. Secondly, effective defence in depth presupposes that castles have been sited with this end in view, and that they form a coherent group under unified control. Practice was normally very different. Anyone who has visited a number of medieval castles will know how admirable their sites often are: how they command distant views, or river crossings, or are placed in situations of great natural strength. But in many cases the castle is quite unrelated to other castles. Many were the results of private enterprise by barons concerned with their own defence and their own private wars. Even those built on the initiative of a prince or a king were often sited with quite other ends in view. The planned defensive systems of King Alfred or of Henry the Fowler were primarily concerned to provide refuges for folk whose land was being pillaged; they also provided defence in depth, but it was a secondary consideration. Castles were also frequently designed as houses for great lords or to be administrative and judicial centres. Those built by governments seem most commonly to have been placed where they could combine the functions of protecting the local population and housing the official who governed the area. The chief Norman royal castles were built at the headquarters of shires, and in early days their castellans were often (though not invariably) the royal sheriffs.

But when due allowance has been made for the very various functions of castles, as administrative and social as well as military centres, it remains true that they were formidable military weapons, and that some of the most remarkable technological advances of the twelfth century were made in the improvement of siege engines and of a castle's defences. The Romans had been used to the idea of employing rams to push down walls, and catapults to throw stones at or over them. The rams were revived; the catapults were improved; and the invention of the trebuchet provided a weapon which could throw a large stone for a short distance with considerable force. More important still were the improved techniques of mining: mines were built under the walls, shored up with timber, which was then burned so that the wall collapsed. And if the base of the wall could not be penetrated, moveable towers were built which could be wheeled up to attack the wall from without; in the longer sieges, such as that of Antioch during the First Crusade, fixed towers were erected over against the walls to harry the defenders and enable a watch to be kept on them. To counter these tactics, larger and thicker walls were built, walls with much enlarged bases; and in the late twelfth and thirteenth centuries a variety of devices were invented to harry the attacker and make his work more difficult.

In other respects warfare remained much what it had been. The castle or the fortified town restricted the movements of mobile field armies; in particular, it was effective against the rapid raids of Magyars, with their lightly armed mounted archers, or the Vikings, with their swift ships, who had had the advantage of striking rapidly and ranging far. Now they tended to find their victims, and the loot for which they came, locked behind strong walls; if they ventured too far, they found garrisons sallying from these fortresses and cutting off their escape. But the main armies of the western monarchs and princes were still armies of mounted knights. The chain armour had to be improved to protect the knight against arrows: in western Europe in the eleventh century the powerful crossbow came to be used, and the crusading armies constantly found themselves rained on by showers of arrows from mounted Turkish archers. But if it came to a pitched battle, the phalanx of heavily armed, well-mounted knights was a very formidable weapon. It is surprising, therefore, how seldom armies joined in pitched battle in the eleventh and twelfth centuries. The English fought on foot at Hastings, and although they certainly used horses for transport, they may normally have fought on foot; Henry I's knights at Tinchebrai in 1106 also dismounted, owing to the nature of the battlefield. Cavalry did not have it all their own way. But the fact that the crusaders—and western monarchs in the twelfth century—did not abandon their style of cavalry strongly suggests that the mounted knight was still a very effective weapon, as well as being increasingly the symbol of social status.

An army consisted, then, primarily of knights, with archers and other infantry as auxiliaries of growing importance; and a king also needed to garrison a number of castles and towns if he were to control his subjects and keep his enemies at bay. For these purposes he could use one of three methods. In the kingdoms of western Europe there was a traditional obligation on all free men to answer the king's call to arms, the *arrière-ban*, when the kingdom was attacked: a right which was rarely invoked in our period, since it produced a cumbersome and inefficient force, which could not be kept long in the field. The English fyrd was used in the Danish wars, but only later, so far as we can tell, as a local militia in emergencies. The French kings were as yet too weak to use the *arrière-ban*, if they had wished to, save in quite exceptional circumstances, as in 1124. The strength of the imperial idea in Germany is illustrated by the special form that the call to the host took there—the duty to attend the king if he went to Rome to be crowned emperor. For this purpose the memory of the *arrière-ban* was preserved; but in practice the imperial armies were not usually recruited in so haphazard a fashion.

Already in Carolingian times the imperial army had had a nucleus of fully trained warriors who served their lord in exchange for holding substantial fiefs. In principle, feudal tenure was the source from which most monarchs and most great lords recruited their armies between the tenth century and the twelfth. In some countries feudal institutions were not fully developed; in many there were still substantial areas of allodial territory. In these a method of recruitment which combined some elements of the old *arrière-ban* and the new feudal bond seems to have operated. The core of the English armies in the early eleventh century consisted of the housecarles, the personal followers of the Danish king, and some proportion of the thegns, the upper classes, who were recruited by no single formula, but often held by quasi-feudal tenure. In Germany the dukes and counts—old royal officers now become semi-independent feudal lords—had obligations to produce knights for the imperial army. But the Saxon emperors reconstructed the army so that the bulk of their troops came from ecclesiastical estates. Bishops and abbots were expected to produce substantial contingents. These consisted largely of *ministeriales*, tenants originally unfree (see p. 105), who in Germany and the Low Countries were assuming increasing importance, and were to be found most frequently on royal and ecclesiastical territories, improving their status by regular military and administrative service.

The weakness of feudal service as a basis for recruiting an army was that it was hedged round with difficult restrictions. Normally a knight expected to serve for about forty days a year at his own expense; the terms of his service might also be restricted—when and where he served, and for how long he would stay after the forty days if the king paid him. The terms of service of the German *ministeriales* are very imperfectly known, and seem to have been longer; even there, dependence on the loyalty and efficiency of widely scattered bishoprics and abbeys could be cumbersome and inefficient. To overcome these difficulties, kings made increasing use of money. They paid their knights to stay beyond their term; they paid mercenaries; and in the late tenth and eleventh centuries we first find evidence of that strange hybrid, the holder of a money fief, or *fief-rente*. The *fief-rente* was a feudal tenure in which an annual rent or money fee replaced the grant of land. It was used for a variety of purposes; most commonly as a retaining fee for a knight who could be called out whenever the king or lord had need of him. Sometimes it was no more than a retaining fee; sometimes, like a normal feudal holding, it paid the knight for some period of service. Normally, the king would expect to pay the holder of *fief-rente* wages as well; he was thus half way to being a mercenary. *Fief-rentes* provided kings with a pool of mercenaries on whom they could call without having to compete in the open market with other war-lords.

'The strength of a state' in the view of a Spanish Muslim of this age 'varies directly as the number of its paid troops.' But the same writer also showed his affinity with the notions of contemporary Christendom by observing that battles were won by a few renowned knights, and the army which had 'even one more famous warrior than its enemy must . . . win'.[1] These ideas are very revealing: they underline the extra-ordinary mixture of military insight and knightly showmanship, games-manship even, which governed medieval warfare.

From the mid eleventh century at latest the paid knight and the mercenary became common. No doubt they had existed before. That they became common then is a striking illustration of the rapid growth in the money economy in our period. From the eleventh century on, the old basis of feudal knighthood became increasingly artificial; and it is a strange irony that the Norman kings, all of whom relied in large measure on money to recruit their armies, should have introduced the most complete feudal structure of the old kind into England. When our period closes both systems were living side by side in uneasy harmony.

Over most of western Europe money was replacing land as the source of troops in the twelfth century. The notable exception to this was Germany. It was suggested, indeed, in the late eleventh century, that the Emperor Henry IV should replace knight-service by a tax, and have an army of mercenaries; it is significant that the suggestion was made by an Italian, Benzo of Alba. Early in the next century, the English Henry I is said to have suggested to his son-in-law, the Emperor Henry V, after the failure of his French campaign in 1124, that he should levy a tax, evidently to improve his army. Yet mercenaries seem still to have formed only a small part of the German army; the *fief-rente* was almost exclusively used to supply garrisons for castles and fortified towns; and as the Church and its *ministeriales* became a less reliable source of troops, the twelfth-century emperors resorted to the practice of strengthening feudal bonds and building up the resources of their own domains. It is probable that Germany was less wealthy than England in comparison to its size, and that it was easier for Henry I to recruit an army of mercenaries than for Henry V. For whatever reason, the contrast outlived our period.

Law and administration

A king's power depended, then, first and foremost on his capacity to recruit armies and to lead them; it also depended on his position as

[1] Quoted in R. Menéndez Pidal, *The Cid and his Spain*, p. 180.

supreme judge and lawgiver in his kingdom. What this meant varied greatly from place to place and from time to time; nor can we make any satisfactory generalizations about the nature of medieval law. Some writers have held that the essential thing about medieval law was that it was discovered, not made; in so far as it was valid and sound, it was a reflection of divine law; it partook of the nature of what in more recent times has been called 'fundamental law'. According to this doctrine, all law must be old and it must be good; if it conforms to both these rules, it cannot be overthrown. A ruler is bound by the good old law; if he breaks it in any serious way, his subjects can rebel, and by formal process compel him to obey the law. Medieval law was indeed profoundly conservative, and no medieval vassal would have accepted the notion that the right of resistance was a law which could be repealed. It was invoked against Henry IV of Germany by the Saxons and the southern dukes; and it was to be invoked against the English King John long after our period closed.

None the less, new law could be and was made. Even allowing that man's capacity to overlook what he does not want to see is almost unlimited, the folk of this age can hardly have failed to observe that new law was being made all the time. The revival of Roman Law in eleventh- and twelfth-century Italy, and of canon law at about the same time, accustomed men to systems of law in which legislation was normal and easy. In England the codes of the Anglo-Saxon kings, although they covered only a fraction of the area covered by custom, and although they contained numerous traditional items, involved some new legislation and made little pretence of not doing so. At the other end of Europe Roger II of Sicily promulgated his codes in 1129 at Melfi and in 1140 at Ariano; they contained much that was traditional, much that was new; and the idea of making some unity in the chaotic laws of his kingdom was especially novel.

On the whole the royal courts of Europe were more concerned to administer than to define the law: as in canon law, there was no clear distinction between legislative and judicial functions, and so the former was normally hidden in the latter. The extent of royal jurisdiction varied enormously: at one extreme lay Roger II, the would-be autocrat, uttering absolutist doctrines out of Justinian; or the English king, who, however tied by custom, had effective control both of the king's court, which retained a wide jurisdiction and was capable, under Henry II, of rapid expansion, and over the old popular courts of the shire and, where they had not fallen into private hands, of the hundred;

at the other extreme was the German king, much of whose jurisdiction had been delegated to the ecclesiastical immunities, and equally much was slipping, in the twelfth century, into princely hands; or the French king, who was expected to do high justice to all who came, but received comparatively few callers from outside the royal domain.

The judicial institutions of Europe were governed by a series of contradictions. Jurisdiction and administration were regarded as essentially one process, and the court in which they were carried out was the central institution of any monarchy or principality: the maintenance of justice and law was in many people's eyes the king's supreme function. Yet the tradition of the Germanic tribes was that judgement should be pronounced by the whole body of freemen, by all the 'suitors', all those who had the right and duty of regular attendance at the court; and the jurisdiction of the old royal and popular courts was cut across here, there and everywhere by the numerous feudal courts erected in increasing numbers on the basis of royal grant or mere usurpation from the ninth century onwards, and in the eleventh and twelfth by the appearance of borough courts and town courts of various kinds and courts which merchants set up to handle their own problems, which could hardly be handled by the warrior president or the yokel suitors of a popular court. Thus jurisdiction was infinitely fragmented; and the confusion was increased by the growing influence and power of the Church courts, which dealt with a large variety of cases, from disputes about marriages to cases involving the clergy's faith and morals. If a cleric engaged in crime, it could be disputed whether a lay or an ecclesiastical court should try him; if there was a dispute about marriage, which carried with it the inheritance of land and other corollaries, lay and Church courts would both be concerned in it. Even when there was not a conflict of jurisdiction, there would often be much coming and going between the courts to ensure that the various aspects of a complex case were handled in unison (see pp. 322 f.). Thus there could be doubt where a case should be tried; there could be, and frequently was, dispute about the competence of courts. In highly feudalized countries, such as France, one could find, in certain times and in certain parts, something like judicial anarchy. Yet it remained critically important that every potential litigant should know in what court, and in what manner, his pleas might be heard. For only in the formal processes of the courts was there any common alternative to the use of force; and in most European countries throughout the period of this book kings and their officers had the greatest difficulty in preventing might from proving stronger than right: disorder was endemic, justice weak—but none the less sought after and admired for being in short supply.

It will help to clarify the confusion a little if some of the tendencies at work in these centuries are noted. In the old popular court, the suitors declared the law and gave judgement, or else passed judgement over to God by making one of the parties submit to an ordeal: to being thrown into a pool, for instance, or made to grasp a red-hot iron; if he sank, or was unmarked, he was innocent; otherwise, he was guilty. In most parts of Europe these courts were waning. In the north, the courts of barons and kings were ousting them, though even in feudal courts the ultimate authority of the body of 'suitors' continued to be widely recognized. In the south, especially in the Italian cities, the influence of Roman Law, which placed far more power in the hands of the magistrates than of the 'suitors', tended to destroy the quasi-democratic character of the old popular courts. In England alone they survived, because the old courts of shire and hundred were defended by the comparatively powerful and comparatively centralized authority of the English and Anglo-Norman kings. They survived to be the essential links between the king and the local communities, out of which grew the special tradition of English government in the later Middle Ages, the principle of 'self-government at the king's command'. But even in England these courts early lost much of their democratic character. The power of the suitors was divided between the sheriff or other officer who presided, and the committees or juries which were chosen to fulfil the various tasks of the body of suitors. The ancestor of the modern jury has been found in a variety of institutions of northern Europe in this period; in truth it seems to be the residuary legatee of the popular courts in general. By the twelfth century, especially in England, juries could be used to provide information, to answer such questions as: who were the notorious criminals of the neighbourhood?—or, who had held a particular plot of land in the recent past? By the late twelfth century, even in England, the function of the suitors had been reduced to this: a committee of them provided information to royal justices in a court which had become effectively or actually an offshoot of the king's court.

In two ways the English development is peculiar. The popular courts survived far longer, and the royal court remained stronger than elsewhere in northern Europe; and in the twelfth century the royal court began to grow in importance, until in later centuries it swallowed the jurisdiction of most other courts. This lay mainly in the future in 1154;

a similar development in France lay wholly in the future. In France and Germany more and more authority had passed into the hands of local and feudal courts, presided over by local lords and their officials, from which these lords drew ample revenues. If justice and administration were part of a single process, so were justice and taxation; for assessments to taxation were fixed in court and the fines and other profits of the courts were extremely lucrative. But the chief function of the feudal court was the regulation of disputes about land. This was as true in England in early Norman times as in France; and the importance of the feudal courts in this respect was only seriously challenged after the mid twelfth century, by the growing use of the right of appeal to a higher court and by the infiltration of the judges of the higher courts into the spheres of the feudal courts.

In the Italian cities the rationalization of legal chaos had taken the form from the late eleventh century onwards of the revival of Roman Law. In the Norman kingdoms, Roger the Great and his legal advisers attempted an even more ambitious rationalization of the extreme diversity of the legal traditions of his subjects. It took time for these changes to become effective. Meanwhile, a wide variety of courts administered a wide variety of laws all over western Europe; and if one asked a man in any part of Europe to whose law he was subject, he might well have answered 'to *my* law'—for law was a personal thing, which a man might carry about with him; it bound him to the courts to which his ancestors had been subject, to the laws of those courts, and gave him the privileges which those courts provided.

Closely linked with justice were the other aspects of administration. In a much governed kingdom like England royal administration included control over the sheriff and other local officers; in some kingdoms it included little more than the issuing of charters and the collecting of somewhat meagre taxes. Even in England the permanent staff of the royal administration was by our standards absurdly small; though it was no doubt enlarged in real life by the hangers-on who gathered round any large household. An account of the establishment of Henry I's household written just after his death opens with the writing office and chapel, still a single department, which organized the king's writs and the king's prayers. The staff listed only consists of the chancellor, one of the greatest of the royal officers, whose wages were five shillings a day, the master of the writing-office, who originally had tenpence a day, but Robert de Sigillo had made himself so indispensable that he had risen into the two shilling class, and the chaplain in charge of the chapel and relics. It is clear that Robert de Sigillo did not write all the royal writs himself, although there is no reason to believe that a twelfth-century English king needed a permanent staff of more than half a dozen clerks, sometimes perhaps even less.[1] The departments which fed the king and organized his armies, and above all his hunting staff, were far larger. The household of Henry I of England, the most literate of its day north of the Alps and the Pyrenees, the centre of an administrative and judicial system which was rapidly growing, was still a mobile headquarters for a chieftain whose principal business was to hunt and to fight.

In the account of Henry I's household there is no reference to the 'chancery'; there was no formal institution under this title at this time, in the English or in any other European kingdom. The office under the chancellor's jurisdiction consisted of *scriptorium*, chapel and relics. Since the household was peripatetic, none of these words denotes a room or a building. But wherever the king was, in one of his palaces or castles, or staying in monastery or cathedral close, or under canvas, space had to be found in which his chancellor and chaplains could do their writing, celebrate mass and maintain the offices of the royal chapel, and preserve the royal collection of relics with due honour and security. This may seem today an odd selection of duties. But it was a common arrangement in the eleventh and twelfth centuries. It derived ultimately from the household organization of the old Frankish monarchs, more immediately from the household of the Saxon kings of Germany.

The word chapel, *capella*, means literally 'a little cloak'; and the cloak from which the word derives was the cloak of St Martin of Tours, after St Denis the chief patron of the Frankish kingdoms. This cloak was the principal relic of the west Frankish kings of Neustria, and wherever the Neustrian kings were, it went with them to adorn whatever building became for the time being the royal chapel. The households of early medieval kings were simple affairs; the permanent staff was small. It was natural and convenient for such writing as had to be done to be performed by the permanent literate officials of the court, the chaplains; and so the tradition arose that royal chaplains could write

---

[1] See T. A. M. Bishop, *Scriptores Regis* (Oxford, 1961), pp. 30 ff. Henry I seems to have had two chancery scribes in regular employment *c.* 1100, at least four *c.* 1130. In Henry II's reign the number rose as high as sixteen, but in his later years it varied from two to five. These are minimum figures: Thomas Becket as chancellor is said to have had fifty-two clerks in all. But there is no reason to believe that the Anglo-Norman kings *needed* more than half a dozen scribes.

royal charters. In fact, a great number of royal charters were not written by royal chaplains, but by scribes of the beneficiaries; and there is grave doubt whether the English monarchs of the tenth and early eleventh centuries employed any professional scribes at all. Edgar may have used the services of monks from leading monasteries.[1] Cnut and Edward the Confessor had competent groups of secular clerks permanently in attendance: the chaplains of Edward formed a large, distinguished and cosmopolitan group. Whether or not they wrote his writs is doubtful. They certainly performed the other functions of the chapel of the contemporary kings of Germany; and it is doubtless significant that some of them were of German origin.

The Saxon and Salian kings had in their household something approaching a school of clerical servants: never large, but always of great importance to them. These men were brought up to do the clerical work of the household, to give the king advice, and eventually to become bishops and perform the duties of royal servants as well as of episcopal pastors in their bishoprics. There was something like a regular *cursus honorum*: the capable chaplain was provided with endowment in the form of canonries and dignities in this and that cathedral, for which he was expected to perform little or no duty, and eventually with a bishopric. A large number, perhaps a high proportion, of German bishops were recruited in this way. The officials of the chapel were the arch-chaplain or arch-chancellor, its honorific head, who was always an archbishop, and from the late tenth century always archbishop of Mainz, and the chancellor, who nearly always became a bishop and commonly an archbishop. For Italy the emperors established a separate hierarchy, anyway of titles, for the chapel and the chaplains were much the same wherever he was.

These arrangements were imitated in France and England. In England the chapel was fully manned in the time of Edward the Confessor (though the title 'chancellor' is generally thought to have been instituted by the Normans). Its close links with the English cathedrals had to wait for the Norman reorganization, which first made possible in England an absenteeism and pluralism on the German model. But the idea of founding fixed royal chapels in strategic places which could provide incomes for royal chaplains was already formed. Thus in Edward's time St Martin-le-Grand in London was founded by Ingelric, apparently a chaplain of the Confessor's of German origin, which in

[1] See P. Chaplais in *A Medieval Miscellany for D. M. Stenton*, ed. P. M. Barnes and C. F. Slade (London, 1962), p. 89.

fact performed this function, and was almost certainly intended to. In Edward's day a *cursus honorum* similar to the German was firmly established. In Edgar's time most of the bishops had been monks; by the mid eleventh century they were mostly, as in Germany, royal chaplains.

The household of Henry I of England had even closer links with France than with Germany. As in France, it contained great lay officials called steward, butler, constable and chamberlain, who controlled its military and domestic affairs; and as in France there was a tendency for these offices to become hereditary. But there was also a tendency in both kingdoms for more and more power to pass into the hands of the chancellor. For most of the reign of Louis VI the chancellor was his favourite Étienne de Garlande, whose brothers held other high offices of state. In the 1120s Étienne overreached himself by combining the offices of chancellor and steward, and the pent-up jealousy of his rivals in the court at last won a hearing from the king. Étienne was removed from his offices and exiled in 1127. But in 1132 he was back as chancellor, though he never aspired to the influence of his earlier days, and the more sober ecclesiastics of the court, in alliance with the papacy, managed to keep him out of a bishopric. The chief ecclesiastical adviser of Louis VI's later years, and of the opening phase of Louis VII's reign, was Suger, the abbot of Saint-Denis, who held no formal office, except during the Second Crusade, when he was regent in the king's absence. After his death in 1151, the leading place in the king's council was taken once more by the royal chancellor, Hugh de Champfleuri, bishop of Soissons. In Hugh's hands were concentrated much of the jurisdiction of the royal court, and control of diplomatic affairs as well as the specific duties of his office, the preservation of the royal seal and the issue of royal documents. After Hugh's dismissal in 1172 Louis VII kept the office vacant for some years: Hugh had been too great a man for it to be wise or safe to raise up a successor to him. We may be sure that the *panache* of the French royal chancellor inspired Thomas Becket to make the office equally great in the court of Henry II, just as it was the quarrel with Becket which no doubt determined Henry II to make the office ineffective after Becket had surrendered the Great Seal on his elevation to Canterbury.

For all their grandeur, the chancellors in Germany, France and England in this period were still essentially officials of the household: even in England the royal chancery did not become a quasi-independent department of state until the turn of the twelfth and thirteenth centuries. Nor were the financial departments in France and Germany in any way independent of the royal household, even though in the nature of things the royal treasury could not be carried round with the king on his travels in quite the way in which the relics were. But in England the financial department was on the way to becoming a formal institution. In Henry I's time its senior officials, the Master Chamberlain and the Treasurer, were still commonly in attendance in the household. But their department, however primitive, was the heir of the treasury which had wielded the Danegelds of Ethelred II and Cnut. Under the presiding genius of Roger, bishop of Salisbury, Henry's most brilliant administrator—said to have been first chosen as chaplain by Henry (whose tastes were different from the Confessor's) for the speed with which he could finish his mass—the English financial departments were achieving something of the efficiency and maturity of their Sicilian counterparts. The treasury at Winchester was the permanent repository; this was coming to be controlled by the Exchequer, the audit department, to which the sheriffs and other officers came twice a year to deliver the royal taxes and to make an account of their stewardship. These accounts were entered on the official 'Pipe Roll'; and the one survivor of these rolls from Henry I's time, that for 1129–30, is far and away the earliest royal account to survive in any European archive; few written accounts were kept in 1130.

The wealth of Henry I set him apart from most European kings; above all it set him apart from his subjects. Their financial resources separated European monarchs from their people in a thoroughly mundane way; the divine aura surrounding the monarchy provided the celestial counterpart, just as relics of the saints jostled with jewels and plate and coins in the royal treasuries.

Divine right: anointing and coronation

The barbarian kings had been a great source of perplexity to the Christian bishops of the early Middle Ages. St Paul had taught that the powers that be were ordained of God, and it was generally held that all power, genuinely held, was God-given, that kings were of God's choosing. Yet one had to admit that the divine selection could take singular forms. This difficulty was never entirely overcome in the Middle Ages; but the camel had already been swallowed by Gregory of Tours 400 years before our period opens, when after describing King Clovis's engaging knaveries, he added the astounding comment: 'God ... increased his kingdom, because he walked before Him in uprightness of heart, doing that which was pleasing in His sight.' The books of Kings and Chronicles, several passages in which are echoed in the dictum, were of great assistance both to the bishops and to the kings; and anyone who wishes to understand medieval kingship should study these books very closely. The kings they portray were a mixture of human heroism, divinely inspired wisdom and very human failings. The prophets they portray were at once more civilized than their masters and more closely in touch with the divine will. A Christian bishop was bound to look in the Bible for precedents for his mode of action; and what he found had many remarkable analogies with his own predicament. These precedents did not settle the balance of power between bishops and kings; but they helped to clarify their different functions; and function was a thing of the highest importance in the complex hierarchy of medieval society.

There may seem to be something excessive and paradoxical in this emphasis on a distant precedent as an important key to medieval kingship. The kings were not simply put on their thrones by churchmen; they were heirs and successors of barbarian chiefs; they ruled by force and fear not by ideals; the fact of politics not the ideals of churchmen were the stuff of their lives. All this is true; yet it is not the whole truth. The feudal king was *primus inter pares* among his vassals, yet he was always much more. The secular foundations of medieval kingship were slender before the twelfth century. The survival of a strong monarchy in Germany in the tenth and eleventh centuries, and the fact that a weak monarchy survived in France at all, bear witness to the importance of the Church and of churchmen in the making of medieval kingship.

When a king had been 'elected', the Church gave him anointing and coronation. By the late tenth century these were established practices in most European monarchies. Otto the Great took special steps to be anointed and crowned king of Germany and emperor; and his younger contemporary Edgar imported a very similar ceremony into England. These ceremonies set the Church's seal on the election, symbolized that the king was God's choice as well as man's, and that he was set apart for the work. In the tenth, eleventh and twelfth centuries the kings of France and England were anointed on the head with chrism, the specially sacred mixture of oil and balsam used in the ordination of priests and the coronation of bishops. This gave their office a quasi-priestly function. At the turn of the eleventh and twelfth centuries the Norman Anonymous (formerly known as the Anonymous of York) wrote that 'the king reigns with Christ', reflecting the common doctrine of the tenth and early eleventh centuries that the king was Christ's vicar, that he was *rex et sacerdos*, that although he could not administer the sacraments, he ruled over the Church as well as over his temporal kingdom, that all authority was vested in him. When the Anonymous wrote this doctrine was under a cloud and his writings are a fascinating mixture of the new logic of the late eleventh century and views of kingship of an extreme conservatism. Times were changing; the popes had abolished the use of chrism in the imperial anointing, had denied the authority of kings over priests; the time would shortly come when the popes themselves claimed to be vicars of Christ, and interpreted the phrase to mean that in the last analysis all earthly authority was mediated through them, not through kings. But we must not be confused by this: a wide variety of views had been held on the relations of popes and emperors, bishops and kings, in the tenth century; a wide variety was still held in the twelfth. In practice, most men thought that each had his own place and function; and though the boundary lines were very variously drawn, most men assumed that it was the duty of *regnum* and *sacerdotium* to co-operate in doing Christ's work. We shall examine the difficulties they encountered in a later chapter (pp. 269 ff.). None the less, it is broadly speaking true that the Church had exalted the monarch in the tenth century, and abased him in the twelfth; that the Church had taught obedience to him in the tenth century when ancient rights of resistance to a king who broke his subjects' rights and liberties still flourished; and that in the twelfth century Church and people exchanged ideas about the bases for the right of resistance.

In tenth-century France leading churchmen looked in something like desperation for an authority which could restore peace to an anarchic country. In tenth-century Germany affairs were somewhat better. But no medieval kingdom would seem even tolerably peaceful to a modern visitor; and it was not until after Otto I's great victory over the Magyars at the Lechfeld in 955 that the fear of invasion and plunder from outside Germany was forgotten. At the end of the tenth century, the highly organized English monarchy was fighting for its life against Scandinavian invaders. In these circumstances it was the business of responsible churchmen to lend support to the monarch in every way they could. There were plenty of cases of unruly or difficult or dissident bishops; but by and large the Church stood by the kings; and in return the kings placed more and more authority and responsibility in the hands of bishops and abbots. Otto the Great's most faithful duke was his brother Bruno, archbishop of Cologne and duke of Lorraine. Otto quite deliberately followed the policy of increasing the estates of the Church, and of granting 'immunities'—that is, of granting to bishops and abbots rights of jurisdiction in their lands which had formerly been vested in the royal prerogative. The bishops and abbots were appointed by the monarch, and he was free to choose whom he would; he did not have to accept hereditary succession, as in other royal offices, such as the dukedoms. The system of government by close liaison with the Church was maintained in Germany by Henry II and Henry III, and under the latter rose to its height. At the same time in England a similar union of king and Church was maintained by Edgar, by Ethelred the Unready when he was his own master, and by Cnut. While the liaison of Church and king remained close, these arrangements worked, at the worldly level at least, to the advantage of both; but if the two powers were ever to split, or their interests seriously to diverge, a mass of tensions might quickly be felt.

Charlemagne and the imperial idea

When a man wished to know what a king should be like, his clerical advisers would give him an expurgated account of the careers of King David, King Solomon and King Hezekiah; if a man aspired to be emperor, he might hear a little about Constantine and Theodosius and other imperial figures of the distant past; but he would hear above all about Charlemagne. Charlemagne was the supreme model for the emperors of this period. He was, indeed, a model for more than them: the French kings had also inherited his throne, and looked back to him as one of their greatest predecessors. The *Chansons de Geste* of the late eleventh and early twelfth centuries centred in the court of Charlemagne; and it was from France that this type of heroic epic spread to Germany. The notion that there was such a country as France, at a time when the royal authority was very little recognized outside the narrow boundaries of the royal domain, the Île de France, was fostered by the legend of Charlemagne.

In France the legend gave prestige to the monarchy; in Germany the monarchs could make some practical attempt to walk in their predecessors' footsteps. This they did in a quite literal way: Otto the Great, at the moment of his accession in 936, went to Aachen to be 'elected' king of the Franks in Charlemagne's own city; he donned Frankish costume for the ceremony of investiture, was anointed and crowned in Charlemagne's basilica. Otto III excavated the stone throne of Charlemagne. Charlemagne's throne, which may still be seen in the basilica at Aachen, gave all the kings of western Europe sooner or later the idea of regarding a throne as an essential symbol of royal greatness. The events of 936 and the imperial coronation of 962 bore witness to Otto I's determination to be Charlemagne *redivivus*. From Otto's time on the ambition to be crowned emperor by the pope was an inevitable ambition for all German kings until long after the end of our period; nor was it ever forgotten that this was in imitation of Charles. Our period opens with the imperial coronation of 962; shortly after its close, in 1165, Frederick Barbarossa had Charlemagne canonized by his anti-pope Paschal III.

So much is clear; can we go further, and say that Otto himself went to Rome to be crowned in order to complete his pilgrimage in Charlemagne's footsteps, that this was his chief motive? The point has been much disputed, and we should be wrong to lay exclusive emphasis on Otto's vision of the past. Even in the realm of symbolism Charles did not provide the only precedent: Otto's father, Henry I, had apparently bought the famous Holy Lance for the cost of a substantial part of what is now Switzerland; and the Holy Lance was viewed as a talisman which would help a king to victory and as a token to be possessed by any candidate to the empire. It was with Otto at the Lechfeld in 955, and it is still among that part of the imperial treasures which is preserved at Vienna.

In the age of Otto the word emperor could be used, roughly speaking, in four different ways. Otto's brother-in-law King Athelstan appears to have called himself by a variety of high sounding titles, emperor (if any of the documents are genuine) and *basileus*, the Greek word for king and the official title of the Byzantine emperor (though it is not clear whether the English realized this). In part this was due to the recent unification of the kingdom; he and his successors were felt to be kings not of one but of a group of kingdoms. In part perhaps it was a translation of the Old English 'Bretwalda', a title held by the high kings of the island from very early days; in part it may have been direct imitation of Byzantium. It was also due to a barbaric delight in high-sounding verbiage, and probably this was the most powerful reason for its use.

Athelstan was an 'emperor' (if he was) because he ruled over several kingdoms; the kings of León-Castile in the eleventh and twelfth centuries were sometimes called emperors for a slightly different reason, that they had aspirations to rule over other peoples. The rest of Spain was held by Muslims, wrongfully, as the Christians saw it; the emperor of León laid claim to the rest of the peninsula.

Otto was lord over many tribes, king of Germany and Italy; he was concerned, too, to subdue Bohemia, to spread German power east of the Elbe, to convert the heathen of north-eastern Europe; if anyone could challenge the prestige of Byzantium, it was he. On these grounds he had as good a claim as either the king of Wessex or of León to call himself an emperor; and his great prestige may well have had something to do with it. But these were not serious grounds for going to Rome to be crowned.

The last person to have the title emperor conferred on him by a pope before 962 had been a minor Italian prince, Berengar I, who had died in 924. Since the division of the empire by the sons of Louis the Pious in 843, there had been a tradition that the imperial crown went with the possession of the middle kingdom, the kingdom of Lothar, Louis the Pious's eldest son. But the tradition rapidly lost substance as, in the course of the late ninth century, the middle kingdom fell to pieces. It is doubtful if the claim of the kings of Burgundy and Italy to bear the title emperor had more substance than the fact that they held the north of Italy and the chief routes over the Alps and were therefore in a position to put pressure on the pope. It is clear that the middle kingdom had strategic importance for a king who wished to preserve German unity; that the Saxon kings had strong practical grounds for wishing to be kings of Lombardy and to hold suzerainty over the kingdom of Burgundy. Only in this way could they counter the ambition of the dukes of Swabia and Bavaria to rule territories south and west of their duchies and to form separate kingdoms of their own. Possession of the imperial title clearly enhanced this interest in Burgundy and Lombardy. Whether they had much bearing on the ambition of Otto and his successors to be emperors may be doubted. The imperial title had no precise political significance; it carried great prestige, but it did not, in itself, help to solve any of these practical problems, which the Saxons could solve only by force.

The Saxon chronicler Widukind, our chief authority for Otto's reign in Germany, ignores the imperial coronation in Rome in 962, and alleges that Otto was acclaimed *imperator*, like a successful general in ancient Rome, by his troops on the field of the Lechfeld. This fiction is a delightful mixture of Saxon piety and attachment to ancient Rome. It has a certain symbolic validity: Otto owed his unique position in great measure to the Lechfeld, and a German monk, however well educated, had difficulty in feeling that this supreme title was conferred by an Italian bishop. But it was not what happened.

An apocalyptic writer of the time (whose works were probably not known to Otto) underlined what was evidently in many people's minds in and after 962. He regarded the imperial coronation as a necessity, for a reason which we should hardly have guessed if he had not told us of it. The reign of Anti-Christ, according to the book of Daniel, was to be preceded by four empires, and these empires were currently interpreted as the Babylonian, the Persian, the Greek, that is, the empire of Alexander the Great and his successors, and the Roman (the Roman had not in fact entered into the calculations of the author of Daniel). It was therefore the duty of a pious Christian monarch to maintain the existence of the Roman Empire so that the reign of Anti-Christ should be postponed until its appointed day. But who had the right and duty of maintaining the Roman Empire? The author wrote before 962; he was in fact a trifle vague about who was to renew it. But he had no doubt that so long as there were Frankish kings to carry on what Frankish kings had begun, the Roman Empire would be maintained and renewed. It was the urgent duty of a Frankish king to consider whether it might not be his destiny to be Roman emperor; in the eyes of many of his pious subjects, Otto could not refuse the call.

We cannot tell whether this point of view was brought to Otto's notice; and both the apocalyptic writer and Widukind represented private opinions. They help us to understand, however, that very many folk took it for granted that Otto would have the ambition to be emperor; and that his empire, whatever it signified, was Roman. We cannot pry deep into Otto's mind; but there can be no doubt that one of the main factors drawing him to Rome was the desire to follow in Charlemagne's footsteps, as he had done in 936. The fact that twenty-six years elapsed between his royal and his imperial coronation may also lead us to deduce that his plans were not solely dominated by dreams of imperial office. Once Otto had been crowned, his successors had precedents both near and far; and the imperial ambition became inevitable, whatever it might mean or whatever it might cost.

It has been objected that Otto and his successors never tried to reconstruct the physical empire of Charles; that they were never lords of France. To this two answers can be given. The first is that they may well have had the ambition: Henry I had been for a time suzerain over France; Otto the Great made Louis IV sit on a less lofty throne than he when they met in 942. 'National' frontiers meant little to the great dynasts of the Middle Ages. Whatever the ambitions of the German kings—and the claim to suzerainty over France was again revived by Henry VI in the twelfth century—political circumstances, the limitation of their resources and the growing significance of the frontier between the kingdoms of France and Germany prevented their realization.

The second answer is that Otto and his successors, at least down to the twelfth century, did not think of the empire in territorial terms. Charlemagne had probably not seen his relation with Byzantium (as we tend to see it) as the relation of 'west' to 'east'. In a similar way, the Saxon and Italian emperors never claimed any particular slice of territory in virtue of their office of emperor.

What then did it signify? What profit did Otto receive from his coronation? He certainly gained something in Italy: a bargaining counter with the Byzantine Empire which occupied nearly half the peninsula, and protection over the Roman states. He received a certain indefinable claim to extend his power in whatever direction he liked. His position vis-à-vis the Church was strengthened. His royal coronation in 936 had already made him (unlike his father) an anointed king, and this could be taken to signify that he had both royal and priestly authority: not the authority to perform sacraments, but God-given authority over clergy as well as people. The crown he had made for his imperial coronation still survives, in the Weltliche Schatzkammer at Vienna. It is a splendid and elaborate affair, surmounted by an arch of metal and precious stones.[1] This arch was made especially high, to enable the crown to be worn on top of a mitre, the low, soft, cloth mitre in use at this time; and the two combined symbolized to Otto his supremacy in Church and State. He does not seem to have felt, any more than Charlemagne, that the imperial coronation added to his authority; it was the supreme symbol of it; and to Otto at least the natural, even inevitable culmination to his career. His contemporary King Edgar postponed his anointing and coronation as king until he thought he had reached a fitting age—thirty, the minimum for the consecration of bishops; Otto postponed his imperial coronation until it was convenient. Neither lost much in authority from the postponement, yet neither would have thought this a ground for not going through with the ceremony.

There were, indeed, good grounds for postponing the coronation, since it added to Otto's responsibilities; it made him protector of Rome and of the Holy See, and although this does not seem to have entered seriously into his calculations in putting the event off till 962, the responsibility involved undoubtedly gave him and his successors much

---

[1] The present arch is a replacement of the time of Conrad II; but there is evidence that the original was of similar shape (P. E. Schramm, *Herrschaftszeichen und Staatssymbolik*, vol. II, Stuttgart, 1955, Chapter 25, and plate 66).

trouble. This was not, of course, the papal view of the matter. The papal tradition had long been that the imperial title was a benefit conferred by the pope; that it carried with it no political authority over Rome, but only a policeman's duty of protecting the Holy See. We must beware of making too precise the opposition between these views. The imperial and papal viewpoints were the extremes; between them lay many positions held by different men at different times. Otto might regard himself as temporal lord of Rome, but he was prepared to grant away large slabs of territory to the pope, as his predecessors had done. The pope might regard himself as in all essentials independent of the emperor, but he was glad to accept the imperial grant. The idea of empire shifted and changed; it was all things to all men. Voltaire observed that the Holy Roman Empire was neither holy nor Roman nor an empire; we may agree to doubt if it was an empire in any geographical sense; but we shall miss its significance if we fail to realize that the *imperium romanum* of the Ottos was in their eyes both holy and Roman. So powerful was this notion that Otto III, going far beyond his grandfather's intentions, made Rome his capital and the *Renovatio imperii Romanorum* his specific aim. But even to Otto III Charlemagne's Aachen was a great centre of pilgrimage.

Against this kind of attitude the papacy slowly came to set its face with real firmness. The emperor provided his own clothes and ornaments; but the pope supplied the oil which anointed him and chose the liturgical form of the ceremony. From the late tenth century on, the aspects of the ceremony which emphasized the sacred character of the imperial office were steadily reduced; the chrism was changed to the less sacred holy oil, which was not used in conferring the orders of priest and bishop. In later centuries, with less success, the popes tried to influence the ceremonies of coronation in other countries, in particular to exclude chrism. In the long run they succeeded in undermining the exceptional position of the emperors and kings of the tenth and early eleventh centuries, in driving a wedge between royal and ecclesiastical authority. But the story was full of twists and turns, and even so late as about 1100 the Norman Anonymous used language about kings which would have delighted, perhaps even mildly embarrassed, Otto I or Henry II. Some of the monarchs of the twelfth century were at least half-educated, in the ecclesiastical sense of the word; but the type of the Emperor Henry II, who took a particular interest in liturgy, and controlled the ceremonies of his court almost as precisely as Charlemagne had done, could no longer be found.

King-making

Such then was the sacral kingship, the 'divinity [that] doth hedge a king'. It was by no means pure matter of theory. Yet we must own that it would have counted for little if the kings who could claim God's support had not already won the support of man. The Church's anointing completed the process of king-making. A king without chrism or crown was perhaps in a dubious position, like a butler without evening dress; but a king who had not been designated and acclaimed indubitably had no position at all.

The terminology of king-making is extremely confusing. Medieval chroniclers tell us, time and again, that kings were *electi*, and try as we may we cannot forget that this is the same as the modern word 'elected'. Between a modern election and tenth- or eleventh-century king-making there is little similarity, except that both could be and often are preceded by prolonged and decisive lobbying; but to complete our confusion there was a gradual shift in the nature of the process between the eleventh and the fourteenth century which transmuted *electio*, early medieval king-making, into something which we can almost recognize as 'election'. We assume that whether the body of electors is small or large, it is specifically defined, and that it has free choice, anyway between the candidates before it, and that its selection is made by a numerical majority. In the Middle Ages 'election', by and large, meant the acknowledgement or acclamation of a candidate already chosen, whether by God, his predecessor, or the man or men who had the first voice in the 'election'. A brief glance at the analogous development in pope-making in this period will help to make the point clear. The pope, like all medieval officials, whether clerical or lay, was chosen by God. He was pope by God's grace, like bishops and kings. In early days the pope was selected, at the human level, by the clergy and people of Rome. In practice the people of Rome came to be represented by a single man, the Roman *patricius*,[1] or emperor, although his rights might be hotly disputed by the Roman nobles. As the office became increasingly important the vagueness of the protocol became increasingly unsatisfactory. In 1059 the papal reformers, in the hope of diminishing lay interference and so of preventing papal schism, issued the famous election decree of Nicholas II. This is a very significant document. Its

---

[1] This title, derived from the functionaries who were effective rulers of the late Roman Empire in the west, was given from time to time to northern kings; it made them guardians of Rome and the Holy See—but the nature of their guardianship was disputed (see p. 284).

essence is succinctly stated in one sentence: when the pope dies 'let the cardinal bishops first deliberate together with most careful thought, and let them soon attach to themselves the other cardinals (*clericos cardinales*); and so let the remaining clergy and the people join in giving assent to the new election'. This decree has one foot in the old world, one in the new. The procedure it assumes is traditional: some person or persons designate, the others who matter assent, the rest acclaim. But it is very precise and definite that the first voice lies with the seven cardinal bishops; and it gives a strong hint that the cardinals are the essential body of electors. The hint was taken, and it became established that the cardinals were the electors (see pp. 262 ff.). The decree, however, was far from satisfactory; from time to time the cardinal bishops gave their first voice to more than one candidate. In 1179 the election was confined to the body of cardinals; and it was laid down that a two-thirds majority made a man pope. This decree, considerably developed, is still in force. It was in its day a revolutionary measure: for the first time the modern idea of election, made by a specified list of electors and settled by a numerical majority, was applied to a major European monarchy.

The other monarchies still, in the main, lived in the old world. All the slight evidence we have about secular elections in the early Middle Ages suggests the same conclusion. Someone designated; the rest assented and acclaimed. There was no question of free choice: on many occasions, no doubt, there was lobbying, in cases of dispute open discussion; but before the election of the anti-king Rudolf of Germany in 1077 (see p. 154) 'election' essentially meant designation and acclamation, a purely formal process.

Beyond that it is difficult to generalize. On the whole the designator had little freedom of choice unless he were himself the king. Kings commonly designated their successors, and had them crowned in their own lifetime to ensure the succession. But even kings were bound by tradition. They were not free, like Roman emperors, to adopt whom they would. They were normally expected—and family affection commonly recommended them—to choose their eldest son or nearest relative. In difficult times they could reasonably avoid suggesting the obvious heir if he was too young or too incompetent. In special cases special traditions were observed. It was sometimes argued that a son born while his father wore the purple of kingship had a better claim than elder sons born when their father was in private station. This, the principle of 'porphyrogeniture', was the special comfort of second or third wives who wished to see their children preferred over the heads of their stepchildren; also of younger sons, like Henry I of England, who may seriously have believed that his claim to the English throne was better than that of either of his elder brothers, Robert or William. Some kings expected or attempted to divide their inheritance among their sons. Thus William the Conqueror left Normandy to Robert but designated William as king of the English. The incompetence of Robert and the fact that England was his own personal conquest might be taken to excuse William's action; and there were always plenty of excuses, sometimes erected into lofty principles by medieval or modern historians, to cover similar cases. In the kingdom of León-Castile, it was still the normal practice, as in Charlemagne's *Francia*, for the kingdom to be divided between the old king's sons; primogeniture had made little headway south of the Pyrenees. It is a striking testimony to the strength of the idea of kingship that this principle was largely forgotten elsewhere in our period; and its effects help us to understand the reason. In León the death of Ferdinand I unleashed a period of civil war marked by intrigue, treachery, perhaps even fratricide, which is reminiscent of Merovingian Gaul in the days of Gregory of Tours. Anyone who cared for peace was likely to set his face against this sort of thing.

We witness, not unnaturally, a constant struggle between the complex forces of tradition, and the instant concerns of the interested parties. No man could call himself king unless the magnates were prepared to accept him. So assent played its part in king-making alongside designation and heredity. It has often been observed that eldest sons frequently did not succeed—never in England between William I and Richard I. This shows how easily heredity could be overcome by designation and by usurpation: it could be argued, odd as it may sound, that all these English kings owed their throne to a mixture of designation and usurpation. But they were all related to their predecessors. The custom of inheritance remained strong. In France it seems even stronger; yet almost every Capetian king had had his title powerfully reinforced by 'election' and coronation in his father's own lifetime. We see in these events a nice mingling of ancient, primitive custom, the urgent needs of the moment, and the play of circumstance and personal affection. What is perhaps most striking is that circumstance and time, and the widening range of ideas, could alter custom quite fundamentally. In England there was never any bar to inheritance through the female line: all the descendants of Matilda, wife of William I, were descended in the female line from the Old English kings, and both Stephen and

Henry II were related to the Conqueror and his wife only through their mothers (see Chart II). In France, meanwhile, the Capetians, for all their weaknesses, never failed to produce a son between the tenth and the thirteenth centuries; so that when Edward III of England came to claim the throne of France, it could be seriously held against him that 'immemorial tradition' was against succession in the female line.

Most interesting of all are the changes which took place in the methods of succession to the German throne. If one had to summarize in a phrase the most sensational change in the political complexion of Europe in our period, the obvious choice would be the collapse of German imperial leadership. Otto the Great was beyond question the foremost monarch in Europe. But in the mid twelfth century John of Salisbury could write, with contempt, 'Who has appointed the Germans to be judges of the nations?' To this one can attach some external causes: the growth of England and Sicily, the greater independence of most of Italy, the cultural hegemony of France, the rise of the papal monarchy, and papal and French leadership in the crusades. Even more striking are the internal causes: the combined effects of civil war and contest with the papacy inside Germany in the late eleventh and early twelfth centuries. Between the eleventh century and the fourteenth Germany became a federation of states; the king-emperor an elected monarch. In the fourteenth century he was elected according to modern notions of the word, by a majority among a specific body of electors. Both these developments lay far in the future in the 1150s, and the immediate prospect seemed to be a revival of German kingly power inspired by the brilliance and *panache* of Barbarossa. In a similar way one could say of the England of Edward I that the revolutionary changes adumbrated under John and Henry III were temporarily obscured by the vivid strength of a powerful king. But the new ideas of government born in the thirteenth century were not forgotten—and so it was with Germany in the eleventh and twelfth. In revolutionary circumstances new ideas of monarchy were given a hearing in 1077; nor could they be entirely forgotten thereafter.

The English John of Salisbury, writing in the 1150s, describes the law of royal succession thus: government is granted to him whom God chooses; divine privilege and human law have made it illegal to depart from a hereditary principle, to choose a king from outside the royal family, if the family walks in the Lord's paths. But the essential thing in the making of a king is to ensure his righteousness, his suitability. These views were supported by reference solely to Old Testament precedent: John, like many other churchmen, had a view of kingship which was essentially based on meditation about the kings and rulers of ancient Israel and Judah; and the mouths of churchmen occasionally uttered strangely revolutionary doctrines. Thus Ælfric, the English homilist of the turn of the tenth and eleventh centuries, observed once, in passing, that a king was freely chosen by the people. Most churchmen were in practice as much attached to custom and tradition as their secular colleagues; but novel doctrines might obtain a hearing and in revolutionary circumstances even be put into practice.

In 1076 it became apparent to the pope and many leading German churchmen that Henry IV was not walking in the Lord's paths (see pp. 276 ff.). Gregory and the German princes planned a formal process—a notion characteristic of the age—to consider whether he could continue to be king. But in the back of their minds as they attempted to justify their plan to depose Henry, they had a vision of Samuel anointing David while Saul yet lived. To Gregory this vision was wholly satisfactory; and it inspired him to his famous prophecy in 1080 that Henry would shortly die. But the German princes and bishops were bound to have certain reservations. If they were to depose Henry, they must invoke a revolutionary doctrine, but if that doctrine was based wholly on the Old Testament, they would place themselves at the mercy of a violent and arbitrary, not to say upstart, Italian cleric. In the event, Canossa saved them from this threat; at Forcheim in March 1077 they proceeded to an act which was revolutionary in fact, but based at every point on German custom, stretched to the furthest possible extent.

In the previous year, basing their action on the right of subjects to rebel against an unjust ruler, the princes had come out against Henry. At Tribur they had made an agreement with him. His flight to Canossa and his submission to the pope were interpreted as breaches of the agreement; they were free to declare him deposed, and they drew up an indictment against him which listed numerous illegal acts which revealed that, so far from defending the law and his people, he had broken the law to the damage of many of his subjects. The papal legates tried to postpone the decision; but the princes argued that the pope had forbidden them to obey Henry, and not reinstated him at Canossa, but merely given him conditional absolution. There was at least an element of prevarication in this; and the German princes were now acting independently of the pope—the legates consented to their acts, but they were not confirmed by Gregory. They proceeded to declare Henry deposed, and to elect a successor in a process which is a strange mixture of new and old. There was something like a real election: carefully organized deliberations were held on who should succeed. Then the archbishop of Mainz designated, as was no doubt traditional, and the clergy and people assented and acclaimed; and to Mainz went King Rudolf to be anointed and crowned. In the process of election some of the princes had wanted to extract special promises from Rudolf. This was forbidden by the papal legates (see p. 283); but it was agreed that certain general promises should be made the subject of an oath by the new king. In this there was nothing revolutionary: German kings had made promises at their coronations before, just as English kings swore a coronation oath. But in the process a very novel doctrine was advanced: that the kingdom was to remain elective, that new kings were to succeed, not by inheritance, but by election.

The election of 1077 was a revolutionary act made in difficult circumstances. The memory of it survived. Rudolf failed; Henry IV was succeeded by Henry V. But in 1125 the archbishop of Mainz designated, and the people acclaimed, a king who was not of the family of his predecessor. The hereditary principle was not forgotten nor altogether repudiated: later in the century it was revived. But David had triumphed over Saul, and might do so again.

In this story we see custom, tradition, religious ideals, faction and personal ambition jostling one another in bewildering fashion. If we ignore any one of these elements we instantly lose touch with the world of the twelfth century. Ideas and ideals were taken seriously; reality invariably fell short of aspiration. Aspirations are none the less worth studying for that; and they have a special interest, since they often represent the meeting-point of the various worlds of ideas, clerical and lay, of this age. In Germany and France we have emphasized how notions of kingship were dominated by memories, true and false, of Charlemagne; how in clerical circles, David and Solomon, Jezebel and Ahab were never forgotten. In an age in which the range of opportunity and ideal was growing for all mankind, it was natural that the range of kingly ideals should develop too. In or about 1069 the rough-hewn king of the Scots, Malcolm III, married a great cosmopolitan lady, St Margaret, a princess of the Old English royal family, brought up in Hungary, who imported into her remote kingdom Hungarian ideas of royal sanctity, French fashions in dress, the international piety of her age, and a powerful sense of monarchic tradition. Her elder children almost all bore the names of her own family—

Edward, Edgar, Edmund, Ethelred and Edith. But after a while names of a different type crept in. Her youngest was called Mary after the queen of Heaven. Some years after her death three of her boys succeeded to the Scottish throne; and their names, Edgar, Alexander and David, reveal Margaret's devotion, not only to the traditions and ideals of her own house, but also to the ideals of Greek and Hebrew kingship, as they were known and understood in eleventh-century Europe.

VII

The Empire, 962–1056

The two centuries between Otto the Great and Frederick Barbarossa witnessed the conversion of the German monarchy from one based on a hierarchy of officials, dukes, counts, bishops and abbots, who were appointed by the king and owed a close allegiance to him, to one in which the king's strength was largely drawn from a smaller, more compact group of feudal vassals, both lay and ecclesiastical. Otto and Frederick both owed much of their strength to the royal domain: the lands over which they retained more or less direct control. They were both heirs of a monarchy of great prestige; both were fervent devotees of the memory of Charlemagne, whose empire Otto revived, and whom Frederick had canonized. But Otto's monarchy was Carolingian indeed. In Germany (in marked contrast to France) there had been a comparatively short interval between the failure of strong Carolingian rule in the late ninth century and the revival of strong rule by the first Saxon king, Henry I, in the years following 919. The dukes were royal officials still, and with many of the lesser officials and nobles, the counts, the kings had, or could reassert, direct relations. Over the bishops and many of the abbots of Germany Otto and his successors were able to exert an authority often very nearly as unquestioned as

BIBLIOGRAPHY. For Chapters VII–XI, see especially the general books in Appendix I and the sources listed above, pp. 3–4. For Germany, see also G. Barraclough, *Mediaeval Germany* (2 vols., Oxford, 1938; vol. II is a valuable selection of trans. essays by German historians) and *The Origins of Modern Germany* (2nd edn., Oxford, 1947); the standard German accounts are R. Holtzmann, *Geschichte der sächsischen Kaiserzeit* (3rd edn., 1955) and K. Hampe, *Deutsche Kaisergeschichte im Zeitalter der Salier und Staufer* (10th edn., Heidelberg, 1959); of the older German classics, perhaps the most rewarding today is A. Hauck, *Kirchengeschichte Deutschlands* (5 vols., 9th edn., 1958–9); for a bibliography, see H. Quirin, *Einführung in das Studium der mittelalterlichen Geschichte* (Braunschweig, 1961), pp. 296ff. For Germany's eastern frontier, J. W. Thompson, *Feudal Germany* (Chicago, 1928), Part II, is still useful.

Charlemagne's had been. His great difficulty was to ensure that the dukes were loyal to him and yet commanded the loyalty of their subjects. Centrifugal tendencies were strong: a duke who was close to Otto might have little authority in his duchy; a powerful duke might be a challenge to Otto's authority.

In the mid twelfth century power was much more widely diffused: a large class of well-endowed nobles had won hereditary control over a large proportion of the old offices, countships and advocacies of monasteries (see pp. 245–6). The old duchies had in great measure been decomposed. In the twelfth century the effects of this were partly hidden by the astonishing concentration of lands and offices in the hands of two men, Frederick himself and Henry the Lion. But this alignment made clear one aspect of the change: that the king depended on his own domain even more than hitherto, and hastened the development of feudal institutions, which made closer the bonds of Frederick and his immediate subordinates, more remote those between Frederick and other great magnates. These changes, and the methods by which successive German kings strove to deal with the changing problems which confronted them, are the themes of this chapter and the next.

The Ottos

By 962 the empire of Charlemagne had long since dissolved; the frontier between what we call France and Germany, though thoroughly ambiguous, was on the way to becoming the most conspicuous political boundary within western Christendom. These facts were perceived, perhaps somewhat dimly perceived, by contemporaries. But it is very doubtful if they played so conspicuous a part in their notion of politics as they seem to us to do, looking back a thousand years later. It is indeed very difficult for us to penetrate into medieval politics; there is so much that we do not know, and what we do know is often very hard to understand. The most we can hope to do is to recover from chronicles and letters and other documents a framework of events. Of these we can make some sense; but we rarely have the sort of detailed information without which a modern historian would not expect to be able to reconstruct a political narrative. We are, by and large, much better informed about the structure of society, about ideas of kingship, about the aspirations of the ruling classes, than we are about the inwardness of their political manœuvres.

The rulers of Europe in 962 were for the most part members of a large, unruly, quarrelsome family circle. Otto the Great's first wife,

Edith, had been sister of Athelstan, king of the English. Queen Edith's sister was apparently queen of Burgundy; the king of France was Athelstan's great-nephew; the king of England was one of the most powerful of Athelstan's successors, his nephew Edgar. After Queen Edith's death Otto married Adelaide, sister-in-law of the queen of Burgundy, widow of the king of Italy; and with her laid successful claim to the Italian kingdom for himself. Germany was full of Otto's relatives: his nephew Henry was duke of Bavaria; an illegitimate son archbishop of Mainz; a cousin archbishop of Trier; his capable brother Bruno was archbishop of Cologne and in effective control of Lorraine, although the duke of Lower Lorraine under Otto II was a brother of the king of France. France was ruled by two dynasties, the Carolingian kings, shortly to disappear, and the dukes of the Franks. King Lothar's grandfather had married one of Athelstan's sisters; Duke Hugh the Great, father of Hugh Capet, had married another. The Church forbade a man to marry his third cousin—or even in theory his sixth. This rule was never fully obeyed, and throughout our period the dynasts who controlled the destinies of Europe were always somewhat more closely intermarried than they ought to have been (see pp. 198, 207–8).

Otto the Great was thus fairly intimately connected with everyone who mattered in the secular politics of Christendom; he even won a Byzantine bride for his son and successor Otto II. Modern historians have been inclined to criticize him for taking too much interest in the affairs of France, Burgundy and Italy; for not concentrating on his proper business of consolidating Germany, the most powerful European kingdom of its day. No doubt Otto was aware of Germany; it was the centre of his power; in effect, the creation of his father and himself. But also, no doubt, he viewed it as in some measure an accident; perhaps even as an accident whose consequences would be temporary. As Charlemagne's successor and as the leading figure in the great family circle, Otto was interested in France, Burgundy and Italy as well as in Germany. Perhaps the politics of Germany compelled him to take this interest: Lorraine was still territory disputed with France; the south German duchies, Swabia and Bavaria, whose control was so difficult, had natural ties of blood, language and geography with Burgundy and Italy; to master Bavaria in particular meant some measure of intervention in Lombardy; to exert authority over Swabia meant more than a measure of control in Burgundy. One further interest of Otto's is beyond dispute. He looked east of the Elbe, to the new lands being conquered and settled by his subordinates in the rule of his own native Saxony. He lifted his

CHART I: THE SAXONS AND SALIANS AND THEIR CONNEXIONS

Kings are shown in capital letters; names in italics also occur elsewhere in the Charts.

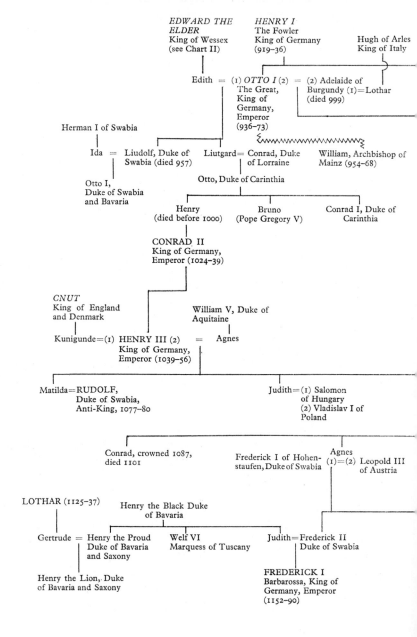

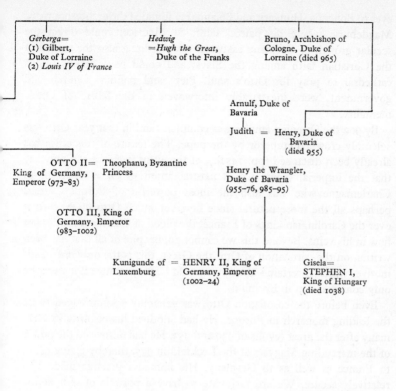

Gerberga=
(1) Gilbert,
Duke of Lorraine
(2) *Louis IV of France*

Hedwig
=*Hugh the Great*,
Duke of the Franks

Bruno, Archbishop of
Cologne, Duke of
Lorraine (died 965)

Arnulf, Duke of
Bavaria

Judith = Henry, Duke of
Bavaria
(died 955)

OTTO II=
King of Germany,
Emperor (973-83)

Theophanu, Byzantine
Princess

Henry the Wrangler,
Duke of Bavaria
(955-76, 985-95)

OTTO III, King of
Germany, Emperor
(983-1002)

Kunigunde of = HENRY II, King of
Luxemburg   Germany, Emperor
(1002-24)

Gisela=
STEPHEN I,
King of Hungary
(died 1038)

HENRY IV, King of
Germany, Emperor
(1056-1106)
Bertha of Savoy (1)=(2) Praxedis
of Kiev

HENRY V=*Matilda*,
King of   daughter of *HENRY I*
Germany,   of England (see Chart
Emperor   II)
(1106-25)

CONRAD III, King
of Germany (1138-52)

eyes to Bohemia, Hungary and Poland. He founded the archbishopric of Magdeburg, where his patron saint, St Maurice, could direct the secular growth of Germany eastwards; could direct also the spread of the Christian faith among the Slavs; and could have canons in his cathedral to pray for Otto's soul. Piety and politics, Church and government, were inextricably interwoven in the fabric of Otto's mentality.

By 962 the Ottonian empire was complete, and in that year Otto was solemnly crowned emperor by the pope. The nature of this office has already been discussed (pp. 145 ff.); of the event itself we can only say that the imperial crown was a natural ambition for a successor of Charlemagne who was also the most powerful of Europe's kings; perhaps all the more natural since however much Otto might lord it over the Carolingian kings of France, the blood of Charlemagne did not flow in his veins. Beyond this we cannot go; in spite of all that has been written on the coronation of Otto the Great, this is the only one of his motives which is certain—though it would be very strange if it were the only consideration in his mind.

Even before the coronation Otto was generally acknowledged to be the leading monarch in Europe. He had subdued his enemies in Germany after the great revolts of 939 and 953. He had destroyed the power of the marauding Magyars at the Lechfeld in 955, thereby giving peace to France as well as to Germany. His immense prestige made him relatively secure. We are fortunate to have a portrait of him at the height of his power from the pen of the Saxon chronicler Widukind. The chronicler has sprinkled his page with flattery, but the portrait is probably not seriously idealized.

He ... was distinguished above all for piety, in all his doings the most resolute of men, always amiable, so long as the kingly dignity is not weakened; liberal in gifts, sparing of sleep, and always talking in his sleep, so that one would think that he was always awake. To his friends he denied nothing; he was loyal beyond the endurance of a man. ... Such was his spirit that after the death of Queen Edith [his first wife] he learnt to read so well ... that he could read and understand whole books. He could talk, besides, in French and Slavonic, but seldom did so. He was an assiduous huntsman, a great hand at draughts (?); he rode a horse with kingly bearing. His fine and royal figure fitted this part—he had a good head of grey hair, and blazing eyes, whose glance shot out like lightning, his complexion was reddish, and he wore his beard, contrary to the old-fashioned way, at full length. His chest was shaggy like a lion's mane; his belly not out of proportion, his gait, once swift, now more measured, his clothing native [Saxon]—he never wore foreign dress.[1]

On the whole, it is a happy tradition which has made of Otto the most attractive monarch of the tenth and eleventh centuries. Like all successful medieval kings, he could engage in violent and ruthless action; atrocities were committed in his name. But he could also be generous, kindly, and forgiving; he was, it seems, an open-handed, open-hearted man; within his limitations imaginative; a man of great tenacity and courage; and it is hard not to be touched by the story of how when his English queen died he consoled himself by learning to read.

Between 962 and 972 Otto was mainly engaged in subduing north and central Italy, and in fighting and negotiating with the Byzantine power in the south. By 972 his control of Rome and the papacy was accepted, and the Byzantine emperor had conceded a few gains to him in south Italy and a princess to be wife to Otto II. The younger Otto was crowned co-emperor by the pope in 967, and in 972 married Theophanu. Theophanu's origin is obscure: it seems that she was not very closely related to the reigning emperors. But Constantinople swallowed its pride in sending a princess to the western barbarians, and in acknowledging an uncouth Saxon—who had no taste for garlic or bath-water—as fellow emperor. The arrangement was a triumph for Otto; it was also his last.

'He left Italy with great glory' writes Widukind;

... he entered Gaul with a victor's wings, and passed through into Germany, and celebrated the Easter of 973 at Quedlinburg, where a great concourse from the different tribes gathered to do joyous honour to his and to his son's return. ... Then he passed on to celebrate the Ascension at Merseburg. ... There he received ambassadors from Africa [whoever they may have been]. ... On the Tuesday before Pentecost he came to the place which is called Memleben. On the following night, as was his custom, he rose at dawn to hear Mattins and Lauds. Then he rested a little; rose to hear mass and tend to some poor men, as was his wont, ate a little and rested again. At dinner time he came down to table happy and cheerful. He went to Vespers, but after the Magnificat he began to feel hot and faint. The princes standing by, when they saw what was happening, made him lie down ... and

[1] Widukind, Book II, Chapter 36.

163

revived him. He asked for the last sacrament, and it was brought to him; and then, without a murmur, in perfect peace, he yielded his spirit to the creator of all. His body was carried to his couch, and although it was late, the news of his death announced to the people. And his people spoke of him with praise and thankfulness; recalled that he had ruled his subjects like a father, and freed them from their enemies, had conquered the proud Avars, Saracens, Danes and Slavs, had subdued Italy, destroyed the shrines of the gods among the neighbouring races, had set up churches and clergy to minister in them; and talking of his many other good deeds, they pressed in to the king's funeral.

Early next morning, though once already anointed king and made emperor by the pope, the emperor's son, sole hope of the whole Church, received again the fealty and homage of his troops. . . . And so, acknowledged king by the whole people, the young Otto moved his father's body to the city which he himself had splendidly constructed, called Magdeburg. Thus, on the nones of May, the Wednesday before Pentecost [7 May 973], died the emperor of the Romans, king of the nations, passing down to the ages many glorious memorials, human and divine.[1]

'Since Charlemagne,' said Thietmar of Merseburg, writing in the early eleventh century about Otto the Great, 'no governor and defender of the realm so great as he has held the royal throne.' The first Otto has cast his shadow over his successors; and his son, Otto II (973–83), and his grandson, Otto III (983–1002), have suffered by the comparison. In fairness one must admit that Otto I ruled for thirty-seven years, whereas the combined total of his successors does not make thirty; that Otto I's first twenty years were exceedingly troubled, while Otto II had only ten, and Otto III, though he reigned in name for nearly twenty, was under twenty-two when he died. The younger Ottos have also been blamed for paying too much attention to Italy, too little to Germany, where the true centre and base of their power lay. Their Italian adventures, as all historians have admitted, were a continuation of those of Otto I; interest in Italy, Rome and the Empire was as inevitable to a German king in the tenth, eleventh or twelfth century as interest in Westminster and Parliament was to the children of eighteenth-century English peers. In any event, the notion that excessive interest in Italy prevented the medieval German monarchy from maturing or

[1] Widukind, Book III, Chapters 75–6.

surviving ignores the astonishing success of a long succession of German kings, from Otto I to Frederick II, and ignores too some of the peculiarities of medieval kingship. It is true that only a king of immense energy or great prestige could make himself effective ruler over an area larger than a single kingdom; and that the energies and concerns of the German kings were spread over a far wider area than most of them could hope to control. But medieval kingdoms were rarely so peaceful or so highly organized that royal power could pass intact, without disorder, to a new king. Otto the Great died at the height of his power; in his later years it was not seriously challenged in Germany; Otto II was anointed king and emperor before his father's death. Even so, it took seven years for the younger Otto to consolidate his rule and suppress rebellion. A new king, that is to say, was bound to establish his personal dominance, to win the personal allegiance of all his leading subjects; to win and to hold them. This involved keeping the ruling class occupied, and keeping his land at peace. But as the normal occupation of the ruling class was war, these two duties were incompatible unless the king engaged in adventures outside the frontiers of his kingdom. The ninth-century German kings had preserved their kingdom intact and relatively strong by regular forays into France. The Ottos pursued adventure on all their frontiers: occasionally to the west, to ensure their control of Lorraine and their superiority over the French kings; more frequently in the east, still more frequently in the south, in Italy. It would be false to attribute these invasions solely or mainly to the need to keep the nobles occupied; but it would be foolish to ignore this motive, and unfair to underestimate the part they played in keeping the German kingdom strong and relatively peaceful in these centuries. Regular campaigning and a constant interest in Italy and eastern Europe were a part of the normal occupations expected of a German monarch of this age.

The permanent staff, the 'civil service', of the Ottos was extremely small, as that of Charlemagne had been. But they exercised power to a great extent by using bishops and abbots as their agents throughout the land, indeed throughout the empire. Even if the institutions of the English monarchy were by the eleventh century more mature and more stable than those of the German (which is far from certain) the German remained, throughout our period, the most powerful in Europe; and it was the alliance with the Church as much as anything else which made this possible. In a similar way the medieval state which attempted, and in large measure vindicated, the right to exercise control over the widest area of any medieval empire, the papal monarchy of the late Middle Ages, exercised its control through the officials of the Church. It is usually idle to speculate on the might-have-beens of history; but if emperor and pope had joined in ruling the world, as Otto III planned that they should, instead of engaging in conflict, the course of European history might have been very different. We shall in due course enumerate reasons why this dream was not fulfilled; but it is hard for a historian writing in the 1960s not to feel that Otto III's dream was a great deal more sensible than the national monarchy which most historians have belaboured him for not creating.

Of the German duchies, Saxony was still Otto II's homeland, though its administration was mainly in the hands of subordinates appointed by his father; Franconia was also in royal hands. Bavaria's duke was Henry II the Wrangler, the quarrelsome son of Otto I's quarrelsome brother, Duke Henry I; Swabia's was another cousin, Otto. Lorraine was divided between Frederick, whose wife was Hugh Capet's sister and Otto II's cousin, and Charles, also Otto's cousin, and brother of the French king; Charles was Otto's appointment, an ingenious expedient, it seems, to divide the allegiance of the French-speaking Lotharingians by setting over them a Carolingian who owed allegiance to the Saxons. Otto and the French King Lothar (954–86) were cousins and brothers-in-law, and bitter enemies. In 978 Lothar broke into Lorraine and nearly captured Otto; in retaliation the emperor invaded France and was only stopped at the gates of Paris by the duke of the Franks, Hugh Capet. Otto had to make a hasty retreat, but Lorraine was now secure; and earlier in the year he had finally suppressed the rebellion of Henry of Bavaria.

These and other troubles occupied the first seven years of Otto II's reign. By 980 he had re-established order, won the submission of the dukes of Bohemia and Poland, and was (for the time being) free of danger from France. He was free at last to turn his attention to Italy and the Mediterranean, where birth and upbringing had given him many interests. His mother was an Italian queen, his wife a Byzantine princess of great intelligence. He himself had been carefully educated. The French chronicler Richer describes a meeting between Otto and Hugh Capet, duke of the Franks, later king of France (987–96), in Rome. It is a symptom of the growing division between Germany and France that they needed an interpreter; and a symptom of Otto's upbringing and outlook that he spoke Latin while Hugh spoke French. There is, too, abundant testimony that Otto enjoyed friendship and intercourse with learned men.

Foremost among these was Gerbert of Aurillac, a Frenchman weaned by the Ottos to their service and allegiance. In Gerbert's letters we enter the atmosphere of cosmopolitan intrigue of Christendom under the Ottos. The letters reveal in approximately equal proportions a zeal for learning of a catholic and voracious sort and a passion for the very highest patronage and favour. Gerbert learned mathematics in Spain, he collected classical manuscripts in France and Germany and Italy. Mathematics had already attracted the attention of Otto I to him; and Gerbert went on embassy to Italy with his master the archbishop of Rheims in the same year that Otto II staged his long postponed journey, 980. Otto was much in need of able and gifted men to help in his plan for governing Italy and appointed Gerbert abbot of Bobbio in northern Italy.

Otto was hoping to establish control in Italy, as in Germany, with the aid of bishops and abbots; he was also trying to gather round him loyal lay magnates like the duke of Tuscany; he planned to subdue the Greeks in south Italy and expel the Muslims. The difficulties were great, and he needed time and good generalship to overcome them. Both were denied him. He was caught in a trap by a Muslim army and suffered a disastrous defeat in 982; and in the midst of active schemes for organizing his empire and renewing the offensive he died in the following year.

Gerbert meanwhile had found Bobbio intractable, and had returned to his old school at Rheims. Here he was ideally placed for joining in the disputes which followed the premature death of Otto II. His genius for intrigue and propaganda played a substantial part in winning the princes of western Germany to accept the succession of Otto III, still only three years old, and the regency of the capable Empress Theophanu. His letters reveal the confusion of a difficult succession. Henry the Wrangler tried to seize the throne for himself, and the emperor's cousins accused one another of treachery. One member of the family who had been very close to Otto I, Bishop Dietrich of Metz, wrote in terms of great violence accusing Duke Charles of Lower Lorraine of every manner of wickedness.

Swell up, grow stout, wax fat, you who, not following the footsteps of your fathers, have wholly forsaken God your Maker. Remember how often my finger restrained your impudent mouth while you were spreading abroad shameful things about the archbishop of Rheims, and more shameful insinuations against the queen by simulating a serpent's hiss. . . . By sweeping out empty dreams and clearing your brow, muddled by the delusive cup, you will . . . finally be able to judge that what you do is nothing and that through the Divine Will what you plot [the control of all Lorraine] must come to naught. . . . Henceforth, unless you repent, by the sword of the Holy Spirit, entrusted to me, I will cut you off along with your putrescent members, and I will abandon both to the inextinguishable fire. . . . May God make foolish the counsel of Achitophel.[1]

As often in violent controversies, the bishop's precise meaning is hidden in the smoke. The rival claims of France and Germany to lordship in Lorraine, the rival claims of Otto and Henry to the German throne, and the rival claims of various members of the royal families to the various segments of Lorraine made the border lands a cauldron of intrigue; and it is perfectly clear that men with a talent for rhetoric in this neighbourhood enjoyed their opportunities for invective to the full. From Charles came the reply, written for him by Gerbert:

To Dietrich, archetype of hypocrites, faithless murderer of emperors and their offspring, and, in general, an enemy to the state. . . . Grown stout, fat and huge, as you rave that I have, by this pressure of my weight I will deflate you, who are blown up with arrogance like an empty bag, as I hasten some advice to you. . . . Not alone, nor in a corner, do I furnish irreproachable fidelity to the son of our Caesar, as you belch forth in your nightly cup of wine. . . . If Judas, who betrayed his Lord for thirty pieces of silver, is considered an apostle, then you who, hoping for a reward—a scandalous reward —have deprived your lord, the hereditary king, of his kingdom may be considered a bishop. . . . You have uttered public perjury. You have exhausted your own city with plundering. You have depopulated the church, entrusted, as you remind me, to yourself. . . . You have piled up mountains of gold. . . .

'We have heard of the pride of Moab, he is exceeding proud. His pride and his arrogancy is more than his strength.'

We fear [added Gerbert in a covering note to Bishop Dietrich] that we incurred the fault of an unfaithful interpreter, since we did not make his speech equal to the impulses of his mind. But, if this effort please you we shall try to do better henceforth, and we shall portray the moods of friends and enemies more carefully to enable you to learn through us with complete confidence what you ought to follow, what to avoid.[2]

[1] H. P. Lattin, *The Letters of Gerbert* (Columbia Records, 1961), no. 39.
[2] *Ibid.*, nos. 40, 41.

This little exchange evidently gave Gerbert pleasure: he preserved all three letters, and many others connected with the accession of Otto III. The duke of Bavaria, meanwhile, had succeeded in kidnapping the baby king; but the majority of the German princes, led by the archbishop of Mainz, the leading ecclesiastical lord of Germany, were against him, and he was forced to submit. He retained Bavaria; Theophanu recovered Otto, and although formally Otto was king-regnant, in practice Theophanu ruled the empire until her death in 991, when her place was taken by her mother-in-law, Adelaide, widow of Otto I; and Adelaide was grandmother regnant until 994, when the young Otto, a mature scholar of fourteen, took over the reins himself.

Gerbert, meanwhile, continued to regard the empire as his spiritual home, and to address appeals for patronage to Theophanu. But his earthly home was Rheims, where French kings were crowned; and the irony of fate gave him a part to play in another royal intrigue. We have first warning of it in a letter of 985.

'We are completing this secret and anonymous letter in a few words [wrote Gerbert to two French notables]: Lothar is king of France in name only; Hugh [Capet] not in name, it is true, but in deed and fact. If with us you had sought his friendship, and had allied his son with the son of Caesar [i.e. Otto III], you would not just now feel the kings of the French to be enemies.'[1] In 986 King Lothar died; his son Louis V followed him in the next year. Under the leadership of Gerbert's principal, the archbishop of Rheims, the holy chrism and the crown of France were transferred to the duke of the Franks, Hugh Capet. Thus was founded one of the longest-lived dynasties in European history; and Gerbert was rewarded, after an interval, with the archbishopric of Rheims. But he received his new office under ambiguous circumstances; his election was questioned by the papacy; and he was eventually compelled in 996 to defend himself in person in Rome. His defence was unsuccessful, but in Italy he met Otto III, who was entranced by Gerbert's charm and learning and readiness to please. Gerbert returned to Rheims; but in the same year his patron Hugh Capet died, and early in 997 his position finally became untenable. He fled to Germany, and appealed to Otto for support. In October 997 Otto himself wrote to Gerbert inviting him to become his tutor; and so began an intimate friendship which profoundly affected the destiny of both men and, in some degree, of Christendom too.

[1] *Ibid.*, no. 55.

Otto was half a Saxon and half a Greek by birth, and very conscious of it.

> We desire you [he said to Gerbert] to show your aversion to Saxon ignorance by not refusing this suggestion [to become his tutor] . . ., but even more we desire you to stimulate our Greek subtlety to zeal for study, because if there is anyone who will arouse it, he will find some shred of the diligence of the Greeks in it. Thanks to this, we humbly ask that the flame of your knowledge may sufficiently fan our spirit until, with God's aid, you cause the lively genius of the Greeks to shine forth.[1]

And so this strangely assorted pair, the young, delicate, ardent, imaginative son of the two races which dominated Christendom, and the 'most skilled of masters crowned in the three branches of philosophy' (physics, ethics and logic)—no ivory-tower professor, but the foremost master of political intrigue of his day—set out together to rule the world.

Gerbert was not the first or the only influence on Otto. Like his hero Charlemagne, Otto was able to gather round him an astonishing proportion of the intellectual, artistic and spiritual leaders of the Europe of his day. Among his friends he numbered St Adalbert, the eminent missionary, who died a martyr in Prussia in 997; St Nilus and St Romuald, leaders of the Italian hermits of the day; Leo of Vercelli, a writer of Latin even more adept than Gerbert. Among these men one may find the first seeds of more than one of the notable movements of the eleventh and twelfth centuries. From Nilus, and even more from Romuald, ultimately stemmed the inspiration of the new monastic movements of the late eleventh century. In Gerbert and Leo one first has serious warning that north-eastern France and northern Italy were to be the centres of a major intellectual revival in the mid eleventh century.

In 996 Otto had paid his first visit to Italy. True to the Ottonian tradition of government, he placed a cousin on the throne of St Peter, subjected Rome and was crowned emperor. Then he returned to Aachen, Charlemagne's Aachen, from which he was called to campaign on the frontiers of Saxony. In spite of his youth his rule was not seriously challenged in Germany until the very end of his reign; and in 998 he was free to return to Italy, taking Gerbert with him.

---

[1] *Letters of Gerbert*, no. 230.

Otto's cousin had had neither the strength nor the tact to hold the papal throne, and he had to be restored in 998 by force. Otto was determined above all to be master of Rome, and he put down his enemies there with some savagery. Otto's pope was restored and Gerbert was established as archbishop of Ravenna. In the next year the pope died, and Otto made Gerbert himself pope. He took the title Sylvester II, after the pope who had served Constantine the Great: he was to be Sylvester to Otto's Constantine. In his role as Constantine and Charlemagne Otto could restore to Rome the undisputed primacy which Constantine had weakened in favour of Byzantium and Charlemagne in favour of Aachen; and the new Constantine could repudiate in formal terms the lavish donation which the old Constantine was supposed to have made to the pope. The 'Donation of Constantine', by which the pope was made temporal ruler of almost anything he chose to claim in western Christendom, was indeed a forgery, a concoction, as we now know, of the eighth century. With one exception, all authorities treated it as genuine before the fifteenth century, however much it might embarrass them. The exception was Otto III. In his solemn grant to Pope Sylvester (written for him, it seems, by Leo of Vercelli) the donation of Constantine was denounced as a forgery; and, even more remarkable, the donations made by Pippin, Charlemagne and Otto the Great, were entirely ignored. Having erased all traces of the false arrangements made by his predecessors, Otto was able to make a new grant 'for the love of Pope Sylvester . . . so that our teacher may have something to offer our lord St Peter on behalf of his pupil', without any surrender being made of the inherent rights of the emperor of the Romans in his own capital.[1]

On Otto's seal was scored the legend '*Renovatio imperii Romanorum*'; the Roman Empire was revived, under the patronage of St Peter; the pope was the instrument of imperial government. This new vision of European monarchy, of the unity of Christendom, was in a way the logical extension of Charlemagne's empire: secular government and the Church were indissolubly bound together; empire was a religious as much as a secular notion. We are often told that Otto was a mere dreamer; that he ought to have realized that his power was based on German troops; that European unity was a mirage. But if we cast our eyes forward to the late thirteenth century may we not ask if the opposite view has not some truth in it? For there we find German unity

[1] The text is in P. E. Schramm, *Kaiser, Rom und Renovatio*, vol. II (Leipzig–Berlin, 1929), pp. 66–7.

and the German kingdom in dissolution; the universal monarchy of the Church a reality. *Realpolitik* has commonly been a mirage; dreams sometimes come true.

In one respect Otto showed himself wiser than most of the rulers of the later papal monarchy. He realized that he could not effectively rule his kingdom by sitting in Rome; like Charlemagne, he must be personally acquainted with every corner of his empire, and all the subject peoples must be aware of him as an actual person. In 999, in true medieval fashion, he made a penitential preparation for his great task: he spent some time staying in the hermitages of south Italy, joining in their austere practices, meditating among the visionaries. Then he made a pilgrimage to the tomb of St Adalbert at Gnesen in Poland. His visit to the relics of the great missionary symbolized the marriage of religion and politics in Otto's designs. Gnesen was made the seat of an archbishop; further missionary work in eastern Europe was organized. Soon after, missions were established in Dalmatia, an archbishopric in Hungary; and the new, Christian ruler of Hungary, St Stephen, was given a crown.

From Gnesen, accompanied by a contingent of Polish troops and a collection of relics, Otto went to his own homeland, Saxony, and then to Aachen. 'He was in doubt where the bones of Charlemagne lay', wrote Thietmar of Merseburg,

'and so he had the floor [of the Basilica or palatine chapel] secretly breached, and ordered workmen to dig where he thought they were. In due course the bones were found seated on the royal throne. Otto removed the golden cross which hung on Charles's neck, and such of the clothes as had not crumbled to dust, and the rest were reinterred with great devotion.'[1]

Then the tour was resumed, and after travelling through Germany Otto returned to Rome.

Otto's power did not rest wholly on German troops. He had secured the personal loyalty of the duke of Poland; he had tried to establish a system of government in Italy which was based on the personal loyalty of some of the native leaders. These foundations, however, needed time to become strong. No sooner was Otto back in Rome than the Romans revolted against him once more. No doubt, given time, he could have reconquered the city; perhaps too he might have been able to deal with the growing discontent in Germany itself. If he had had the physical

[1] Thietmar of Merseburg, *Chronicon*, Book IV, Chapter 47 (29).

strength of Charlemagne he might have lived another fifty years. In the event he lived only a few months, and died of a fever in January 1002. A year later his pope died too.

From Henry II to Henry III

On Otto's death the German princes, following the lead of the archbishop of Mainz, with whom lay the first voice in an 'election', chose Henry duke of Bavaria, his cousin, to succeed him. Henry was the son of Henry the Wrangler, but was himself a conscientious man, the first of the Henrys of Bavaria to be consistently loyal to an Otto. Indeed, he evidently much admired Otto III, whom in some ways he resembled: *'tantus imperator, talis Caesar'* were the words used of Otto III in one of Henry's charters.

Henry was well educated, and as much at home among clerks as among laymen. Like Charlemagne he took a personal, and somewhat dictatorial interest in the affairs of the Church, even in matters of liturgy. He was present at a synod in Rome in 1014, and startled the Roman clergy by enquiring why they did not sing the Creed in the Mass, as was the custom in Germany. They tried to defend their practice, which was indeed ancient, by pointing out that the Roman Church had never been tainted with heresy, and so it was quite unnecessary. The emperor, characteristically, pressed his point; and to him, it seems, the Creed owes its place in the Roman Missal. He was in general noted for his piety; for his interest in relics; for his concern for the wellbeing of the Church. But he stood no nonsense. He reallocated the resources of the German monasteries with a high hand. He permitted the form of episcopal election to be complied with; but it was very rare for a German bishop to be elected in his reign who was not his candidate; many were members of his own 'chapel', his circle of clerks. He overrode elections which were not according to his wishes. He expected the Church to help him in government as much as any German king before or later. His favourite project was the foundation of the cathedral and see of Bamberg, where he was buried. In founding it he was imitating his great-uncle, Otto the Great. Bamberg, like Magdeburg, was a centre of missionary work; it had been Henry's favourite city since his youth. Added to all this, his new bishopric provided him with a copious and reliable force of knights.

Henry's piety and honesty were not forgotten. After his death miracles were reported at his tomb, and Pope Eugenius III was moved to canonize him in the mid twelfth century. His sanctity caused some embarrassment to German historians of the nineteenth century, concerned to emphasize that Henry was also an efficient man of action. Henry's friend and chronicler, Thietmar of Merseburg, writing while Henry was still alive, noted that in one of his many illnesses Henry saw visions. This story was relegated to a contemptuous footnote by Albert Hauck; but it is in fact highly probable that Henry was something of a dreamer as well as a man of action. Like the English King Alfred, he was subject to constant illness, perhaps in part of nervous origin. But once on his feet again, he returned to the ceaseless round of war and government.

The greater part of Henry's reign was spent in consolidating his power in Germany. He could never aspire, perhaps never wanted to aspire, to the kind of empire devised by Otto III. Henry was rarely free of trouble within Germany. It was not, in the main, the great dukes who caused him trouble. Most of these were his relatives by blood or marriage, and chance frequently gave him the task of appointing a new duke, who thus commonly owed his strength to royal nomination rather than to traditional power within his duchy. The Ottonian conception of the duke as a royal officer, not an independent dynast, looked like bearing fruit. But this carried with it, in a country so little united as eleventh-century Germany, a concomitant danger. The lesser nobility, especially the counts, viewed themselves as the genuine, independent potentates of the country. No strong traditional bond or strict duty of feudal service bound them to the dukes; and it was with the lesser nobility, even in his own duchy of Bavaria, that Henry found himself constantly at war. He never had to face a major coalition, such as had faced Otto I in his early years and again in the early 950s, in the years before the Lechfeld. Equally, he was never so secure from rebellion as Otto in his last years. Strong even to the point of being overbearing with churchmen, Henry could be extremely diplomatic with his secular colleagues and subjects; but he never won their complete, unambiguous loyalty.

In his later years these troubles died down. But he had long since realized that he could not hope to rule the eastern and the southern parts of his empire as Otto III had done; and he sanctified his own sense of the limitation of his aims by translating Otto's '*Renovatio imperii romanorum*' into '*Renovatio regni Francorum*'—'*rex Francorum*' still remained the official title of the kings both of Germany and of France. This did not mean that he abandoned his claims in Italy and the east. But after Otto III's death the duke of Poland, Boleslav the Mighty (992–1025), was able to build up a considerable independent power, and Henry's efforts to subdue him, in campaign after campaign from 1005 to 1018, came to nothing. With the king of Hungary, St Stephen, his relations were better; and Bohemia, which was in confusion, caused him no trouble. In Italy, however, another petty monarch had arisen. It took two campaigns to subdue him effectively, and restore the old system of imperial control through faithful bishops and marquesses. On the second of these, in 1014, Henry was crowned emperor by the pope. The office meant much to him; he was a true successor of the Ottos. But his concern was not to revive Otto III's government based on Rome, but a government which in some measure could work without him. In 1012 a lay member of one of the great Roman noble families took the papal throne as Benedict VIII. Benedict was of the Tusculani; in the conflict with the rival Crescentii which inevitably followed, Benedict sought and won the support of Henry. Benedict was a pope after Henry's heart. A good soldier, capable of ruling the papal states on his own account, he was also an honest man, prepared to play the part of pope without involving himself in the scandals which had surrounded earlier popes of his house. Henry treated Benedict not as a subordinate but as a colleague; together they directed the affairs of central Italy and held synods for the reform of the Church. Henry was probably the more spiritually minded of the two; both wished to see good order established in the Church, simony and clerical marriage put down, monasteries reformed, efficiency restored. Neither had any deep notion of what 'reform' involved, nor where the ideas of reform might lead. Under Henry's rule the famous canonist Burchard, bishop of Worms, put together his compilation of the authorities of canon law. He was a firm supporter of Henry and had little interest in papal primacy; but in his book, side by side with evidence of respect for royal power, are set out the authorities which supported the freedom of the Church from lay control—and especially freedom of election of bishops and abbots, which so many chapters and communities tried or thought of trying to vindicate against Henry II, with little success. Observant churchmen throughout Europe were beginning to be seriously aware of this paradox; and the time was not far off when it would be brought to the notice even of kings.

The death of Henry II in 1024 is reckoned to mark the end of the Saxon dynasty; Conrad II (1024–39) was the first of the Salians. But in truth the accession of Henry II marked a clearer break than that of Conrad; and neither was a catastrophic event in the history of German kingship. Henry left no close relations; but after some preliminary lobbying, and less dispute than in 1002, the archbishop of Mainz designated, and the princes accepted, a Franconian count, Henry's nearest cousin, as king.

The event is described at length and in dignified words by the new king's biographer. He tells us that only two candidates were seriously considered; two Conrads, cousins of Henry and of each other. He describes how the leading men of the kingdom were long undecided between them; how the two Conrads met, and the elder (if there is any truth in the well-found speech Wipo puts into his mouth) pointed out to his namesake that 'the votes, wishes and consent of Franks, Lotharingians, Saxons, Bavarians and Swabians' were directed towards the two of them, but if they did not agree to submit to the people's decision, they would doubtless elect a third as king. So the two Conrads embraced one another, and the formality of 'election', or, as it might more appropriately be called, of designation and acclamation, could proceed.

> The archbishop of Mainz, whose decision was to be taken before the others', when asked by the people what seemed good to him, with a full heart and cheerful voice acknowledged and chose the elder Conrad as his lord and king and governor and defender of the realm. This decision the other archbishops and men in holy orders followed without hesitation. The younger Conrad, after brief discussion with the Lotharingians, came back at once and happily acknowledged the elder as lord and king; and the king took him by the hand, and made him sit next to himself.[1]

There followed the repetition of the words of acknowledgement, from the folk of all the different segments of the kingdom; and the old empress, Henry II's widow ('so far as a lady has authority to do so'), confirmed the election by handing to him the regalia, which Henry had given into her care. In the end, even the archbishop of Cologne and those Lotharingians most loyal to the younger Conrad submitted and Conrad and his queen were duly anointed and crowned.

The Saxon emperors had enjoyed the resources of enormous family estates as well as the domain of the crown. Conrad's family estates were modest. They lay in Franconia and so gave his dynasty its name;[2] but

---

[1] Wipo, *Gesta Chuonradi imperatoris*, Chapter 2 (my own translation).

[2] Conrad was a Franconian, i.e., a Frank in the original sense, a son of the original Frankish homeland; and it was for this reason that he came later to be called the 'Salic'—Salic or Salian being taken in later tradition to be a synonym for Frankish, although the homeland of the 'Salian Franks' lay far to the north-west of Franconia.

they gave it little else. None the less, his own capacity, and the very full use he made of the resources of the crown, enabled him to become perhaps the most secure and the most feared of his line. He lacked Henry II's education, and his treatment of the Church has earned him the reputation among modern historians of being something approaching a militant anti-clerical between the two pious Henrys. This is doubtful; it seems more likely that he treated the Church very much as Henry II had treated it. The difference was that the undercurrent of criticism was growing, certain traditional practices were no longer so leniently regarded, and Conrad could not silence detractors by a reputation for personal sanctity. Early in his reign he accepted a substantial gift from a man whom he had made a bishop. Henry II had apparently regarded ecclesiastical property as his own, and such gifts as a normal part of what was due to him. Conrad was less fortunate. Even his biographer, Wipo, accuses him of simony, of selling ecclesiastical offices (see p. 254); and Conrad, we are told, promised to behave more suitably in future. Of the new ideas about reform which were maturing in his time, Conrad had little conception. He was an honest man, concerned that the Church should support and obey him, and that its affairs should be in good order. So far, he was simply imitating Henry II. His care for the affairs of the Church, however, was much less than Henry's outside the frontiers of Germany. The papacy passed to Benedict VIII's brother, then to his nephew; and they were Tusculani of the old school, interested in the local politics of Rome; prepared to enjoy occasional moments of grandeur, as when Conrad himself came to Rome in 1027 to be crowned emperor, but equally ready to cast off the pretence of spiritual primacy as soon as he was gone. So the Tusculani were left to their devices until some years after Conrad's death.

In Italy Conrad attempted to secure peace by forming marriage alliances with the local lay potentates; he forged closer links than Henry II had done, and he even intervened in the affairs of south Italy. In the east, he reasserted his supremacy over Poland, put down rebellion in Bohemia, but was forced to accept the growing independence of Hungary. Conrad's journey to Rome in 1027 coincided with a pilgrimage made by the other leading European monarch of the day, Cnut of Denmark, England and Norway. This meeting under singularly propitious circumstances gave Conrad the opportunity to settle the affairs of his northern frontier with Denmark.

Thus Conrad was both more fortunate and more successful than Henry II in subduing and making peace with subject states and neighbours. Within Germany itself he had little opposition. A clever and active soldier, he was a master of the sudden coup, of strong and forceful and effective action. A would-be rebel found himself attacked or arrested before his plans could mature. The nobles feared him, and submitted. But already there were signs of a growing division of interest and activity between king and nobles. Increasingly, the royal armies came to depend on levies from the estates of the Church and the royal domain. Unfree tenants of king and Church, the *ministeriales*, were trained and endowed as knights, given royal offices, promoted to power and wealth. Meanwhile, the great noble families no longer looked on royal office, especially on the office of duke in the old 'tribal' duchies, as the source of their power. They built up their private domains, recruited their own private armies; and over these the king had virtually no control. Occasionally—but more and more rarely—the whole nobility were called out to accompany the emperor to his coronation in Rome or for some other similar purpose. For the time being, royal control over the Church, which had grown stronger than ever before under Henry II, ensured that the king had the largest and most stable following of any prince in the land. But if the loyalty of the Church should waver, or the lay nobles find an opportunity to acquire ecclesiastical followings themselves, this power would be drastically weakened.

There was little sign of such a trend in the days of Conrad II and his son Henry III (1039–56). Henry's name and his upbringing are interesting testimony to the admiration of Conrad and his wife for Conrad's predecessor. Henry was well educated, as were all the German kings from Otto II to Henry IV except Conrad II. His interest in the Church was personal and close; he felt a vocation to regulate its affairs such as Otto III and Henry II had had; he gathered men of learning about him, and enjoyed their conversation. Two famous acts mark the character of the man and of his reign. In 1043 he determined to imitate the movement for a 'Peace of God' which had sprung up in France in an attempt to put down anarchy and private warfare. In France it had been preached by archbishops and bishops. In Germany it was Henry III himself who mounted the pulpit in Constance in 1043 and directed and implored his subjects to forgive each other their trespasses and be at peace; in earnest of which he himself made a public act of forgiveness and penitence. Three years later, in 1046, by his personal intervention he inaugurated the papal reform.

One of Henry's favourite churchmen was Bruno, bishop of Toul, whom he eventually made pope. Bruno was at once an ardent reformer and a capable and active warrior; and so was his master. Henry had been a successful general at the age of sixteen; and although only twenty-two at his accession, and under forty at his death, he had a considerable list of military successes to his name. For most of his reign Germany was peaceful. In his time the old office of 'tribal' duke virtually disappeared, for a space. Henry was himself duke of Franconia, Swabia and Bavaria; and the duchies in Saxony and eastern Bavaria (Carinthia) were glorified countships created by the Ottos. Lorraine alone remained. It had been divided under the later Ottos; reunited under Duke Gozelo by Conrad II; then divided again by Henry III. Gozelo's son Godfrey, reduced to the duchy of Upper Lorraine, rebelled and plotted rebellion until well after Henry III's death; but while Henry lived, the menace was easily kept in check. A series of campaigns made him effective overlord of Bohemia, Poland and Hungary. In his later years Hungary won her independence; and his attempts to reorganize the German duchies led to some further difficulties. Henry could not imitate Otto the Great in distributing high offices among his close relations; because of close relations he had none. A sister of Otto III's (a distant relative of his own) was married to the count-palatine of the Rhine. To two of her sons he gave Swabia and Bavaria; a third was archbishop of Cologne, and Henry's closest confidant. His Bavarian appointment revealed once again the difficulty of delegating power effectively in tenth- and eleventh-century Germany. Duke Conrad owed his position entirely to Henry, and was not strong enough to sustain it. He fell out with a leading bishop, and Henry was compelled to remove him. The most serious discontent in Germany, however, was in Saxony; this was only maturing in Henry's later years; it was left as a *damnosa hereditas* to destroy the authority of Henry IV.

In Italy, meanwhile, Henry III had prepared a yet more dangerous snare for his son's feet. The story of how Henry III deposed three popes and substituted his own nominee must be told elsewhere (p. 251); but Henry's reign and achievement cannot be seen in perspective without mention of the papal reform. Henry's action has aroused much controversy then and since. There were those at the time who said that what he had done at Sutri and Rome was improper; that the Church should be free of lay control. Pope Leo IX himself was happy to work in collaboration with the emperor, and so, it seems, were most of his associates. Whether this happy union could last must in any case have been doubtful; in the event it was shattered more rapidly than anyone could have foreseen.

VIII

From the Salians to the Hohenstaufen

Henry IV

Henry III, like Henry II, suffered from frequent illness. In 1056, still under forty, he died, leaving government in the hands of his widow, and an heir only six years old. The Empress Agnes was a remarkable link between the old world and the new. Her father was count of Poitou and duke of Aquitaine, her mother successively duchess of Aquitaine and countess of Anjou, a great feudal baron in her own right. A conscientious ruler had normally to look far afield for a wife in the eleventh century, owing to the strict rules of the Church about whom a man might not marry; and Henry III somehow chanced on Agnes, a lady of cosmopolitan outlook and piety like his own. Her friends included the abbot of Cluny and St Peter Damian, the Italian ascetic in whom all the religious movements of the century met. Unfortunately for her and for Germany, she lacked close friends of adequate ability in her husband's kingdom, and noblemen great and small had a taste of independent power which they did not quickly forget when Henry IV came of age. The dissidence of Saxony was in no way curbed; and the southern duchies were given to men who had no strong attachment to her or to her family, and were to prove Henry's most dangerous enemies— Rudolf of Rheinfelden, duke of Swabia, Berthold of Zähringen, duke of Carinthia, and Otto of Nordheim, himself a Saxon, duke of Bavaria.

In 1062 the young king was kidnapped by the archbishop of Cologne, and shipped to the archbishop's city. The empress retired, and presently crossed the Alps to Italy, to find a more congenial career in piety and almsgiving. She presently became the centre of a small circle of devoted ladies who gave unstinted support to the revived papacy. The bitter irony of Agnes's fate was to be ambassador between her son and Gregory VII, to both of whom she was devoted. When she died in 1077,

BIBLIOGRAPHY: see Chapter VII, p. 157.

she, and the world, had travelled far from the Aquitaine of her child-hood.[1]

The son of the Church's great reformer was being brought up, mean-while, among a gaggle of worldly prelates who broke any faith he might have had in the probity of bishops. The archbishop of Cologne acted as self-appointed regent from 1062 to 1064, when he took it upon himself to go to Rome to settle a papal schism; having confirmed the reforming Pope Alexander II on his throne, he returned to find that the arch-bishop of Bremen had stolen his authority. The archbishop of Mainz, nominally the leading figure in the German Church, was too weak to intervene. Bremen and Cologne continued to dispute for supremacy until Henry himself took over the government in the year of doom 1066. They had meanwhile succeeded in preparing the ground for the most powerful conflict of Henry's reign. The province of Bremen looked out into the Baltic, and Adalbert, when not engaged in German politics, did notable work in developing the missionary tradition of his Church. But its base, and the source of its wealth, lay in Germany, mainly in eastern Saxony, bordered on the west by the province of Cologne, to the south-east by Magdeburg. Anno of Cologne, the more hardened intri-guer of the two, succeeded in planting a nephew in the bishopric of Halberstadt, the old home of Adalbert of Bremen in south-eastern Saxony, and a brother at Magdeburg. These made common cause with the east Saxon nobles, and were frequently in rebellion against Henry IV.

Eastern Saxony was already the scene of conflict, then, before Henry became effective monarch. Nor could he ignore it. Here lay many of the richest lands of the royal domain, and here, in the Harz mountains, lay silver mines of great importance to the royal treasury, and the royal city of Goslar, for economic and strategic reasons—and perhaps too out of sheer sentiment—a favourite of the king's. Throughout Germany the nobles had been feathering their nests in the minority; Henry's legacy was extremely difficult.

Even so, it is likely enough that he would have succeeded, as his predecessors had done, in reviving monarchic power and reasserting the imperial supremacy in eastern Europe, but for his misfortune in being confronted by two implacable enemies: his own temperament, and Pope Gregory VII.

The character of Henry remains, indeed, an enigma. Like his great antagonist, he was much admired by his friends and vilified by his enemies. But Gregory wore his heart on his sleeve; however difficult it

[1] On Agnes, see Southern, *Making of the Middle Ages*, pp. 76-8.

may be to give him a fair judgement, it is not difficult to make contact with him (see pp. 265 ff.). Henry is altogether more enigmatic. It may well be that he had a secretive element in him, fostered by his fearful upbringing; and a layman, even so literate a layman as Henry, very rarely speaks to us with his own voice.

Henry's enemies accused him of every vice. Some of this was the common form of controversy; and Henry's friends were almost equally scurrilous about Gregory. But when all allowances have been made, it seems clear that not all the charges were ungrounded. At the least, Henry sowed his wild oats. Early in his reign he tried to repudiate his wife, Bertha, and although he seems to have taken her back with a tolerably good grace in the end, his family was never a happy one. In 1087 his eldest son Conrad was elected and crowned at Henry's behest to secure the succession; but in the event it only added to the number of his enemies. After Conrad's death Henry's next heir, the future Henry V, executed a scheme of calculated treachery which reduced his father to impotence. It may well be that the young Henry wished to save Germany from further misgovernment; but that is little excuse. Similarly, one may pity Henry IV for his misfortunes, but it is quite clear that he was not a good father nor an easy man to serve.

Good qualities he had. If we cannot entirely dismiss the charges of vice, so, equally, we cannot ignore entirely the stories told by his friends of his acts of charity, and even of mercy. It is clear that many non-partisans much admired him. But he was not trusted by those who knew him. He had charm, but a temper which was a terror to his friends. He had a sharp intelligence and an educated, or at least half-educated mind. But he was arbitrary and incapable of patience. Like Gregory, he tended to extreme action. At the turn of 1075 and 1076 he did not wait until the Saxon revolt was fully settled before proceeding to violent measures against the pope; in the 1080s he did not wait till he had fully settled the civil war in Germany before pressing home his attack on Gregory once more. The result was that he was never fully master in his own house, and his obstinate attachment to his anti-popes left him out on a limb when Europe was answering Pope Urban's call to the First Crusade and applauding its success. Again like Gregory, he died in the ruins of his empire. The arbitrary, mercurial element in his temper helps to explain why the rule of one who in many ways seems the most brilliant and attractive of the Salians should have been so disastrous. Yet in other respects friend and foe alike portray the type of the great military leader of this age—with fine and commanding presence, penetrating eyes, attractive and yet terrifying; much like the English Henry II, and yet somehow more mysterious, more remote.

The strength of Henry's predecessors had lain partly in their personal prestige, partly in the prestige of their office; also in the material foundations of the German monarchy—wide royal domains, the personal possessions of the king, his power to call constantly on the support of the bishops as officials, on bishoprics and abbeys as sources of troops and funds; and, on occasion, on all the German princes. Finally, the great dukes were his officers, and his power over them, and his power to act within their duchies, had never been forgotten. The prestige of the monarchy remained high, and Henry did everything he could to enhance it; at times his own personal prestige helped him too, at other times his reputation proved more of a hindrance. For some generations, the power of the great dukes had been dwindling; the lesser nobility, who were not subjected to royal rule by any feudal bond, nor tied by any consistent duty of service to him, were able to build up their own domains, to foster in their own interest local separatist feeling against the king. The king's minority encouraged them, and in one particular gave them a new opportunity for gaining at the crown's expense. In the days of Henry II and Henry III the appointment of bishops had lain almost exclusively in royal hands; bishops were royal servants. The minority meant that men like Anno of Cologne could foster their private dynastic ambitions; it is no chance that his brother of Magdeburg was Henry's most consistent enemy among the German bishops. And Henry made this weakness infinitely worse by showing no inclination to follow his father in being a patron of reform and good order in the Church, and by alienating the pope, who might otherwise have helped to restore his control over the German bishops. Even over the abbeys the nobility were beginning to win a larger measure of patronage.

Henry met the threats to his authority by methods old and new. His emphasis on his own office, the grip he tried to keep on all new appointments to bishoprics and royal abbeys, his efforts to exploit all the traditional powers of the crown, have led to his being described as the last king of the old, conventional, kind. His notable efforts, especially in his earlier years, to restore and build up the royal domain, to ally himself to the developing cities, to develop royal towns like Goslar and assets like its silver mines, have led to his being described as an original, revolutionary monarch. Both views are much exaggerated. He was not, could never be, a king after the model of his father, though he lived constantly under the illusion that the revival of his father's power was within his grasp. At the same time he was bound to live largely under his father's shadow. He was an intelligent, imaginative man, who made the best of what lay to his hands; his idea of kingship was traditional; he had some notion of how the resources of his kingship could be improved. But his temperament, the malice of his enemies and sheer misfortune prevented his achieving his desires.

In 1070 Otto of Bavaria was driven to rebel, and deprived of his duchy. The outcome was that Otto returned to his native Saxony to plot further rebellion, and in the new duke of Bavaria, Welf, Henry raised another potential enemy. In 1073 east Saxony broke into revolt, inspired in large measure by Otto; and the rebels won the support of the southern dukes. Henry was forced to give way; and in 1074 he agreed to demolish the castles by which he had been striving to enlarge his authority in Saxony, and secure his domain there. But the Saxons agreed to his terms somewhat too readily for their allies: the southern dukes felt that they had been deserted, and in the next round were to be found on Henry's side. This was characteristic of German politics. In Germany, as in some measure in all European kingdoms, it was reckoned that subjects could resist their ruler if his rule was intolerably oppressive or unjust; but subjection and obedience were normal. Thus even the Saxons, with a strong tradition of independence, were commonly in a hurry to make peace with the king once their demands had been met. The coalitions against Henry often dissolved as rapidly, and as unexpectedly, as they formed.

In 1075 Henry triumphed in Saxony, with the aid of the southern dukes, and the support of the pope, Gregory VII (1073–85). His victory made him too confident; and when affairs in Milan led to a brush with the pope, Henry proceeded at once to extreme measures. These and the context of the great quarrel between Henry and Gregory must be left to another page (p. 276). The events of 1076 and 1077 formed the central drama of Henry's reign. In January 1076 he and a number of German bishops declared Gregory deposed; in February Gregory excommunicated the king and suspended him from office. The southern dukes, meanwhile, found Henry's victory over the Saxons too complete for their own security; and for once the papal ban had full effect. It led to an alliance between the southern dukes and the dissident Saxons; and in the wake of this alliance the German bishops, many of them inclined to feel that they had proceeded too far against Gregory, were glad of a chance to be reconciled to the pope. The princes sat in judgement on Henry at Tribur in October 1076, and planned to summon the pope to Augsburg in February to help them settle the affairs of the German monarchy.

It had always been assumed hitherto that the German kingdom would pass by some sort of hereditary succession when it could. In difficult circumstances, as in 1002, a change of dynasty might be adumbrated; but only extreme circumstances would lead the German princes to meditate seriously on deposing a king and electing a successor from outside his family. Disillusionment, fear and ambition may have put such an idea in the heads of the princes before this. It was the intervention of the pope, with his talk of sitting in judgement on Henry's suitability to reign, that seemed to put it in the realm of practical politics. Even so, the southern dukes welcomed Gregory's intervention for the help it gave them, not because they were convinced that a pope should settle the affairs of Germany. They were planning revolution, and like many revolutionaries, their actions heightened such conservative susceptibilities as they retained. In mid-winter 1076–7 Henry made his famous journey over the Alps to Canossa, where, with extreme difficulty, he won absolution from the pope. The German princes felt that Gregory had betrayed them, even though he still insisted as firmly as ever that Henry must submit to judgement. But Henry had forced a draw. He could not prevent papal legates joining the princes at Forcheim in March; he could not prevent the princes electing Rudolf of Swabia king of Germany. But the pope had not come in person, nor could he endorse what his legates accepted; Canossa had given Gregory obligations to Henry, and so Henry's enemies were for a time, and in some measure, divided.

In 1080 the pope eventually declared for Rudolf; but in October 1080, after long civil war, Rudolf was heavily defeated at Hohenmölsen, and died of his wounds soon after. With the pope's blessing a successor was elected, the Lotharingian Count Herman of Salm. But he made little headway, and in the year of his election, 1081, Henry felt safe enough to venture to Rome.

The rule of King Rudolf was shortlived; but the consequences of his election did not die with him. A revolutionary situation produced a novel solution; the German princes were facing, in even more extreme form, the sort of problem the English barons faced in dealing with King John in 1215, or with Henry III in 1258. As in thirteenth-century England, their immediate success was shortlived; but the memory of what they had done lived on. Rudolf made grandiose promises on his election. In some degree all medieval kings made promises; but

Rudolf set a precedent which was followed even by Henry V; and Henry V was compelled to follow it because he could not be unaware that after 1077 the succession of a king would never be quite the automatic event it had often been before. Forcheim made a difference to German kingship. We do wrong to read into it the cause of the collapse of the monarchy in the thirteenth century, or the triumph of the principle of election. But we should do equally wrong to ignore its significance. Henry's contest with Gregory enabled his enemies in Germany to proceed to more extreme measures than would probably have occurred to them otherwise. This was one of its most serious consequences; it also weakened his hold over the Church in numerous ways, and gave the German nobles opportunities to prosper at his expense.

All this was only possible because the contest coincided with a civil war which had started before Henry and Gregory had become implacable enemies. The contest with the pope, indeed, was a vital ally of the German civil war; but it was primarily the civil war, following hard upon the long minority, which made this a disastrous period in the history of the German monarchy. Even so, in the 1080s Henry came near to restoring his power in Germany.

In 1081 he invaded Italy; in 1084 he at last succeeded in capturing Rome. He established an anti-pope in the Holy City, who crowned him emperor; and Gregory was only saved from capture by the arrival of a large relieving force under the leader of the Normans in south Italy, Robert Guiscard. Henry was forced to retreat, but for the time being he could enjoy the revival of his authority in north Italy and a rule almost undisputed in Germany.

The most persistent enemy of Henry III had been Godfrey of Lorraine, who in his later years had married into Tuscany; and his wife's Tuscan inheritance was now in the hands of their daughter, the Countess Matilda, the lady of Canossa, who had been second only to the Empress Agnes in her devotion to Gregory VII. In 1089 she married the son of Welf of Bavaria, and in 1091 Henry came once more to Italy to deal with this dangerous alliance between the most powerful survivor of the southern dukes and the most devoted of the papal supporters among the Italian nobility. But on this occasion his own domestic infelicity was his undoing. The Empress Bertha had died in 1087, and soon after he married a Russian princess, Praxedis, in an attempt to recover his father's prestige and authority in the east. In 1093 Welf and Matilda succeeded in winning to their side both the Empress Praxedis and Henry's eldest son, Conrad. The conspirators formed an alliance with a group of Lombard cities, and Conrad (already, at his father's behest, king of Germany) was crowned king of Italy. Welf closed the Alpine passes, and Henry was bottled up in Verona until 1097.

By 1097 the alliance of Welf and Matilda had collapsed: he was hoping to become an Italian prince, she was only concerned to find allies for the pope. Once Welf had realized that he would gain nothing further from her, he opened the Alpine passes, and Henry could return to a Germany once more restored to peace. But peace had still to be paid for: the Saxon nobles were confirmed in their independence; the southern duchies also gained in independence. Berthold, son of Berthold of Carinthia, was given a new duchy, that of Zähringen. This duchy was not a territorial unit, nor yet an empty title. Henry recognized Berthold's hold over his own inheritance and over the estates of his father-in-law, the ex-king Rudolf; he was left a free hand in acquiring rights of advocacy in the monasteries of south-western Germany, where most of his estates lay; he was made lord of the imperial city of Zürich. Zürich represented one of the foundations of Zähringer power: they were lords of many cities in southern Germany and in what was later to become Switzerland. Their cities, their monasteries and their landed properties made them the most formidable territorial magnates in the area of the Black Forest, and Theodor Mayer has shown in a famous study how they attempted in the twelfth century to dominate southern Swabia, and to consolidate their domain.[1] The activity of the Zähringer was characteristic of the rising power of a German nobility, larger in numbers, more precisely based on landed domains, than that of the old ducal families.

It was by accepting the terms of men like the new duke of Zähringen and the east Saxon nobles that Henry restored peace to Germany in 1099; nor could he now hope for an early recovery of power in the east or in Italy. Pope Paschal II confirmed Henry's excommunication and deposition; and so Henry continued to set up anti-popes to support his illusory imperial authority. Royal authority seemed to be dissolving, and this was no doubt one of the motives which stirred Henry's unscrupulous son to rebel against his father. The events of 1104–6 are best read in the *Life of Henry IV*, written by one of his clerks after his death to stir sympathy for the dead king's memory. The book as a whole is a suave and clever piece of advocacy. There is little directly false in it; but it is highly selective. It highlights his successes, passes lightly over

[1] Translated in G. Barraclough, *Mediaeval Germany*, vol. II, Chapter VI.

his failures; dwells lovingly on his victorious stay in Rome in 1084, then passes hastily to the restoration of peace at the turn of the century. The events of 1104–6 fill well over a third of the whole. The author tells how the German nobles grew weary of peace, accustomed as they were to the exercise of local warfare; how they found in the younger Henry a suitable anti-king; how by every kind of trick they seduced him (though one fears he was an apt pupil); how he travelled through Germany, gathering support as he went, and drew many of the leading magnates to his cause; how in 1105 the loyalty of the cities of the Rhineland preserved the old king; how the son summoned his father to a parley and imprisoned him; how Henry IV escaped and was able to defend himself; of the vicissitudes of his last months; and of how death released him from the vortex of treachery in which he was caught up.

> You are happy, Emperor Henry . . . who have changed a violent kingdom for one of peace, . . . an earthly for a heavenly. Now at last you reign, now you wear a crown which your heir cannot snatch from you nor your enemy hold in envy. . . . And behold [concludes the author] there you have the deeds of the Emperor Henry, his alms to the poor, the turns of his fortune, his death: which I could not write, nor you read, without tears.[1]

Henry V

As part of his plan for undoing his father, Henry V had been reconciled to the Church. The reconciliation was, however, incomplete; as will be described in a later chapter (pp. 287ff.), Henry made no surrender on lay investiture until 1122. He came into Italy in 1110 with a large army, was crowned emperor and for a time held the pope prisoner (1111). But Henry's victory was temporary; he soon had to release the pope and to leave Italy, and although he came to Italy again he was never able to exert authority there as the earlier Salians had been accustomed to; still less in eastern Europe.

Most of Henry's reign was spent in attempting to restore his power in Germany, by building up the royal domain, by entering into competition with the nobles for the advocacies (see pp. 245–6) of monasteries, and in trying to put down open rebellion. In his efforts to restore royal power, he was, like his father, competing with the now entrenched nobility; but the situation was transformed by a concentration of power of a new kind. There was at this time a tendency for the old duchies to

---

[1] *Vita Heinrici IV imperatoris, ad fin.* (my own translation).

revive, in alliance with new princely families. Thus Swabia was now in the hands of the Hohenstaufen, who were able to consolidate their power by building up their family domains. Apart from the lands of the house of Zähringen, Frederick II of Hohenstaufen was able to exert effective sway throughout Swabia; his own lands and castles and towns formed a powerful nucleus for his rule, and the lesser nobility were made to accept his overlordship. He was, however, also nephew of Henry V and gave his uncle little trouble. The duke of Swabia was not only nephew of the king, he was son-in-law of Henry the Black, younger brother of Welf V and duke of Bavaria. Once again, as in the days of the Ottos, power was being concentrated into the hands of one large family; and the family circle was still further enlarged when, after Henry V's death, the son and heir of Henry of Bavaria married the daughter and heiress of Lothar of Saxony, Henry V's successor as king (1125-38).

As in the days of the Ottos, the family was an unruly one; the alliance of Bavaria and Saxony was the source of future conflict. But the concentration of power into the hands of the Hohenstaufen and Welfs made possible a striking revival in the power of the German monarchy in the mid twelfth century. Its foundation was in many respects quite different from that of the old Salian monarchy; its power over bishoprics and abbeys was always more restricted; it could no longer treat the dukes as royal officers in the old manner. It ruled through the strength of its domain, and the strength of a growing, personal, 'feudal' bond between king and nobility, especially between the king and lesser nobility; it ruled—in this respect like its predecessor—also by the traditional prestige of the royal office and the personal prestige of the king. The change only became explicit with Frederick Barbarossa (1152-90) and Henry VI (1190-7), the most powerful of the German kings of the twelfth century, but the tendency was already in evidence in the reign of Henry V. The weakness of Barbarossa's rule was that this feudal relationship, which provided him with so much of his support, could also be developed in the interests of a rival; and the heir of the Welfs, Henry the Lion, duke of Saxony and Bavaria, could build up a domain and a following as powerful as the king's. The fall of Henry the Lion in 1180 showed that the royal office, anyway in the hands of a Barbarossa, was still immensely powerful; but Henry's challenge had showed that the king had also to compete with his most powerful subjects in the game of collecting castles, lands, cities and vassals.

This, too, had been seen on a smaller scale in the reign of Henry V.

During Henry's reign Bavaria was quiescent, Swabia friendly to the king, but Saxony definitely hostile. The old 'tribal' duchy had been absorbed into the monarchy of the Saxon kings; but the title duke had been given to the Billungs, the leading counts on the frontier of Saxony, by Otto the Great. The last of the Billungs died in 1106, and Henry V gave his dukedom to Count Lothar of Supplinburg. The new duke entered into the traditions of his office and of the Saxon people; built up his domains and his power in Saxony, and showed no intention of furthering the designs of his maker; and in his opposition to Henry he had an unexpected ally in Henry's other most notable creation, Adalbert archbishop of Mainz. In his later years the king was at loggerheads with one of the most powerful of his bishops and one of the most powerful of his dukes. By the end of the reign Lothar had succeeded in preventing Henry from exercising royal rights of supervision over the Saxon nobility; in the last few years he virtually ignored the king.

Henry, meanwhile, had been reasserting his authority in Lorraine, and casting envious glances over France. In 1114 he had married Matilda, daughter of Henry I of England; the marriage was childless, but it involved the emperor in the schemes of his powerful and ambitious father-in-law. In 1124 a great plan was made for the two Henrys to join in an attack on the French king; Henry V's share of the takings was to be an accession of land to Lorraine. Louis VI countered by calling out the French feudal levy, and the princes of France, who normally paid little heed to their allegiance to the king, rallied to the call. Henry V was compelled to make a hasty retreat. His father-in-law recommended him to retrieve the situation by levying a tax and hiring a new, mercenary army of greater efficiency; but the Germans, if they reflected on the setback, may have noted that the feudal bond had its advantages.

The rise of the Hohenstaufen

In the past, the normal procedure when a king was dying had been that he designated his successor, and after his death the archbishop of Mainz repeated the designation, and the rest of the princes accepted and acknowledged the new king; in many cases he had already been anointed and crowned in his father's lifetime. Henry V and the archbishop of Mainz, however, were at loggerheads, and the political situation, combined with memories of Forcheim, gave the archbishop the victory. Henry designated his nephew Frederick of Swabia; the archbishop designated Lothar of Saxony. The accession of Lothar, now allied to the Bavarian duke, marked the establishment of the rivalry between the two great houses which dominated Germany until the early thirteenth century, and whose names remained a battle cry for many generations: on one side Lothar's son-in-law and heir, on the other the duke of Swabia. In 1125 the duke of Bavaria was Henry the Black; his son, Lothar's son-in-law, was Henry the Proud; the child of Henry the Proud's marriage was to be Henry the Lion. In spite of this, they were known, from their forebears, as the Welfs. The dukes of Swabia were commonly known as the Hohenstaufen; but their battle cry was taken from the old family home of Weiblingen. In Italy in a later age these were translated into the party labels 'Guelph' and 'Ghibelline'.

German politics for the rest of our period and beyond were dominated by these two great families. From 1126 the Guelf leader was Henry the Proud; later his place was taken by his brother Welf VI; from the late 1140s Welf and Henry's son, Henry the Lion, together guided the family fortunes; during most of Barbarossa's reign Henry the Lion was lord of the whole inheritance of the Welfs. Under Lothar the Hohenstaufen were led by Duke Frederick II and his brother Conrad; when Frederick died, his own son Frederick was too young to succeed him, and it was Conrad who headed the family until his own death in 1152. Then the roles were reversed: Conrad's eldest surviving son was a small boy, and so it was his nephew who succeeded and raised the Hohenstaufen to the summit of their power as the Emperor Frederick I, Barbarossa (1152–90).

Between 1125 and 1152 fortune's wheel made several turns. The accession of Lothar and his alliance with the Welfs seemed to bar the advancement of the Hohenstaufen. But before the end of the year they had fallen out over the inheritance of Henry V, which Lothar claimed successfully to be royal domain, while Henry's nephews asserted that it was their personal heritage. In 1126 Lothar took the field against them, but was defeated. In 1127 Conrad had himself proclaimed king; and he tried to consolidate his power by attaching the kingdom of Italy to his German possessions. This embroiled him with the pope as well as with Lothar and, when Conrad's Italian allies deserted him in 1130, he was forced to abandon his Italian adventure; in Germany meanwhile Lothar had been making headway against Conrad's brother. In the 1130s it seemed that the Hohenstaufen were in decline; Lothar and the Welfs in the ascendant. But in December 1137 Lothar died, and the events of 1125 were reversed. Lothar had designated his nephew, Henry the Proud. There was no archbishop of Mainz; the archbishop of Cologne was newly elected; and so effective designation fell to the archbishop of Trier. In collaboration with a papal legate, he designated Conrad of Hohenstaufen at a meeting of princes in which the Welf duchies of Bavaria and Saxony were not represented.

Conrad had won; and he attempted to follow up his victory by separating the Welfs from their dukedoms. In Saxony he was unsuccessful: Henry the Proud died in 1139, but his young son, Henry the Lion, though a minor, was accepted as duke. In Bavaria Welf VI failed to recover the dukedom. But the large family domain made the Welfs a formidable power none the less, and Conrad was never able to subdue them. From 1147 to 1149 he was absent on the Second Crusade; most of the rest of his reign was spent trying to put down disorder in Germany. Alone of the German kings in the period covered by this book he never wore the imperial crown. The journey to Rome was planned, but he died before it could be accomplished.

Throughout the period since the minority of Henry IV and his civil wars had broken the continuity of imperial rule, the German kings had never forgotten their claims to overlordship in eastern Europe and in Italy; but circumstances had prevented them from asserting their ancient position for more than brief interludes. At the beginning of his reign Lothar failed to enforce his will even in Bohemia. At its close, at the height of his prestige, his suzerainty was recognized by Bohemia, Poland and Denmark. Conrad's adventures in the east were marked with a little success; but he too could not command obedience for any prolonged period; and Hungary stood aloof from them both. None the less, the twelfth century marked a decisive turning-point in the relations between Germany and her eastern neighbours. Imperial suzerainty might not amount to much; but the stage was prepared for the decisive act of the *Drang nach Osten*. The advance of Germany's eastern frontier by permanent conquest and settlement had begun in the tenth century, then petered out. In the twelfth it began again in earnest: great lords like Henry the Lion carved out large domains for themselves east of the Elbe, and they peopled them with peasant settlers from many parts of Germany. This was one aspect of the large movement of colonization which is so marked a feature of the age. In the main these events belong to the second half of the century, but they were already beginning before the death of Conrad III. Meanwhile, in the reigns of Lothar and Conrad III, the east counted for less than the south.

Power in Italy lay mainly in the hands of the Lombard cities, the pope and the Norman kingdom of Naples and Sicily. Against these a

German king had little chance of making his claims effective. None the less, there were some of the Italian nobles and bishops who remembered their allegiance to the emperor; others who found it politic to make alliance with him; and if he appeared at the head of a formidable army, he could for a space restore the glory of the Ottos. But as his columns disappeared over the Alpine passes, the memory of his presence faded rapidly.

In 1130 there had ended the premature Italian monarchy of Conrad of Hohenstaufen. In the same year occurred the disputed election to the papacy which established Innocent II and Anacletus II as rival popes. By 1133 (as will be described in another chapter, p. 291) Lothar had agreed to support Innocent and was prepared to escort the pope to Rome for the imperial coronation. Lothar was not strong enough at this moment to make Rome secure for his candidate, and Roger of Sicily, who had been raised from duke to king by Anacletus, was implacably hostile. In 1136-7 Lothar came again, with a more substantial army. He established Innocent in Rome, and, in alliance with Norman rebels, drove Roger out of Italy; for the time being 'King' Roger was confined to Sicily. Late in 1137, shortly after leaving Italy, Lothar died. Innocent was now accepted as pope over most of Europe and by 1139 the schism was ended, in spite of further difficulties and humiliations which Innocent had had to suffer from Roger of Sicily. Conrad III was never able to come to the help of Innocent and his successors in their difficulties. Frederick Barbarossa did indeed attempt to restore German power in Italy. But he came as a conqueror, as the pope's enemy; and remarkable as were Barbarossa's achievements, he was never able to be king of Italy after the model of Otto III or Henry III, and he was defeated in the end. For the time being the most formidable political power in Italy was the kingdom of the Normans.

IX

The Kingdom of the French

The resources of the monarchy

The areas which we call France and Germany—although their frontiers have shifted considerably in the intervening centuries—were the two most substantial of the segments into which the empire of Charlemagne became divided. Apart from the difference in language which divided them then as it divides them now, two very notable differences between these two kingdoms have been observed. First, that the German monarchy, in spite of vicissitudes, remained strong, and was able in the tenth century to reassert its sway all over Germany, while the French monarchy was sinking into impotence; second, that specifically feudal institutions, the personal bond closely linked with the tenure of land and military service, developed much earlier and more fully in France than in Germany (see pp. 99f., 105). France was as much a feudal country in the late tenth and eleventh centuries as it ever became; northern France was the most highly feudalized area in Europe. In Germany feudal institutions made far less headway until the late eleventh and twelfth centuries; only at the very end of our period did they come to have vital consequence for the German monarchy.

BIBLIOGRAPHY. The outstanding sources are Richer, Gerbert's *Letters,* Orderic and Suger's *Life of Louis VI* (see Chapter II). For a recent summary, see R. Fawtier, *The Capetian Kings of France,* trans. L. Butler and R. J. Adam (London, 1960); C. Petit-Dutaillis, *The Feudal Monarchy in France and England* (English trans., London, 1936) is very useful; the classic is A. Luchaire, *Histoire des institutions monarchiques de la France sous les premiers Capétiens* (2 vols., 2nd edn., Paris, 1891). Of the numerous histories of individual principalities, see especially F.-L. Ganshof, *La Flandre sous les premiers comtes* (3rd edn., Brussels, 1949); L. Halphen, *Le comté d'Anjou au XIe siècle* (Paris, 1906), cf. Southern, *Making of the Middle Ages,* pp. 80ff.; D. Douglas, *The Rise of Normandy* (British Academy, 1947); and see works by Lot and Fawtier and Newman listed above, p. 124. There are detailed studies of Philip I by A. Fliche, *Le règne de Philippe Ier, roi de France* (Paris, 1912) and of Louis VI by A. Luchaire, *Louis VI le Gros* (Paris, 1890).

The explanation of these differences lies outside our ken; it must suffice to observe that in the ninth century the German monarchy had remained strong by exploiting the weakness of the French; that German kings had been able to work off the bellicose tendencies of their subjects by adventure in France; that the German monarchy was held between 919 and 1056 by a succession of men of ability and prestige which it would be hard to parallel in European history; and that northern France was the land of vassals and feudal institutions even in the heyday of the Carolingians.

In the second half of the tenth century the French kingdom was ruled by two rival dynasties: the Carolingian kings and the dukes of the Franks. The arrangement was in some ways reminiscent of the days when the Carolingians had been mayors of the palace and the last of the Merovingians had exercised formal royal functions. But the last of the Carolingians were by no means nonentities. The letters of Gerbert and the chronicle of Richer make it abundantly clear that Lothar (954–86) and Louis V (986–7) were men to be reckoned with. On the other hand, no taboo stood between the dukes of the Franks and the throne. Hugh the Great's father and uncle had been kings for a time, as had his brother-in-law; he had married in succession a sister of Athelstan, king of the English, and a sister of Otto the Great. Only a minor revolution was needed to make him or his son a king.

Perhaps the most conspicuous difference between the situation in the late tenth century and the situation in the eighth was that the combined resources of the monarchy and the dukedom were very much inferior to those of the Carolingian mayors of the palace. The royal domain was a shadow of what it had been; the dukes, though they still held broad acres, were constantly forced to alienate land in order to win support or reward their supporters. Hugh the Great's son, Hugh Capet, was more formidable than the king: it was he who turned Otto II back from his attack on Paris. But he brought no great power to the French throne when he succeeded the childless Louis V in 987. One tremendous asset the Capetians enjoyed: like the Abbé Siéyès during the Terror, they survived. No Saxon or Salian took much account of the Capetian kings, and they can only have appeared formidable to the last of the Hohenstaufen. But when all these great men were buried, the successors of Hugh Capet were still reigning in France, and lords of a much stronger kingdom than the German kings could command.

The end of the story would have seemed incredible enough to Hugh Capet in 987. The history of his kingdom and that of his successors down to the mid twelfth century was that of the narrow royal domain (see Map 4), less than half what his great-grandfather had enjoyed; on its fortunes impinged those of a group of north French princes, counts of Flanders, Anjou, Blois and Champagne and dukes of Normandy. The dukes of Burgundy—lords of that part of the old Burgundian kingdom which lay inside the French boundaries[1]—usually paid little attention to the king. The lords of the south paid even less; they rarely troubled to attend his court. In the tenth century the counts of Toulouse and Poitou contended for the title duke of Aquitaine, which carried with it a claim to lordship throughout southern France, the lands of the Langue d'oc. Poitou won, but it was not until the twelfth century that there was any real pretence that Toulouse was subject to Poitou; on the contrary, the count of Toulouse was happily engaged in building an empire on the shores of the Mediterranean. Farther south the counts of Barcelona occasionally recognized French overlordship when they hoped for some particular favour from France; but in the main their destinies lay with the Spanish kingdoms.

Poitou and Aquitaine formed what was almost an independent principality down to 1137, when the tenth Duke William bequeathed his heiress and his duchy to the French king. The fifth William had tried to win the crown of Italy for his son in the early eleventh century; and after his death his daughter became Henry III's empress. The ninth William, at the end of the eleventh century, was the first of the troubadours, and left a tradition of cultivated patronage and of vernacular literature which his granddaughter, Eleanor, successively queen of France and England, was to foster. Thus the house of Poitou played its part in the history of Europe; but on the affairs of Hugh Capet and his descendants it rarely impinged.

The power of the early Capetians, such as it was, depended on the tradition of the monarchy, into which they were anointed and crowned, on their relations with the Church, and on their domain. It was never forgotten that they, like the German kings, were the successors of Charlemagne. Their office had memories, could on occasion assume a grandeur, far beyond its normal strength. The history of the French kingdom is indeed peculiarly difficult for us to grasp. The military resources of the king were no greater than those of several of his vassals; it was rare for the great vassals to obey their king, though they might on

---

[1] See map 5, where the boundaries of the duchy and the kingdom (including the county, the later 'Franche comté') are shown; only the duchy lay within the borders of France in this period.

occasion form alliances with him. In the mid and late twelfth century the monarchy was crushed almost out of existence by the power of the Angevin kings of England. And yet in the struggle of Capetian and Angevin it was the Capetians who won. Much of this story lies beyond our horizon; much of it is due to the play of circumstance. But it owes something to the power of the idea of kingship. This idea was always of significance. In the late eleventh and early twelfth centuries it saw a marked revival. The most fashionable vernacular literature of the period was the *Chansons de Geste*; the *Chansons*' centre was the ocurt of Charlemagne; their country '*la douce France*'. The brilliant statesman abbot of Saint-Denis, Suger, built up the traditions of his house, the Westminster Abbey of the French kings, and of his king together; his associates appropriated versions of the Charlemagne legend to do honour to St Denis and his warrior King Louis. Was it the popularity of Louis VI which gave such vogue to the legend of Charlemagne in and around his court? Or was it the legend of Charlemagne which helped to make his court a centre of loyalty? It would be naïve to answer either question affirmatively without any qualification; but wrong to say firmly no to either. It is significant that Louis VI accompanied his famous summons in 1124 which gathered the feudal host to the discomfiture of the Emperor Henry V with a solemn visit to Saint-Denis. For in the Saint-Denis of Abbot Suger were gathered symbols of many of the supports of his monarchy, particularly the traditional prestige of his kingship and the value of his relation to the Church.

The German kings of the tenth and early eleventh centuries ruled in large measure through the Church. This the Capetian kings could only do on a limited scale, since their influence over the Church was not strong outside the royal domain. There were, however, enclaves over a wide area of northern France where semi-independent bishops and archbishops owed an allegiance to the French king stronger than any tie they had to the local feudatories. Thus at various times the kings could assert their authority at Tours, Beauvais, Laon and above all in Rheims, where Hugh Capet himself established Gerbert, and where Hugh and his successors reckoned to be anointed and crowned.

The principalities of northern France

But his hold on these bishoprics was precarious; often the bishops were independent men with their own policies, often too they were subjected to pressure from the counts whose territories surrounded them. The most notable developments in northern France in the eleventh century were the growth and consolidation of the principalities. The royal domain saw some development in this period, and in many respects became as it were one among the principalities. More sensational was the growth of Normandy, which came to its height under William the Conqueror in the mid and late eleventh century; its story belongs to another chapter (see pp. 218 ff.). In Anjou meanwhile, the counts had already entered into legend in the tenth century; the careers of Fulk the Black (987–1040) and Geoffrey the Hammer (Martel, 1040–60) enlarged its boundaries and made it one of the strongest principalities in France. Fulk was a great castle builder, a ruthless soldier, with a touch perhaps of megalomania which came out in his acts of piety as clearly as in his acts of violence. He founded two abbeys and endowed them richly, and went two, probably three, times on pilgrimage to Jerusalem. One of his companions on this dangerous adventure was the duke of Normandy, Robert I, head of the only family in France comparable in force and cunning to the house of Anjou. The example of his father's old companion was not lost on Robert's son, William the Conqueror. In many ways his career of conquest, castle-building and abbey-building was reminiscent of Fulk's —save that William played for higher stakes, and managed too to leave a reputation for piety without making a pilgrimage to any more distant shrine than that of St David, at the south-western corner of Wales.

The power of Anjou was established by Fulk. His successor completed the programme of aggrandizement by capturing Tours in 1044 and laying hold on the Touraine. He would have liked to round off his county by adding Maine; but Maine lay between him and Normandy, and over it Norman and Angevin fought until the two houses were united in the mid twelfth century.

One of the most curious incidents in the extraordinary career of William the Conqueror was the way in which he—normally a faithful son of Holy Church—fought a papal ban for many years in his determination to marry Matilda of Flanders. He was an obstinate man, and in the later stages the bond of affection between them may well have strengthened his resolve. But he was fighting for the plan (so far as one can tell) before they had ever met; and it is clear that the political advantages of the match were of much consequence to him; partly, it may be, because Matilda was (rather remotely) of the English royal stock, mainly, no doubt, because William wished to cement an alliance with the greatest power in northern France. In later years this alliance proved its worth: William's father-in-law, the count of Flanders, was

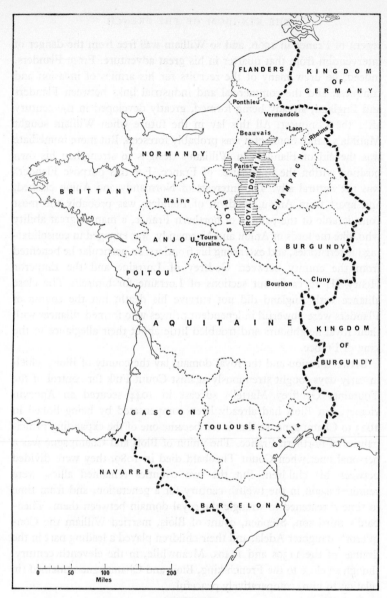

4. FRANCE

The boundaries are approximately those of the late eleventh century. The royal domain is shaded (this area does not include bishoprics, like Rheims and Laon, under royal influence). The area round the north and east of the royal domain and Champagne consisted of a number of small counties, etc., not controlled by any of the great feudatories. The thick, dotted line represents the frontier of the kingdom: but it was much less clearly defined than appears on a map of this kind.

regent of France in 1066, and so William was free from the danger of intervention from that quarter in his great adventure. From Flanders, indeed, he drew many of the recruits for his armies of invasion and conquest; and the commercial and industrial links between Flanders and England, already being formed, greatly developed in the century after the Conquest. All this lay in the future when William sought Matilda's hand. Some of it was probably foreseen. But more immediate was the aid of Flanders in William's designs to strengthen his own position within the boundaries of France. For this purpose Flanders was the natural ally. The interests of Normandy and Anjou clashed; and apart from Anjou, Baldwin of Flanders was probably the most considerable of the princes of northern France, a man of great ability who, like the lords of Anjou and Normandy, was engaged in consolidating his territories, and extending his frontiers. In particular he benefited from the enmity between Godfrey of Lorraine and the Emperor Henry III to carve out sections of Lorraine for himself. The close alliance with England did not survive his death; but the counts of Flanders were powerful independent princes who formed alliances with their royal neighbours and troubled little about their allegiance to the king of France.

Between Anjou and the royal domain lay the county of Blois, which in early days fought strenuously against Count Fulk for control of the Touraine. Geoffrey Martel's success in 1044 secured an Angevin victory, but Blois had already been compensated by being linked in 1023 to Champagne, so that it too became one of the expanding principalities of northern France. The union of Blois and Champagne was a personal one; when Count Theobald died in 1089, they were divided between his children. But the two counties remained allies, were reunited again in the twelfth century for a generation, and from time to time threatened to strangle the royal domain between them. Theobald's third son, Stephen, count of Blois, married William the Conqueror's daughter Adela, and their children played a leading part in the dramas of the 1130s and 1140s. Meanwhile, in the eleventh century, though so close to the French king, Blois and Champagne remained (in relation to him) comparatively peaceful.

The Capetian kings

Such was the pattern of great principalities which can be traced in the ruins of the Carolingian kingdom and the duchy of Hugh the Great as the eleventh century advanced. Surrounded by these mighty opposites, Hugh Capet and his successors did not succeed in doing much more than holding their own. In the west Hugh made an alliance with Normandy which lasted into the 1040s, and left Anjou and Blois to cancel each other out. In the east, he threw all his energy into maintaining control over the bishopric of Laon and the archbishopric of Rheims, both threatened by the Carolingian Duke Charles of Lower Lorraine. The intrigues of Charles, and the way in which Gerbert became involved, first as master of the schools of Rheims then as archbishop, have already been described (pp. 167ff.). Hugh succeeded in capturing Duke Charles, and kept him in prison till his death; Hugh's son, however, had to give way before the papal ban on Gerbert's election. But in the end Rheims remained, somewhat uneasily, within the royal sphere of influence, although both Laon and Rheims were separated from the royal domain by the county of Champagne.

Hugh Capet's three successors, Robert II, 'the pious' (996–1031), Henry I (1031–60) and Philip I (1060–1108), have fared ill at the hands of historians. Their reigns were long and ineffective; the domain was troubled by serious disorder. French kingship looked like becoming a petty affair. None the less, however discreditably, the kings survived; each of them had some unexpected success to his credit; each of them could on occasion wield power in excess of what the royal domain seemed able to support. The idea of monarchy never died, and proved capable of substantial revival, shortly after Philip's death, in the hands of two kings of sterling character but very mediocre ability, Louis VI and Louis VII. In the end, by a curious twist of fortune, the French monarchy came near to total destruction in the mid twelfth century, at a point when it was also nearer than ever since 996 to real power.

The soubriquets of kings and princes are often strangely misapplied. Fulk the Black and Geoffrey the Hammer were named appropriately enough; but they were in their peculiar way no less pious than Robert the Pious of France, who revealed his piety shortly after his accession by marrying his cousin Bertha against the Church's ban, and later by dismissing her when his resolve collapsed. The marriage set him at loggerheads with the Church and compelled him to give way over Rheims; Gerbert had his revenge when, as pope, he in his turn compelled Robert to give way over Bertha. Robert then married a second time, and quarrelled with his second wife. Bertha had previously been countess of Blois, and in Robert's later years her indignant son was count of Blois and Champagne, to Robert's acute discomfort. But for all this there was some compensation. Robert's second wife was a

Provençal, and Robert's kingship for a time had some influence, perhaps rather mistily, in the south. In Burgundy he succeeded, after strenuous efforts, in winning the duchy for himself. After he had made peace with Gerbert, he was able in some measure to exploit his natural advantages in relations with the Church: for Robert was an educated man, who could argue with his bishops on the doctrine of the Eucharist, and might have been expected to rule that part of the French Church which owed direct allegiance to him as his contemporary and friend, Henry II of Germany, ruled his. Robert was not a man of Henry's strength; none the less, his government, for all its vicissitudes, was not wholly unsuccessful.

Robert's last achievement was in securing the succession to his elder surviving son, Henry I, against the wishes of his queen, who favoured their younger son Robert. Henry was forced to make Robert duke of Burgundy; but he was able to heal the old feud with Blois, and in the early 1040s, with his alliance with Normandy as strong as ever, his position seemed tolerably secure.

Henry was an indefatigable soldier. But he knew well that his own power was not sufficient by itself, and that he must rule by playing off one of the great princes against another. His method seems to have been that as soon as one of his allies, with his aid, showed signs of achieving too much power, he rapidly changed sides—so far as we can judge at this distance of time, too rapidly; the princes answered this technique by using him in their turn when it suited them, but ignoring him when it did not. In the early 1040s he invested Geoffrey Martel with Tours, and encouraged him to take it from the count of Blois; he also found other ways of weakening the old enemy of Blois-Champagne. Then, in the mid 1140s, Henry decided that Anjou had grown enough. Normandy, meanwhile, the traditional ally of the king, was in confusion. The boy-duke, William (the future Conqueror) had come almost to years of discretion, but was faced by a dangerous revolt. Henry marched to his aid, and the revolt was suppressed. William, in his turn, joined the king in a campaign against Anjou. In an instant the king changed sides again, and fostered every hint of revolt, every chance to weaken the young duke of Normandy. In 1053–4 he organized a grand alliance among the French princes, in which Burgundy, Champagne and even Aquitaine joined, to attack and humble William. The invaders came in great force in two columns, one north, one south of the Seine. The northern column was soundly beaten at the battle of Mortemer in 1054; and the news of this disaster (enlarged, if the story is to be believed,

by a messenger cunningly sent into the king's camp by Duke William)
sent the royal column flying back in panic. In 1058 Henry tried again,
this time in company with Geoffrey of Anjou; but once again he failed.
It was his last major campaign. In 1060 both Henry and Geoffrey died;
William was left to pursue his schemes unmolested, and Baldwin of
Flanders ruled the royal domain on behalf of the boy-king Philip I.

Apart from allowing William to invade England, Baldwin fostered
Philip's interests with skill and care; and when Philip grew up, he
proved to have something of his father's vigour as a soldier, combined
with a cunning and adroitness comparable to William the Conqueror's.
But he lacked the resources or the allies for great enterprises, and as the
years passed, he became increasingly lethargic, a decline in some way
associated with his increasing girth—although his son, Louis VI, like
many others before and since, combined extreme stoutness with constant activity till near the end of his life. Philip might have achieved
more if he had been prepared to come to terms with the reformed
Church. But he wished to rule his bishops in the old-fashioned way,
and to enjoy the fruits of simony, and at the same time acquired a
reputation for immorality and lack of scruple remarkable even in that
age. He was even accused of brigandage. By open simony and resistance
to papal decrees, he drew on him the anger of Gregory VII and his
legate, Hugh of Die, archbishop of Lyons. The authority of the French
kings over such bishops as acknowledged it was still an important pillar
of the monarchy; bishops and archbishops over an area substantially
wider than the royal domain still acknowledged allegiance to them; and
Philip thought, not unreasonably, that surrender to papal authority
would damage his prestige and authority irreparably. It is a strange
irony that his son and grandson were to build up the prestige of the
French monarchy, in great measure, by submitting to the very humiliation which Philip had resisted.

In 1080 Philip's archbishop of Rheims was deposed, a humiliation
even more serious for Philip than Gerbert's deposition had been for
Robert II. In 1092, to complete his own discomfiture, Philip involved
himself in a matrimonial scandal from which he could hardly hope to
escape unscathed. He put away his wife and eloped with the countess
of Anjou. The Countess Bertrada must have been a remarkable woman,
since she succeeded in controlling both her old husband and her new.
Fulk made a show of violence, then amicably joined the family circle in
the French court. The papal legate was not so easily tamed. He laid
Philip under ban of excommunication; and Philip was compelled to sit

by while the best of his vassals went off in glory to the First Crusade. There was a certain similarity between the kingdoms of France and Germany at this time: in both an ageing, excommunicate king observed the decay of his rule; and in both an active heir took over the reins of government.

There, however, the resemblance ended; for Louis took over with his father's consent. From 1100 he was king-elect; in 1103 even Bertrada, his step-mother, was reconciled to this event; and in 1104 a curtain of respectability was drawn over the old king: his liaison with Bertrada was officially declared closed; the Church lifted its ban; and they continued to live (so far as we know) exactly as before, save that Bertrada had renounced her spite against Louis, and he could now reign undisturbed by her intrigues.

Louis VI (1108–37) has been as kindly treated by historians as his predecessor has been vilified. Physically, they were alike: 'eloquent, tall, of pale complexion and stout' Orderic describes him (noting elsewhere that his paleness was due to Bertrada's poisons); and he became known as 'Louis the Fat'; one English chronicler, indeed, noting the stoutness of Louis and his father, observed that both had made their belly their god. In spite of this, Louis remained until 1135 extremely active; only at the very end of his life did he become physically incapable; and he never subsided into the lethargy of his father's last years. Louis was an ardent, conscientious, attractive man and as fortunate as his father was unlucky. In his earlier years he attempted to carry on his father's resistance to what he regarded as papal encroachment. But even before Philip's death he had given up lay investiture (see p. 287) and come to terms with the papacy. When Leo IX had come to France in 1049, he had been studiously ignored by Henry I; when Urban II came to preach the crusade in 1095, Philip I was under his ban; when Paschal II came in 1107, he and the king and king-designate met and conferred in most friendly fashion at Saint-Denis. This scene was witnessed by a young monk of the abbey, on whom its significance was not lost; and in Louis VI's later years Church and king united to strengthen royal authority, and Abbot Suger as leading royal minister was able to act as an effective propagandist of monarchical power.

The churchmanship of Louis was perhaps of a somewhat old-fashioned kind. The independently minded Bishop Ivo of Chartres, who was ready to defend the king against the pope on lay investiture, attacked him fiercely for permitting the favourite minister of his earlier years to continue his immoral manner of life. In his later years Louis was on friendly terms with two of the most famous of his clerical subjects, Suger, abbot of Saint-Denis, and St Bernard, abbot of Clairvaux. With Suger, a monk of the old school, and a man, like Ivo, who stood for moderate reform and cool friendship with rather than obedience to the papacy, Louis formed the closest ties. Suger became his chief minister, by faithful service ensured Louis's temporal success, and by writing his biography ensured his approbation by posterity. To the ardours of Bernard, Louis was more resistant. But Louis and Suger both wished to see good order in the Church, and Louis was a conventional man who valued the Church's prayers. He had, furthermore, two considerable strokes of fortune. In his early years the papacy was inclined to view his activities with indulgent favour, since he neither resembled nor abetted the Emperor Henry V; and in his later years Pope Innocent II found in Louis his chief secular supporter. After the double election to the papacy in 1130, Bernard, by brilliant advocacy, convinced the kings of France and England that Innocent was the rightful pope. Louis found himself the papacy's most favoured secular monarch and died in the glow of papal favour.

Meanwhile Louis had taken considerable pains to restore order in his domain, and the royal estates gained considerably from the peace which he enforced. Louis had little sense of the value of royal towns, and was often at loggerheads with them in their growing desire for independence; nor was he swift to crush men who, like himself, enjoyed the sports of war. But he liked good order, and so in the end he put down the disorderly barons of his domain; and the towns flourished in spite of his suspicion of them. The domain was much more prosperous when he died than at the opening of the century.

Meanwhile the favour of the Church and the propaganda of Suger were steadily reviving the prestige of the crown. Paschal II at Saint-Denis in 1107 had reminded Louis that he was Charlemagne's successor; and in his time the *Chansons de Geste* had their greatest popularity. A notion of France as a united kingdom was, somewhat mysteriously, growing up in various parts of the land. It was enhanced by a growing sense of enmity with the Germans. These factors were revealed in a striking way in 1124, when Henry V, in alliance with Henry of England and Normandy, planned a large-scale invasion. At a solemn council in Saint-Denis, in the presence of the relics of the patron saint of France, Louis took a standard from Saint-Denis as his banner against the enemy; and summoned the feudal array of the whole of France. Contingents came from almost all the great feudatories of northern France, including Theobald of Blois, who had been at war with Louis (see pp. 98, 126–7). A great army gathered at Rheims, and Henry V found it expedient to abandon his invasion. Later again, at the very end of his reign, Louis received an even more striking compliment to his kingship. Duke William X of Aquitaine died in 1137, on a pilgrimage to St James of Compostella; and on his death-bed he bequeathed his daughter and heiress Eleanor to Louis's son, the future Louis VII, and his duchy to Louis himself. The two Louis accepted their legacies with alacrity, and the kingdom of France received a notable accession of strength. It was the fate of Eleanor to be married both to Louis VII of France and to Henry II of England, and to bring each great power and great misfortunes. She was the supreme symbol of the fact that marriage was more potent than war or political intrigue in deciding the fortunes of great offices in the twelfth century; her career revealed very clearly why the marriage market played so large a part in the calculations of kings and princes; it was also a reminder that marriage is not merely a game —that domestic infelicity can destroy the most politic unions.

Meanwhile the legacy of Aquitaine and Eleanor cast a pleasant glow over the evening of Louis's life; in July the younger Louis and Eleanor were married; on 1 August the father died, and Abbot Suger found room for his substantial remains in Louis's chosen place between the altar of the Holy Trinity and the altar of the Martyrs in the abbey church of Saint-Denis.

Louis VI had, perhaps, deserved his moment of triumph; but there was thunder in the air. To change the metaphor, the marriage market had been exceptionally active in his later years, and the effects were beginning to work themselves out. Henry I of England and Normandy had married his daughter to the Emperor Henry V. By the time of Henry V's death (1125), Matilda was Henry I's sole surviving, legitimate child. She was therefore hustled back from her imperial widowhood, designated heiress to his kingdom, and married to the young count of Anjou. No one but Henry was pleased with this marriage. The empress felt disparaged (see p. 97); the count rapidly tired of her; the French king was horrified at the alliance of the two most dangerous dynasties in France; and the English barons were alarmed at the prospect of an Angevin king, and annoyed that they had not been consulted. But in the early 1130s the marriage was patched up for a short time and Matilda began to have children. In 1133 her first son, the future Henry II of England, was born. In 1135 Henry I died. At this juncture, Henry and Geoffrey of Anjou, supported by his wife, were at war; and in the confusion following Henry's death, his eldest nephew, Theobald, count of Blois and Champagne, nearly succeeded him. It would be a nice point to decide whether an alliance of Normandy and England with Anjou was more or less dangerous to Louis VI than an alliance of Normandy and England with Blois-Champagne. Luckily for him, neither took place in 1135. Theobald's younger brother, Stephen, who had made a career for himself in his uncle Henry's court, kingdom and duchy, and so had become the best endowed baron of England and Normandy, made a swift and successful bid for the English throne. Stephen and Theobald might be brothers, but at least their territories were not united under a single ruler. Louis decided that Stephen was preferable to Matilda and Geoffrey, and lent him his support.

Louis VII was commonly referred to by John of Salisbury and others of Thomas Becket's supporters in the 1160s as 'the most Christian king'; he might well be, for his generous patronage and defence of the exiled archbishop saved Becket and his clerks from extinction. But even some years before the crisis began, John had already referred to him as 'a prince whose memory will be sweet and blessed'; and Louis's popularity, especially with the Church, is many times confirmed. This was the general view of the mature Louis. But he only achieved the eminence of his later years after passing through a difficult apprenticeship. The young Louis was sensitive and impulsive, keen to do his duty, swift to take offence. At first, it seems, he was ruled by Eleanor. Suger remained head of the administration; but effective power was in the hands of Eleanor and Ralph count of Vermandois, who divorced his first wife to marry Eleanor's sister. Ralph's first wife was niece to the count of Blois-Champagne, and this scandal brought Count Theobald and St Bernard into conflict with the royal family. Louis made a raid into Champagne, in the course of which his army set fire to the town of Vitry-sur-Marne, and a church in which the citizens had taken refuge was burnt down. Bernard and Suger between them brought Louis to his senses; and the shock of his sacrilege combined with the influence of the saint to turn him into a new course. In the years which followed Louis and Eleanor drew apart, and Bernard became the dominant influence on the king's impressionable mind. Under his inspiration Louis went on the Second Crusade in 1147–9. This imposed further strains on his marriage. He suspected Eleanor of infidelity in Antioch, and public rumour (rightly or wrongly) confirmed him in his jealousy. They reminded each other that they were related within the forbidden degrees of consanguinity. On their return the pope attempted to heal the breach, for a time successfully. But in 1152 Louis was finally exasperated, and an ecclesiastical council declared the marriage null.

In 1137 Stephen of Blois was king of England and duke of Normandy. In the year which followed his grip on both weakened. By 1144 Normandy was lost, conquered by Geoffrey of Anjou and, although Stephen was successful in the end in preventing the countess of Anjou from making herself effective queen in England, his hold on the country was never undisputed, and he had little hope of recovering Normandy. In 1150 Geoffrey made Normandy over to his son Henry; in 1151 Geoffrey died, and Henry joined Anjou to Normandy; in 1152 Queen Eleanor, rejoicing in her freedom, instantly joined Aquitaine to Anjou and Normandy by marrying Henry. In 1153 Henry invaded England, and was recognized as Stephen's heir; and in December 1154 Henry was anointed and crowned king of the English. With the brilliant and violent young Angevin lord of a far greater domain than Louis's, it might well seem that the French monarchy was doomed. But through all the vicissitudes of his long contest with Henry, Louis had three advantages. Even Henry admitted that Louis was king, and as such his overlord; so that when Henry was at the gates of Toulouse in 1159 the arrival of Louis was sufficient to make him pause in his assault: with his overlord he had (at that moment) no quarrel. Secondly, Henry and Eleanor in due course quarrelled, and Eleanor taught her sons to hate their father, or at least to rebel against him, so that Louis VII and his successor, Philip II Augustus, found powerful allies within the Angevin brood. And thirdly, the constant friendship of Louis with the Church in his later years, and the popularity which was evidently already his when John of Salisbury was a student in Paris, kept on his side responsible churchmen and others who were not committed. At considerable risk he gave shelter in the 1160s to the two most dangerous exiles in Europe, Pope Alexander III and Thomas Becket, archbishop of Canterbury. This marked Louis out as the sincere and genuine friend of the papacy, 'the most Christian king', and he and his successors could count, for several generations to come, on the friendship of the papacy. Even Philip II, who fell under the papal ban for much the same reason as had Philip I, found the pope less implacable to him than to his rivals in papal disfavour, the kings of Germany and England.

None of this could have been foreseen in 1152; the future seemed to lie wholly with the heir of the Normans and Angevins.

X

Britain and the Vikings, 959–1035

Under Otto the Great, the German monarchy was the most powerful and the most respected in Europe. By his victory on the Lechfeld he had freed Europe of the last of the barbarian invasions until the coming of the Mongols in the mid thirteenth century, and his coronation at Rome in 962 finally confirmed in a fitting manner his claim to be Charlemagne's successor. But his glory was in part a personal success, and his heirs could only sustain his imperial power by adding their own personal successes to his. In a similar way the smaller, though in some ways more closely knit, kingdom of England achieved a summit of power in the mid tenth century, which could only be sustained by the personal prestige of its monarchs.

The heirs of King Alfred had steadily extended their rule over the whole of what we call England. King Edgar (959–75) could claim the full allegiance of English and Danish subjects, within the boundaries of England, and was acknowledged overlord by virtually all the princes in

BIBLIOGRAPHY (to Chapters X–XI). On England, F. Barlow, *Feudal Kingdom of England, 1042–1216* (Longmans' History of England, 1955), Sir Frank Stenton, *Anglo-Saxon England* and A. L. Poole, *From Domesday Book to Magna Carta* (Oxford History of England, 1943, 1951, with full bibliographies); on Domesday Book, F. W. Maitland, *Domesday Book and Beyond* (Cambridge, 1897); V. H. Galbraith, *The Making of Domesday Book* (Oxford, 1961). On Wales, Scotland and Ireland: J. E. Lloyd, *History of Wales . . . to the Edwardian Conquest* (3rd edn., 2 vols., London, 1939); J. G. Edwards, 'The Normans and the Welsh March', *Proceedings of the British Academy*, vol. XLII (1956); W. Croft Dickinson, *Scotland from the Earliest Times to 1603* (Edinburgh, 1961); R. L. G. Ritchie, *The Normans in Scotland* (London, 1954); E. Curtis, *History of Medieval Ireland* (4th edn., London, 1942); G. W. S. Barrow, *Feudal Britain* (London, 1956). On the Vikings, see Chapter III. On the Normans in general, C. H. Haskins, *The Normans in European History* (Harvard, 1915); in Normandy, D. C. Douglas, *The Rise of Normandy* (British Academy, 1947), C. H. Haskins, *Norman Institutions* (Harvard, 1918); in South Italy and Sicily, E. Curtis, *Roger of Sicily and the Normans in Lower Italy, 1016–1154* (New York the island; nor were the princes of Man and of Ireland unaware of him. In some ways one may liken the distribution of power in the British Isles in this age to that on Germany's eastern frontiers. Bohemia, Hungary and Poland owed to the German king an allegiance somewhat similar to that which was admitted by the seven Welsh and Scottish kings who submitted to Edgar at Chester in 973. A powerful king received this allegiance, though he might sometimes have to fight for it; a weak king was ignored by the more distant princes. The links, more-over, were made closer in the eleventh and especially in the twelfth century by settlement, of Germans in many parts of eastern Europe, by Anglo-Normans in Wales, Scotland, and eventually in Ireland. The suzerainty of a quasi-imperial power over small kingdoms, sometimes of different race and language, is indeed characteristic of the period.

The difference, however, is as striking as the similarity. Though there were rivers in the north and mountains in the south, no substantial natural frontier divided Germany from the east. In particular, northern Germany and Poland both form parts of the north European plain; the manner of life of mankind in both is substantially the same, and religion and economics gave them a common interest. The heart of England lay in the south-east and in the agrarian claylands of the Midlands; the heart of Wales and Scotland in the highland zone, whose manner of life was fundamentally different. The Roman invaders, used to crossing real mountains, had treated the British hills with contempt when they first arrived, as we can see from the line of some of the Roman roads. But even the Romans learned in course of time that a powerful frontier separates the English lowlands from the English highlands. The Romans conquered Wales, with difficulty, but never subdued the Scottish highlands. In the eleventh and twelfth centuries, although English kings often commanded the temporary submission of Welsh and Scots princes, they never came near full conquest of either.

Although the frontiers, in a general way, were preserved, they fluctuated considerably from time to time. In earlier centuries what we call Scotland had been divided approximately into three: Strathclyde, in south-west and west, the true kingdom of the Scots, that is, of the Irish settled in Scotland; the ancient Pictish kingdom in the north, whose successor in the tenth century was the kingdom of Alba, Shake-speare's Albany, commonly known as the kingdom of the Scots; and the

and London, 1912), C. Cahen, *Le régime féodal de l'Italie normande* (Paris, 1940)—the classic is F. Chalandon, *Histoire de la domination normande en Italie et en Sicile* (2 vols., Paris, 1907).

northern limb of the English kingdom of Northumbria, which stretched
to the Firth of Forth, and had a long and much-debated frontier with
Strathclyde to its west.

In the ninth century the history of all the British Isles had been
dominated by Viking attacks. Norwegians and Danes settled in large
numbers in various parts of the islands, notably in Ireland, western
Scotland and north-western England, and north-eastern England: much
of Yorkshire, Lincolnshire, the East Midlands and East Anglia came to
be the Danelaw, although Danish settlement was clearly much thicker
in the northern portion of this large area. Even where the Vikings
did not settle, they raided; and their raids, among other things, came
near to destroying the old, monastically organized Welsh Church,
and did irreparable damage to the Irish Church too.

The Vikings were pirates, traders and settlers; sometimes one
activity predominated, sometimes another; on the whole piracy came
first and trade (as we normally use the term) last. But in every capacity
they profoundly affected the life of all the countries they visited. They
gave new life to the sea routes surrounding Britain, and a new orientation. They destroyed old political arrangements. They helped to speed
the formation of new groupings, and out of the chaos they had made, a
new order arose. The formation of a united English kingdom owes
much to them; so does that of a united kingdom of the Scots; and so,
even in Wales, does the tendency towards union, however ephemeral.

By the time of Edgar the Viking settlements were firmly established,
and the first round of invasions was over. The earlier invaders had
destroyed all the English kingdoms save Wessex, and so, in the process
of survival and of reconquest, the kingdom of Wessex became the
kingdom of England. Edgar's predecessors had conquered the Danes
and the Norse within the boundaries of England; they had destroyed
even the last of the Viking kingdoms in this area, the Norse kingdom
of York, and the Danes had begun to settle down to be English citizens. Edgar gave great impetus to the process of settlement, by putting
his whole prestige behind the revival of the English Church, which
was (among other things) engaged in converting the pagan Vikings;
by building ships and making a serious effort to command the
sea highways; and by treating Danes and English as equally his subjects.
The Danes were allowed to enjoy their own customs and laws, so long
as they obeyed and served the king of the English.

Even so, Edgar could not hope to be king of a united England in any
full sense of the words, still less of a united Britain. One of his chief

CHART II: THE KINGS OF ENGLAND, FRANCE AND SCOTLAND

Kings are shown in capital letters; names in italics also occur elsewhere in the Charts.

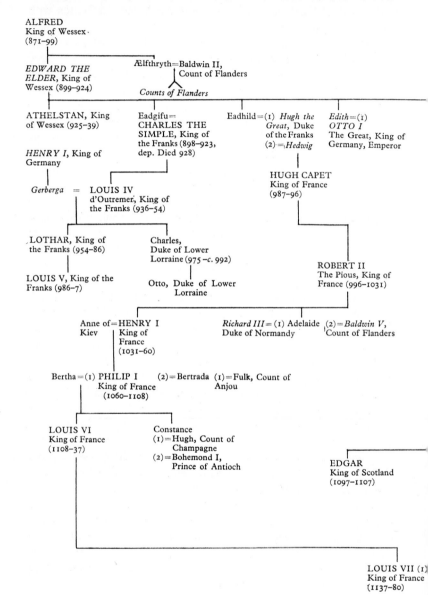

ALFRED
King of Wessex ·
(871–99)

EDWARD THE
ELDER, King of
Wessex (899–924)

Ælfthryth=Baldwin II,
Count of Flanders

Counts of Flanders

ATHELSTAN, King
of Wessex (925–39)

HENRY I, King of
Germany

Eadgifu=
CHARLES THE
SIMPLE, King of
the Franks (898–923,
dep. Died 928)

Eadhild=(1) *Hugh the
Great*, Duke
of the Franks
(2) = *Hedwig*

Edith = (1)
OTTO I
The Great, King of
Germany, Emperor

HUGH CAPET
King of France
(987–96)

Gerberga = LOUIS IV
d'Outremer, King of
the Franks (936–54)

LOTHAR, King of
the Franks (954–86)

Charles,
Duke of Lower
Lorraine (975 –c. 992)

ROBERT II
The Pious, King of
France (996–1031)

LOUIS V, King of the
Franks (986–7)

Otto, Duke of Lower
Lorraine

Anne of=HENRY I
Kiev   King of
France
(1031–60)

Richard III = (1) Adelaide
Duke of Normandy

(2) = *Baldwin V*,
Count of Flanders

Bertha = (1) PHILIP I
King of France
(1060–1108)

(2) = Bertrada (1) = Fulk, Count of
Anjou

LOUIS VI
King of France
(1108–37)

Constance
(1) = Hugh, Count of
Champagne
(2) = Bohemond I,
Prince of Antioch

EDGAR
King of Scotland
(1097–1107)

LOUIS VII (1)
King of France
(1137–80)

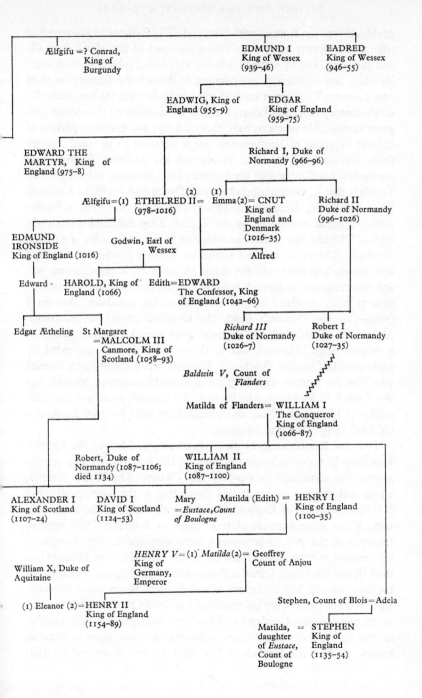

problems was the frontier with Scotland. The Romans in the past had tried two different methods of ruling this part of the island: by walls and garrisons, and by setting up buffer kingdoms, subject to their over-lordship, but sufficiently independent to defend the frontier on their own account. The former method was wholly beyond the resources of a tenth-century king; and Edgar, while he lived, followed the second with great success. He seems to have reckoned that the northern portion of the old kingdom of Northumbria was too distant to be ruled directly from Wessex, and in order to shorten his northern frontier, and strengthen his alliance with the northern king, he seems to have granted Lothian, that is, Northumbria between Tweed and Forth, to Kenneth, the Scottish king. Kenneth was already king of the Scots and of Strath-clyde—a union engineered by the English King Edmund a few years earlier. The addition of Lothian bade fair to make him ruler of a united Scotland. The union was not secure for another generation: Scotland and Strathclyde fell apart, but King Malcolm II, Kenneth's son, was able to strengthen his family's hold on Lothian and to ensure the succes-sion to both Scotland and Strathclyde of his grandson, Duncan I (1034–40). On Duncan's death the kingdom passed to his cousin Macbeth; and, although Shakespeare's play gives a distorted picture of a tangled reign, Macbeth was in the end ousted and succeeded by Malcolm III Canmore (1058–93). Malcolm was a rough-hewn warrior who kept the frontier with England in violent fluctuation; his wife was the English St Margaret, who brought the Scottish court into the main stream of European culture and educated her sons to make Scotland a civilized, Anglo-Norman kingdom.

Thus the English kings of the tenth century had helped the Scottish kingdoms to unity and new strength, in the hope of winning an ally against the continued pressure of the Vikings. The Welsh frontier, which was to be as uncertain and fluctuating as the Scottish after the Norman Conquest of England, was relatively stable in the tenth cen-tury. Wales never came so close to union as Scotland. From time to time one of the princes achieved a temporary dominance throughout the country, but the union almost invariably died with him. In 949 or 950 died Hywel the Good, friend and associate of the English Athelstan; in his later years he had held north as well as south Wales under his sway. At the end of the century his grandson Maredudd repeated this success; in the mid eleventh Gruffydd ap Llywelyn, sprung from a different line in the dynasty of south Wales, achieved an even more substantial power, holding the English at bay until he was destroyed by Earl

Harold in 1063. But these personal hegemonies did not last long enough to counteract the centrifugal tendency so powerful in Welsh institutions and traditions, the disunity implanted, as on a larger scale in the Spanish peninsula, by nature.

In Ireland in earlier centuries had been reproduced, with many differences, a political organization similar to that in England: many independent kingdoms owing some kind of allegiance to one 'high king'. The Norse settlements brought a new kind of life to Ireland; in the eleventh century the settlers built towns and many of them became peaceful merchants; they throve above all on the traditional traffic of the Irish Sea, the slave trade. But neither by infection nor reaction did the Vikings in Ireland help the island to unity. The line of 'high kings' continued. But the last of them to have any power died in 1014, and the Irish kingdoms remained in confusion, and the Irish Church in decay, until the mid twelfth century. In the late eleventh century the Norman leaders in England cast glances across the sea; and their Irish Viking cousins cast glances back; the church in Dublin established relations with Archbishop Lanfranc. But these manœuvres were no more than portents.

The English kingdom was more closely knit than the German, and the tenth-century kings were able to build up a system of local government, based on the shires and hundreds, which enabled them to rule, through royal officers and local notables, more directly and effectively than any other European kings of the age. Edgar's power was much more effective in the midlands and the south-east than elsewhere: it was here that the growing towns, with walls, markets and mints to coin money, were mainly situated; it was in this part of the country that most of the bishops and all the monks lived. The English monastic revival was under way before Edgar's accession; but his patronage, and his close alliance with its promoters, Dunstan of Canterbury, Ethelwold of Winchester and Oswald of Worcester and York, were of fundamental importance in ensuring its success and securing his kingship. The monasteries did not perform quite the same role as those of Germany, since there was less devolution of authority and jurisdiction to bishops and abbots in England than in Germany (see pp. 165–6); government was somewhat more centralized. But the close alliance of king and Church was equally essential; the bishops formed a powerful nucleus in the royal councils of men dedicated (on the whole) to peace and good order; the monasteries were the recruiting ground of most English bishops in the late tenth century; and the bishops were engaged in organizing the conversion of the Danes, an essential part of the process of subduing them to be faithful subjects of the English crown. This is only a very partial account of the monastic revival, which meant much to the community at large in the resurrection of spiritual ideals, the fostering of letters and the formation of schools of drawing and painting which made England a leading centre of European art. The reign of Edgar may be taken as the high tide of Old English monarchy.

Whether we blame Edgar or not—and it seems a little hard to pass judgement on a man who dies at the age of thirty-two for not making adequate dispositions for his succession—his death was followed by the dissipation of his power. His elder son, Edward, succeeded; after three years of intrigue Edward was murdered and Ethelred II, Unræd, or 'no-counsel', succeeded. The two kings were boys at the time of these events; but Ethelred never succeeded in reviving his father's power or restoring unity to the country. He was rarely free from the threat of treachery, and in the 980s and 990s Danish raids started once again.

It is not clear why the Danes turned their attention to England at this juncture, although no doubt they were quickly made aware that England under Ethelred II was a possible prey. The main efforts of the Vikings had been directed to the Baltic lands, and to Russia; they had planted trading stations and garrisons along the Baltic coast, of which Jomsborg, in the Wendish territory at the mouth of the Oder, is the most famous because its garrison became the heroes of a later saga. The leading Viking of this period, Harold Bluetooth, king of Denmark, had held some kind of sway over Norway as well, and under pressure from Otto II had organized the conversion of the Danes to Christianity. This may well have been one of the causes of the resentment which enabled his son Swein to rebel against him and seize his throne shortly before his death.

In the 990s the Danes raided regularly into England. In 994 they were led by the two most famous Vikings of the age, Swein and Olaf Tryggvason, who seems to have picked up his Christianity in England, and soon after tried to carve out a kingdom for himself in Norway. There was a certain unity in the Viking world. Vikings of diverse origin would fight in the same raiding parties; powerful kings like Harold would unite Denmark and Norway. But anarchy frequently reasserted itself, helped by the violence and the feuds which were the stuff of Viking life. Meanwhile Swein and Olaf grew rich on English tribute; Ethelred found it easier to use the fine organization of his mints to coin silver pennies with which to buy the Danes off than to raise armies which he could trust to fight them.

In the end Swein's rapacity and ambition, and the defection of the lieutenant to whom he had delegated control of the English raids, decided Swein in 1013 to come again to England in person and make himself king. In this he was successful, but in the moment of triumph, early in 1014, he died. For a brief space Ethelred and his son Edmund Ironside were able to resume control; but in the next year Swein's son, Cnut, assisted by many of the leading Vikings of the age, resumed the offensive; after some vicissitudes, both Ethelred and Edmund died in 1016, and Cnut was left undisputed master of England. On his brother's death soon after Cnut became king of Denmark; at various times he was king of Norway and ruler of some parts of Sweden. He was the leading monarch of northern Europe, and was duly treated as such by pope and emperor when he made his famous pilgrimage to Rome in 1027.

Cnut was well aware of his dual role: he ruled in Scandinavia as a Viking war-lord, by fear and force; and he ruled in England by a mixture of force and tradition. In England, after a somewhat violent start, he made strenuous efforts to conform to the practices and traditions of the dynasty of Alfred. This duality perplexes the historian; but Cnut seems to have learned to live the double life with remarkable success. It enabled him to unite the Danish and English elements in his English kingdom as they had never been united before. Edgar's kingdom had survived the weakness of Ethelred, to be revived, almost intact, by Cnut. One innovation he made: he allowed a great concentration of landed wealth and power in the hands of a few great ealdormen, or earls (jarls) as they were called in honour of the Danish origin of their master and patron and of the Viking nature of their power. Some of Cnut's earls were of Danish, some of English origin. Under a weaker king they could achieve a sway in the country as formidable as that of the most powerful of the German dukes.

Cnut was still comparatively young when he died in 1035. He had entered into legend in his lifetime, but on his death his empire entered into chaos.

XI

The Normans

In Normandy

In 1154 a king of Norman ancestry, ruling an empire in southern Europe, died; in the same year another succeeded to the English throne, and so completed an empire which included a great part of France. The kingdom of Roger the Great and the empire of Henry II were the most highly organized, maturely governed principalities in Europe. Roger was heir to the legal wisdom and administrative traditions of Greeks and Muslims; before Henry died his financial administration and the law administered in his court were described in two great manuals, of a sophistication which would have left Cnut or the Conqueror gasping. The Normans had an astonishing success, not only as conquerors but in adapting themselves to the institutions of the countries they conquered and adapting those institutions, once assimilated, to their own grandiose designs.

The Norman duchy in the tenth century was a chaotic Viking principality. Hegemony lay with the family of Count Rollo, but their power was little more stable than that of the Norse or Danish jarls in their homeland. The early eleventh century saw the beginning of a serious development towards a more highly organized, feudalized principality on the model of Normandy's neighbours. Normandy, indeed, could teach the counts of Anjou nothing in violence, cruelty, fraud or cunning; as patrons of monasteries, Duke Richard I and Richard II outbid Count Fulk, though he was not far behind. Normandy became an important centre of monastic life in the early eleventh century, under the inspiration of St William of Volpiano and Dijon, and his successor at Fécamp, Abbot John (1028–78). This revival helped the dukes to restore order. But their lay followers still resembled Viking pirates more than French feudatories; and the organization of the duchy

BIBLIOGRAPHY: see Chapter X, pp. 209–10.

into holdings of land in exchange for military service, the formation of a stable aristocracy, though under way in the first third of the century, was not completed until the reign of Duke William the Conqueror (1035–87).

To the Vikings good order had always been synonymous with poverty and want. The establishment of some semblance of order in Normandy, and in particular the introduction of a system of landholding which, to a considerable extent, concentrated an inheritance in the hands of an eldest son, and left the younger children landless, raised serious problems for many Norman warrior families; problems which the traditional Viking love of adventure and of wandering helped to solve. The story of Tancred de Hauteville, who had twelve sons and a modest patrimony, might serve as an example of the difficulties of a feudal knight and of a Norman feudal knight in particular; it is, however, more than a mere example, because his sons were the effective founders of the Norman principalities in Italy and Sicily, and Roger the Great himself was his grandson.

It is clear that the Norman warriors were prolific and land-hungry; we should know that in any case from the way they spread over England after 1066. But their adventures in Italy were even more remarkable: here a comparatively small body of Norman freelance warriors, far from their homeland and in a strange climate, were able to weld in two generations one of the most anarchic segments of Europe into a strong kingdom. There is a certain contrast between their achievement in Italy and in England. In England they took over and adapted native institutions; and in Scotland, under the patronage of the Anglo-Scottish royal house, they partially transplanted Anglo-Norman customs and manner of life. But Wales they attempted to conquer without success; and it is noticeable that while they infiltrated into the Welsh Church and adapted it to their own models, they failed to adapt the secular institutions, or rather the fragmentation, the *morcellement*, of Wales; failed to assimilate Welsh and English. 'They perpetuated *morcellement* and called it the march.'[1] The Normans in south Italy found an inheritance even more civilized than that of their brothers in England; but also disunity, divergence of language, race and tradition of an extreme kind. Here they succeeded, as they did not in Wales, in bringing the various elements into one harmonious picture.

[1] J. G. Edwards, 'The Normans and the Welsh March', *Proceedings of the British Academy*, vol. XLII (1956), p. 177.

In Italy and Sicily

At the opening of the eleventh century, south Italy was regarded in Byzantium as part of the eastern Roman Empire. In Apulia and Calabria the Greeks ruled indeed. Sicily was a Muslim island, though its inhabitants represented many different strata in the island's varied history. Amalfi, Naples and Gaeta were independent city states, enjoying a modest but increasing mercantile prosperity. Salerno, Capua and Benevento were the headquarters of old Lombard principalities, owing allegiance—so the Greeks thought—to Byzantium, but in practice independent. South Italy was too remote from the centres of power of the eastern or the western emperors or the Fatimites to be under anyone's effective control; and it was therefore a paradise for the landless adventurer.

In the year 1016 a party of Norman pilgrims, returning, if the legend is to be believed, from Jerusalem, landed in south Italy. They encountered two Italian princes in great need of help, the prince of Salerno, who was striving to repel a Muslim attack, and a rebel against the Greeks called Melo, who had won from the Emperor Henry II recognition as duke of Apulia, but no help of any practical consequence. Both princes, it seems, were inspired to send messengers to Normandy to appeal for recruits in their wars. Some Normans came, then more, until by the 1040s they had established themselves as mercenaries and bandits whom Greek, Muslim and Lombard rulers had learned to respect and fear. It was some time before they began to form principalities on their own account. They fought for whichever power was willing to pay them. The familiar story of earlier barbarian conquests soon began to repeat itself. The mercenaries became too powerful for their employers; they lived off the land, and when they were not sufficiently provided they took to loot on their own account. The three eldest sons of Tancred de Hauteville had been conspicuous among the Normans since the late 1030s; in the late 1040s they were joined by the eldest son of Tancred's second marriage. His brothers were inclined to treat him as the ugly sisters treated Cinderella. But Robert Guiscard was a brigand of genius. Stories gathered round him like those of Robin Hood or the heroes of the American west. It was said that he once leant over in his saddle to give a ceremonial embrace to a Greek city governor who had come to a parley, gathered the Greek in his arms and swept him to the ground, while his followers ambushed the governor's escort; and again, that he put one of his followers in a coffin and staged a fictitious funeral procession into a monastery in a nearby town, as a preliminary to looting both monastery and town. As so often, truth is as strange as fiction. From 1053, when the most forceful of his elder brothers died, Robert was the chief of the Norman leaders in Italy; in 1059 Pope Nicholas II invested him with the duchies of Apulia, Calabria and Sicily. This was a paper transaction, an attempt to buy off Robert and his colleague and rival, Richard of Capua, from their threatened attacks on Benevento, the papal vassal-state. But when he died in 1085, Guiscard was lord of south Italy in fact; overlord of the ruler of Sicily, his brother; neither Capua nor the pope could offer him any resistance; and his piratical raids into Greece and the eastern Mediterranean had made him the terror of Byzantium.

The papacy was slow to offer the Normans recognition; it could hardly look with favour on bandits. In 1053 Leo IX tried to subdue them in a campaign which he led in person; the result was that he was captured and compelled to come to an arrangement. This might not have lasted; but the death of Henry III deprived the popes of any hope of protection from the emperor for many years to come, and so Nicholas II, by the treaty of Melfi of 1059, recognized Guiscard and his rival of Capua, and empowered them to conquer south Italy from the Greeks and Sicily from the Muslims. It was with a papal blessing that Roger, Guiscard's younger brother, invaded Sicily in 1061.

In the 1060s and 1070s Guiscard was the dominant figure in Italian politics. His attacks on Benevento made his relations with the popes uneasy; there was no visible limit to his ambitions or to his adventures. In the 1080s Pope Gregory VII was compelled to ask him for help against Henry IV; and in 1084–5 the pope had to submit to the humiliation of having his city laid waste by his Norman rescuers, and being carried away to die in exile at Salerno.

Roger, meanwhile, had been pressing slowly forward with the conquest of Sicily, and after Guiscard's death the centre of interest moves to his court. Richard of Capua died in 1078; his successors retained his inheritance, but could never challenge the power of the house of Tancred. When Robert Guiscard died in 1085, his inheritance and hegemony passed nominally to his elder son Roger Borsa (1085–1111). But as the years passed Roger Borsa's difficulties increased; and although the First Crusade carried off his brilliant brother Bohemond to be conqueror and prince of Antioch, Borsa's overlordship steadily became more fictitious. When Roger I of Sicily died in 1101, he was effective overlord of the Norman Empire in the Mediterranean; and in

Sicily he had built up a principality which could rival in organization and efficiency that of his fellow-countryman of England.

From 1103 (after two years in which his elder son had been count) to 1154 Sicily was ruled by Roger's second son, Roger II, Roger 'the Great'. For some years his rule was nominal, since he was a child at the time of his father's death. But the state his father had constructed in Sicily survived the minority, and provided Roger II with a stable base throughout the fluctuations of his stormy career. From 1112, when he officially came of age, or perhaps rather 1113, when his mother went off to be queen of Jerusalem, Roger was effective ruler of Sicily. Norman, Greek, Muslim and native Sicilian elements jostled one another in his island principality; and being born in the south, not, like his father, in Normandy, he appreciated the value of each. Greeks and Muslims were accustomed to organized government, and Roger left administration largely in Greek hands; only the Normans favoured anarchy, but they soon learned the strength of Roger's hand. It was many years before he could entirely trust his Norman followers; meanwhile, he could not dispense with them, since they still provided the core of his armies. And although Roger was thoroughly at home in his Mediterranean empire, he never quite forgot that he was a Norman: towards the end of his life one of his right-hand men, his chancellor, was the Anglo-Norman Robert of Salisbury. Meanwhile he was lord of an island stronghold placed in the middle of the known world, where the interests of eastern and western emperors, of pope and caliph, met.

In 1111 Roger II's uncle Roger Borsa died and the mainland duchies passed to his son William, who ruled them or failed to rule them from 1111 to 1127. The old cities and the new Norman baronies enjoyed the benefits of anarchy. It was therefore a rude shock to them when William died and Roger claimed his inheritance; for they knew the lord of Sicily to be a strong, ambitious ruler who would leave them little of their independence. The position of the cities was ambiguous: freedom they craved, to follow their own interests and development; but they also needed peace, or at any rate peace on land, freedom from the brigandage of the Norman lords. Roger was therefore able to bribe Salerno to open its gates to him; and there he was proclaimed duke. But the cities, like the barons, found him a somewhat overbearing master. He would grant privileges with a lavish hand when he needed allies, but limit them when he felt secure. In the long run the towns submitted to him politically, and he in turn fostered their mercantile privileges. In the long run too he won the allegiance of the Norman barons of the mainland, but it was a long tortuous course, with many twists and turns, which led to the triumphs of his last years.

In 1129 he put down the first rebellion, which had been backed by the pope, and the pope was compelled to recognize Roger's succession. In 1130 began the papal schism, and in Roger the anti-pope Anacletus II found a ready ally—in return for a concession very precious to him. Anacletus gave Roger the title 'king of Sicily and of the duchies of Apulia and Calabria'; and Roger's determination to keep his hard-won title kept Anacletus from total extinction for some years after almost all the rest of western Christendom had turned against him. At one point Roger paid dearly for his defence of the anti-pope. He was still not secure in south Italy, and in 1137 he was ousted by an alliance between rebel barons and the Emperor Lothar. For a time his empire was confined to Sicily; but only for a time, and by 1140 he was at the height of his power. First, Lothar died, before the end of 1137. In 1138 Anacletus died, and although a successor struggled to maintain his paparchy for a brief space, a *rapprochement* between Innocent and Roger was now possible. Innocent found a short cut to this by himself taking the field in 1139 with the intention of punishing the schismatic Norman. But Innocent, like Leo IX, succeeded only in falling into his enemy's hands, and once again the Norman leader, with every show of humility and respect, extracted from his spiritual father the uttermost farthing. The pope pretended to ignore what Anacletus had done, but in effect he confirmed it; Roger was now king of Sicily, and he and his sons became the pope's liegemen.

In 1140, in a solemn royal council at Ariano, Roger the Great issued a revised code of laws. In it Norman feudal elements can be found; also elements of Greek and Muslim origin; and the whole is contained in a legal framework inspired by Roman Law. Some Italian cities had been governed by Roman Law long before this, and traces of it could be found in earlier barbarian codes. But Sicily was the first European kingdom to return to the allegiance to Roman Law—not completely, and yet in sufficient measure for it to be something of an anticipation of the 'reception' of Roman Law in northern countries at the end of the Middle Ages. It symbolized the fact that Sicily was becoming the most highly organized and the most autocratic of the European kingdoms. No doubt the code exaggerated this; medieval legislation was always two steps ahead of reality. But Roger II in his later years certainly ruled the most mature royal government in western Europe. In spite of the distance, it retained quite close links with the other leading monarchy of the period, that of the Normans in England. John of Salisbury, in one of his letters, tells a friend of his distaste for 'the wine of Falerno or Palermo or of Greece, which the chancellor of the king of Sicily used to give me to the peril of my life and my salvation', and in his *Policraticus* he describes a gargantuan feast which he enjoyed, or endured, in the same kingdom, and which he likened to the Feast of Trimalchio, when he visited it as a clerk of the archbishop of Canterbury in Roger II's later years. The chancellor was the Anglo-Norman Robert of Salisbury, and the Sicilian court (among other things) was clearly associated in John's mind with the union of Norman blood with Mediterranean, if not oriental, luxury. This blending had more mundane aspects. In the second half of the twelfth century one of the leading officials of the English Exchequer was Thomas Brown, who had served his apprentice-ship in the Sicilian treasury. Henry II of England was well aware that he had much to learn from the king of Sicily, and their common interests were cemented when Roger's grandson, William II, became Henry's son-in-law. The links can be exaggerated: a long and dangerous journey lay between the two kingdoms, and it is difficult to tell, when we see similarities, whether it is direct imitation or the parallel development of the Norman genius which we are witnessing. On the whole, however, communication between them has probably been under- rather than over-emphasized by modern historians.

The Normans in England

The second wife of Ethelred II was a Norman princess, Emma, daughter of Duke Richard I of Normandy and so aunt of Robert I (1027–35), William the Conqueror's father. When Ethelred died, Cnut married Emma, and after Cnut's death in 1035 all the English kings, with two exceptions, were closely related to the Norman ducal house. After an interval in which Cnut's son by his English mistress, Harold I (1035–40), ruled over England, while his son by Emma, Harthacnut, ruled in Denmark, Harthacnut succeeded to both (1040–2). But in 1042 he followed Harold to the grave, and Emma's surviving son by Ethelred, Edward 'the Confessor', seemed the only candidate. Edward had spent his youth in exile, largely, it seems, in Normandy; he had never expected to be king, and he was not at home in England. He was never master in his own house. In his early years the survivors of the leading earls of Cnut's day tried to dominate him; and the domineering Godwin of Wessex married Edward to his daughter. In 1051 Edward had a chance to show his hand. He and Godwin quarrelled; the king was able to isolate his father-in-law, and send him into exile with all his family; even the queen was packed off to a convent. A Norman was made archbishop of Canterbury, and Edward's cousin, William the Conqueror, according to the most probable story, was designated Edward's heir. The king's success was shortlived. In 1052 Godwin returned; the archbishop was sent back to Normandy; the queen restored; and no more was heard, so far as we know, of Duke William's succession. But Edward had no children, and the succession was still unsettled; nor was William himself likely to forget that he had been Edward's chosen heir.

It is doubtful if his claim was taken very seriously by many folk in England or in Normandy in the late 1050s. After Godwin's death in 1053, Edward seems to have come to an accommodation with the earl's children: especially with Harold, who acted as 'under-king' in Edward's later years, though always careful to pander to the king's taste for hunting and church-building, and not to attempt to monopolize power as his father had tried to do; with Tostig, who was made earl of Northumbria; and with Edith, now securely established as queen, though still childless. Edward continued to indulge his taste for foreign ecclesiastics, though as many of them were German or French (in a wider sense) as were Norman. And the succession was as unsettled as ever.

The events of 1066 are brilliantly portrayed in the Bayeux Tapestry. It opens with a prelude: the mysterious visit of Earl Harold to Normandy in or about 1064, culminating in his equally mysterious oath to Duke William. It then portrays, with great magnificence, the death-bed of the Confessor; the coronation of Harold; the instant preparations of William; the crossing of his fleet to Pevensey; the formation of his base at Hastings; the march to 'Battle' and the close-fought struggle with Harold's army, ending in the defeat of the 'perjured' Harold and the flight of the English from the field. All this took place between January and October 1066. Even so, the Tapestry leaves out many critical events. It does not tell us of Earl Tostig's deposition from the earldom of Northumbria at the end of 1065, of his flight and conspiracy with the king of Norway, who also claimed the English throne. It does not therefore reveal to the full Harold's difficulties in 1066—how he expected an attack not from one but from three enemies; how he kept his fleet patrolling the Channel all summer, and then dismissed it just as the attacks were mounting; how the king of Norway, Harold

Hardrada, the most famous Viking warrior of the age, came first and was defeated and killed, with Tostig, at Stamford Bridge, less than three weeks before the battle of Hastings. Nor does it show the aftermath: William's slow progress through the home counties; the reluctance of the English leaders to accept him; the final surrender; the coronation on Christmas Day in Westminster Abbey amid the flames of the surrounding houses, set on fire by the Norman troops in fear of the English, whose cries of acclamation they had misinterpreted; still less does it show the years in which William secured his conquest against disaffection and revolt.

The rapid vicissitudes of 1066 contradicted what one would regard as reasonable prediction. Harold had secured the throne, in all probability, because he was generally regarded as the one man who could hold the kingdom against the Norman and Norwegian threats: the alternative seemed to be foreign invasion and civil war. Harold seems to have been chiefly afraid of William; yet to us looking back Harold Hardrada's appears the more serious challenge; one cannot help feeling that if William had landed first, the English king at the end of 1066 would have been one Harold or the other. William seems to have had an obstinate determination to be king of England which overruled the caution of his advisers and the sense of the situation which was normally his. He had inherited Normandy as a boy of seven; he had had all the difficulties of a lonely minority among a ferocious baronage. He had been lucky to survive. The Normans were sufficiently Viking to overlook his illegitimate birth; sufficiently civilized to be prepared, in the end, to submit to strong government. The Conqueror, in his turn, was ruthless and realistic enough to succeed in Normandy, sufficient of a dreamer to dare to invade England.

The rest of the story is equally remarkable, though by no means so improbable. The English quickly learned that William was not to be trifled with. From time to time English and Normans conspired together in rebellion against him; and his answer to rebellion left large areas scarred with devastation, sometimes for a generation or two. In the end the English losses at Hastings and in the rebellions left only a handful of pre-Conquest thegns in possession of their properties; the vast bulk of the secular lands of pre-Conquest England passed to Norman barons, or barons from other parts of northern France who had joined in the adventure. A new upper class meant a reorganization of relationships in the English hierarchy of tenure. This is not the place to embark on the controversies as to the effect of the Norman Conquest

on English society:[1] suffice it to say that in the hurly-burly of redistributing the estates of the English aristocracy, the Conqueror and his
associates introduced into England as near an approximation to a
'system' of feudalism as Europe ever knew; that is to say, a society in
which all land was held of the king, and the large bulk of it was held in
exchange for defined military service. There was a plan behind this, of
a kind; but it was defined and reshaped in accordance with a rough and
ready appreciation of a complex and difficult situation; and in the
process the Norman preserved as much of Old English institutions, and
even social organization, as was compatible with conquest and expro-
priation by a warrior class with its own customary arrangements. The
tendency to feudal institutions was in many respects very marked before
the Conquest; much more so after it—yet many local customs and
variations survived. At the end of his life, in the famous Domesday
Survey (1086), the Conqueror arranged for a comprehensive investigation of the outcome of all the upheavals. The pattern of English tenure
was revealed to him, and to us—chaotic, as we should expect after the
forcible, only partly controlled replacement of one ruling class by
another; and yet showing that for all the disputes the process had been
sufficiently controlled for the commissioners to get, in the vast majority
of cases, a perfectly clear and unambiguous answer to the question:
who holds this land? Domesday, indeed, is more than a record of
tenure; it reveals, in crude statistics, yet with more clarity than any
other monarch of the age could hope to have it, the value of the lands
and villages of almost the whole country. It could be used as a check
on taxation, as well as on tenurial disputes; and in a general way it told
King William what he had won.

Domesday Book has been preserved from the moment of its com-
pletion among the records of the English government, in two volumes:
the first contains the returns, in a finally digested form, for all but the
counties of East Anglia. Volume II contains the returns for East Anglia
in a slightly fuller form: probably it was delivered in the royal treasury
too late to be digested in the same form as Volume I. Volume I is the

[1] The controversies centre on the question how profoundly the Norman
Conquest affected English life, society and institutions. The most debated of
all, perhaps, is the question whether English society was feudal or quasi-feudal
before the Conquest: on this see the bibliographical article of J. C. Holt in
Economic History Review, 2nd series, vol. XIV (1961–2). See also the general
books cited above; V. H. Galbraith, *Studies in the Public Records* (Edinburgh,
1958); David Douglas, *The Norman Conquest and British Historians* (Glasgow,
1946).

work of a single scribe, probably an Englishman; probably also the presiding genius (under the king) of the enterprise. Domesday is a monument of the marriage of Norman ruthlessness and energy with the traditions of literacy and orderly central government which had been characteristic of the Old English monarchy. This can easily be exaggerated: the size of the royal household, the number of officials and clerks regularly employed by Edward the Confessor or William the Conqueror would hardly fill a corner in a single department in modern Whitehall. But the mature efficiency of the apparatus which minted coins and collected them to pay the enormous Danegelds of Ethelred or Cnut, or put together in a single book the Domesday statistics for the greater part of England, would have filled the kings of France and Germany of this age with envy and won at least a nod of respect from the Muslims in Spain and in Sicily.

The Normans and Britain

The Normans never conquered the other kingdoms of the British Isles, although they were far poorer and weaker (in any obvious, material sense) than England, which they conquered in a day. They never tried to conquer Ireland or Scotland: in Ireland they tried from time to time, rather remotely, to exert influence; intervention they never attempted before the reign of Henry II. On Scotland they exerted influence more consistently; and Scotland underwent, in its own way, a Norman conquest. But it was not a violent conquest, nor the result of deliberate action by the English kings. The Conqueror and his sons, indeed, received less recognition from the Scots than had Athelstan or Edgar. The Scottish infiltration was due to circumstances. St Margaret had brought English influences to the Scottish court; and her sons held the throne throughout the first half of the twelfth century. David I, in particular (1124–53), was a cosmopolitan ruler of great imagination. He enjoyed an English earldom as well as his Scottish kingdom, and was at home in the court of his brother-in-law Henry I of England; he was also, in return, a powerful influence on his great-nephew, Henry II. In his English earldom and his Scottish court, David gathered round him a growing circle of Anglo-Norman, or Norman-Scottish barons and knights, who peacefully normanized south-eastern Scotland—Lothian, once part of English Northumbria, now the centre of David's power. David also encouraged the development of the Scottish Church, in this carrying on his mother's work, and he was the founder and refounder of monasteries on a spectacular scale. But the process meant no surrender to England: it was indeed at this time that the Scottish Church vindicated its independence of the English, although this was not recognized finally until the end of the century and the archbishop of York retained one small foothold for a while longer.

In the late eleventh century, Archbishop Lanfranc of Canterbury had tried to build up a large ecclesiastical empire by claiming (successfully, for a time) primacy over York and exerting influence in Wales, Scotland and Ireland. In the twelfth century Scotland, though much influenced by the English Church, broke free. In the same century the Irish Church was completely remodelled under the leadership of St Malachy in direct affiliation to Rome; Lanfranc's influence was not revived by his successors. In Wales alone the Norman kings and the Norman archbishops attempted total conquest; and in large measure, although the kings failed, the archbishops succeeded. The Welsh Church had been reduced to chaos, it seems, by the Viking attacks; a revival was under way in the late eleventh century, which received a considerable fillip when Henry I appointed his wife's chancellor, Bernard, bishop of St Davids in 1115. Bernard was quickly won to an appreciation of the traditions of his cathedral, and claimed independence of Canterbury and primacy in Wales. Both claims were lost in the twelfth century after a prolonged dispute lasting well after the death of Bishop Bernard; both were revived earlier in the present century, when Bernard's claims became once again a matter of actual concern, and the Church in Wales is now an independent province of the Anglican communion, although St Davids has not vindicated its primacy.

The absorption of the Anglo-Norman Bernard in Welsh aspirations is an interesting reflection of the complexity of the history of Wales in this period. William I set up great lords on its frontiers, to rule the marchland and to conquer Wales. Some of these lordships, notably the earldoms of Chester and (for a time) of Shrewsbury, formed semi-independent principalities. William I himself went on a pilgrimage to St Davids which was clearly not solely of spiritual significance. But the resistance of the Welsh was far more stubborn than the Normans seem to have anticipated; gains in Wales were far less profitable than in the richer lands of England; and adventure in Wales tended to be less fashionable at this time than in France or the East. As the eleventh century turned into the twelfth, it must none the less have seemed that the Norman conquest of Wales was about to be completed. Under the patronage of William II and Henry I, the marcher lords conquered the whole of south Wales and much of central Wales; and the earls of Chester and Shrewsbury were pressing into the north and centre. The advance was checked from time to time; some of the marcher lords fell victim to death or excessive ambition, or both. But there were few indications in the reign of Henry I that the whole movement was to fail. When he died, however, the piled-up resentment of the Welsh found its opportunity, and the most powerful of the marchers were diverted to adventure in England. The Welsh had already found a brilliant leader in Gruffydd ap Cynan, who revived the power of the old kingdom of Gwynedd, and his son Owain Gwynedd (1137–70) opened his reign by being one of the chief leaders in the great rebellions of the late 1130s; even after the succession of Henry II he was able on two occasions to resist royal invasion from England. The Normans kept south Wales and a part of the marchlands they had conquered; but the north and centre retained their freedom. The Celtic peoples had kept their independence of the rulers of the south-east of Britain in the past largely because of the fundamental frontier which divided the peoples of the lowlands from those of the highland zone. It is interesting to observe that the Normans, descendants of the Viking peoples who had successfully conquered and settled so much of the highland zone in earlier centuries, had become sufficiently acclimatized to Normandy and to feudal conditions to become, in England, men of the lowlands, and to prove incapable of adapting themselves successfully to warfare in the highlands.

William II, Henry I and Stephen

In 1066, from one point of view, the English throne had merely passed from one branch of the Norman ducal family to another. This is not a merely paradoxical way of describing the event. The great dynasts of Europe were often closely related to one another in that age as more recently; and family feeling was often as powerful with them as sense of 'nationality'. Duke William claimed the English throne essentially because he regarded himself as Edward's designated successor; but it is very improbable that he would have been designated, or would have taken his claim seriously, if he had not been Edward's cousin. None the less, from the point of view of the majority of Englishmen, and of Europe at large, one of Europe's leading kingdoms had been violently conquered and (so far as its upper class was concerned) ruthlessly resettled by the leaders of a French principality and their allies from other parts of western Europe. The story of the relations between the

Normans and the English in the decades after the Conquest used to be told in vivid, not to say lurid detail, until it was shown that the chief medieval source for reconstructing the hidden agony of the English people, 'Ingulph of Crowland', was a late medieval forgery. Since then historians have steered clear of this fascinating but difficult theme. We can see the English reaction reflected in the splendid epitaph written for the Conqueror by the author of one of the versions of the *Anglo-Saxon Chronicle*. One can see that all feared him; that many hated him; that he was regarded as ruthless and stark; but that many, too, respected him for his strong sense of justice and for his piety. This and other indications remind us of a period of adjustment which must have been for many very difficult and trying. There is no reason to imagine any large-scale hidden conflict, still less a class war. The bulk of the English people remained struggling peasantry; the Norman lords were more ruthless perhaps, more inclined to bind the peasants to the soil; but equally, less inclined to leave them as mere slaves, not at all inclined to remain a caste apart. Thus we see in the twelfth century an interesting paradox. In many European countries the old, fluid nobility was tending to harden into an aristocratic caste;[1] in England, the one country in which the warrior classes were, on the whole, racially distinct from the rest, this tendency was less marked. There is no single explanation for this. But there are copious indications that after the first shock the two races tended to meet and mingle as rapidly as they could. The English on the make became normanized, spoke French, gave their children French names. The Normans intermarried with their subjects and even learned their language. Before long even the kings followed this practice.

The Conqueror's wife, Matilda, was a descendant, in the female line, from King Alfred.[2] This may well have weighed with William in his choice of bride, and it meant that William II and Henry I had slightly more hereditary claim to the English throne than their father. But they both had an elder brother, William for the whole and Henry for most of his reign, who was slow to abandon his idea of becoming king himself. Robert II succeeded the Conqueror as duke of Normandy without serious question. But he and his father had been on bad terms and, since Robert was known to be incompetent, William had designated his second son and namesake to succeed him in England. This he did, with the aid of the old king's right-hand man, Archbishop Lanfranc. It was

[1] But see p. 90n.
[2] Her ancestor, Count Baldwin II, married Alfred's daughter Ælfthryth.

some years before William II's throne was secure; but in course of time he revealed himself as the equal of his father in strength and ruthlessness. There was one marked difference between them. William I had been, especially in his later years, the friend of churchmen; he had even been trusted by Pope Gregory VII as a friend of ecclesiastical reform. He would not stand opposition from the Church, but he was a pious man who liked to enjoy its respect. William II, like his father, was happy in the camp and the hunting field; but unlike him he was profoundly unhappy in church. He disliked clerical influences at court—unless they were thoroughly worldly—and only submitted to the conventional demands of the Church when he was in fear of death. He owed much to Lanfranc, and tolerated him while he lived. When he died, William kept the see vacant and enjoyed its revenues. But in 1093 he fell seriously ill, and became suddenly convinced that he must fill the see with Anselm, the saintly abbot of Bec in Normandy, whom a number of magnates had already pointed out as the most suitable candidate. Anselm was forced into accepting it; the king recovered; and the inevitable quarrel followed. Rufus felt that he had been tricked into filling the see, and tricked again into filling it with the kind of cleric he particularly disliked; and Anselm, who was by nature a peacemaker and an academic, although he had no wish to fall out with Rufus, felt bound to stand by the rights of his see and office, which the king now set himself to attack with every weapon in his armoury. Anselm had foreseen the trouble: he likened himself to an old sheep being yoked to an untamed bull. He was, however, far from being a sheep: he had a mind of great incisiveness and a determination to hold to essential points of principle. Eventually Anselm asked, and was granted, leave to consult the pope; in effect, he went into exile. William was free to carry on his knightly adventures, and Anselm, in retirement at Lyons, and in his native Italy, to finish the greatest of his books, the *Cur Deus homo*.

In the meantime the First Crusade had been launched, and Duke Robert had set off for the East, having pawned his duchy to Rufus. The latter now engaged in continental adventure, and planned campaigns in central France. But on an August day in 1100, while hunting in the New Forest, he was killed by an arrow. Contemporaries attributed the arrow, at the human level, to accident; *sub specie aeternitatis* to his sins. Both judgements have been questioned by modern historians.[1]

Whether or not Henry I had conspired for the removal of his brother,

[1] For a recent discussion of various views, see C. Brooke, *The Saxon and Norman Kings* (London, 1963), Chapter 11.

he was singularly fortunate in the moment of Rufus's death. Duke Robert was on the verge of returning from the East; he was the accepted heir; unlike Rufus, he was married, and might well have a child. But a few weeks before Robert's arrival, Rufus died, and Henry with great rapidity made himself master of England, had himself crowned, and summoned Anselm to return to England. Robert did not accept defeat; but as the years passed fortune turned against him. Henry cemented his throne by marrying Edith or Matilda, as she came to be called, daughter of St Margaret of Scotland and so a princess of the Old English line; and in Normandy and France he gathered allies for a trial of strength against Robert. In 1106 he defeated Robert at the Battle of Tinchebrai, and kept him in a British prison for the rest of his life, treating him as Alfonso VI of Castile had treated his brother Garcia (see p. 377).

Henry I was the ablest of the Conqueror's sons. He was like his father in his ruthlessness and in his imaginativeness as an administrator. The strength of the Old English monarchy had lain in close links between central and local government. The old shire courts were strengthened, the old sheriffdoms made more amenable to royal control by being removed from the hands of the substantial barons who had held them in the previous reigns and placed in those of laymen and even clerics close to the king. The financial organization achieved a new sophistication under Henry's favourite administrator, Roger, bishop of Salisbury.

The doubt as to his right to the throne evidently made Henry all the keener to surround himself with men who were his own creations; to make his court reflect his own glory, not that of his father or his brother. This inclined him to endow new baronies, to raise men of the second rank to be his closest counsellors; and the patronage he exercised in large measure altered the nature of the English baronage. In addition, Henry had his favourites, and he had very numerous illegitimate children. His senior illegitimate son Robert he made earl of Gloucester; even more lavish was his endowment of his nephew Stephen of Blois, who was clearly his chief favourite. There is indeed a marked difference between his generous treatment of Stephen and his harsh treatment of his daughter Matilda, who after the disaster of the *White Ship* in 1120, when his son and heir William and many courtiers were drowned, was his only surviving legitimate child. Matilda was sent as a child to be Henry V's empress; and when after Henry V's death her position looked like becoming comfortable and dignified, she was dragged back to be England's heiress, which meant, in effect, to be married to whoever her father decided should succeed him. To her own and the barons' disgust, she was married to the count of Anjou. After a pause in which even her father tired of the match, she took to living with her husband; and in 1135, when their first-born, the future Henry II, was two years old, she supported her husband in a war against her father. Under these circumstances the old king died; and it may be that Matilda's harsh rejoinder to the harsh treatment she had received decided him in the end against her claim to the throne.

This is far from certain; but whether his uncle had designated him or not, Stephen of Blois succeeded in taking the English throne (1135–54), and for a time it looked as if he would inherit the whole Norman Empire. Stephen had charm and courage; but he was not sufficiently ruthless or persistent to destroy opposition; nor did he command the trust or allegiance of the Anglo-Norman barons as a whole. Matilda and her husband found it easier to be allies than to live together. They set to work to dismember Stephen's empire. Matilda landed in England in 1139, and support gathered round her, led by her half-brother, Robert of Gloucester. In 1141 she was nearly successful: her allies captured Stephen, and she marched to London intending to be crowned queen. But Matilda, at this stage of her career, behaved like an empress when she was not quite a queen, and alienated a good deal of support. Within a week London became too hot for her; and within a year Stephen had to be released. Her power was confined once more to the south-west, the counties surrounding her brother's headquarters in Bristol and Gloucester. In 1147 Earl Robert died; in 1148 the empress retired to Normandy. Her husband, meanwhile, had conquered Normandy in her name, and their eldest son was growing to years, if not of discretion, at least of generalship. He made a series of raids on England; in 1149 he was invested with Normandy by his father; in 1152, as recounted elsewhere (p. 208), he married Eleanor, the ex-queen of France; in 1153 he compelled Stephen to accept him as his heir; and in December 1154 the ageing archbishop of Canterbury, Theobald (another ex-abbot of Bec), who had struggled to keep the English Church united in the days of the anarchy and to restore peace, anointed and crowned the young Henry II, duke of Normandy and Aquitaine and (by his father's death) count of Anjou, as king of the English.

In Stephen's reign England had suffered something like anarchy as well as civil war. The anarchy was sporadic; it affected such areas as East Anglia, where the barons engaged in private war, or the south midlands, disputed territory between Stephen and Matilda, far more

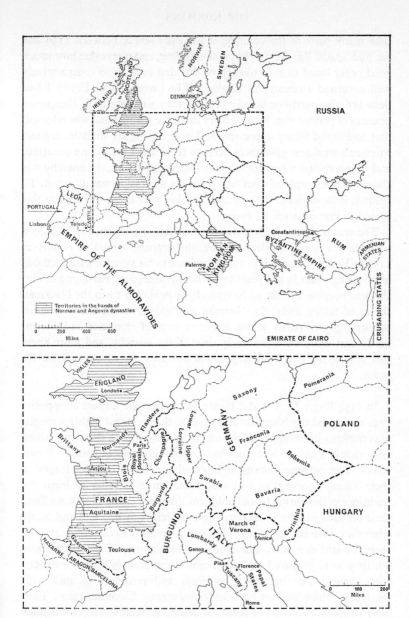

5. EUROPE IN 1154

235

than many parts of the country; it was only severe between 1139 and the mid 1140s. But it brought great suffering; and it revealed how much good order owed to the strength of the king even in so comparatively well governed a country as England. The barons under Henry I had been orderly, partly or largely because they were afraid of the consequences of private war. When Henry died, the strong hand was released; they had found Henry oppressive and were hoping for an easier régime; Stephen's weakness gave them heart to rebel when the excuse occurred, and to ignore him when opportunity offered; above all, the anarchy was the classical example of what happened if a succession was disputed. To study it is to see why such enormous pains were taken throughout this period to prevent such an event.

The anarchy, once begun, was not easy finally to quench. It is indeed somewhat mysterious why the English baronage agreed so readily in 1153 to Henry's succession, and submitted to his very forceful methods of restoring order in the years following his accession. Partly, no doubt, this was because as duke of Normandy he held over them the blackmail threat of taking away the Norman possessions which many English barons enjoyed; partly it was his own force of character and charm, partly that some were genuinely tired of the anarchy, and more knew that among the people at large there was an even stronger desire for peace.

In 1154 Roger II died and Henry II came to the throne: at opposite ends of Europe the Normans had created the two most highly wrought governments in Europe; but the earlier careers of both these men show very clearly that the Normans had become creators in spite of themselves. The Norman barons of England and Sicily had not forgotten their Viking ancestry; or had only forgotten it in order to learn the traditions of the unruly feudal nobles of France. Yet one cannot attribute their creative success in making the monarchies of England and Sicily what they were in the late twelfth century entirely to chance or even to their brilliant dynasties. The Normans had energy, adaptability; above all, they were prepared to mingle and intermarry with their subjects; they showed that natural friendliness and readiness to mix with foreigners which has not been universal among European races. They were ruthless, and did not cease for several generations to be brigands at heart. But by and large they were tolerant, of other folk, of other ways of life, and even, in the end, of civilization.

XII

Monasticism and Papal Reform

Cluny, Gorze and Glastonbury

It is commonly said that the beginnings of a great religious revival can be seen in many movements of the late tenth and early eleventh centuries. In some senses this must be true. It may be that it is misleading to judge a religious movement by its outward manifestation; that what the historian can view is superficial evidence; that at a deeper level it is meaningless to say that one age is 'more religious' than another. But whether we apply the crude external test—the evidence of interest in the outward exercises of religion—or the test of maturity and subtlety in religious thought and sentiment, few historians would care to deny that a great change, a great development took place between the tenth and the twelfth centuries. Its deep springs and origins, as with all such movements, lie hidden from us. We can trace many of the sources of its inspiration; why they should have bubbled over at this moment rather than at that is beyond our comprehension. The best we can do is

BIBLIOGRAPHY (to Chapters XII and XIII). On monasticism in general, see Dom Cuthbert Butler, *Benedictine Monachism* (new edn., London, 1961); Dom David Knowles, *Monastic Order in England* (Cambridge, 1940); G. G. Coulton, *Five Centuries of Religion*, vol. I (Cambridge, 1923); on Cluny, Joan Evans, *Monastic Life at Cluny* (Oxford, 1931); on Gorze and the Lotharingian reforms modern views have been substantially altered by K. Hallinger, *Gorze-Kluny* (2 vols., Rome, 1950–1), whose findings are not readily available in English. On John of Fécamp, A. Wilmart, *Auteurs spirituels et textes dévots du moyen âge latin* (Paris, 1932). Wilmart's book has numerous sidelights on the religious history of the period, and is the principal monument to a great scholar. The same can be said of the *Liturgica Historica* (Oxford, 1918) of Edmund Bishop, one of the greatest of English medievalists. On the *Eigenkirchen*, U. Stutz in G. Barraclough, *Mediaeval Germany* (Oxford, 1938), vol. II, pp. 35–70.

On the papal reform and the disputes it engendered, *Cambridge Medieval History*, vol. V; H. X. Arquillière, *Saint Grégoire VII: essai sur sa conception du pouvoir pontifical* (Paris, 1934); J. P. Whitney, *Hildebrandine Essays* (Cambridge, 1932); G. Tellenbach, *Church, State and Christian Society at the time of the* to make some guesses, and our guesses will be wide of the mark if they do not help us to understand two facts about this movement: that it was accompanied by widespread popular enthusiasm,[1] and that the inspiration of the movement, in its origins, was mainly monastic. It seems that the troubled conditions of the ninth and early tenth centuries had made some men long for greater peace in the world; had made others long for a chance to retreat from it; that these unsettled conditions had, however, made it exceedingly difficult for existing communities to sustain a regular monastic life. As the tenth century proceeded more settled conditions and royal and princely patrons made the monastic revival possible; and the urge found its means of expression.

All this is probably true; but it is not the whole truth, and we shall be more profitably engaged inspecting the movement itself.

There are in monastic history two constant tensions. Does the community look inward, concern itself with its own life and worship, the salvation of its own members? Or outward, and perform some special function in the world at large? And does the community exist for communal activity, for communal worship and approach to God; or to provide the framework within which the individual may work out his own approach to God? This tension is between what St Benedict called the cenobitic or communal and anchorite or hermit lives.

The expression of the monastic ideal in these centuries was very diverse; but all the organized monastic orders owed something to the sixth-century *Rule* of St Benedict of Nursia, and most monastic communities claimed to model themselves first and foremost on Benedict's prescriptions. The *Rule* of St Benedict (sixth century) is one of the foremost documents for an understanding of the period: it was known

---

[1] See Chapter XVI.

Investiture Contest (trans. R. F. Bennett, Oxford, 1940); A. Fliche, *La querelle des investitures* (Paris, 1946) and *La réforme grégorienne* (3 vols., Louvain-Paris, 1924–37). On the doctrines, W. Ullmann, *The growth of papal government in the Middle Ages* (London, 1955); Z. N. Brooke, *Lay investiture and its relation to the conflicts of Empire and Papacy* (British Academy, 1939); there are useful summaries in R. W. and A. J. Carlyle, *History of Mediaeval Political Theory in the West*, vol. IV (Edinburgh, 1922). For the English Church before 1066, F. Barlow, *The English Church, 1000–1066* (London, 1963), and for the Investiture contest, Z. N. Brooke, *The English Church and the Papacy from the Conquest to the reign of John* (Cambridge, 1931); R. W. Southern, *St Anselm and His Biographer* (Cambridge, 1963); for the effects of the contest in Germany, P. Joachimsen in Barraclough, *Mediaeval Germany*, vol. II, pp. 95–129. For sources, see Chapter II; also W. Fritz, *Quellen zum Wormser Konkordat* (Berlin, 1955: in Latin).

by heart over many centuries by countless thousands of monks and formed the basis of their lives. To the question whether a monastery was inward- or outward-looking Benedict's answer appears at first sight to be unambiguous. The community described by Benedict is a self-contained island of devotion in a barbarous world, subject to the patriarchal control of its abbot, engaged in communal worship, private prayer and devotion, work and reading. No doubt it was always held that the prayers of the monks benefited their secular neighbours, and were indispensable to their secular benefactors; and in practice Benedictine communities have very frequently been centres of Christian influence, of culture and learning, and of teaching; but this is not inherent in the *Rule*, and was secondary in the early days of Benedictine history. A Benedictine house may look outward into the world; it always looks inward, to its own life, to its own ceaseless round of worship.

In the controversies between Cenobites and Anchorites St Benedict's fundamental position was clear: 'Let us by God's help set down a *Rule* for Cenobites, who are the most steadfast (*fortissimum*) kind of monks.' The emphasis of the *Rule*, furthermore, is on communal activity. But at the end, in a famous passage, Benedict reintroduces the hermit ideal, not under that name, but by reference to the works of Cassian, the eastern monk who at the turn of the fourth and fifth centuries had displayed and interpreted the work of the anchorites of the Egyptian and Syrian desert to the west, in the manner of life of his community at Marseilles, and in his *Institutes* and *Collations*.

We have written this *Rule*, that, by its observance in monasteries, we may show that we have in some measure uprightness of manners or the beginning of the religious life. But for such as hasten onward to the perfection of holy life there are the teachings of the Holy Fathers, the observance whereof leads a man to the heights of perfection. For what page or what passage of the divinely inspired books of the Old and the New Testament is not a most perfect rule for man's life? Or what book is there of the Holy Catholic Fathers that doth not proclaim this, that by a direct course we may come to our Creator? Also, what else are the *Collations* of the Fathers, their *Institutes* [Cassian's books], their *Lives* [St Jerome's Lives of the fathers of the desert] and the *Rule* of our holy father St Basil, but examples of the virtues, of the good living and obedience of monks? But to us who are slothful, and lead bad and negligent lives, they are matter for shame and confusion.

Do thou, therefore, whosoever thou art who hasteneth forward to the heavenly country, accomplish first, by the help of Christ, this little *Rule* written for beginners, and then at length shalt thou come, under God's guidance, to the lofty heights of doctrine and virtue, which we have spoken of above.[1]

Thus Benedict insisted on the communal life of the *Rule* as the foundation for all, but looked on the individual approach to God as the higher flight for the few. In a sense, then, he gave his blessing to both species of monasticism; and so the tension has always existed where his *Rule* was seriously considered and followed. But the higher flights of mystical doctrine, as in Cassian, represented something more sophisticated than was easily recovered in most centuries of the early Middle Ages. Cassian's elaborate mystical doctrine was comparatively little regarded before it was picked up again by the great Italian hermits of the eleventh century, especially St Peter Damian, and subsequently by the Benedictine reformers of the twelfth century, especially St Bernard of Clairvaux; from them the tradition was to be continuous to the Spanish mystics of the Counter-Reformation.

This is not to say, however, that the tendency was solely for monasteries to grow more inward-looking as time passed, or for their concern for individual progress to become exclusive. Strangely enough the revival of the anchorite ideal went hand in hand with a renewed interest in the relations of the monk and the world. It is well known that the latter culminated in the rise of a new type of monastic order in the thirteenth century, the Orders of Friars. But in the life and ideal of St Francis both tendencies appear; and the story was told—apocryphal maybe, but well found—that St Francis passed through a crisis in his early years in which he took the advice of St Clare and Brother Sylvester whether to become a hermit or a preacher.

Most of the monastic movements of our period placed the *Rule* of St Benedict at the basis of their plan of life. This was already traditional. The *Rule* had been widely read, widely honoured in early centuries; it was, however, the activity of another Benedict, St Benedict of Aniane, who was made a kind of dictator among the monasteries of the Frankish Empire by Charlemagne and Louis the Pious in the early ninth century, which set the *Rule* on the pedestal it has occupied ever since. Benedict of Aniane produced a series of regulations for the life of monks, whose

[1] *The Rule of St Benedict*, trans. F. A. Gasquet (London, 1936), pp. 9, 123-4 (slightly adapted).

basic character may be summarized as follows: the *Rule* was to be universally accepted, but the *Rule* interpreted and elaborated in the light of more recent tradition; manual work was dropped from the monastic day, to be performed by peasant tenants and servants; there was to be no education provided save for members of the community; the liturgy was to be something far more elaborate than had been envisaged by the first Benedict. Some monasteries were in fact centres of learning, very notably so in the days of the Carolingian renaissance. But there was no idea, then or later, that monastic houses should automatically be centres of learning. Spiritual reading was a part of the daily round; scholarship an occasional extra. It was chiefly the elaboration of the *opus Dei*, the communal worship in the conventual church, which swallowed up the time given in the *Rule* to manual labour.

The work of St Benedict of Aniane, to outward appearance, soon perished. The empire decayed, and with it the monastic life he had tried to establish; many of his monasteries were destroyed or deserted in the disorders of the ninth century. But he had left a clear impression in the minds of responsible churchmen of the kind of life which should be led in a well-run monastery; and this bore fruit, all over western Europe, in the tenth century. The centres from which the new movements sprang lay in Burgundy, Lorraine and England, and the fact that they all got under way within a single generation suggests that they were not entirely independent of one another; the English, indeed, was openly modelled on the Burgundian and the Lotharingian, though it had many native roots as well. The connexions between the others were more tenuous, and may amount to little more than that all were products of the same age and climate of opinion; and that all looked for instruction to Benedict of Aniane.

Most famous of these foundations was the Burgundian abbey of Cluny, founded, strangely enough, by a duke of Aquitaine, in 910. Shortly after came the re-establishment of Brogne, in Lower Lorraine (*c.* 920), and of Gorze in Upper Lorraine (*c.* 933); and the revival of monastic life at Glastonbury by St Dunstan (*c.* 940). By the middle of the century the foundation, endowment or revival of monasteries was fashionable once again among the lay aristocracy and the bishops of western Europe; and its popularity grew as the centuries passed, reaching its climax in the twelfth. Meanwhile, there had also appeared a growing number of men and women prepared to be recruits for these foundations; and, what was of particular importance, a number of folk of special capacity and fervour to act as leaders and inspirers of the movements. When King Alfred of Wessex had attempted to revive monasticism in the late ninth century, he had failed; he established, in effect, only one, struggling community, mainly recruited from abroad. In the mid tenth century, under the leadership of St Dunstan (archbishop of Canterbury, 960–88), St Ethelwold (bishop of Winchester, 963–84) and St Oswald (bishop of Worcester, 960–92, also archbishop of York, 972–92), recruits gathered quickly, sufficient to form between thirty and forty houses. We may be sure that these monasteries could not have grown up without the patronage of the kings, especially of King Edgar (959–75). Equally, they could not have grown and flourished without a steady supply of recruits. Such a supply could be found in most of western Europe at this date; and from now on the history of many monasteries was continuous until the end of the Middle Ages, whatever might be the vicissitudes in their external fortune and internal observance. The number of recruits was small compared to what it later became; but they had an influence in the Church out of proportion to their numbers; and in an age when the monastic life offered one of the very few alternatives to the life of war and the chase, it is hardly surprising that the monasteries drew many talented recruits.

The two most influential centres of reform were Cluny and Gorze. In early days, neither made any attempt to imitate Benedict of Aniane in acquiring authority over other houses. The abbot of Cluny or Gorze would be asked to take over the reform or revival or foundation of a house; to supply it with some monks, anyway for a time, to instruct it in the monastic life. Customs would be imported from Cluny and Gorze, and a bond of friendship established; but once the house was on its feet it retained the traditional independence of the old Benedictine monasteries. It was only in the mid and late eleventh century that Cluny began to acquire daughter houses which remained in subjection to her; not an order constitutionally governed, like the later religious orders of Cîteaux and the rest, but a congregation of houses under one single head, under the patriarchal governance of the abbot of Cluny.

In many ways Gorze and Cluny were very similar, and this has led to their being confused by some modern historians; others, in the recent reaction against this, have exaggerated their differences. Looking back from the twelfth century, the movements must have seemed very similar. The tradition of Benedict of Aniane ruled in both. The *Rule* of Benedict of Nursia was the norm, but the *Rule* with many additions and modifications. Gorze and Cluny accepted the liturgical development, the increasing time allotted to the *Opus Dei*; they did not attempt to revive manual labour; they expected to teach their own 'oblates'—children placed in the monasteries to be brought up as monks—but not other children. They laid emphasis on the communal aspect of the Benedictine tradition; they were inward-looking.

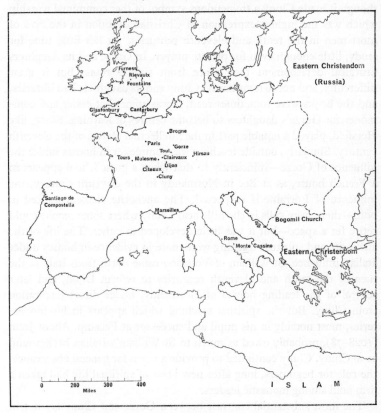

Eastern Christendom
(Russia)

Furness
Rievaulx
Fountains

Glastonbury Canterbury

Brogne

Paris
Toul. Gorze
Tours Molesme. Clairvaux Hirsau
Cîteaux Dijon
Cluny

Santiago de
Compostella

Marseilles

Bogomil Church

Rome
Monte Cassino

Eastern Christendom

0   200   300   400
Miles

I S L A M

6. MONASTERIES AND PILGRIM CENTRES

None the less, there were differences in emphasis and in practice. Many of these were details of observance, the sort of thing which would have seemed to a monk of Gorze visiting Cluny to set him in a foreign world, but which seem to us a thousand years later to be trivial. Some of the differences are more perceptible. The liturgical development was more marked at Cluny; in the end it outstripped everything else, growing like a snowball down to the twelfth century. Cluny was dedicated to St Peter. The night office on the eve of the patronal festival, the

Feast of St Peter and St Paul, started before dark on 28 June and continued till daybreak on the 29th; sleep had to be fitted in on the summer afternoon of 28 June, and the offices of the preceding days telescoped to fit. The calendar had outgrown nature, and the liturgical round, though it made Cluny a tremendous symbol of that communal worship which was the highest expression of Christian devotion in the eyes of most men in the tenth and eleventh centuries, yet left little time for study, little enough even for private prayer. In Gorze and its daughters liturgical development took place from similar roots; but it grew differently, and not so luxuriantly. Cluny and its daughters had libraries, and the books were sometimes read; it was somewhat easier and commoner for Gorze's daughters to become centres of learning. Some, like Hersfeld, played a notable part in the intellectual revival of the eleventh century. Similarly, outside teaching was commoner in houses under the influence of Gorze—sufficiently so that when a great school appears in a French house, as at Bec in Normandy in the eleventh century, the influence of Lorraine is suspected. The anchorite element existed in both—there were cells in the hills near Cluny where some monks could retire for a space—but it was little developed in either. The life of the anchorite and spiritual teaching were more in evidence in houses under Italian influence. St William of Volpiano came north from Italy at the turn of the tenth and eleventh centuries to reform Dijon, and later several of the leading houses of Normandy, under direct inspiration from Cluny. But the spiritual teaching which appears in his monasteries, most notably in his pupil and successor at Fécamp, Abbot John (1028–78), probably owed as much to St William's Italian background as to Cluny. Cluny continued to provide a norm for general observance, the rule for beginners, long after new ideas of spiritual life had taken a firm hold among monastic leaders.

The most substantial contrast between Gorze and Cluny lay not in interior observance but in organization. So far as relations between monasteries were concerned, there was no difference in early days; it was only in the later years of Abbot Odilo (994–1048) and the early years of Abbot Hugh (1049–1109) that Cluny began to gather its children in permanent unity. But if the technique was in origin the same, the sphere of influence was to a remarkable extent distinct. Directly or indirectly Gorze was responsible in the tenth, eleventh and very early twelfth centuries for the reform of over 160 houses, a few in northern France, Belgium, Switzerland and Austria,[1] two in Italy, but

---

[1] Most of Switzerland and all Austria were then within Germany.

the overwhelming majority in Germany. In the same period Cluny reformed houses in Belgium, Italy and Spain; but the overwhelming majority were in France and Burgundy, especially in the south of France.[1] In the late eleventh century, however, they began to overlap more than hitherto, owing to the infiltration of Cluniac influence into Germany in the person of the great Abbot William of Hirsau. Abbeys reformed under the influence of Hirsau and its daughters can be found all over Germany. But with this exception Cluny's influence remained within its old frontiers; and of the priories which were founded in direct subordination to Cluny after the mid eleventh century, about 100 were in Britain, Spain and Italy, over 800 in France and Switzerland.

The question is sometimes asked: which had the greater influence, Gorze or Cluny? To this in the nature of things there can be no answer; one cannot weigh the largely imponderable influence of these two great movements. In sheer statistics, in numbers of houses and monks affected, it is probable that Cluny had the more impressive record. But in the history of monasticism one must be content to say that they exerted parallel influence, mainly in different areas; in their influence on the world at large one can say that their functions were quite distinct. In their relation to the lay world lies their last, and most striking difference of all.

The Gorze houses owed their existence and their wealth to the generosity of the kings and princes of Germany, above all to the kings. Four-fifths of the 140 Gorze houses in existence in the mid eleventh century were subject to the king or to a bishop. The Emperor Otto the Great and his successors restored the fortunes of abbeys and founded new ones. In England, too, there was a close link between the king and the leading ealdormen and the new abbeys, and the king retained a considerable measure of control over their affairs. But Edgar's influence was due, in a general sense, to his position as king and as founder. In Germany the position of the founder or advocate was more extensive still. The advocacy was a hereditary office, carrying rights of jurisdiction in the abbey's lands; the advocate, in practice, was appointed by the king or some other great magnate who had authority over the abbey;

[1] Cluny lay in the part of Burgundy in dispute between France and Germany. It was normally reckoned to be within the duchy of Burgundy, and so within the kingdom of France—as opposed to the kingdom of Burgundy, which was in the empire, and whose king, from Conrad II's time on, was also king of Germany. But the Maconnaise was definitely a border country, owing little allegiance in this period to any king. Burgundy, duchy and kingdom, was on the whole in the Cluniac sphere of influence.

and the advocate's powers substantially reduced the freedom of the abbey to run its own temporal affairs—to manage its vassals, farm its estates, organize its law-courts—and dispose of its own income. At the same time the advocate saved the abbey from many of the responsibilities which consumed the time and energy of abbots elsewhere. This kind of advocacy was peculiar to Germany. But in many parts of Europe the relations of kings and other lay patrons to their abbeys were close.

The position of Cluny was the extreme opposite. Here is an extract from the charter of Cluny's founder, Duke William of Aquitaine (910):

> It has pleased us to set forth in this testament that from this day forward the monks united in congregation at Cluny shall be wholly freed from our power, from that of our kindred, and from the jurisdiction of royal greatness, and shall never submit to the yoke of any earthly power. I beg and pray that no secular prince, no count, no bishop, no pontiff of the Roman Church, by God and through God and all his saints, under threat of the awful day of judgement, may ever invade the possessions of these servants of God. Let him not sell, nor diminish, nor exchange, nor take any thing which is theirs; let him set up no ruler over them against their will. That this prohibition may bind the bold and evil with straiter bonds, once again I say it, and add: I conjure you, ye Holy Apostles and glorious princes of the Earth, Peter and Paul; and thou, pontiff of pontiffs of the Apostolic See, do ye cut off from the communion of the Holy Catholic Church and from life eternal, by the canonical and apostolic authority received from God, those who steal, invade or sell these things which I give to you with eager wish and a joyful heart. Be ye guardians and defenders of Cluny and of the servants of God who shall dwell there, and of their goods that are destined for the giving of alms, for the imitation of the loving-kindness and mercy of our most Holy Redeemer. . . .

And Duke William pronounced a thundering curse on anyone who violated his provisions.[1]

In this document Duke William appealed to the pope and to the Roman apostles to protect his abbey, and Cluny duly received papal support. This culminated in 998 or 999, when the pope granted Cluny exemption from the jurisdiction of its local bishop. Both Duke William's grant of secular exemption and the pope's grant of episcopal exemption

[1] Joan Evans, *Monastic Life at Cluny*, p. 6.

could be paralleled by earlier arrangements in other houses; but neither had been common hitherto. The fame of Cluny helped to make these privileges well known and widely sought after; and it was the ambition of many of Cluny's daughters to share her privileges; in this some succeeded in one way or another; and in the eleventh and twelfth centuries many houses in different parts of Europe discovered or invented ancient grounds for exemption from episcopal control; many, if not most, of them forged privileges in support of their claims.

The most obvious difference between the circumstances of Duke William's Cluny and the German royal monasteries was that the latter were controlled and protected by a comparatively stable government, at least by the most stable and powerful protector they could have discovered. When Cluny was founded, large stretches of France and Burgundy were in a state of anarchy, and the great principalities which restored some semblance of order were only beginning to emerge, or re-emerge. The condition of affairs was emphasized by the fact that Cluny was founded by the duke of Aquitaine. But Cluny is in Burgundy. Later dukes of Aquitaine had no jurisdiction in Burgundy, and would hardly have provided Cluny with the support and patronage a monastery needed; Cluny would have suffered from being permanently attached to the family of its founder. Fortunately for Cluny, her early abbots were great men who were on terms of friendship with kings, bishops and counts, and could command widespread patronage. The early abbots were in theory elected by the community; in practice they were designated by their predecessors. It was this which made possible the striking succession of long-lived abbots: the new abbot was usually a young man of outstanding ability who had been observed and brought up to the task by his predecessor. Their youth is underlined by their length of tenure: two abbots between them spanned the whole eleventh century, St Odilo (994–1048) and St Hugh (1049–1109). Both were on terms of personal friendship with more than one of the emperors of the day; but the emperors did not employ them in the reform of their own abbeys. It was no coincidence that the frontier of France and Germany[1] was also the frontier between the sphere of influence of Gorze and of Cluny.

The idea had been current all over western Christendom down to the eleventh century that churches—whether bishoprics, abbeys or parish churches—could be, and normally were, the property of the lay patron and founder ;to put it another way, bishops, abbots and parish priests

[1] If we reckon the area of Cluny itself a part of France: see above, p. 245 n.

were life tenants and vassals of the secular overlord. For this institution we have no elegant word in English, and so we have adopted the German *Eigenkirchen*, made famous by the fundamental studies of Ulrich Stutz; this we sometimes render 'proprietary church'. Stutz saw its roots in pre-Christian Teutonic custom, and believed it to be a specifically Teutonic institution; but it has been found in regions where Teutonic influence was remote or virtually unknown, and all that we can say with safety is that it was characteristic of western Christendom in the centuries preceding the papal reform. In the tenth and eleventh centuries the royal bishoprics and abbeys of Germany were the most notable examples of *Eigenkirchen*; Cluny and the houses which secured similar privileges were the most notable exceptions.

The kings of Germany treated the bishoprics, and even more the abbeys, as part of the royal domain. They claimed exclusive control over the appointment of bishops and abbots; and although there were a few bishoprics which escaped them at first, by the time of Henry II (1002–24) elections regularly took place in the royal court, and were concluded by a most elaborate ceremony of investiture with ring and (for bishops) pastoral staff. Henry also took in hand the reform of his monasteries a good deal more energetically than his predecessors had done. He incurred great unpopularity with the monks by redistributing their property—improving the endowments of the poorer houses, stripping the richer ones of many of their properties and even suppressing about fourteen. In these activities Henry was supported by a pious sense of duty to see that his monasteries were efficient both temporally and spiritually, and a lofty sense of his own office and its rights. It is difficult to distinguish temporal and spiritual concerns in his actions, as in those of most of the Saxon line. His associate and chronicler Bishop Thietmar of Merseburg takes all this for granted. In describing the foundation of the archbishopric of Magdeburg by Otto I, Thietmar characteristically gives the motives of Otto's favourite scheme as 'the hope of eternal reward and the defence of the country': the archbishop would be a marcher lord, his city a centre of defence on the eastern frontier of Germany, and also, one may add, a base for eastward expansion, settlement and missionary enterprise. The same motive was evident in Henry II's foundation of the bishopric of Bamberg, in his favourite city in east Franconia, also intended to be a bulwark against invasion from the east. Bishops and abbots were royal officers; the bishops were largely recruited from Henry's court school and chapel (see pp. 138–9), where they were trained up for the administrative and military duties which they would have to undertake as bishops. From the lands of bishoprics and abbeys came (in all probability) the majority of the royal armies, and from the abbeys came taxes in the shape of supplies for the court; since the bishops were exempt from some of these taxes, Henry made a practice of staying in episcopal cities, and so receiving in hospitality what he could not obtain by direct taxation. His grip on the Church enabled him to govern with a less elaborate central organization than the kings of England of the day. The English kings, for example, kept a close grip on the issue of coin, insisting on central control of the dies from which money was struck. In Germany coining was decentralized, passed in the main by the king to the bishops. To us the difference seems substantial; royal control much less. It is doubtful whether Henry would have agreed. He was God's vicar (as Thietmar described him); the bishops were his men; Church and kingdom were one. He was even referred to, like Henry VIII of England, as 'head of the Church'. He could hardly foresee that within a generation of his death this position would be seriously challenged. There were voices raised while he lived against his high-handed government of the Church, against the confusion of spiritual and temporal which his methods assumed. But they appeared to be only discontented grumblers. Henry II can be forgiven for not foreseeing Canossa.

The origins of the Papal Reform

Cluny has been the centre of two disputes among modern historians: one concerns its relations with Gorze and the other movements of monastic reform of the tenth and eleventh centuries; the other its relation to the papal reform. It used to be the convention to call the latter the 'Cluniac' reform, as if its inspiration stemmed from Cluny; in more recent times it has been called the 'Gregorian' reform, after Pope Gregory VII (1073–85), who was its most famous, though not its first leader. The title 'Cluniac reform' gravely exaggerates the importance of Cluny; 'Gregorian reform' somewhat exaggerates the influence of Gregory. For that reason I prefer the neutral 'papal reform'. The papacy was at the centre of reforming currents from the mid eleventh century on; and although the reform of the papal Curia was only the centre of a much wider movement—so that even the colourless label 'papal' is not free from objection—reform at the centre was the process which made possible the drastic revolution in the Church's government and outlook.

The association of Cluny with the papal reform received its plausibility from three circumstances: the great fame of Cluny among historians of the period; the chronology of the movement—the revival of the papacy in the heyday of Cluny's influence; and the notion that Pope Gregory VII himself had been a monk of Cluny. Pope Gregory had been a monk;[1] so had most of the leaders of the papal reform; so were most leading churchmen who had the leisure to think and to write in the tenth and early eleventh centuries. The monastic inspiration of the papal reform cannot be doubted. But it is unlikely that Gregory had been professed at Cluny. His friend Bishop Bonizo of Sutri tells us that he had, but he lends his story artistic verisimilitude by telling how the abbot of Cluny presented the young Hildebrand (as he then was called) to Pope Leo IX (1049–54) on his way from Germany to Italy to become Pope. With his genius for inaccuracy Bonizo has chosen the only month in the eleventh century when Cluny had no abbot; and there are grounds for thinking that Hildebrand was a monk, not at Cluny, but at Cologne. As for the other grounds for associating Cluny and papal reform, Cluny's fame no longer dominates the age as it once did; we see it more in perspective now, and we can observe that it was not from Cluny, but from Lorraine and from Italy that the monks whom Leo IX gathered round him came. The chronological relation survives: it was the movements of the tenth and early eleventh centuries which provided the atmosphere which made papal reform possible; these movements were mainly monastic or inspired by monks; and Cluny still holds a dignified place among them. We shall be able to make this more precise as we proceed.

The history of the papacy in the tenth and early eleventh centuries is dominated by the efforts of local factions to seize and keep control of Rome and its greatest office; efforts which might have been successful but for the incursion from time to time of an emperor determined to restore the office to a show of dignity or at least to obedience to the

---

[1] Though only for a very short time, two years (1047–8) at the outside, and it is difficult to believe that this was a vital experience in his life. Bonizo's assertion that he was a monk at Cluny has been defended by G. B. Borino ('Quando e dove si fece monaco Ildebrando', *Miscellanea Giovanni Mercati*, vol. v, Vatican City, 1946). It cannot be disproved; but Bonizo's unsupported testimony is worth very little, quite apart from the confusion of his account; and a passage in the *Register*, Book I, no. 79, 'ob recordationem discipline, qua tempore antecessoris vestri in ecclesia Coloniensi enutriti sumus', clearly implies that he was a monk at Cologne—a view which fits very nicely with Hildebrand's movements in 1047–8. (I owe this suggestion to the late Professor Z. N. Brooke.)

emperor rather than to a local family. In 954 had died Alberic, son of Marozia, who had been herself the daughter, as well as the mistress, of different popes. From Alberic descended the family which held the papacy most frequently between 954 and 1046, known as the Tusculani, because their leader in the late tenth century was the count of Tusculum. Their chief rivals were the Crescentii, whose first leader, John Crescentius, ruled in Rome for a time in the 980s and 990s.

Otto the Great was crowned in 962 by Alberic's son, Pope John XII; but they soon fell out, and after some vicissitudes imperial nominees of tolerable respectability, but no great importance, reigned till 984. By 985 John Crescentius was dominant in Rome; his rule lasted till 996, when Otto III came to Rome and set up his cousin Bruno as Pope Gregory V. But Crescentius soon revolted and set up his own anti-pope; both were savagely treated by Otto in 998, when he had Crescentius hanged and the anti-pope mutilated. Gregory was followed by the famous Gerbert, Sylvester II; but after the death of emperor (1002) and pope (1003) the local nobility resumed its sway. After a Crescentian interlude, the Tusculan family ruled the papacy in the person of Benedict VIII (1012–24); in him they had at last found a pope keen to combine local politics with a show of respectability, and his alliance with the Emperor Henry II kept him securely on the throne; for a time the papacy was an institution of European significance once again. But this happy arrangement did not survive the death of Benedict and Henry. Finally, in Benedict IX (1032–46) the Tusculan house found once again a pope worthy of its origin.

The subjection of the papacy to local faction again reduced its activities to the level of farce. The Tusculan Benedict IX grew weary of his own mismanagement, and it was alleged that he wished to retire and take a wife; so he sold the papacy to John Gratian, who took the name Gregory VI, and evidently had a serious wish to reform it. There was already another pope in the shape of Sylvester III, who had been set up by the Crescentii as a rival to Benedict in faction and folly; and when Benedict repudiated his arrangement with Gregory, there were three popes pontificating simultaneously. At the synod of Sutri, Henry III arranged for the deposition of Gregory who, though the only respectable pope of the three, had bought his way into office and so was clearly guilty of 'simony' (see p. 254). Sylvester was brushed aside; Benedict was removed, though whether with or without the formality of a synod is not quite certain; and the bishop of Bamberg was elected in their place.

It was often noticed in the Middle Ages that the climate of Italy, and especially of Rome, could be very destructive to those unused to Mediterranean heat and malarial swamps. Henry III nominated two Germans as pope in rapid succession; both died within a year of their election. At the end of 1048 Henry nominated his cousin and friend Bishop Bruno of Toul, in Lorraine, and Bruno's arrival and coronation in Rome as Pope Leo IX on 12 February 1049 marked the effective beginning of the papal reform.

The papal reform, whichever way one looks at it, was one of the most dramatic and startling events of the Middle Ages; the sudden emergence of the papacy, reformed, transformed, as a central organization for the direction and improvement of the Church. Many of its sources can be traced. Something has been said of the monastic reform which preceded it and there will be more to say in a later chapter of the intellectual revival which accompanied it; but these do not dim its dramatic quality, any more than listing the causes of the French Revolution abolishes the excitement of the event.

The reformers themselves were an oddly assorted group of men, with divergent ideas and often with divergent motives. But their impact on the contemporary world was that of a group of prophets come to make Europe live up to its spiritual vocation. It took time for this to be apparent, still longer for all the tensions they let loose to be felt; but the main ingredients were already present in the papal Curia before the death of Pope Leo IX. The second half of the eleventh century was in many ways the heroic age of papal history, the time when the medieval papacy was most evidently in touch with the roots of its inspiration. What the reformers achieved was no doubt less dramatic; but it was remarkable enough. Hitherto the papacy had been a venerable institution, the preserver of the tradition of St Peter in the Church, the custodian of his shrine and of an immeasurable treasury of relics. Rome had been a distant goal of pilgrimage, of immense prestige, to those who had lived at a distance; those who lived near had observed rather more of the difference between the Rome of legend and the papacy of present fact, the toy of local faction. The reformers brought the papacy to the notice of the whole of Europe; made an organized government out of it, which, like all effective governments, was respected, disliked, and sometimes obeyed. The reformers' work, however, went deeper than that; and its numerous ramifications appear in almost every chapter of this book.

I have purposely avoided any attempt to sketch the character of the

Church at large in the tenth and early eleventh centuries. Historians of the papal reform have often repeated the rhetoric of contemporaries on the depravities of the clergy of their day. It is doubtless true that the secular clergy, especially those who served the parishes, were ignorant men, with no very lofty standards of life; it may also be true that marriage was a normal practice among them, in spite of the canons forbidding it. But both these generalizations were as true in the late twelfth as in the eleventh century, so far as the documents can inform us—and may have been largely true for centuries to come. The educated secular clergy were probably very few in number; monks were more numerous and, although the reforms of the tenth and eleventh centuries often lacked staying-power in individual monasteries, the monastic ideal was in higher repute than for many centuries before. The assimilation of clergy and laity was an abuse which stirred the reformers' anger. We have seen how the German kings treated clergy as royal officers, and blurred any distinction there might have been between the spiritual and the temporal. No doubt there were objections, on any Christian standard, to a bishop whose life was spent in warfare; though before we become too censorious, let us remember, first, how much effort for the welfare of their flock as well as for their kings many of the great administrator-bishops of tenth- and eleventh-century Germany made; let us remember too that Leo IX himself was a noted warrior as well as a reformer. In many ways we are very ignorant of the state of the Church in 1049; what we do know suggests that it deserves understanding as well as reproach; that it had its ideals, which were in many ways very different from those of the reformers; and yet that the reformers had taken on an immensely formidable task in trying to make it live up to its Christian vocation as they understood it.

In analysing the inspiration of the reformers, one can lay emphasis on their interest in the law; one can deny that they were concerned to reform, and can assert that they were first and foremost policemen, concerned to enforce an already existing law. Or again, they can be seen in a theological context, as men who had a theological vision of how the Church should be run, and were impelled to organize radical change because they were influenced by new theological trends. Finally, one can see them as practical men, with a clear vision of the specific weaknesses and specific needs of the Church of their day. None of these views, by itself, is adequate. In some of the reformers, one or another predominated; all were present to some degree in most; if we wish to give a broad analysis of the principles of the movement, we must give a large place to all three. Let us examine some of the basic principles, and see how they were related to these various springs of inspiration.

All the reformers wished to see the eradication of simony and clerical marriage and incontinence, and the enforcement of the primacy of the Holy See. Simony meant the sale and purchase of offices in the Church, a practice very widespread at this time. It was contrary to canon law, the law of the Church; a formidable collection of authorities could be assembled to condemn it. An office in the Church carried with it the right to administer sacraments; and the theological development of the time was laying special emphasis on the sacraments. The right to administer them carried with it the right to mediate the gift of the Holy Ghost; and so simony was reckoned to involve the sale of the Holy Ghost, a notion so blasphemous that some of the reformers felt that those who engaged in it must be theologically unsound; hence they condemned simony not merely as a sin, but as a heresy. Simony took its name from Simon Magus, who appears from the Acts of the Apostles to have been the first Christian to attempt it. By a misunderstanding of another passage in Acts, the failure to preserve clerical celibacy was sometimes known as Nicolaism, after Nicholas the deacon of Antioch. Marriage had long been forbidden to the clergy by canon law: to mention no earlier enactments, a letter of Pope Leo I had specifically enjoined celibacy on all in subdeacon's orders or above; and this had commonly been accepted as the norm by reformers, and was to be the basis of the reformed canon law on the subject in the late eleventh and twelfth centuries. There were, however, a number of respectable authorities which suggested qualifications to this, and even some which seemed to permit clerical marriage; and the married clergy (unlike the open simonist) had several ingenious and powerful defenders in the early generations of reform. If one had to generalize on the situation before 1049, one could say that the academic tradition of the Church condemned clerical marriage; traditional practice (outside the monasteries) had made it respectable. Theological tides were running against it; the enhanced value set on the sacraments underlined the meaning of ordination, enhanced the sacredness of the person who administered the Eucharist. It was urged that he should be separated for the work, set apart from the entanglements of the world; and almost all medieval reformers inherited from St Jerome the notion that the petticoat was the supreme symbol of the snares of the world.

This separation of clergy from layfolk must of necessity be reflected, in an age so deeply conscious of hierarchy, in one's view of the Church's higher offices; above all of the papacy. The theological trend tended, therefore, to enhance the position of the pope. Even stronger was the legal support for papal supremacy. In practice, the emperors had dominated the papacy, whenever they were near enough to keep watch on the pope's activities, in the late tenth and early eleventh centuries. But the Papal Curia had a tradition, never forgotten for any great length of time, of claiming independence of secular authority: of viewing the emperor as a protector, but only in the sense of a bodyguard; of claiming the ultimate supremacy of spiritual over temporal, of papacy over empire. This issue was not discussed by Henry III and Leo IX; and Leo and several of his supporters would not have thought of exerting their independence, still less their superiority, over him. But even in Leo's time there were signs that the emperor might have raised a rival to his own authority, and voices were heard criticizing what had been done at Sutri. Meanwhile, the creation of the papal monarchy as an effective organ of government was beginning; and was bound in the end to challenge the old order.

Theology and law cannot be too clearly separated in this age and in this field; and they both combined to support a demand for *libertas*, which is a frequent and recurring theme. In medieval usage, *libertas* meant *privilege*, and it was normally used to cover all the special rights and privileges of the different orders of society, or of individual men, of communities, offices and institutions. The *libertas* of the Gorze monasteries meant their privilege of royal favour and patronage; the *libertas* of Cluny meant its freedom from secular entanglement. The papal reformers demanded *libertas* for the Roman Church and for all the Churches and all the clergy: freedom from secular control; independence of action; freedom to pursue a wholly spiritual vocation; in a word, disengagement.

It has commonly been argued by Christian thinkers that if the Church becomes too much concerned with the other world, it loses all contact with this; that the clergy must be worldly or they cannot mingle adequately with their lay parishioners. It seems highly probable that heretical preachers were so widely welcomed in the twelfth century because, after the first flush of the papal reform, its effect was to make the clergy more aloof, the educated segment of the clergy more removed than ever from the layfolk of Christendom. None the less, there is a reverse to this argument. If it is held that the clergy are there to set the laity a standard, to set before them the Christian life in their own lives as well as in the sacraments they perform, it clearly matters that the laity should see some distinction between layman and cleric; that the clergy should not be wholly indistinguishable in manner of life from the laity. No doubt this argument tends to give the rank-and-file clergy of the eleventh century a far more elevated moral function than they commonly performed, or than most men expected them to perform. But in some degree it clearly ran in the reformers' minds.

The human race has never been so savagely denounced as in St Peter Damian's *Book of Gomorrah*, save perhaps in the last book of *Gulliver's Travels*, which it somewhat resembles. An overwhelming sense of sin, and a sense that, under God's providence, the clergy had the vocation to attempt the superhuman task of lifting mankind from the appalling depravity of its ways, inspired Damian, and, in only a slightly less measure, his colleagues. They feared above all assimilation, since they held that if the clergy became wholly assimilated to the world, they would accept the whole gamut of the world's abominable standards. The grip of the world on a man was held to be especially symbolized by the influence of money and of the other sex. There was some humanity, but no chivalry among the reformers. At the high level, simony was part of the machinery by which bishoprics and abbeys had become largely secular offices in many parts of Europe; and if the emperor's treatment of the German Church, and of such parts of the Italian as he could control, had often been free from simony, it led no less to assimilation of the things of the world and of the Church; so that some reformers reckoned all lay interference as wicked as simony itself. At the lower level there was danger of an even more complete assimilation. The high offices of the Church were not hereditary, and it did not suit kings or princes that they should be; the higher clergy were commonly, though not invariably, celibate. Among the lower clergy the growth of the parish church which was also an *Eigenkirche* of the local lord had tended to encourage the growth of a class of clergy who were little different in manner of life from their secular neighbours. The lord of a village built a parish church on his domain; he was its owner; the priest who served it was his vassal, his servant; the lord could do what he liked with priest and altar. The system became exceedingly widespread in the century and a half after the break-up of the Carolingian Empire. These clergy seem (so far as we can tell) quite often to have married and passed their benefices from father to son like any other small vassal holding. Over these clerks the bishops could assert a little control, since they alone could ordain them; but because there were no seminaries or theological colleges and no means of training the ordinary parish clergy, and because many of the bishops were themselves essentially men of the world, there was little chance of new, different or higher standards passing through to the clergy. These factors encouraged the reformers to campaign for the abolition of simony and clerical marriage; and for the enforcement of the supremacy of the Holy See as the instrument for reform. They help to explain why it was these particular aspects of the law on which the reformers laid so much stress, why so much of their research into the authorities for canon law was concerned with these three points.

Such was the programme: I have given a simplified account of it; but it was in fact, like all effective programmes, a simple one. It had to be, because it was difficult enough to get the reformers to agree on anything; indeed, they fought among themselves on the definition of simony, on whether orders conferred by simoniac bishops were authentic and valid; on the influence to be allowed to the emperor in the affairs of the Church. But they agreed in the main on what we have outlined. If we analyse the writings of the reformers (which are quite voluminous) we find that with the exception of Peter Damian the bulk of what they have to say centres on these three things: the eradication of clerical marriage and simony and the establishment of the supremacy of the Holy See.

As bishop of Toul, Leo IX had represented what was best in the old régime: he had managed to combine the role of a noted warrior bishop with that of a distinguished pastor and reformer of clerical abuses. As pope his military adventures continued; but the only serious result was a defeat at the hands of the Normans in south Italy in 1053, which had the ironical result of forcing the papacy to accept the Normans as respectable citizens, and in the long run, as the papacy's best allies. It was for his reforming activities that Leo's pontificate was memorable.

In many directions Leo laid down the paths which his successors were to tread; he was a pioneer, and it is only the first beginnings which can be discerned during his time. In a few ways his activities had decisive effect. Thus he attempted to enforce his authority in Constantinople; his legate Humbert, later cardinal bishop of Silva Candida, was not the most tactful of ambassadors, and gave the patriarch and his associates the idea that Leo was simply trying to rap a tiresome subordinate official over the knuckles. This led to breach of relations between East and West; not, as used to be supposed, a formal schism— yet one may date from 1054 as well as from any other point in the preceding centuries the beginnings of a real division between the Churches.

More positive was the mark left by Leo in the management of the Holy See itself. He began the process of converting it from a local bishopric to the central offices of a world-wide Church. He reorganized the chancery to cope with his greatly increased correspondence; wrote to kings, princes, bishops and lesser fry; interfered as few of his predecessors had done since the time of Gregory the Great. He began the slow process of restoring the papal finances, so that they could supply a revenue commensurate with the needs of the greatest court in Europe. He made the Roman synod, hitherto an intermittent meeting of the bishops of southern Italy and Sicily (the papal province), into a regular institution, more widely representative, an organ for regular discussion; in some respects similar to the Tudor parliament, a place where the monarch could air his views, advertise his intentions, make solemn his proclamations. The Roman synod became an annual event, and was maintained by Leo's successors, when possible, and above all by Gregory VII. After Gregory's death the synod became less frequent, and in the twelfth century its functions were divided: the routine came to be performed by the cardinals in consistory, the occasional solemn pronouncements by the general councils of the Lateran, of Rheims, Tours and elsewhere, summoned by the pope, presided over and receiving their authority from the pope.

Councils were occasionally held north of the Alps in the twelfth century; but this was generally because political events had compelled the pope to leave Rome. A strange tradition tied the medieval papacy to the Holy City—strange, because most monarchs reckoned to rule by constant travelling, by making themselves personally known to their subjects. One of the few popes deliberately to do this was Leo IX himself. He took the papacy on tour. Accompanied by his team of assistants, and by a superb retinue of archbishops, bishops and princes, he toured Europe, preaching reform, denouncing abuses, seeing to all the details of improvement himself. He brought the papacy to the notice of all Europe: he tested its prestige, and found that it was very high. Clearly, like Baal, it had slept and needed waking; equally clearly, it was far from extinct. Nothing, indeed, reveals the atmosphere of the papal reform or explains the basis of its success so lucidly as the well-known story of Leo's council at Rheims in 1049.[1]

It had been arranged that the pope should perform two ceremonies

---

[1] The story is brilliantly told by R. W. Southern, *Making of the Middle Ages*, pp. 125–7; but it must be told again, for the papal reform cannot be understood without it.

while he was at Rheims: translate the bones of St Remigius, or St Rémi, the patron saint of the town, to a new church built in the saint's honour, which he was also to consecrate; and secondly, hold a council for the reform of the French Church. The French king, Henry I, was not interested in reform and distrusted the pope; he refused to come to Rheims, and his example was followed by the bulk of the French bishops and abbots. The attendance at the council was thin and a high proportion of the bishops who were present had no good reputation. They were hardly the material, nor a synod of them the occasion, for inaugurating a great spiritual revival—or so one would have thought. But Leo could count on the enthusiasm of the populace, which was tremendous; and he had a yet stronger weapon in the relics to be translated. The bones of St Remigius were carried round the town amid general rejoicing and the intense veneration normally accorded to relics in general, and to the relics of the local saint in particular; then they were carried into the church. Instead of immediately immuring them in their new resting place, however, Leo ordered them to be laid on the High Altar, and by this dramatic gesture Leo opened the council and ensured its success.

The council lasted three days, and all its proceedings were carried out in the presence of St Remigius. From the outset the initiative lay with the pope and worldly bargaining was given no chance. First of all the papal chancellor (on Leo's behalf) rose and made the seemingly innocent request that all present should declare whether they had paid any money for their offices, that is, had committed simony. Hardly a soul stirred; not only were many of them guilty, but the host himself, the archbishop of Rheims, had been insulted, and by the guest of honour. The archbishop was let off with a caution, and summoned to answer the charge on a later occasion. One of the guilty bishops tried to make a fight of it; but one of his defending counsel was struck dumb in the act of defending him, and he had no resource but to flee, which he did under cover of darkness. Three other guilty bishops were reinstated after confession. The council was brought to a close with a number of rigorous decrees, and Christendom had received a shock from which it was not to be permitted to recover.

Two weapons which Leo possessed still have to be mentioned, perhaps the most important of all: the intellectual revival which ultimately grew into the twelfth-century renaissance, and the circle of his assistants and helpers, the embryo of the future college of cardinals. Leo himself when he came to Rome was bridging the gap between the reformers of Lorraine and the first beginnings of intellectual revival in Italy. He brought with him a group of northerners educated in schools like Liége (which were among the few really flourishing in the north of Europe at the time) and imbued with the spirit of reform; and he met in Italy some of the products of another intellectual revival, as cultivated as that of the north. The development of the papal reform went hand in hand with the intellectual revival. It was to become in due course the papacy's most potent weapon, especially when the revival of law got under way. Legal education accustomed educated clerics all over Europe to a canon law at whose heart lay the principle of papal supremacy. The greatest representative in Leo's day ultimately became the greatest ornament of the Roman Curia and cardinal bishop of Ostia; but Peter Damian did not come to Rome till some years after Leo's death. Peter was a strange man, somewhat akin to St Jerome in his combination of asceticism and a passion for the classics. He was not so much the sensitive egoist as Jerome, nor so great a scholar; he was something like a mixture of Dean Swift and St John of the Cross, fierce and gentle, sardonic and modest all in one. His heroism could quell single-handed a riot in Milan; but by nature he was a hermit, and the greatest mystic of the century.

Leo's most considerable task was the transformation of the Roman Curia from an organ of local government into the central offices of the world-wide Church. Such conversions are not completed all in a minute, and there was probably little external change in his time. We have not to deal with new institutions, but with their tiny seeds sown in old ones. In particular, Leo is credited with the foundation of the college of cardinals; but the change was only just beginning in his brief pontificate. What he did was to inaugurate the policy of summoning able men from distant corners of Europe to assist the pope, and of giving important jobs in the Curia to such new arrivals; clearer signs of the development of the cardinals appear under his successors, when Leo's protégés were the leading figures in the Curia.

Of these, four deserve individual mention. They were all four monks. Frederick of Lorraine, brother of a duke, was chancellor of the Roman See under Leo, abbot of Monte Cassino (St Benedict's own monastery, at this time in close touch with the Roman Curia), and Pope Stephen IX from 1057 to 1058, when he died. Humbert of Silva Candida was also brought south by Leo. He was a man of big ideas, quite a distinguished theologian, a grandiloquent writer; and also a man of great force of character and much practical ability. He acted as Leo's legate—not altogether tactfully—in 1054; played an important part in the secretarial work of the papal chancery; became cardinal bishop of Silva Candida in 1057; was the leading figure in the Curia under Pope Nicholas II (1059–61), and died at the height of his influence in 1061. His great book was an attack on simony, the most extreme statement of the reformers' position. Humbert regarded the holy orders administered by simoniac bishops as invalid; he thought that the Church should be independent in all its operations of the State, and disapproved of Henry III's intervention in papal elections; he may have started the idea, which soon after became common, that the cardinals co-operated with the pope in ruling the Church and in some unspecified way shared his supremacy. Peter Damian thought simoniac orders valid; regarded the co-operation of Church and State as normal and inevitable and Henry III's intervention proper; he described the cardinals as the Senate of the Roman Church; he was almost as learned as Humbert in the sources of canon law; but he was not fundamentally interested in constitutional theory. Hildebrand's views before he became pope are very imperfectly known: as pope he took Damian's position on simoniac orders, Humbert's position on the relations of Church and State, and he reckoned that the papacy was an autocracy, that the pope could act entirely on his own initiative. We can see that with a group of powerful personalities of this kind in control of affairs the Curia must have been an exciting and difficult place; there is no doubt that they often disagreed among themselves. But they made a powerful nucleus for the reform of the Church.

The pope's immediate subordinates had two special functions, of great importance to the reformed papacy: they acted as his legates, as his representatives or ambassadors, and when he died they took the initiative in electing his successor. The vision of an itinerant pope, who visited every corner of his ecclesiastical dominions, was rarely seen after the death of Leo IX. His successors usually kept in touch with distant lands by letter, by embassy and above all by sending legates. The legate derived his authority from the pope, in whose name he acted; but his work was only likely to be effective if he himself was a man to be reckoned with. Pope Nicholas I in the ninth century had found himself pitifully hamstrung in his grand designs because his messengers were weak men without prestige, who could be bullied or bought. It was the singular strength of the reformed papacy in its early days that it could send men like Peter Damian and Hildebrand. The frequent sending of messengers kept Rome in touch; and it meant that the best men in the

Curia could be used for foreign service and yet not lost to the Curia. It was soon realized, however, that for steady and constant pressure for reform and for imposing the apostolic will a permanent, a standing legate was a more powerful weapon. From Gregory VII's time the principle was to use a standing legate when a suitable one was available, and to send legates from Rome from time to time where no standing legate could be found. Gregory's most eminent standing legate was Hugh of Die, to whom he gave the senior archbishopric of France,[1] that of Lyons. Hugh was a strong reformer, though a somewhat autocratic and unpopular person; he proved a very faithful and useful servant of the Holy See.

In the early Church a bishop was elected 'by clergy and people', and it was many centuries before this phrase became more precisely defined. The canon lawyers of the eleventh and twelfth centuries redefined the process by saying that a bishop should be elected by the clergy of his cathedral chapter; that the 'people' had only the function of hearing who had been elected, and applauding the divinely inspired selection. In a similar way, the election decrees of 1059 and 1179 confined the election of the pope to the college of cardinals; that of 1179 made a man pope who had secured two-thirds of the votes of the cardinals. Both developments represented a major innovation. In the election of bishops the normal process had been for the local representative of the people, who was taken to be the king or secular prince in control of the bishopric, to nominate, and for the clergy of the diocese, often represented by the leading members of the chapter, to accept and to confirm. In Rome there had been a running dispute between the emperors and the Roman nobles as to which should be considered the effective nominators; the Roman clergy, in most cases, simply confirmed the election of whoever was presented to them. The Roman nobles, being on the spot, had more often affected the election than the emperor; but when the emperor took a personal interest in the election, his will generally overrode local intrigue. Thus Otto I had nominated Leo VIII and John XIII; Otto III, Gregory V and Sylvester II; and Henry III nominated four popes in succession. But the regency after his death was too weak to sustain his policies in Italy; and the position of the reformers became precarious. The next pope was one of their number, Stephen IX (1057–8); but his death was followed by schism. The Roman nobles set up

---

[1] Strictly, Lyons was not in France at this time, but its claim to primacy stretched over all 'Gaul', and Hugh of Die's jurisdiction as legate likewise extended over France.

Benedict X; the reformers Nicholas II; by great good fortune Stephen IX's brother Godfrey of Lorraine was in control of much of northern Italy at the time; he came to the reformers' aid, and established Nicholas in Rome in January 1059. In the same year, under the inspiration of Cardinal Humbert, the first election decree was passed.

The election decree of 1059 placed the initiative in the hands of the cardinal bishops; gave the cardinals and the Roman clergy at large the right to elect; made no mention of the Roman nobles; gave the emperor the right merely to be informed of the election. Needless to say, it was not immediately acceptable to the secular powers. The Roman nobles fought against it, but were in the end reduced to using their powers of influence among the clergy; the emperors put a forged version into circulation which much enhanced their importance. In the end neither succeeded, but the struggle was still going on when our period ended.

The initiative lay with the cardinal bishops; but the other cardinals gave their voices next, and the custom rapidly grew up of excluding the rest of the Roman clergy from anything but formal acclamation. To this extent the decree of 1179 only confirmed existing practice; in making precise the majority principle in the election, it innovated. Thus the period between 1059 and 1179 had seen a steady development in the self-consciousness of the body of cardinals. It is premature as yet to call them a 'college'; they had not yet received their special costume; it could still be argued that a cardinal priest or a cardinal deacon was inferior in status to any bishop. But the cardinals were becoming in a variety of ways the papal chapter, and the Senate of the Catholic Church.

Who were the cardinals? They owe their strange title and status to the curious fact that the pope has no cathedral. As bishop of Rome the Basilica of St John Lateran is his cathedral; as pope, if he has one at all, it is an amalgamation of the five major basilican churches (the Lateran, St Peter's, St Paul's without the walls, San Lorenzo and Sta Maria Maggiore) and the 'titular churches', the original parish churches of Rome, built for the most part on the sites of houses in which Roman Christians worshipped in secret when Christianity was a proscribed religion. As the centuries passed a curious anomaly appeared. The titular churches had parish priests; the basilicas had only one, the pope himself. The papal staff consisted of seven deacons, lesser fry apart. In order to provide the pope with an adequate staff of subordinate clergy, it was decided to make the priests of the titular churches officiate in the basilicas as well. This contradicted a fundamental principle of early canon law, that a man could only serve one church. The same principle applied, in a more rigid form, to a diocese: a priest or bishop ordained in one diocese could not be translated to another. But it often happened —for instance, when a new diocese was established in the mission field —that this had to be done. To overcome the difficulty, the process of incardination was devised: a priest was temporarily attached to two dioceses; he became, as it were, a hinge between the two, or, more precisely, was incorporated as into a mortice joint, for the Latin *cardo* means both hinge and mortice. In a similar way, the Roman titular priests, and a group of seven local bishops, were incardinated into the Roman basilicas, and so became mortice-like or hinge-like, *cardinales*. For centuries their functions were wholly or primarily liturgical, although it happened from time to time, especially in the late tenth and early eleventh centuries, that a leading office in the Curia might be given to a cardinal bishop. It was only after the papal reform, however, that the idea arose of using these established offices to provide dignity and a livelihood to the new circle of the pope's advisers; and in this way the political importance of the cardinals began. By the eleventh century the original meaning of *cardinalis* had been forgotten; analogy with other uses of the adjective had suggested that it implied the notion of a turning-point or, more generally, of importance; following in the footsteps of the cardinal winds and the cardinal virtues, the cardinal bishops and priests were not unnaturally tempted to regard themselves as bishops and priests of a special eminence; and priests and even archdeacons in cathedral chapters up and down Europe imitated their greatness, so that the word cardinal came to be widely used. But as the Roman cardinals grew in self-esteem, they regarded their titles more jealously; and in due course the popes were compelled to suppress all rival cardinals.[1]

This was a period when the offices of the Church multiplied and crystallized. Just as the college of cardinals grew out of established offices, so the changes in other institutions at this time were usually a natural development from existing seeds, fertilized by the movement for ecclesiastical revival and reform. In many parts of Europe bishops had been assisted by archdeacons and archpriests in the administration of their sees; and the diverse organization of cathedral chapters in different parts of Europe was the product of a long historical growth. The functions of archdeacons became crystallized in the eleventh and

---

[1] This is based on S. Kuttner, 'Cardinalis: the History of a Canonical Concept', *Traditio*, vol. III (1945), pp. 129–214.

twelfth centuries, as did the dignity and revenues of deans, provosts and canons of cathedrals. Only in England does one see a self-conscious revolution, with the implanting of French institutions on English soil by the first generations of Norman bishops. By and large the diocese divided into archdeaconries, and the cathedral chapter, led by dean, precentor and other officials, peopled by canons who derived independent incomes from their 'prebends', were the work of the Norman bishops, led by St Osmund of Salisbury. When the archdeaconries were divided into rural deaneries is not precisely clear; but by the middle of the twelfth century the pattern was probably complete, and the English dioceses, like those over most of western Europe, were ruled, as Trollope observed of Barchester, either by the bishop or by the archdeacon.

No doubt when Alexander II was pope and Hildebrand archdeacon, the see of Rome was ruled by both combined. Hildebrand held the anomalous office, soon to disappear, of 'cardinal archdeacon'. At this time, however, the other deacons were not called cardinal. The seven deacons of Rome were the pope's original staff; they had never served elsewhere and so never acquired the title cardinal. In the mid and late eleventh century they began to feel that they were losing cast. If they had known more of the early history of their office, they might well have felt like the elder brother of the prodigal son. In due course they too assumed the title cardinal; and so by the early twelfth century the chapter of cardinals became a distinct body of men, with seven bishops, twenty-eight priests and eighteen deacons—or at least, with that as a potential maximum, because it often happened that the total fell below, sometimes much below, that figure. But the significance of this, and the fluctuations in the college's numbers, belong to the history of a later age. In our period the cardinals came to expect that they should elect the pope and that he should consult them, in formal consistory, on matters of importance; most of the popes accepted this view, the most notable exception being Gregory VII.

And to Gregory, or rather to Hildebrand, we must now turn; for there are few aspects of Leo IX's work so significant as his employment of the young Hildebrand, and the institutions of the papacy in the eleventh century are of secondary importance beside the two towering figures of the papal reform, Leo IX and Gregory VII. Of the two, perhaps unjustly, Gregory is the more famous. He is certainly the more difficult to estimate; the most exciting, the most disputed figure of the century. Of Roman family and a chaplain to Pope Gregory VI, he accompanied his old master north of the Alps when Gregory VI had been deposed by the synod of Sutri, and subsequently became a monk, probably at Cologne. His existence somehow came to the notice of Leo IX, who took him back to Rome when he became pope in 1049. In 1059 he became archdeacon, a post which seems to have involved him in administration and politics; and from then on he was certainly one of the leading figures in the Curia. It used to be said that Hildebrand was the power behind the throne for years before he actually became pope, and there is no doubt that he was an influential figure, perhaps the most influential figure after the death of Cardinal Humbert in 1061, and a leading legate and administrator. But Hildebrand was too forceful and too individual a character ever to be exactly a power behind the scenes; and his later criticisms of some of the acts of Alexander II (1061–73) show that he had not himself been sole director of affairs. When Hildebrand became pope there was little evidence of new policies; the emphasis on papal power as the instrument of ecclesiastical reform was the same as ever, the attack on simony and clerical marriage carried on. The programme was the same, but there was a new tempo, a new bustle about affairs, a more vivid and electric inspiration behind the activities of the Holy See. His enemies said the pope was possessed by a demon; and Gregory's friend Peter Damian, who was fascinated by the force and magnetic compulsion of the man, described him as 'my holy Satan'.

Gregory was a Roman born. It will be disputed till the end of time who his earthly parents were; but there can be little doubt that his spiritual father was St Peter. Under the great apostle's protection he had been brought up, and as pope he felt himself to be, in a deep and personal way, St Peter's vicar, even St Peter himself acting in the world. This gave him an overwhelming sense of responsibility and authority: his authority was Peter's, his model, not the apostle who fled from his Master's trial, but the prophets of the Old Testament who rebuked kings to their face, and whom God justified by visible acts of power; above all, Elijah. So sure was he of the end to be attained, and that God was on his side, that he could be violently overbearing in expressing his authority, and remarkably careless about the means he employed. Thus in the end he drove the majority of his cardinals into opposition, and caused fearful suffering in Germany and Italy by preaching Holy War against his Christian opponents. It is right that he should be a disputed figure: there is much evidence, overwhelming evidence, of his single-mindedness, of his faith; there is much evidence too that he constantly associated his own opinions and interests—if it is possible to distinguish his interests from those of his see—with God's will, and rode roughshod over difficulties and over other men's sufferings. The eleventh century could hardly claim to be the papacy's heroic age without him; it was well, however, for Christendom, and for the papacy itself, that he did not altogether succeed. These are value judgements; but it would be cynical for a historian to ignore that great issues were involved in Gregory's life and work.

St Ignatius Loyola was a soldier before he was a churchman: in Gregory the roles seem almost to be reversed—he was a man of God turned soldier; but his soldiering always remained a matter for his dreams. He was intelligent and well informed, though not widely read or academically inclined. He knew his canon law, he knew well some passages of the early fathers; above all, his letters are full of quotations from the Bible, and more from the Old Testament than the New. The words of the prophets were always on his lips. Contemporaries compared him with Elijah and the comparison was singularly apt: a major prophet, but a very militant one. His favourite quotation was from Jeremiah: 'Cursed be he who keepeth back his sword from blood'—'Maledictus homo qui prohibet gladium suum a sanguine.' It is true that he regularly went on to draw out Gregory the Great's interpretation: 'That is, who keepeth back the word of admonition from attacking the worldly'; but the military nature of the metaphor evidently appealed to him. His letters are full of military metaphors; and also of the fury and exaltation of enthusiasm: he is impatient and imperious, but very human; human in his intense friendships, and human in his fits of despondency, when he despairs of himself and of his superhuman task. Like Elijah on Mount Horeb, he cries: 'There is not a righteous man left'; and on his death-bed, when he seemed utterly to have failed, and when many of his friends and associates had deserted him: 'I have loved righteousness and hated iniquity, and therefore I die in exile.'

Righteousness, justice, *iustitia*, was a key word in Gregory's vocabulary. He wished to see justice done to every man; and sometimes he extended it to give it the full flavour of its Hebrew and Christian inheritance, and revealed his longing to see established the righteousness of the divine order on earth. There was nothing new in these ideas, but Gregory gave them a force of his own. His letters were addressed to all the countries of Europe, especially to France and Germany. He wrote to France as to a country already converted, as if the work set in motion by Leo IX's councils had borne fruit: there was little mention of simony and clerical marriage; the letters were full of the details of reform and administration and legal decisions. In his letters to Germany, however, he made it clear that everything was still to do; they spoke more of principles and fundamentals, of simony and clerical marriage, and less of concrete details over which Gregory could not as yet hope to exercise control. They also spoke, with growing fire and insistence, of the shortcomings of King Henry IV and his advisers.

XIII

The Papal Conflicts

Gregory VII and Henry IV: The issues

At the turn of 1075 and 1076 tension between Gregory VII and Henry IV was transformed into open war; and empire and papacy were not at peace with one another until Gregory had been dead thirty-seven years and Henry sixteen. After Henry's death lay investiture rapidly became the main point of open dispute; and it is a remarkable coincidence that the first stringent papal decree against it had been promulgated in precisely the year, 1075, when irreconcilable conflict first broke out. And so the conflicts of these years, together with those in England and elsewhere, have commonly been given the label 'investiture contests'. The issues were always both wider and deeper, however, than investiture, especially between the original contestants.

The great conflict inspired a no less remarkable pamphlet war, and from it we can discover with some precision the intellectual roots of the dispute. These pamphlets show us how wide a divergence of views was held on the relations of secular and spiritual power, of *regnum* and *sacerdotium*, of Church and State. Any notion that medieval thought was homogeneous, or mental horizons narrow is rapidly dispelled by the most superficial acquaintance with the massive volumes of the *Libelli de lite* in the German *Monumenta*. Yet even so, the range of opinion is not fully disclosed. There are eloquent defences of a variety of lay views as well as those of the pope and his adherents; but the lay views are generally rationalized by ingenious clerical minds. The strength of conservative lay opinion, which the pope had outraged, is indeed particularly difficult to recover. But a brief analysis of the outlook of some of the anti-imperial writers will do something towards uncovering it, hidden in the writers' presuppositions and prejudices. In the late eleventh century, then, opinions on the relations between the two powers were especially diverse; as the intellectual revival matured, this

BIBLIOGRAPHY: see Chapter XII, p. 237.

variety tended to be subdued. Theoretical acceptance of papal headship became more widespread; the more fanciful and eccentric anti-papal theories were dropped, or went underground. The excitement of eleventh-century controversy was not revived before the days of Dante and Marsilio of Padua at the turn of the thirteenth and fourteenth centuries. But at the level of practice and prejudice the controversy never died.

The papal position was, intellectually, the more coherent and firmly established, although it would be wrong to assume that it was coherently or uniformly understood and interpreted by all its defenders. In spite of all the vicissitudes of time it was firmly based on what Leo the Great and Gelasius I had said in the fifth century, as it had been interpreted by a succession of popes in the interval. All authority on earth comes from God, and is mediated by the activity in the world of what St Augustine had called the Heavenly City—that is, God's activity in the minds and hearts of men as well as in earthly institutions; but especially, in the view of most medieval writers, in the Church. The Christian commonwealth is one, under one head, Christ. But on earth it sub-serves two rather different ends: man's spiritual end, his eternal life, and his earthly, mortal, temporal life; in crude terms often misunder-stood, his soul and his body. To these two ends, in practice, by divine dispensation, correspond two systems of authority. Temporal authority, granted to lay princes, kings, and emperors, is exercised over men's bodies; its business is to protect and foster their earthly lives, their temporal wellbeing. Spiritual authority is mediated through the bishops and the clergy at large, whose business it is to see to the spiritual well-being of man. But since man's spiritual end (so the argument ran) is of more moment than his temporal and temporary existence in the world, the clergy perform a higher function than the laity; where their spheres overlap, where above all they come into conflict, the spiritual authority must take precedence.

The special position of the papacy had many historical roots. Rome was the ancient, traditional hub of civilization in the western world; it contained the tombs of more early martyrs than any other city; it was the goal of countless pilgrims. But its special position, in its own theory, depended on three things. The pope was the successor of St Peter, inheritor of all the rights which Christ had granted to Peter. In strict theory the pope received these rights as Peter's successor, direct from Christ; and as Peter had been prince of the apostles, the source of the other apostles' authority, the authority of other bishops was derived from the supreme authority of the pope. A saying of Leo the Great, somewhat modified by the author of the Pseudo-Isidorian Decretals in the ninth century, declared that other bishops have pastoral care attributed to them, the papacy alone has plenitude of power: strong words, however their meaning might be disputed. In practice the pope claimed to act not so much as Peter's successor, but as his representative, his *alter ego*; to act as if with Peter's own hands and voice, and with the voice of all his successors. For Rome, it was claimed, had never deviated from the faith: the pope was the arbiter in matters of faith and doctrine, and the supreme judge of appeal in all spiritual matters in Christendom, the fount of justice and law.

It had been generally held, not only by the popes, that all authority came from Christ. Priests and bishops were 'vicars of Christ'; kings and emperors, in a different way, were also 'vicars of Christ'. But these types of authority, though distinguished often enough in practice, had never been seen as wholly distinct. In the Book of Genesis men read about Melchizedek, priest and king, of Salem; and Melchizedek was taken to be a type of Christ, his authority the same as that which Christ delegated to earthly rulers, spiritual and secular. Thus Charlemagne, like some of the earthly rulers who followed and imitated him, was referred to as '*rex et sacerdos*', 'king and priest'. This notion was firmly repudiated by the papacy. In the long run the popes themselves appropriated these titles and claims. From the mid twelfth century popes were occasionally referred to, and occasionally referred to themselves, as vicars of Christ. The title, and the relationship to Melchizedek, were a favourite part of the mental furniture of Pope Innocent III (1198–1216). Their precise significance has been much disputed. Theoretically, it would seem that Innocent claimed that all authority was mediated from Christ through the pope; but he did not regard this mediation as adding to his practical authority. He was called to spiritual government, kings to temporal.

There were, however, numerous situations in which Innocent III, like the eleventh-century popes, felt bound to intervene in temporal affairs. They reckoned that it was their right and duty to intervene where moral issues were involved, that is to say, where temporal and spiritual jurisdiction overlapped; and as popes they exercised certain kinds of temporal rule. They were lords of the papal patrimony, the states in central Italy which tradition, and imperial grant, had given them. Some European kingdoms, especially those lying on the fringes, acknowledged papal overlordship; a pope like Gregory VII delighted to receive these royal homages, though in the main they had little significance. The pope and cardinals anointed and crowned the emperor. This did not give them the right to choose emperors; but it was almost inevitable that they should claim, if disputes arose, the right to vet the candidate presented to them. But it was when they reckoned that moral issues were involved that the medieval popes most frequently intervened, *ratione peccati*, on ground of sin, in temporal affairs.

Ancient chronicles and canonical authorities could produce plenty of precedent for papal intervention in the affairs of kings, and for ecclesiastical denunciation of the moral offences of rulers. Gregory VII had a collection of such authorities made; and the famous *Dictatus pape* (the 'pope's memo') which he had entered in his *Register* in 1075, was almost certainly an index of this collection. Here are a few of its items: 'That the Roman church was founded by the Lord alone; That the Roman pontiff alone is called by right universal; That he alone can depose or reconcile bishops; . . . That it is lawful for him to depose emperors; . . . That he can absolve from their fealty the subjects of wicked rulers.' Gregory made no claim to intervene in the normal operations of secular government; most popes, and most of Gregory's supporters, regarded such intervention as extremely abnormal. But in the fury of his exaltation Gregory tended to lose sight of these rather subtle distinctions; and in the loftiest statements of his claims, his letter to Bishop Herman of Metz in 1081 justifying the deposition of Henry IV, he pointed out that a pope had 'deposed a king of the Franks not so much for his wickedness as because he was not suitable (*utilis*, useful) for such lofty power, and set Pippin, the father of the Emperor Charlemagne, in his place and absolved the Franks from the oath of fidelity which they had made to him'. The history is somewhat tendentious; the principle is not strictly incompatible with normal papal doctrine of the time; but *utilitas* is capable of very wide interpretation.

The papal view had coherence and a long and respectable tradition behind it. The anti-papal view, or rather views, were supported by a conservative fervour and a knowledge of precedent in which history genuine and false was mixed in about the same proportions as in the papal argument. It was indeed true that Charlemagne had regulated the affairs of the Church, sat in judgement on a pope, and even resolved doctrinal issues; nor could it be hidden from Henry IV that his father had deposed three popes and appointed three more; whatever formalities had been observed, it was common knowledge that this in fact had happened, less than a generation before Gregory claimed, in his turn, to depose Henry III's son and successor. The imperial crown was a lofty symbol of temporal authority, made purposely high so that a cloth mitre, symbol of ecclesiastical authority, could be worn beneath it. The traditional respect due to kings, and a powerful awareness of how much the alliance of kings and bishops meant for good order, government and peace in the precarious politics of Christendom, inclined most men of goodwill throughout the eleventh and twelfth centuries to advocate moderate courses. When the pope was in conflict with a king, it was rare for the king's subjects to be entirely united in their king's support, but he could always rely on a substantial measure of obedience; it was equally rare for the cardinals to be united in support of papal policy—though no pope before the fourteenth century alienated his followers so effectively as the autocratic Gregory VII.

On top of this passionate conservatism, deeply felt and, in an age devoted to custom and tradition, securely based, various clever men built a superstructure of theory. Their theories were naturally diverse; three examples will give some impression of their different methods. The Italian Bishop Benzo of Alba addressed a long poem to Henry IV, in which he revived the *Renovatio imperii Romanorum* of Otto III with all the brilliance made possible by eleventh-century humanism. The unity of the Roman world, of Christendom, centres in the emperor, the successor of the Caesars. A dazzling vision of Roman greatness is presented to us, in which statesmen of ancient Rome, Charlemagne and others form the background and support to the empire of Henry III and Henry IV; and Hildebrand and his accomplices are treated with a ferocious scurrility scarcely imaginable outside the young and untamed satire of the eleventh century and the violence engendered by the contest of Henry and Gregory. No doubt Benzo's vision was in its way as absurd as his invective; and yet both are intelligible in an Italian of this age. For men like Benzo were intensely aware of the Roman past; they lived in its ruins; it breathed down their necks; they were brought up to believe that Otto III and Henry III had truly revived it; and they saw Hildebrand as the latest factious, degenerate Roman bent on the destruction of the true Rome. Nor was Hildebrand the only pope to discover that a prophet may be without honour in his own land. The Italians were too close to the popes to regard them as venerable and remote; the proverb 'familiarity breeds contempt' was already current.

Very different, yet equally brilliant and equally fantastical were the arguments developed by the Norman Anonymous of the turn of the eleventh and twelfth centuries, who used to be known as the 'Anonymous of York'. These are the private speculations of an extremely clever Norman cleric who applied the new dialectic of Lanfranc and Anselm to disproving all the propositions of the papal reform; above all, to defending, and inflating, the sacred nature of kingship. The Anonymous wrote in the interest of the Anglo-Norman kings, and so the vision of Rome which lies at the heart of Benzo's satire is absent; his emphasis is all on kingship. The rite of anointing and coronation symbolizes the divine gift of kingly power, which sets kings above priests as Christ's vicars. The king is Christ's *figura et imago*.

Benzo and the Anonymous answered the papal claim, in effect, by ignoring it. To Benzo Rome is the centre of earthly authority; to the Anonymous, it is the king, whose power, derived directly from Christ, sets him above all ecclesiastical potentates. There was a third way in which the problem of papal power might be tackled—a way more in accord with the practice of earlier centuries, and which was to become in the end the normal doctrine of more recent times. This was the notion that the two powers were equal and separate. It is a remarkable witness of the power of the notion that Christendom was a single commonwealth that this conception was very slow to take firm root among the theorists of the eleventh century. It appears in effect twice only, in radical form, in the surviving literature. It is fully developed in the *Liber de unitate ecclesie conservanda*, written in support of Henry IV at the end of the eleventh century, and it is adumbrated in the letters in which Henry or one of his chaplains blew the embers of the contest into full flame in January 1076.

1073–7: the road to Canossa

By 1073 the first two phases of the reign of Henry IV were over: the minority, which had given the German nobles a taste of independence and a liking for intrigue, and the first seven years of personal rule, which had shown them that Henry was determined to be every inch a king, taught them to dislike his ingenious schemes for strengthening royal power and tightening royal control, and to fear his brittle, mercurial temper. In 1073 the honeymoon of his reign was at an end: the Saxons came out in revolt and Gregory VII ascended the papal throne.

Even before Gregory's accession, the first breach between pope and emperor had taken place, and the cause of it, significantly enough, was trouble in Milan. The seat of the leading archbishopric of northern

Italy, with its long tradition of grandeur and independence, was of special consequence to an emperor trying to assert his power in the Lombard plain, and equally so to a pope trying to assert his primacy. The growing wealth of the Italian cities led not unnaturally to social tensions (see pp. 115 ff.). The leading clergy of Milan were scions of the local noble families; they were also addicted to simony and marriage, which seemed to them the dignified customs of their ancestors, to the papal reformers scandal and sin. Henry III had appointed a member of the lesser nobility as archbishop, in the hope of keeping the various factions in balance; but this he notably failed to do. At the moment of Henry's death serious trouble was on the way. The *popolani*, merchants and artisans, led by two nobles, Landulf and Ariald, agitated for the reform of the clergy. No one can say where religious fervour ended and social and political jealousy began: the 'rag-pickers', the *Patarini*, as their enemies called them, had a mob at their command; but they were skilfully and intelligently led, and they won the alliance of Anselm of Lucca (the future Pope Alexander II), and were supported from time to time by the most powerful legates Rome could send, Peter Damian and Hildebrand. In 1059 Anselm of Lucca and Peter Damian put down simony and clerical marriage with a strong hand, and faced without flinching a riotous mob raised by the nobles and the ladies of Milan. But the struggle continued. Landulf died; Ariald was murdered; the *Patarini* found a new leader in Landulf's brother Erlembald, and Anselm, meanwhile, had ascended the papal throne. In 1071 the archbishop of Milan died. His chosen successor was promptly invested with staff and ring by the young Henry IV, anxious to assert his rights; and a rival candidate put up by Erlembald was declared the rightful archbishop in a Roman synod.

These events took place in 1071 and 1072. Early in 1073 the pope excommunicated five of the counsellors of Henry IV. To blame a king's wicked counsellors was a conventional way of putting pressure on him; though one may doubt whether Henry, in his early twenties, relished the implication that he was not responsible for his actions. The Saxon revolt brought the dispute to an end. Soon after Gregory's accession Henry wrote to him acknowledging his errors, and submitting in the matter of the archbishopric of Milan. Gregory was never a good judge of men, and he was captivated by Henry's charm, even at a distance. He dreamed of an alliance similar to that of Leo IX and Henry III; he planned to lead in person a great crusade to recover Jerusalem; he even suggested to Henry that he should manage the affairs of Christendom while the pope was absent in the East. But at the end of 1075 all these dreams were shattered.

Battle was joined once again over the affairs of Milan. In Milan were united two of the major issues between Henry and Gregory: the delicate political balance in Italy, and the problem, always peculiarly vital both to the papal reformers and the German kings, of episcopal appointments. Probably by misadventure the issue of appointments was exacerbated in 1075; for at the Lenten synod Gregory had promulgated his first decree against 'lay investiture'. The practice of lay intervention in the election of bishops and abbots had been strenuously attacked by earlier councils. This was the first time that a pope had specifically condemned the outward and visible sign of royal intervention in these appointments: the practice which had grown up in recent centuries whereby a king handed to a newly appointed bishop his ring and pastoral staff as a symbol that he was giving him the bishopric. This is the practice which we know as lay investiture. Its significance was much disputed at the time; it was even claimed that the king did no more than grant the temporal authority and properties of the see or abbey by this act. But since the ring was the symbol of episcopal ordination and the staff of the bishop's pastoral care, the ceremony was bound to be offensive to the reformers; and a dispute about such symbols was bound to be a matter of extreme delicacy for lay and spiritual powers alike. In 1075 the decree against lay investiture was a minor irritant; by the end of the century it had become the centre of the whole dispute.

Gregory foresaw that this decree would not be welcome, and hesitated to make it public until he had sounded Henry's reaction. As often happened, the slow passage of news from southern to northern Europe added to the confusion which ensued. For the political situation was radically altered in the summer of 1075. Henry saw that victory over the Saxon rebels was near; he no longer felt so dependent on papal goodwill. Erlembald, by an unlucky accident, was killed in a riot at much the same time, and the old nobility reasserted its power in the Milanese Church. Henry was offered another new archbishop; the temptation was too strong, and he sent an embassy to give this new candidate investiture. Henry, that is, lent his authority to schism in Milan in as offensive a manner as could be devised, and it was clear that he was planning forcible intervention in Italian politics as soon as Saxony was finally quelled. In October the Saxon rebels submitted. In December Gregory denounced Henry's adventures in Milan and threatened him with excommunication.

Henry was not without allies within the ranks of the clergy. Some of the German bishops took obedience to the king for granted; some took almost equally seriously their allegiance to the pope. But the leaders of the German Church, Siegfried of Mainz and Liemar of Bremen, men brought up to admire the system of Henry III and Leo IX, were happy with neither of the protagonists. As far back as 1065 a royal chaplain called Herman had become bishop of Bamberg by blatant simony. Henry III would never have consented to such an arrangement, while Henry IV at no period of his life could seriously comprehend the feelings it aroused. In 1074 papal legates had come to Germany to deal with Herman and the Saxon revolt, and a complex situation ensued. The king needed Herman's troops for his Saxon campaign; Liemar regarded Herman as beyond the pale and refused to use chrism and holy oil consecrated by him; but Liemar and Siegfried were equally suspicious of the papal legates, and refused to summon a synod in which they rightly suspected the legates intended to proceed to the reform of the German Church. That was a matter which lay near Liemar's heart; but it was not to be conducted by upstart Romans. So Herman escaped deposition.

The Bamberg affair was settled by the canons of Bamberg cathedral, who finally rebelled against Herman, and compelled the king to be rid of him. Their rebellion coincided with the crisis of the Saxon war, and Henry and the archbishops eventually concluded that papal support was more valuable than Herman's vassals. And so they made a show of submission. But neither Henry nor the leading German clergy felt any affection for the person of Gregory.

The depth of their feelings, and the paradoxes of their situation, were revealed in the vicissitudes of 1076. On 24 January a number of German bishops met at Worms and declared Gregory deposed. With tortuous rhetoric Henry, or one of his chaplains, opened his mind to the pope.

Our Lord Jesus Christ called us to royal power; but called you *not* to priesthood. By these steps you climbed: by guile, a thing abominable to the monastic profession, you won money, by money favour, by favour the power of the sword, and by the sword you came to the throne of peace. From peace's throne you have destroyed peace: you have armed subjects against their rulers, have taught (yourself uncalled) that our bishops (called by God) are to be despised; you have set laymen over priests. . . . Me too, anointed to kingly power, although unworthy, among the Lord's anointed, you have touched—

me whom the tradition of the holy fathers has taught am to be judged by God alone, and cannot be deposed for any crime, save only heresy. . . . The true pope St Peter cries out: 'Fear God, honour the king'; but you, who fear not God, do me, whom he has set up, dishonour. . . . By judgement of all our bishops and of ourself you are condemned: come down, depart from the papal seat which you have claimed. Let another sit upon St Peter's throne, one who will not cloak violence with a pretence of religion, but will teach the pure doctrine of St Peter. I, Henry, by God's grace king, with all our bishops say to you: come down, come down![1]

And in like vein Henry wrote to the bishops not present at Worms to summon them to another synod to confirm the sentence; in this letter he made explicit his claim, as king, to be wholly exempt from the jurisdiction and authority of a true pope, let alone of the usurper Hildebrand. Henry's sentence was confirmed by the bishops of Lombardy. But the second German synod never met.

Henry's letter was delivered to Gregory at the Lenten Synod in Rome; and the pope lost no time in answering the challenge. In solemn mood he addressed the living master of the Roman see.

Blessed Peter, prince of the apostles, . . . hear your servant, we beseech you, whom you have tended from his childhood, and freed till today from the hand of wicked men, who hated and hate me for my faithfulness to you. You are my witness, and my Lady the mother of God, and Blessed Paul your brother, among all the saints, that your holy Roman Church dragged me unwillingly to its government; that I had no thought to climb your throne as a robber, and would rather have ended my days as a pilgrim [i.e. as a monk] than seize your place with worldly cunning for earthly glory. I believe that it is of your grace, not by my deeds, that it has pleased you, and still pleases you that the Christian folk specially committed to your care should obey me, acting on your behalf. And it is of your favour that I have the power, given you by God, of binding and loosing in Heaven and on earth. Trusting in this faith, for the honour and defence of your Church, on behalf of God almighty, Father, Son and Holy Ghost, by your power and authority, I take from King Henry, son of the Emperor Henry, who has risen against your Church with pride unheard of, the government of the whole kingdom of the Germans

---

[1] Henry IV's letter 12 (ed. C. Erdmann, *Die Briefe Heinrichs IV, Monumenta Germaniae Historica*, Leipzig, 1937: my own translation).

and the Italians, and I free all Christian people from any oath they have made or shall make to him, and I forbid any to serve him as king. Let him who tries to lessen the honour of your Church himself lose the honour which he seems to have. As a Christian he has yet spurned to obey and has not returned to God, whom he has set on one side by intercourse with excommunicates and by despising the warnings I sent him for his good, as you are witness, and by attempting to rend your Church . . .; and so on your behalf I bind him with the chain of anathema, and I bind him thus out of the faith I have in you, that the nations may know and acknowledge that you are Peter and on your rock the Son of the living God has built his Church and the gates of Hell shall not prevail against it.[1]

With the gates of Hell clanging about their ears, the German bishops began to have second thoughts. Many of the German princes seized with delight the chance to undo Henry's too decisive victory in the previous year. The southern dukes allied with the Saxon counts, who were released from prison with the collusion of some of Henry's enemies and Gregory's supporters. The leading bishops hastened to cross the Alps to ask for pardon, some inspired by the politics of the German rebels, some by genuine concern at Gregory's thunders, some by both. The German princes delighted to find rebellion so unexpectedly hallowed, and in the autumn had the pleasure of sitting in judgement on Henry at the diet of Tribur. They declared that Henry would be deposed if he did not receive absolution by 22 February 1077, the anniversary of the sentence against him; they invited the pope to join them at Augsburg on 2 February in a solemn discussion of whether Henry was fit to reign. The situation was immensely gratifying both to the princes and the pope. The plan had only one weakness. Henry had been broken by condemnation from the throne of mercy; for mercy he could still appeal.

Henry determined to cross the Alps; the southern dukes closed the passes. But Henry succeeded in slipping through Burgundy, and after Christmas he made for the Mount Cenis pass. Lampert of Hersfeld describes his journey thus:

> When the difficulty of obtaining permission to proceed had been overcome, another difficulty followed. It was a very bitter winter, and

---

[1] Gregory VII, *Register*, bk. III, no. 10a (ed. E. Caspar, *Monumenta Germaniae Historica*, Berlin, 1920-3, pp. 270-1: my own translation).

the lofty mountains which he had to cross were so covered with snow and ice, that neither horse nor foot could take a step on the steep and slippery slope without danger. But the anniversary of the king's excommunication drew near and would suffer no delay, since unless he were absolved from anathema before that day, he knew that by common sentence of the princes his cause would be lost for ever, and his kingdom forfeit. . . . And so he hired natives expert in the Alpine passes to guide him up the steep mountain and over the drifts of snow, and lighten the harshness of the journey with such skill as they possessed. With great difficulty they reached the summit, but they could get no farther because . . . the slippery ice seemed to deny any possibility of descent. But straining every nerve, now scrambling on hands and feet, now leaning on the shoulders of their guides, now staggering and slipping and falling, sometimes in great danger, they just managed to reach the plains below. The queen and the other ladies of their company were sat on oxhides and dragged down by the leaders of the company. . . .

When the news spread through Italy that the king had come . . . the bishops and counts of Italy flocked eagerly to him, and received him with the honour due to a king, so that within a few days an army of great size had gathered. Ever since the beginning of his reign they had been looking forward to his arrival in Italy, since the kingdom had been plagued with crimes, sedition and war; and they hoped that the king's authority would curb every excess. . . . Besides, rumour had it that he was coming with violent courage to depose the pope, and they were delighted to have an opportunity suitably to avenge their own injury against the man who had previously excommunicated them too.

Meanwhile the pope had been invited by the German princes . . . to discuss the royal case with them at Augsburg at Candlemas, and in spite of the dissuasions of the Roman nobles, he had left Rome and made what haste he could to be there on the day appointed, accompanied by the Countess Matilda [the daughter of Henry III's enemy, Duke Godfrey of Lorraine, herself lady of Tuscany, and one of the small group of noblewomen, led by Henry IV's own mother, the Empress Agnes, who were Gregory's most devoted and consistent supporters]. . . . When he was on his way, he learnt without warning that the king was already in Italy, and on Matilda's advice he turned aside to a strongly fortified castle named Canossa, to wait until the king's intention might be plain—whether he came to beg forgiveness or to revenge himself by force of arms for his excommunication. . . .

[In due course] King Henry summoned the Countess Matilda to confer with him and sent her back to the pope laden with prayers and promises, and with her his mother-in-law and her son and the Marquis Ezzo [of Este] and the abbot of Cluny [St Hugh, Henry's godfather] and a number of other Italian princes, whose authority he thought would weigh with the pope; and he begged the pope to absolve him from his excommunication and not to trust the German princes too hastily, since envy rather than justice had fired them to accuse him. When the pope heard their message, he said that it was quite improper and contrary to canon law that a case should be tried in the absence of the accusers; but that if Henry was confident of his innocence, he could without any trace of fear confidently meet him on the appointed day at Augsburg . . .; and that he would hear the statements of both sides, undiverted by favour or hatred, and give as just a judgement, in accordance with the canons, as he could on every issue. . . . To this they replied that . . . the day approached, and if it was once passed, the princes, according to the law of the palace, would no longer treat him as king, nor listen to his pleas. . . . The king would obey anything which the pope required of him, he would answer in full to every point on whatever day at whatever place the pope might instruct him, if only he would absolve him meanwhile and restore him to the grace of the holy communion. . . . A long time the pope held out, fearing the inconstancy of youth in the king, and his readiness to plunge where his flatterers directed. But at last he was overborne by their urgent appeal and the weight of their views. 'If he is truly repentant of his deed,' he said, 'let him surrender into our power his crown and the other royal insignia as proof of the genuine sincerity of his penitence, and confess himself after so stubborn a fault unworthy of the name and honour of a king.' This seemed too hard to the ambassadors; and when they insisted vigorously that he should soften his sentence and not destroy a reed shaken by the wind with a judgement of such extreme austerity, he at last, with ill grace, agreed that the king could come and, if he did true penance, wipe away by obedience to the decrees of the Holy See the guilt he had incurred by contempt of the Holy See. He came as was commanded; and since the castle was protected by a triple wall, he was received within the second circuit; . . . stripped of his royal robes, with nothing kingly about him, entirely without display, barefoot, fasting from morning till evening he awaited the judgement of the pope. A second day he did it, then a third; and finally on the fourth he was admitted to the presence, and after much discussion finally absolved. . . .[1]

Lampert's account has often been assailed: the crossing of the Mont Cenis, it has been said, is too dramatic; the triple walls of the castle at Canossa improved the story, but cannot really have existed. Long ago, however, C. W. Previté-Orton 'after going over the old track', pronounced in favour of Lampert's description of the pass. 'What Lampert does not bring out, perhaps, is that the dangerous parts to the ordinary traveller were quite short, the drop to the level Novalesa valley being steep. Further, the transport by sledges, . . . a kind of tobogganing, was a speciality of the Mont Cenis route.'[2] And more recently excavation has revealed that Canossa did indeed have a triple wall. But Lampert's account of the oath sworn by Henry to the pope cannot be so fully accepted: he has not indeed falsified the oath, but drawn out and made explicit everything which seemed to him implicit in what Henry actually swore. This is recorded in Gregory's *Register*, and was very simple. He swore to submit to Gregory's judgement on the dispute between himself and the magnates of Germany, or else to come to an agreement with them by Gregory's counsel, and if the pope wished to come north of the Alps he guaranteed him a safe-conduct. In return the pope agreed to release Henry from his excommunication. He did not restore him to full monarchic power. He regarded Henry as suspended from his office, until his suitability for it should have been tested and judged. But to communion he was restored.

Nor was Henry's word rashly accepted. The abbot of Cluny, since he refused to swear on account of his monastic profession, placed his trust in the eyes of God who seeth all things. The bishops of Zeitz and Vercelli, the marquis Ezzo and the other princes of the agreement, in the presence of relics of the saints, confirmed on oath that Henry would do as he promised and not be diverted by any hardship or change of fortune.

When he had absolved him from excommunication, the pope celebrated mass, and after the holy sacrifice he called the king with

[1] Lampert of Hersfeld, *Annales*, pp. 285 ff. (my own translation).
[2] C. W. Previté-Orton, *Early History of the House of Savoy* (Cambridge, 1912), p. 239 n. On the castle at Canossa, see L. Tondelli in *Studi Gregoriani*, ed. G. B. Borino, vol. IV (Rome, 1952), pp. 365–71.

the throng who were present to the altar, and laying his hand on the Lord's body

he made a lengthy speech exculpating himself from the charges made by Henry's supporters; then ate a part of the host, and called on the king to make a similar oath to his innocence and good intentions, and to eat the rest. Henry refused; but the pope was reasonably well satisfied, concluded his mass, entertained the king to dinner, and sent him on his way.[1]

1077–1106

The humiliation of Henry IV at Canossa made a deep impression on contemporaries. The king, whose father had deposed and appointed popes, had himself submitted to a papal ban, and sworn to accept papal judgement; the roles of the principal players at Sutri were reversed; papal autonomy, even papal supremacy, had been visibly successful. The relations of pope and emperor would never be quite the same again.

But in the immediate political situation Henry IV was the victor at Canossa. His plight had been due to an alliance between pope and south-German dukes and Saxon rebels; even in January 1077 the Lombard bishops and many of the Lombard nobles rallied to him. The pope could only count on wholehearted support in Germany so long as his ban was a major political weapon in the rebels' cause. When it was lifted, he was no longer useful to them. Gregory claimed, furthermore, that he should sit in judgement on Henry; nor was this claim welcome among the German princes. If the pope pronounced in Henry's favour, their cause was lost; if he pronounced against Henry, the new king would be king by papal favour, a situation which could only be accepted in extreme circumstances. Something of this Gregory understood; hence his long hesitation at Canossa. When Henry was absolved, the German rebels declared themselves betrayed, and proceeded to the election of Rudolf, duke of Swabia, at Forcheim in March 1077 (see pp. 154ff.). The election was accepted by Gregory's legates on the spot; but Gregory was compelled to repudiate their action. Henry had not been formally deposed; however much Gregory might wish to ally himself with Rudolf, he was committed to allowing Henry to defend himself in a legal process. The pope longed for this process to take place and cast himself for the role of the judge. But it was much in the interests of the contestants that nothing of the kind should happen. The unhappy pope found himself compelled to sit on the fence.

[1] Lampert, pp. 294–8.

At last, in the Lenten synod of 1080, he pronounced sentence. At Canossa Henry had promised to submit to papal judgement; but the council in which this was to happen had never met, and Gregory felt that this was Henry's fault—not without justification, although in fact Rudolf was also reluctant to let it meet. Once again, in an even more elaborate harangue, the pope placed his ban on Henry; this time he was formally and definitively deposed, and Paul as well as Peter were admonished to see to it that the judgement took effect. Then the pope, in prophetic exaltation, forecast that within a year Henry would be dead. The prophesy was not well conceived; for in the same year Rudolf died, and Henry had still a quarter of a century to live.

With Rudolf's death the issue was virtually settled. The rebels presently elected a successor to Rudolf, but he had little chance of success. Meanwhile Henry was proceeding once more to extreme measures against Gregory. Gregory's sentence was pronounced in Lent 1080; at Easter Henry and the German nobles and bishops pronounced Gregory deposed; in June, at Brixen, strengthened by a numerous band of Italian bishops, the king, *patricius* of the Romans (see p. 150 n.), and his followers confirmed their sentence and, acting on a version of the papal election decree which had been conveniently forged in the imperial interest in the 1060s or 1070s, elected the archbishop of Ravenna as pope (or anti-pope, as he is usually reckoned) Clement III —a nice reminder of Clement II, nominated by Henry III to succeed the deposed Gregory VI in 1046.

From 1080 on Henry was never without a pope of his own. The men who succeeded Clement III after his death in 1100 were shadowy figures, and even Clement, in his later years, counted for little. But in the 1080s and early 1090s it was by no means clear which pope would be finally accepted. Clement was too obviously a creature of the German king to be welcomed by the other potentates of Europe. But from time to time a man like William II of England found it highly convenient to use the excuse of the papal schism to keep his country temporarily free of allegiance to any pope. Furthermore, if Clement had little chance of winning new adherents, Gregory in his later years was adept at alienating his, and in the 1080s Henry IV was at the height of his power. Hungary, Serbia and Croatia for a time submitted to Clement, perhaps even for a very short time England too. Henry came to Italy in 1081, and laid siege to Rome: in 1084 he at last succeeded in capturing it, and Clement could crown Henry emperor, and establish his Curia in Rome itself. By now most of Gregory's cardinals had deserted him, including old reformers like Hugh Candidus, a German associate of Leo IX, who felt, as many felt, that Gregory ought to strive to resurrect the old alliance of empire and papacy, not to foment discord. Even the papal chancellor left Gregory, and in his last years the *Register* fell into chaos. From the old papal fortress, the Castel Sant'Angelo, Gregory looked on impotently while his enemy and his rival occupied his throne. From this ignominy he was rescued by the leader of the Normans in south Italy, Robert Guiscard; to him Gregory had often appealed, but Guiscard had other fish to fry, and came only when it suited him. And when he came Rome felt, for the first time, what it was like to be attacked by a Viking horde. The city was sacked as never before since the early days of the Republic, and Gregory, a Roman of the Romans, had to flee with his new patron. On 25 May 1085 he died at Salerno, contemplating the ruin of his work.

It was fortunate for the reformed papacy that Gregory did not live longer. As it was, there was a long vacancy; then the abbot of Monte Cassino was elected, but failed to establish himself in Rome; and finally one of the few cardinals constantly faithful to Gregory was elected as Pope Urban II in March 1088. Urban was an ardent reformer; he was a Cluniac; he was a Frenchman; he was also a diplomat and a man who had all the political sense which Gregory VII had lacked, as well as not a little of his prophetic vision. It was not unnatural that he should be able to rally all the people to whom Clement III was for one reason or another obnoxious. Even so it was slow work, and for several years touch and go. He was able to take immediate advantage of political unrest in northern Italy. The cities had seen too much of Henry IV; the yoke of imperial government was heavy on them. Even Henry's archbishop of Milan was prepared to join forces with Urban. In 1089 Urban was re-established in Rome itself; and in the following years he imitated Leo IX and took the papacy on tour, in those countries where his allegiance was accepted, especially in France. In 1095 he was helped by a great stroke of fortune: the Byzantine emperor appealed to him for help. In reply Urban launched the First Crusade—declared holy war, not, as Gregory had done, against Christian foes, but against the heathen, and drew under the papal banner the enthusiasts and the discontented of all Europe. The success of the crusade was a substantial moral victory for Urban; and Henry IV, who never acknowledged Urban as pope, suffered thereby. Urban, meanwhile, repeated with stronger emphasis than ever the decrees against lay investiture; and peace between empire and papacy seemed still remote.

The Investiture issue in England and France

Urban's successor, Paschal II (1099–1118), was a saintly, unworldly man, whose reign saw some extraordinary successes, some equally astonishing failures. In England and France the issue of investiture was settled. It is a curious fact that when Urban II had launched the First Crusade he was in open dispute with the kings of Germany and France, and the king of England, who did not recognize him, was shortly also to be at loggerheads with him. In England the anti-clerical William II, tricked (as he thought) into accepting the saintly Anselm as arch-bishop of Canterbury in 1093, was bent on getting rid of him; a series of disputes led to Anselm's exile from 1097 to 1100. When Henry I succeeded in 1100, he immediately summoned Anselm to return; but the old archbishop had meanwhile attended a series of councils in which Urban and Paschal had reiterated Gregory VII's condemnation of lay investiture, and made it clear that bishops ought to do no homage to kings; that the Church's property was free of secular control. These views were not acceptable to Henry I and, when Anselm refused to consecrate bishops who had received investiture at Henry's hands, conflict was inevitable once more. But neither party wished it to continue indefinitely, and before long a compromise was found. It was put to Henry that the ceremony of investiture could reasonably be given up, so long as homage was done by a new bishop for his temporal possessions. This was based on the notion that the main body of a bishop's lands were 'temporalities', as distinct from purely ecclesiastical revenues, like tithes and offerings, which only a churchman could receive, the 'spiritu-alities'. The notion became current that while the spiritualities were wholly under ecclesiastical control, the temporalities, having been originally a gift of the king's ancestors, were held of the king. This also meant that during a vacancy the king could claim, as he had long done, that the temporalities of the see returned to him; that he could administer them and enjoy their proceeds until a new bishop was installed. The idea of 'temporalities' was clean contrary to the decrees of Paschal; but it gained wide currency, and was the basis of the practice in most European countries in the later Middle Ages. To avoid controversy, all that was proposed in 1105–6, however, was that Henry I should give up lay investiture so long as he could receive the homage of bishops. Anselm hesitated to accept a compromise, but the pope, to Anselm's surprise, accepted it. In 1107 Anselm was able to return to England; Henry I had sworn not to invest with ring and staff again; in return Anselm agreed not to refuse consecration to a bishop-elect who had done homage to the king. In practice Henry continued to appoint the English bishops; but the surrender of the old symbol was a powerful reminder that bishops were not simply royal nominees; that the power of the pope counted as it had not counted a hundred years before.

In France meanwhile lay investiture had been given up without any open rupture. A dispute there had been, but on a different issue. Philip I eloped with the countess of Anjou and, although the ferocious count accepted his loss with remarkable docility, the pope was less accommodating. Urban II excommunicated the king, and peace was only restored in 1104, when Philip repudiated the lady (see pp. 203-4). This crisis added to the many difficulties of Philip's later years; and the French monarchy was in any case far weaker than the English or the German. Gregory VII's old ally, Hugh of Lyons, had denounced lay investiture strongly in the 1090s. The investiture, and also the homage of bishops, where politically desirable, were defended by the famous canon lawyer, Bishop Ivo of Chartres. Ivo was too eminent and too respected for the pope to wish to proceed directly against him. Nor was it necessary, for he was indeed only fighting a rearguard action so that King Philip, or rather King Louis—for Philip's son and heir, already elected and crowned, came increasingly to wield the sceptre in his father's dotage—could gracefully retreat. By 1107 investiture had been given up; homage was only asked for in special cases, and that too soon lapsed. But Louis continued to exercise his customary authority in the election of bishops in the royal domain, and to attempt to spread his influence outside the Île de France, not without a measure of success.

Pope and emperor, 1106-22

In the midst of these démarches Henry IV of Germany died. In his last years his eldest surviving son, the future Henry V, had tried to anticipate his father's death and take over the reins of government (see pp. 187-8). He was therefore prepared to ignore his father's anti-popes, and acknowledge Paschal. But when he succeeded his father in 1106, it became clear that he was not going immediately to surrender investiture. In 1107 Paschal was in France; and at the Council of Troyes his bloodless victory in that kingdom was confirmed by yet another decree against lay investiture. This decree was mainly aimed at the German king; and Paschal improved the occasion by excommunicating the German bishops, technically on the ground that they had refused to answer his summons to a council in 1106. But Henry V knew that the majority of the German bishops were still as disinclined as ever to accept papal intervention; and so he remained firm on the issue of investiture while France and England were withdrawing from the conflict.

In 1110 Henry came with a large army to Rome to be crowned emperor. At the same time he tried to interest the pope in the distinction, coming increasingly into fashion, between 'spiritualities' and 'temporalities'—investiture, he claimed, solely pertained to temporalities. Out of these discussions a scheme of dazzling originality was devised: pope and emperor agreed to an arrangement whereby Henry would surrender investiture and the bishops all their temporalities. This scheme provoked, not unnaturally, a wild outcry. The bishops were horrified; the lay princes almost equally outraged by this attempt to split the German nobility down the middle, to destroy, in effect, the ecclesiastical nobility of Germany. The supporters of pope and emperor told both, in no uncertain terms, that the scheme must be abandoned; Henry rapidly kidnapped the pope and extracted from him, momentarily, total surrender. Paschal, under duress, granted to Henry the right to invest, and crowned him emperor.

Henry V had succeeded by a trick. As soon as his army had left the environs of Rome, the pope was bound to repudiate an arrangement palpably extorted by force. Henry, however, was obstinate as well as violent, and between him and Paschal there could be no peace. For a while they ignored one another; then in 1116–17 Henry came to Italy again with his wife, the English Matilda, intending to have her crowned by his side. This was done, but by a complacent archbishop; Paschal had fled.

In the next year Paschal died. Henry, meanwhile, was beset with difficulties in Germany, and he could not ignore the fact that his colleagues in England and France had lost little or nothing by submission to the pope. Henry I of England was his father-in-law, and always ready with good advice. In 1119 he was addressed in person by one of Louis's leading bishops, the famous teacher William of Champeaux.

> If you wish to have true peace, my lord king, [he said] you should entirely give up investiture of bishoprics and abbeys. You can take it as certain that you will lose nothing in royal power by this; for see, I was elected bishop in the French kingdom, and received nothing from the king's hands either before or after consecration, and yet in tribute, in military service, in customary payments and in everything

THE CONCORDAT OF WORMS

pertaining to the commonweal, and for all the properties which were granted of old to God's Church by the Christian kings, I do as faithful service as your bishops in your kingdom—whom you have hitherto embroiled in this conflict, not to say in excommunication, by continuing to invest.[1]

Henry, meanwhile, had proceeded once again to extreme measures. In 1118 he set up the archbishop who had crowned him in 1117 as an anti-pope; open conflict had once more broken out. But to the German princes, as to William of Champeaux, it now seemed pointless. In 1121 they drove Henry to accept a compromise in all points closely similar to that which his wiser father-in-law had accepted many years before. This was made formal at Worms in 1122, in the famous Concordat. Once again, the surrender of investiture was complete; it was made in a solemn and permanent grant to the pope, sealed with a golden seal. But as in 1107, the papal letter outlining the papal concessions was an informal thing, a personal grant to Henry alone. Henry of Germany was no more troubled by this than Henry of England. He and his supporters could claim that everything contained in it was the ancient custom of the realm; in practice it would outlive the reigning prince. Even if it did not, they could still draw comfort from the assurance of William of Champeaux; and Henry V meanwhile, with papal permission, could hold elections in his own presence and grant the 'temporalities' by touch of his sceptre.

The investiture contests had many consequences. Lay investiture was utterly destroyed, but the conflict on who should appoint bishops continued unabated throughout the Middle Ages. The practices permitted to Henry I of England continued, in spite of the interlude of weak government under his successor; those permitted to Henry V gradually fell into desuetude. This difference is a symptom of the different history of the English and the German monarchies; and the weakening grasp of the German kings over the German bishops only meant occasionally, and sporadically, that papal influence was increased. It was to the new German nobility that the real surrender was made.

But the great battles of the late eleventh and early twelfth centuries had deeper and larger significance than can be deduced from the political consequences of the treaties which ended them. In Germany, the contest, coinciding with bitter civil war, had gone far to destroy the

[1] Quoted by A. Becker, *Studien zum Investiturproblem in Frankreich* (Saarbrücken, 1955), p. 133.

old German monarchy; at Forcheim in 1077 a new world, a new idea of monarchy, had looked in for a moment on the Salian garden. The old alliance of king and Church could never be quite the same again. The English king, who was always favoured by the circumstance that the pope had more dangerous enemies nearer home, was able to retain much of the substance of his power. The French king found a new support for his in an alliance, at first a somewhat uneasy alliance, with the pope. It was the emperor who was hardest hit. His government of Germany had depended on close alliance with the Church, on his quasi-monopoly of control over the Church. The Lombard bishops were in the main faithful to Henry IV against Gregory VII. But they could not for ever support a distant and weakening imperial authority, nor be for ever impervious to the new trends in ecclesiastical thought and law. Above all, the rising power of the Italian cities was making the interests of Germany and Italy more divergent than hitherto, and giving the Italians a new taste for liberty. In Germany itself the growing strength and independence of the nobility, counts and lesser dukes, provided a permanent challenge to royal supremacy; and the bonds established between the nobility and the monasteries reformed under the inspiration of Hirsau in the late eleventh and early twelfth centuries was a dangerous threat to royal control over the Church. William of Hirsau was a genuine reformer, who embarked on his work without a preconceived plan. In due course he came under the influence of Cluny and of Gregory VII. These influences opened the way to a system extremely congenial to the princely benefactors who patronized his movement. The houses reformed under the influence of Hirsau were independent of royal and often of episcopal control, directly subjected to the papacy; but this left room for a peculiar kind of lay advocacy, developed from that of the old German monasteries, different in that it owed nothing to the king. The effect was to build up a large group of immunities, of enclaves of ecclesiastical property owing no allegiance to the king. This was one of many ways in which the contest of empire and papacy lent aid to the other tendencies leading to the decline of the Salian Empire.

Hirsau has two faces: it has a constitutional significance and a religious interest, as one of many movements of monastic reform in this age. It reminds us that if from one point of view the contests described in this chapter were political and constitutional, from another they represented the coming-of-age of a powerful religious movement. Christianity has always claimed to be a revolutionary religion; occasionally it is seen to be so.

The papacy, 1122–53

In 1123 Pope Calixtus II celebrated the end of the investiture conflicts by presiding over a general council in Rome, the First Lateran Council, in which definitive decrees were passed against lay investiture and other measures taken for the reform of the Church. For thirty years the popes were on relatively good terms with the great powers of northern Europe, and the conflicts with Frederick Barbarossa and Henry II of England lie beyond our horizon. But the papacy was not, for most of this time, at peace. It had still to struggle to find a *modus vivendi*, with itself, with Roger of Sicily, and with the people of Rome.

In 1130 the peninsula and the Church were thrown into confusion by a disputed election to the papacy. The older cardinals, survivors of the heroic age of the reform, in alliance with one of the Roman factions, elected Peter Pierleoni, son of one of the Roman families closest to Gregory VII, as Anacletus II. The younger cardinals, many of them French, supported by another Roman faction, that of the Frangipani, elected Gregory Papareschi as Innocent II (1130–43). Ecclesiastical and political threads were interwoven in this election; and the weakness of the election decree of 1059 was demonstrated once more. Innocent seems to have had a majority among the cardinal bishops, with whom the initiative in the election lay; but among the cardinals at large a minority. Anacletus held Rome and won the allegiance of the Norman leader in the south. But Innocent was able to establish himself in France, take advantage of his French adherents, and win the advocacy of St Bernard of Clairvaux, whose eloquent voice and magical pen were instantly at his service. Bernard was convinced that Innocent was the more suitable candidate, and so God's choice; and he carried much of western Europe with him. Some he convinced, others found it easier to agree than to argue with St Bernard. Eventually the Emperor Lothar also agreed.

Lothar's first visit to Italy, in 1133, won him the imperial crown, but no sort of security for Innocent. His second visit, in 1136–7, was a more prolonged and successful affair; Roger of Sicily was driven out of Italy altogether. In 1137 Lothar withdrew, and promptly died; but in 1138 he was followed to the grave by Anacletus, whose successor as antipope soon abdicated. Innocent was left in possession of the field. The end of the investiture contest had been celebrated in the First Lateran Council; in 1139, at the Second, Innocent II celebrated the end of the schism. Once again important decrees were passed; bishops and abbots came from all over Europe; the papal supremacy and unity were reasserted.

Innocent's triumph, however, did not give him political security. In 1139 Roger of Sicily recovered his hold on south Italy. Like Leo IX many years before, Innocent took the field against the Norman leader in person, and with similar results. Innocent was captured and, although he was treated with profound respect, he was not released until he had confirmed Roger in the royal dignity which Roger had extorted from Anacletus II as the price of his support. In his later years Roger the Great was to be a useful ally to the papacy.

An ally, indeed, was what the popes especially needed, since their temporal power was being challenged at home, and Conrad III was never strong enough to come in person to protect them. In 1143 the merchants and artisans of Rome established a commune, as had so many other Italian cities, and tried to assert their independence both of the pope and of the old Roman nobility. In traditional Roman fashion, they established a senate on the capitol. Innocent II died shortly after its invention; neither of his successors lasted more than a few months; and it was still in active occupation of the city when the cardinals chose Bernard of Pisa, a Cistercian abbot and disciple of Bernard of Clair-vaux, as the new pope. He took the name Eugenius III (1145–53), and the opening years of this attractive, capable, earnest pope saw the re-establishment of his authority in Rome. The Roman economy depended to a great extent on the throng of visitors and the flow of gifts which came to the papal Curia, and the evident determination of the pope to absent himself from Rome until the senate came to terms weakened his enemies. If the pope had been able to stay longer in Rome he might have settled the city more permanently. But in 1147–8 he went to France, to organize the preaching of the Second Crusade and to hold another general council, at Rheims in 1148; and while he was absent from Rome, the senate revived, under the inspiration of a fervent preacher of pronounced puritanical views, Arnold of Brescia. At one time an abbot, and at another a pupil of Abelard in Paris, Arnold's increasingly anti-hierarchical views had led to his expulsion first from France and later from Zürich. He was brought before Eugenius III, who set him to do a penance in Rome. It was a disastrous solution, for Arnold took to preaching again; he was soon in alliance with would-be rebel leaders and he remained at liberty until after Eugenius's death; his denunciations of pope and cardinals became increasingly fervent. The pope, meanwhile, was reluctant to let himself be too dependent on the Sicilian alliance, since he feared the power of Roger II and disliked his ecclesiastical policies; but, as Conrad III never came, he was forced to make some use of Roger. The situation in Rome was still unsettled, and Arnold of Brescia still at large, when Eugenius died in 1153. It was the brief alliance of Pope Hadrian IV and Frederick Barbarossa in 1155 which led to Arnold's downfall: the trouble-maker was hanged, with the connivance of the senate, the emperor and the pope. Peace in Rome had been won, but with the aid of a far more dangerous enemy.

This brief survey of papal history between 1122 and 1153 has been mainly concerned with political events. The enumeration of difficulties and disasters, however, presents the papacy of the early twelfth century in quite a false perspective. Although conservative opinion acted still as a powerful check on papal authority, and although the papacy had been compelled to compromise on many aspects of lay patronage and lay control in the Church, the papal monarchy was now securely established; the papacy was still regarded as the natural centre, the natural ally, of spiritual movements by all save a few radicals like Arnold of Brescia. While Innocent II struggled with Anacletus and Roger, Master Gratian was writing his *Decretum* in seclusion at Bologna; and in the person of Eugenius III, St Bernard and the Cistercians captured the papal throne —'men say', wrote Bernard in jest to the pope, 'that I am pope, not you'. The movements represented by Bernard and Gratian are of more significance for papal history, broadly viewed, than the political troubles of the popes; and to them we must now turn.

XIV

The New Monastic Orders

The monastic movements of the eleventh and twelfth centuries will always be most closely associated with the Cistercian Order and the name of St Bernard of Clairvaux (1090–1153). The Cistercians came to be more widespread, more influential than any other order; their fame was based not only on their zeal for purity and simplicity, but also on their skill at organization. Our growing knowledge of the other orders of their time must not be allowed to abolish our sense of their originality. But equally, we must not allow the glamour of Cîteaux, the splendid ruins of her numerous daughter-houses or the eloquence of Bernard to hide from us the preparation which Cîteaux had in the eleventh century; or the context of religious revival in which she was born.

In the late tenth and early eleventh centuries the anchorite life was reviving in popularity in many parts of Italy. One of the first hermits of whom we have information was St Romuald of Ravenna, who died in 1027. Romuald, like many of the spiritual leaders of the generations

BIBLIOGRAPHY. Indispensable is Dom David Knowles, *Monastic Order in England* (Cambridge, 1940), which deals fully with the continental background to the Cistercian and other monastic movements; on St Bernard and on Cîteaux and Cluny see D. Knowles, *The Historian and Character and other Essays* (Cambridge, 1963), Chapters 3 and 4, and Bernard's *Letters* (trans. B. S. James, London, 1953). On the canons regular, see J. C. Dickinson, *The Origins of the Austin Canons and their introduction into England* (London, 1950); H. M. Colvin, *The White Canons in England* (Oxford, 1951) [i.e. the Premonstratensians]; R. Graham, *S. Gilbert of Sempringham and the Gilbertines* (London, 1901). On Odo of Tournai, see C. Dereine in *Revue d'histoire ecclésiastique*, vol. LIV (1959), pp. 41–65. On the controversies surrounding the date (1097 or 1098) and circumstances of the foundation of Cîteaux see J. A. Lefèvre in *Revue d'histoire ecclésiastique*, vol. LI (1956), pp. 5–41; C. Dereine in *Cîteaux*, vol. X (1959), pp. 125–39. On Christina of Markyate, C. H. Talbot, *The Life of Christina of Markyate* (Oxford, 1959). There is a useful selection of Peter Damian's spiritual teaching in St Peter Damian, *Selected Writings on the Spiritual Life*, ed. Patricia McNulty (London, 1959); see also J. Leclercq, *S. Pierre Damien* (Rome, 1960).

which followed him, was a wanderer. He started life in a house under Cluniac influence but left his community in search of greater solitude. Wherever he went he left behind him a trail of hermitages under his inspiration. He founded no coherent rule of life or order, but his influence was picked up here and there by an eminent follower. Most famous of all was St Peter Damian, who always remained a recluse at heart even when cardinal bishop of Ostia, and eventually retired to Fonte Avellana, one of Romuald's hermitages, to end his life there. Romuald's other principal centre of influence was Camaldoli, which in the late eleventh century became the centre of a regular order of monks and anchorites, who had as the basis of their life the literal observance of the *Rule* of St Benedict, and who, none the less, treated it (in St Benedict's own words) as 'a little rule for beginners'.

Two things made this kind of development possible: the popularity of the monastic ideal and the intellectual revival. Religious revival and enthusiasm were in the air. We understand nothing of this period unless we realize the immense popularity of the monastic ideal and of the religious life; a popularity already widespread, under the influence of Cluny, Gorze, Brogne and Glastonbury, when St Romuald was a child, but which was steadily growing for over a century after his death. Many of the papal reformers were themselves monks; and monasticism was their norm for the religious life. It was partly this which made them campaign so fervently for the enforcement of celibacy; and it explains their concern to drive all clergy not actively engaged in parish work— and even some who were—into monasteries. Hildebrand and Damian helped to start the movement for converting communities of clerks and canons into 'canons regular', which blossomed in the late eleventh century in the formation of numerous houses of canons following the *Rule* of St Augustine. This *Rule*, which had been considerably re-written over the centuries since Augustine had written it, still remained somewhat vague and unspecific; to remedy this, the earliest Augustinian houses developed a series of customs which were regularly observed in conjunction with the *Rule*. The outcome was a form of monasticism little different in origin from the Benedictine, into which countless small communities were swept. In England and Wales, for instance, the first half of the twelfth century saw the establishment of about fifty Cistercian houses and nearly a hundred Augustinian; but the number of religious in each (excluding lay brothers) was roughly the same: about 1,400–1,500.

The monastic life was popular with secular patrons as well as with would-be religious. On the whole, the opinion tended to be that the more fervent the Order, the more efficacious its prayers would be—and so the more worth supporting. This accounts for the paradox that many communities founded in poverty and hardship were provided with almost crushing endowments quite soon after their foundation. Patronage could often be a nuisance. The Norman barons who invaded England provided their favourite Norman abbeys with lands and churches near their new headquarters in England, and often seem to have expected the monks to serve these churches in person. The monks no doubt served the parishioners and the benefactor well. But it was contrary to the basic tenets of the monastic Order, and often tiresome for the monks to perform. We must not exaggerate: service of layfolk, close links with patrons, were part of the ethos of eleventh-century monasticism and were widely accepted. It was only in the newer orders that the laity were excluded from monastic churches, and an attempt made to separate the monks wholly from the world.

Nor were prayers the only benefits which monastic houses could offer their patrons. They could be homes for surplus children. In the past these had usually been placed in the community as children, and brought up to the profession and, although they could not take solemn vows till they came to years of discretion, they usually had little alternative but to accept the vocation chosen by their parents. This practice was also condemned by the new orders, but it took a long time to die; and even then, the monasteries provided the chief outlet for those who did not wish for, or for some reason could not engage in, the hurly-burly of feudal life. Aversion to marriage, for example, led some women to enter nunneries, but there were clearly many social reasons, which we cannot fully analyse, which enhanced the popularity of the monastic life in this age.

There was, however, more to it than that. In the eleventh and twelfth centuries the monastic life was attracting many of the best minds of the day, much as the friars were to do in the thirteenth century. If the thirteenth century produced St Thomas Aquinas and St Bonaventure, the eleventh produced St Peter Damian, Lanfranc, prior of Bec and archbishop of Canterbury (1070–89) and St Anselm, abbot of Bec and archbishop of Canterbury (1093–1109); the twelfth century St Bernard, St Ailred of Rievaulx, most famous of the English Cistercians, Hugh of St Victor, of the distinguished Augustinian house of St Victor in Paris, Master Gratian, the Camaldolese monk of Bologna, who has been called the father of the science of canon law.

These were all men of intellectual eminence, and have been specifically chosen to underline the connexion between the monasteries of this period and the intellectual revival. No order of this time, old or new, was specifically learned; St Dominic in the early thirteenth century was the first founder of a religious order to set a special premium on learning. But in the period between 1050 and 1150 the monastic orders old and new drew in great numbers of intellectual leaders and famous teachers. As we shall see, the intellectual revival was by no means confined within the walls of monasteries in this period; most of the large schools and most active centres of intellectual life, even then, were secular. But in weight and range of scholarly production, the monks for most of this century retained their preponderance; it was the age *par excellence* of monastic learning; and it was only in the second half of the twelfth century that the balance was finally tipped in favour of the seculars. It is not too much to say that the intellectual revival was an essential part of the background to the rise of the new orders.

St Romuald, who had felt strongly the influence of Byzantine monastic ideals, had been a close reader of the lives of the desert fathers; Peter Damian similarly. As time passed, a wider range of antique literature became ever more widely read; and the books were studied with new eyes. A heightened intellectual awareness and sophistication enabled men to read even familiar books, like the *Rule* of St Benedict, as if they had not been read before. The monks of Gorze and Cluny could not imagine the *Rule* apart from Benedict of Aniane, just as most men in the eleventh century could not imagine the figure of Christ apart from the aura of theology and conventional art with which the centuries had surrounded him. The founders of Camaldoli stripped the original Benedict of his accretions and looked straight at what they saw, and so demanded greater simplicity, less liturgical magnificence, a place for manual work. Peter Damian was one of the first to consider, though with a profoundly devotional imagination, the human life and human setting of Jesus; from this stemmed the cult of the human Jesus and of the Blessed Virgin which is so marked a development of the twelfth and thirteenth centuries, in which the central names were St Bernard and St Francis. A man like Damian was inspired by his interest in books and in people: if he had not been converted to the religious life, we should remember him as the first of the medieval humanists, in the tradition which was to lead to Abelard and John of Salisbury (see pp. 319–20). In some ways there came to be opposition and conflict between intellectual leaders and religious reformers; the conflict of Bernard and

Abelard is the most famous example of this. These tensions should not obscure from us the fundamental link: Abelard and his like were inspired by reading ancient works of philosophy and logic with new eyes; Damian and Bernard—two of the finest Latinists, it may be noted, of the Middle Ages—were also inspired, in great measure, by books. One of the most active schools in the intellectual revival of the eleventh century was that of Rheims; and it was from Rheims that an eminent scholar, Master Bruno, came south to found La Grande Chartreuse. In doing so Bruno may have buried his books, but not his learning.

The later disputes between Cluny and Cîteaux have led historians to see too rigid a distinction between the old world and the new. Not infrequently the new ideas fermented within Cluniac walls, and sometimes led to schism in the community. Some historians, having observed these facts, have tried to abolish the originality of the new movements altogether. This is quite false. A world of ideas separates the old Cluny from the new Cîteaux; the new ideas and impulses proceeded like tracks in the snow, now clear and distinct, now crossing one another, now inextricably confused; the label 'Cluniac' does not guarantee that the old ideas are untouched by the new, any more than Cîteaux herself succeeded in putting behind her all that was characteristic of the old.

Thus Odo of Tournai, who never ceased to be the monk of a house of Cluniac customs, was inspired by the reading of Cassian in the 1090s to demand a reform which included the following points: a home in a more deserted place, poverty and simplicity even in church, a strict novitiate (or apprenticeship) for novices, manual work and systematic hospitality of the old and poor. A few years earlier, a group of bandits who lived in a wild spot at Affligem in Belgium, preying on the road from Cologne to Bruges, had become converted and established themselves as monks in the same wilderness. The monks of Affligem incorporated Cluniac customs in their way of life a little later; but their original inspiration was to a life of solitude and poverty, and to the care of the poor. It was to be a haven of refuge and solitude: in marked distinction from older foundations, layfolk were specifically excluded from the services in the monastic church. The life of the community, however, was open to every kind of person, and in early years it attracted 230 recruits, monks, nuns and lay brothers. The lay brothers, as at Hirsau in Germany a few years earlier, were illiterate layfolk, who could become members of the community and engage in manual work for its support, but were not expected to engage in the full liturgical life of the choir monk. Affligem was an early example of a type of inspiration common in this age; only the attempt to mingle monks and nuns was rare—though even that was made the basis of a new order by the English Gilbert of Sempringham in the mid twelfth century; and it serves to underline a basic feature of these movements, that they attempted to provide a haven for the many, while yet insisting on celibacy and on austerity which might seem to make them attractive only to a few. In practice Affligem became a haven for the many, and surrendered some of its primitive observance in the process.

Farther south, perhaps under direct influence from Italy, groups of hermits were becoming more common. From them sprang many of the religious movements of the age, orthodox and unorthodox. In a rocky and desolate valley near Grenoble, Bruno and his companions formed the Chartreuse in 1084. In due course they developed, not into a community of the traditional kind, but into an organized order of hermits, living in cells within a common boundary wall, meeting only occasionally in chapel and chapterhouse. A comparatively small order of hermits, the Carthusians, have remained from that day to this, and their life is still substantially what it was. At about the same time a group of hermits were living on the borders of Brittany and Maine; as time passed they came to form the nucleus of two monastic communities of notable fervour and austerity, Tiron (1109) and Savigny (1112). Both became centres of small orders, which spread in their own area and in England. Savigny in particular became the mother of a group of English abbeys, of which the most famous was that founded by Henry I's favourite nephew, Count Stephen—later king—in the peninsula of Furness (at Tulketh, 1124, Furness, 1127). But a little over twenty years after the foundation of Furness, Savigny and all its children submitted to the rising star of Cîteaux, and were absorbed into the Cistercian order.

In the third quarter of the eleventh century another similar hermit group gathered at Colan in Burgundy, near Langres. About 1075 they formed themselves into a community under a superior named Robert, a Benedictine abbot already of high reputation. Robert established them in circumstances of extreme discomfort at Molesme, and ruled them for twenty years without external signs of friction. Molesme was looked up to as a model of sanctity and fervour; local secular princes and lords regarded its prayers as highly efficacious and endowed it; and the abbot began to grow restless under the pressure of success. Again the desert called him: like so many of the great monastic leaders of the Middle Ages, he preached stability but was restless himself. In 1097 or 1098 he led an exodus from Molesme to found a new monastery—

Novum Monasterium was what they called it at first—not far away, in the next diocese. Once again Robert encountered extreme hardship, which was what he was seeking; and he had provided himself also with a new challenge, since he had no one's permission to leave Molesme. In 1098 the new community received a measure of recognition; but the monks of Molesme protested that their abbot had absconded without their leave or consent; the benefactors of Molesme protested that their house was losing prestige and its prayers their efficacy. Robert was forced to return, and with him went some of his companions. The new monastery struggled on, and obtained recognition and papal protection under Abbots Alberic and Stephen Harding. But from 1100 to 1112 the little community of Cîteaux, as it came to be called, was dwindling in numbers. There was little sign that it would form the nucleus of a new order; it seemed hardly likely, indeed, that it would survive. But it already had within its walls the organizing talent of the English Abbot Stephen Harding; and in 1112 its fortunes were transformed by the arrival of a young Burgundian nobleman with a team of fellow-recruits. After Bernard's coming Cîteaux rapidly climbed to fame. He spent only three years as a monk of Cîteaux, then went out to be first abbot of the third daughter house, Clairvaux. When he died in 1153, still abbot of Clairvaux, Cistercian houses were to be found in every corner of Europe; they numbered many hundreds, and their inmates many thousands; they had transformed the monastic scene of Europe, and played their part in city and village as well as in the wilderness where they preferred to live. They had even captured the Holy See in the person of Pope Eugenius III (1145–53); and their influence had inspired the founding of new orders of canons and of knights.

The Cistercian order, then, began as one among many attempts to find a more ascetic life, further removed from the world than that provided by the older monastic communities. What set it apart from the rest was partly the vivid inspiration of St Bernard, partly the genius of its organization. This was outlined in the *Carta Caritatis*, the 'charter of divine love', a treatise in which administrative regulations and inspired spiritual direction somehow contrive to live in harmony; in its original form at least it was the work of St Stephen Harding. The Cistercians demanded, first of all, a return to the *Rule* of St Benedict; they set out to make their monasteries what Benedict had expected them to be, little islands apart from the world where monks could worship God in community and as individuals, undisturbed by the anxieties and passions of secular life.

The old monastic communities, save for the dependent priories of Cluny and a few others, were jealous of their own independence; sometimes they were even independent of their bishop. They depended entirely on their own resources for the maintenance of their standards and way of life; and this, as much experience had shown, was precarious. Under a capable abbot they flourished; but if they let in too many unsuitable recruits, and if they became subject to inferior leadership, they tended to wane. The Cistercian founders wished to devise a system which did not depend wholly on one man, as did Cluny, and which yet bound the houses of a growing order together. This they provided by the system of visitation and of General Chapters. Every house was subject to visitation by the abbot of the mother house once a year, and Cîteaux herself by the abbots of her four eldest foundations. The visitors had power to remedy anything they found amiss; their action could be swift and effective. Every year, furthermore, the abbots of all the houses of the Order gathered in general chapter at Cîteaux; and the general chapter was the supreme authority of the Order where all essential matters of policy were decided and discussed. The system had its weaknesses: it involved the abbots in much travelling; and in due course the annual general chapter became an intolerable burden on abbots from countries far removed from France, or even, sometimes, at war with France; and the whole system had to be modified. But these difficulties still lay in the future in 1150; and the Cistercian organization was regarded as a model, then and later, which many orders imitated.

The return to the *Rule* carried with it many corollaries. The Cistercians preferred remote, deserted sites and lonely valleys, where they could be alone and self-sufficient—and visitors to Fountains, Rievaulx Tintern, or to hundreds of other houses in England, France, Spain, Germany, Italy and Austria will know how well they chose their sites. Yet it was not the beauty of the scene which primarily attracted them to the Skell or the Wye, but its remoteness; and they chose a river valley, by preference, where there was both sound, dry ground for their large and solid church, and running water to provide supplies for the conduits and drains for the domestic offices; the Cistercians, practical in all things, were pioneers of efficient civil engineering. In course of time they became so prolific that waste spaces could not always be found for them. They reckoned, even so, to till their own lands and not to live off rents, tithes or the labour of serfs. Quite soon they had to compromise a little; eventually they consented to be rentiers; but in early days they carried their convictions to the point of frequently ejecting sitting tenants. When their patrons could not find them wood or fertile waste to clear, they gave them villages; and these the Cistercians moved and resettled. But in principle, they preferred a natural waste.

They went out, like the monks of Egypt and Syria, into the desert. 'Believe one who has proved it,' wrote St Bernard, 'you will find among the woods something you never found in books. Stones and trees will teach you a lesson you never heard from masters in the school. Think you that honey cannot be drawn from the rock, and oil from the hardest stone? Do not the mountains drop sweetness and the hills flow with milk and honey, and the valleys abound with corn?'[1] This is not nature mysticism, but the call of solitude; and the milk and the honey is not to be literally interpreted, because the life of a Cistercian monk was extremely hard—physically as cold and comfortless and austere as man can well endure. A monk of Rievaulx who found he had no vocation for it called it

> that death without end which the cloistered always endure. . . . Everything here and in my nature are opposed to each other. I cannot endure the daily tasks. The sight of it all revolts me. I am tormented and crushed down by the length of the vigils, I often succumb to the manual labour. The food cleaves to my mouth, more bitter than wormwood. The rough clothing cuts through my skin and flesh down to my very bones. More than this, my will is always hankering after other things, it longs for the delights of the world and sighs unceasingly for its loves and affections and pleasures.[2]

The monotony and rigour of the Cistercian life in its early days were extreme; and the account of the physical suffering incurred by St Bernard and St Ailred of Rievaulx is painful to read.

And the rewards? These, too, may be read in Ailred's *Life*, or in the blazing eloquence of Bernard's *Letters*; and in our own day they have been analysed in some of the finest pages of Dom David Knowles's *Monastic Order in England*. These pages must be read, and cannot be summarized; and they must be read by all who have an interest in the twelfth century, for no one can see the ruins, or the survivors, of the countless Cistercian foundations made in the first half of the twelfth century, without being made very forcibly aware of the problem of the Cistercian appeal. A brief extract must suffice.

[1] Quoted Knowles, *Monastic Order*, p. 221 (slightly adapted).
[2] *Walter Daniel's Life of Ailred*, ed. and trans. Sir Maurice Powicke (Nelson's Medieval Texts, 1950), pp. 36, 30.

In addition to the simple and potent appeal of evangelical perfection . . . there was the life of patient and useful labour, which showed its gradual but enduring result as the original 'waste howling wilderness' by the banks of Rye or Aire, or in the marshes of Howden or Lindsey, began to bud and blossom as a Carmel. . . . Then there was the absolute identity of treatment and occupation, which contrasted strongly with the hierarchy of officials and obedientiaries among the black monks, separated as the communities were, a little later, into the officials on the one hand and the 'monks of the cloister' on the other. Also, there was the peace of these lonely yet populous houses. . . .

There was, moreover, another appeal that must have been very strong in individual cases, an appeal that came from Clairvaux rather than from Cîteaux. This was the invitation to the mystical life which Bernard never ceased to make in his later years. . . .

When to these many appeals were added the incalculable advantages of a clear, uniform and comprehensive rule of life, of a system of government of unrivalled excellence, and of the presence in their midst of the man who was the greatest spiritual force of his century, and when all these advantages existed in a virile and unfolding society that, from Rome to Edinburgh, Hungary to the Pyrenees, was becoming more and more homogeneous in culture and institutions, the *succès fou* of Cîteaux was all but inevitable. . . . It could be said that the world threatened to become one vast Cîteaux.[1]

There are times, as one reads St Bernard's letters, when one feels that the saint really wished to see the world turn into Cîteaux. This was not true, anyway not the whole truth; like St Francis a century later, Bernard was much concerned with finding a vocation for those who could not and should not submit utterly to the monastic life. The Cistercian houses were essentially tucked away from the world. There was room for men to preach and go on missionary journeys; and Bernard gave much encouragement to his friend St Norbert, founder of the Premonstratensian canons, reformed Augustinians who were intended to be partly monastic, partly active and apostolic in their way of life; Norbert himself became archbishop of Magdeburg and the organizer of missionary work on the eastern frontier of Germany, especially in Brandenburg. Norbert was indeed no legislator, and there was a fundamental ambiguity whether his order was to be primarily

[1] Knowles, pp. 222–4.

active or primarily monastic. Norbert was a missionary, and the preaching element never disappeared; but in due course the order became increasingly static; and its 'apostolic', evangelizing functions were taken over in the next century by the friars.

There was a place too for men who wished to combine the monastic and the military life. St Bernard was reluctant to preach the Second Crusade, but this was not because of any doubts about the value of what Christian knights were accomplishing in Spain and the Holy Land. Cistercian encouragement helped in the growth of the orders of Templars and Hospitallers, formed in Jerusalem in the early twelfth century and dedicated to the defence of the kingdom, and also in the development of the orders of knights which grew up in the Spanish peninsula.

The knights in these orders took vows of celibacy and obedience. Within St Bernard's view of the world there was room even for the married man; and especially if that man was prepared to be a patron of the monastic orders. For the success of Cîteaux is unthinkable without the numerous lay patrons who endowed it, sometimes with wildernesses, often with property already yielding a valuable return. Some were small men who could give only a rood or a little labour in the building of a monastery, in return for the monks' prayers; but the patrons included many of the great, such as King David of Scotland, the lifelong friend of Ailred of Rievaulx, who founded or refounded over a dozen monasteries, a majority of them Cistercian.

Bernard's hand, directly or through his disciples, was everywhere; so much so that we are in danger of losing all sense of proportion and attributing to him religious influences which were quite independent, just as his brilliance tends to blind us to the achievements of his predecessors. We can hardly imagine the early twelfth century without him; yet it is clear that much of the active religious life of the age was spontaneous, would have been there if he had not lived. The Cistercians were certainly on the crest of the wave. Their own growth was the most sensational in the monastic history of the century. The wave was a tidal wave, and swept many apart from the Cistercians in it. We may indeed feel that Bernard had some responsibility for the earthquake which made the wave tidal. Yet we can hardly doubt that there would have been a wave without him.

We cannot hope to isolate the personal influence of Bernard. The life of Christina of Markyate, an English hermit of the early twelfth century, gives a very vivid account of the urge to the religious life, and the struggles it involved, for a lady of moderately well-to-do family; Christina formed no order, nor even a regular community, but she was a not uncharacteristic product of the religious movements of her age. Her major struggles were over by 1120 and there is no trace of Bernard's influence in her life. In the early 1130s Master Gilbert of Sempringham, the son of a Norman knight, who had succeeded to his father's property, but owing to physical deformity could not lead a military life and so had been brought up a cleric, organized a small community of female recluses who wished to live in the precinct of his church at Sempringham. A new turn was given to Gilbert's thoughts by a visit from his friend William, the first abbot of Rievaulx and one of St Bernard's most fervent disciples. William was accompanied by some of his lay brothers, and these gave Gilbert the idea of a double community, of praying canons and praying and working nuns—or rather, perhaps, a triple community, since the out-of-door work was performed by male lay brothers, because 'without the help of man the woman's care availeth little'.[1] Gilbert, indeed, attempted to affiliate his community to the Cistercians. This was refused; but with Bernard's help he drew up a rule, and he was established as head of his little order by Bernard's disciple, Pope Eugenius III (1147). The order was never large, and never spread outside England, but in its combination of a spontaneous movement among religious-minded folk, male and female, and Cistercian influence, it is very characteristic of its period.

In general chapter at Cîteaux in 1147, Gilbert of Sempringham met Pope Eugenius, St Bernard, St Malachy, the reformer of the Irish church, and many other leaders of the spiritual movements of the day. Yet we do well to remember that it was not Bernard's influence which had brought him there, but that of William of Rievaulx and the Cistercian way of life. In the next century one of the early Franciscans, who joined the Order of Friars Minor in Francis's own lifetime, later in life told the story of how he had regarded Francis as a human being until one day, a few years after the saint's death, he was carrying some of his relics, and the reverence with which the friars treated him made him suddenly realize that Francis was not a mere man. The story was told by the brother against himself, with gentle and characteristic irony; but it reminds us that the wild success of the friars, like that of the Cistercians, was due to the appeal of their way of life fully as much as to the magnetism of their leaders. And so the final word should be with a Cistercian

[1] St Gilbert's *Life*, quoted Rose Graham, p. 12.

of the rank and file, a novice of the 1140s—speaking, it must be admitted, with the tongue of St Ailred:

> Our food is scanty, our garments rough; our drink is from the stream and our sleep often upon our book. Under our tired limbs there is but a hard mat; when sleep is sweetest we must rise at a bell's bidding. . . . Self-will has no scope; there is no moment for idleness or dissipation. . . . Everywhere peace, everywhere serenity, and a marvellous freedom from the tumult of the world. Such unity and concord is there among the brethren, that each thing seems to belong to all, and all to each. . . . To put all in brief, no perfection expressed in the words of the gospel or of the apostles, or in the writings of the Fathers, or in the sayings of the monks of old, is wanting to our order and our way of life.[1]

[1] Ailred, *Speculum Caritatis*, Book I, Chapter 17, quoted Knowles, pp. 220–1.

XV

Schools and Scholarship

The schools

The intellectual world, the world of ideas, of the upper, educated clergy, was something profoundly different from that of the rank and file of the parish priests, still more different from that of the laity. The educated cleric had access to the heritage of the classics, to some part of the thought of Plato and Aristotle, to the fathers of the Church; and the best minds, throughout our period, were able to make something of their own out of what they read and studied. Nevertheless, the intellectual world of the twelfth century was markedly different from that of the tenth. It was at once larger and more sophisticated, larger above all in the sense that far more young men of talent had the opportunity to enter it. The flourishing schools of the eleventh century, like Chartres and Bec, were comparatively few in number; the great scholars of the tenth century had been lonely figures like Gerbert. In the twelfth century the number of schools and scholars grew so rapidly that by its

BIBLIOGRAPHY. For bibliography, see E. Gilson, *History of Christian Philosophy in the Middle Ages* (London, 1955), which is a general outline on a substantial scale; for a shorter introduction, D. Knowles, *Evolution of Medieval Thought* (London, 1962); older, but still interesting, is R. L. Poole, *Illustrations of the History of Medieval Thought and Learning* (2nd edn., London, 1920); see also G. Leff, *Medieval Thought* (Harmondsworth, 1958); Beryl Smalley, *Study of the Bible in the Middle Ages* (2nd edn., Oxford, 1952). On the schools, see G. Paré, A. Brunet, P. Tremblay, *La renaissance du XIIe siècle* (Paris, 1933), H. Rashdall, *Universities of Europe in the Middle Ages* (ed. F. M. Powicke and A. B. Emden, 3 vols., Oxford, 1936); on the revival as a whole, C. H. Haskins, *The Renaissance of the Twelfth Century* (Harvard, 1927). This aspect of the period is dealt with at length in R. W. Southern's *Making of the Middle Ages*. On literature, J. De Ghellinck, *L'essor de la littérature latine au XIIe siècle* (Brussels–Paris, 1946); F. J. E. Raby, *History of Christian-Latin Poetry* (2nd edn., Oxford, 1953) and *History of Secular Latin Poetry in the Middle Ages* (2nd edn., 2 vols., Oxford, 1957); H. Waddell, *The Wandering Scholars* (London, 1927). On humanism, D. Knowles in *The Historian and* close the schools had become institutions, were crystallizing as schools and universities, with a pattern of syllabuses and degrees.

In the year 1140, at the instance of St Bernard, Peter Abelard's teaching was condemned by the pope, and the famous master driven to seek retirement as a monk at Cluny, where he died two years later. About the same time a monk of the order of Camaldoli at Bologna, called Gratian, issued the first edition of his *Concordia discordantium canonum*, or the *Decretum*, which became the standard textbook of canon law for the medieval schools, and remained the accepted repository of the early authorities of canon law down to 1917.[1] Chartres still held the disciples of the Chancellor Bernard, an eminent grammarian and student of Latin literature, who had died in 1130. Soon after 1140 the elderly Adelard of Bath was dedicating a treatise on the astrolabe to the future Henry II of England—writing up a part of the scientific and philosophical learning acquired by a lifetime of travel in France, probably Spain, Italy, Sicily, Greece and Asia Minor. These four men represented diverse branches of learning and diverse attitudes to it; and the range of opportunity open to a student at the time is illustrated by the career of a young fellow-countryman of Adelard's, John of Salisbury, who sat at Bernard's feet at Chartres and Abelard's at Paris; attended the lectures of many other leading masters; made the acquaintance of Bernard of Clairvaux; and at some stage received a training in the new canon law.

The chief schools attended by John of Salisbury, at Chartres and Paris, were associated with cathedrals. Cathedrals had been the traditional centres of teaching; many monasteries too had large libraries and schools for their own child-monks; a few had schools to which out-

---

[1] Not, technically, the official repository, because it was the work of a private scholar; but in practice the official collections of *Decretals*, from Gregory IX's on, were supplements to Gratian.

Character and other essays (Cambridge, 1963), Chapter 2; H. Liebeschütz, *Mediaeval Humanism in the life and writings of John of Salisbury* (London, 1950). On canon law, Z. N. Brooke, *English Church and the Papacy* (see Chapter XI); on the Anstey case, P. M. Barnes in *A medieval miscellany for D. M. Stenton* (Pipe Roll Society, 1962), Chapter I.

For individual figures: R. W. Southern, *St Anselm and his biographer* (Cambridge, 1963); J. G. Sikes, *Peter Abailard* (Cambridge, 1932); E. Gilson, *Heloise and Abelard* (English trans., London, 1953) and *The Mystical theology of St Bernard* (English trans., London, 1940); D. Knowles, 'St Bernard of Clairvaux', *Historian and Character*, Chapter 3; C. C. J. Webb, *John of Salisbury* (London, 1932); S. Kuttner, *Harmony from Dissonance* (Latrobe, 1960) (on Gratian and the canonists); see also articles in *Dictionnaire de théologie catholique*.

siders came. In Italy the lay schools of the towns still lived on, and the tradition of learning was far less dominantly ecclesiastical. Elsewhere education was always organized from above, by the Church and by the teachers; in Italy one sees the curious spectacle of schools being reorganized by guilds of students; and of professors forming rival guilds to protect themselves against their student-employers.

Chartres and Paris were schools of a traditional kind. Their eminence, however, depended on the fame of individual masters; and this was the period, *par excellence*, when students travelled in search of a great master, not just from lecture room to lecture room, but from city to city, if need be from one part of Europe to another. When John of Salisbury went to Chartres its celebrity was long-standing; a succession of teachers, from Fulbert, chancellor and bishop in the early eleventh century, to the masters of his own day, had preserved its traditions as a school; and latterly it had made a special reputation as the home of grammar and rhetoric. The fame of Paris was more recent. Two generations earlier, John would probably not have gone to Paris, but to Bec, where the Italian scholar-monks Lanfranc and Anselm taught in the mid and late eleventh century; by John's time Bec, as a school, was forgotten. A generation later, Chartres too was forgotten as a school. Paris and Bologna lived on, to be joined by great schools old and new. Each of them came to form the nucleus of a university, an established centre of learning, no longer dependent on the individual talent of a great master.

John of Salisbury went to Chartres to learn grammar and rhetoric, to Paris to learn logic and theology. The choice of subjects, by our standards, was narrow; but the course was very broad. From late Roman times until the scientific revolution of the seventeenth and eighteenth centuries the 'liberal arts' reigned as the basic studies of any curriculum; with the vocational studies, theology, law, and medicine, as higher subjects to which the men trained in 'arts' should then go on. The liberal arts were seven, divided between the three, the trivium, which no university man could evade—grammar, rhetoric and logic—and the four, the quadrivium, in which many men dabbled but only a few became proficient, geometry, arithmetic, astronomy and music. Grammar, which included a basic knowledge of literature, rhetoric and logic formed the solid base of education.

Grammar, rhetoric and dialectic

The content of learning altered comparatively little. John of Salisbury, perhaps the most widely read scholar of the twelfth century, can astonish us by his more abstruse reading—he was the only scholar before Petrarch to refer to Petronius' *Feast of Trimalchio*, he knew more of Macrobius than we do, and can bemuse us by his whimsical invention of a new work by Plutarch. But the nucleus of his library consisted of the Bible, the Latin fathers, especially Augustine and Jerome, much of the classics, Virgil, Ovid, Lucan, Juvenal, Horace, Seneca and the philosophical works of Cicero; the late Roman *savants*, Macrobius and Martianus Capella; Plato's *Timaeus* and other works known from extracts in the fathers; Aristotle, in the main, from Boethius (the new translations were only just beginning); as well as more recent literature, which included the writings of St Bernard. All but the last were available to a tenth-century scholar if, like Gerbert, he was prepared to gather books from many libraries. The attitude to older literature, too, had a strongly traditional flavour. John quoted with approval Bernard of Chartres's famous comparison of the modern to a dwarf, who, so long as he remained seated on the shoulders of the ancient giants, could see farther than they, but on his own was lost. There was some dispute whether pagan classics should be admitted as 'authorities'; some of the learned ascetics, like Peter Damian, revived St Jerome's condemnation of secular learning. In a famous passage St Bernard of Clairvaux emphasized that the apostles should be our teachers: 'What have the holy apostles taught us? Not the art of fishing, nor tent-making or anything of this kind; not how to read Plato, nor to deal in the subtleties of Aristotle, not to be always learning, and never come to the knowledge of truth. *They taught me how to live*.'[1] Bernard elsewhere inveighs against the study of philosophy, which leads to vainglory. This is not because he was anti-intellectual; but because he felt that secular learning had its place in the scheme of learning, that it was a comparatively humble place, and that it should be kept there—and further that he, as a Cistercian monk, was concerned with it only as a means to divine learning. Such a means it had always been taken to be; and scholars in every age, from Augustine at the turn of the fourth and fifth centuries and Cassiodorus in the sixth, to John of Salisbury in the twelfth, insisted that the liberal arts were an essential foundation to the understanding of the Christian revelation enshrined in the Bible. St Bernard himself provides a very impressive example of its uses.

Bernard was an ascetic and a Puritan, who not only, like all his order, renounced ornament and ostentation and all the symbols of wealth, but

[1] Cited by C. Mohrmann in *S. Bernardi Opera*, ed. J. Leclercq and others, vol. II (Rome, 1958), p. x.

went some distance to persecute these symbols—inspiring regulations which forbade even the illuminating of manuscripts, in which Cîteaux had shone. He refused to be bound by the rules of metre, so that his verse (as Gregory of Tours said of King Chilperic's) had no feet to stand on. But this was a special, and characteristic, eccentricity. For his prose was not only inspired by a burning zeal; it was composed with the conscious skill of an artist in rhetoric.[1] There were not perhaps many medieval writers of whom one could say with conviction that Latin would have been a poorer language if they had not written; but Bernard was surely one of them. It has long been realized that the themes and metres of rhythmic Latin verse added a new medium to the language and brought out an aspect of Latin which had been hidden in its classical days. Bernard wrote no verse worthy of the name, but the poetic rhythms of his prose, and his skill in marrying ideas to expression, inspired new generations of poets—inspired, for example, the famous sequence '*Dulcis Iesu memoria*' which was for long attributed to Bernard himself. Both language and sentiment owed much to him.

Bernard's literary technique was most carefully cultivated. The various versions of his *Sermons on the Song of Songs* show how he and his secretaries worked and reworked the material, until the elaborate structure of the final version was produced. His style was individual, but could be imitated; and he had once to apologize to the abbot of Cluny for a letter sent in his name, written in his style, which he had never set eyes on. The range of his literary effects is wide. He can pile up the imagery like a grotesque, baroque fountain; he can spill words with as prodigal a hand as St Augustine. For years he fought to have Archbishop William of York unseated, on what he thought were powerful grounds. At the height of the dispute he went to Rome to argue the case; he returned believing it settled, only to learn that William's uncle, the princely Henry of Blois, bishop of Winchester and papal legate, had intervened again to save his nephew. The transition from triumph to exalted fury is most skilfully portrayed in a letter written to the pope's successor soon after, and with an economy difficult to render in English.

> I returned home to my own affairs from that excellent meeting of your Curia strengthened by the grace of God and delighting in your own most efficacious help as a rich man delights in his treasure. Since then ... I have been waiting to see if the flower of the decision you made

[1] On St Bernard's style, see Mohrmann, *S. Bernardi Opera*, vol. II, pp. ixff.

in Rome would bear the appropriate fruit in Winchester, so that the cup of my joy might be filled. Gladness is mingled with anxiety when the vine is still in flower. . . . Hence we read in the Canticle: 'Let us see if the flowers be ready to bring forth fruit.' I have been watching the vine at Winchester, the second Rome as it is called in their song, to see if it brought forth grapes and lo 'it is turned into the bitterness of a strange vine and has brought forth wild grapes'. O happy Winchester, O second Rome, happy in your choice of so great a name! O city so powerful that you can withstand the authority of your mighty fathers in Curia, change their decrees, pervert their judgements, defame truth, and with a great voice confirm what Rome has most rightly judged shall not be confirmed without the prescribed condition. . . . Yet that Philistine in a spirit of turbulence does not blush to set up that idol Dagon next to the very ark of the Lord. Surely he has the effrontery of the harlot spoken of by Jeremias the prophet. What will not 'the cursed lust for gold' drive a man to do! Winchester has arrogated to herself the venerable name of Rome, and not only the name but the prerogatives as well. . . . O father, O glory of Rome, O upholder of justice, who carries alone the burden of so many great affairs, who protects the republic of the Church with the arms of justice, and adorns her life with virtues, we in our weakness call upon you to avenge these outrages, to make for yourself a whip of cords and upset with the strong hand of Rome the tables of those who buy and sell and drive them forth from the temple. . . . Behold here, here, I say, is the enemy, here is the man who walks before Satan, the son of perdition, the man who disrupts all rights and laws. This is the man who has 'set his face against heaven', who has repudiated, reprobated, rejected, and renounced the just judgement of the apostle, confirmed, consolidated, promulgated, and clearly defined in solemn conclave. . . . Would that the song in which they sing that Winchester is greater than Rome could be silenced on their lips. . . . Lest such contumacy should become a custom and an example, lest the dignity of Rome should be torn to shreds, lest the authority of Peter succumb to these new and great humiliations, lest religion should grow cold in the diocese of York, yea, lest it be wholly up-rooted and scattered to the winds, let Rome in the sole interest of justice, crush the contumacy of this stubborn man, and with the hammer of severity throw down that idol he has set up, and break his throne to pieces. If any of them should come to Rome for the pallium [an archbishop's scarf of office], it behoves your Holiness manfully to resist them, despising Ananias and Sapphira with their money bags. For we fear and dread lest that old whore of Winchester should be asked in some way by the new prophet he has set up to share in the government, yea in the full power of the diocese. Therefore be prudent and crush the head of the serpent that lies in wait for your heel in that realm lest the Church there should succumb and be totally suppressed. May your Holiness grow and flourish.[1]

It was an age when a man commonly used such language about an opponent; and if Bernard was exceptionally fiery when roused, we may be sure that the whore of Winchester was not entirely crushed, and gave as good as he received. But there is certainly a strain of fantasy in this piling up of rhetorical flourishes, and brilliant and daring use of biblical phrases; nor was it out of character for him to slip in a hidden phrase from Virgil: 'the cursed lust for gold'. But Bernard had other weapons in his armoury. Here is a letter to a king, Henry I of England, on the foundation of Rievaulx abbey by Bernard's own monks.

In your land there is an outpost of my Lord and your Lord, an outpost which he has preferred to die for than to lose. I have proposed to occupy it and I am sending men from my army who will, if it is not displeasing to you, claim it, recover it, and restore it with a strong hand. For this purpose I have sent ahead these men who now stand before you to reconnoitre. They will investigate the situation carefully and report back to me faithfully. Help them as messengers of your Lord and in their persons fulfil your duties as a vassal of their Lord. And may he for his honour, the salvation of your soul, and the health and peace of your kingdom, bring you safe and happy to a good and peaceful end.[2]

The imagery is here, but subdued and tamed; Bernard had met King Henry, but they were not old friends; dignity and simplicity were appropriate to the occasion.

If we could ask St Bernard in person why he condemned ornament in buildings but not in language, he might perhaps have given two answers. He could have said that his highly coloured, personal language was the tradition of the fathers of the Church; that, as a dwarf on their shoulders, he could do no other than be carried along by them. He

---

[1] B. S. James, *The Letters of St Bernard of Clairvaux* (London, 1953), no. 204, pp. 275–6, slightly adapted (to Pope Lucius II; on the context, see Knowles, *Historian and Character*, Chapter 5).

[2] James, no. 95, pp. 141–2.

could say further that he had the responsibility to make his points in the way most effective, most appropriate to the occasion. Plato and Aristotle were not for him, maybe; but he never doubted that rhetoric well-applied paid homage to God; and in this he showed himself a man of his own age and a true disciple of St Augustine. The artistry of his rhetoric gave him a closer bond with Augustine than any of his contemporaries. Bernard's vocabulary is less rich than Augustine's; his syntax is simpler. Bernard was conscious of the effort involved in making Latin a living language once again. The use of Latin had never died; but it had become a learned language in the interval between the fifth and the eleventh centuries; and it was only in the eleventh and twelfth centuries that it became once again widely spoken, truly alive again; even then it could only recover its old life in the hands of men like Bernard. Some of the learned Latinists of the age enjoyed reviving the obscurities of late Latin; men like Bernard preferred the simpler tradition of Christian Latin, and in certain ways made it simpler still. But within his limits Bernard was the master of his language; he had no contact with the new tradition of theological writing growing up in his time which went far to making Latin a purely technical, desiccated instrument of expression in the thirteenth and fourteenth centuries.

Augustine was very widely read at the time, but mainly for his theological treatises. Only a few read the *Confessions*, by which he is best known to us; the few who did, however, were profoundly influenced. In the personal writings of Bernard we see the influence of the personal writings of Augustine. It comes out not only in his language but in his readiness to express his own most personal emotions. This partly helps to explain the strangest paradox of all in St Bernard: austere as he was, he allowed free play to certain human emotions, and he laid special emphasis on the humanity of Jesus, meditating on his human life and human context, developing the devotion to his human mother; even, in the process, doing something to humanize the austerity of medieval theology.

'Rather would I have risked my life, Gerard,' he wrote in his famous lament on the death of one of his brothers, 'than lose your presence—who zealously roused my studies in the Lord, a faithful helper, shrewd examiner. Why, I ask, have we loved, have we lost one another?' Characteristically, Bernard draws his hearers after him from the vale of misery into a tremendous climax of triumph over death. Equally exuberant were his early homilies in praise of the Blessed Virgin. Towards the end of his life, in the later *Sermons on the Song of Songs*, a quieter, more sober note is heard; but he remained a magician with words to the end, never failing in striking antitheses, in rich imagery.

The emphasis on the humanity of Jesus was not new; nor the readiness to express human emotion in glowing Latin. The former thread attaches Bernard to St Anselm, whom strangely he seems not to have read; the latter to Peter Abelard, whom he is well known to have persecuted. These two paradoxes will help us to understand much about the intellectual climate of the age, its variety and its vigour. Anselm came from Aosta in Italy, spent the bulk of his life as monk and abbot of Bec, and died archbishop of Canterbury (1093–1109). He was in touch with several of the intellectual and devotional centres of Europe of the mid and late eleventh century. In his meditations he fostered the concern with the human Jesus which had already appeared in the writings of Peter Damian. Like Bernard, he was deeply influenced by Augustine. Unlike Bernard, he was fascinated by the possibilities of 'dialectic', or what we should call logic.

This, the third subject of the trivium, was coming into its own in Anselm's youth. Gerbert had studied logic, as he studied everything else; to him, as to his successors down to the late twelfth century, logic was founded on Aristotle, as transmitted by Boethius's *Commentaries* (sixth century). But logic was in Gerbert's eyes a mere tool of rhetoric, and inferior to it. At Chartres grammar and rhetoric were queens of the arts; both were expanded to include a very wide range of classical and patristic literature and learning. But logic was much less studied. Characteristically, the one pupil of Fulbert of Chartres who attained celebrity as a logician, Berengar of Tours, always kept his logic closely linked to his study of grammar and of language. R. W. Southern writes of him:

> he would have called himself a grammarian—that is to say, he was interested in the meanings and derivations of words, in the relation between language and reality, and in the rules of eloquence. Of his eloquence, which is well-attested, we have little evidence; but that he was a fanatical speculative grammarian, anxious to push the conclusions of his subject as far as possible and to apply them to the clarifying of dogma, there can be no doubt.[1]

The clarifying of dogma led Berengar into sacramental theology; and his attempt to define the nature of the Eucharist—in reaction against the growing tendency to emphasize the reality of Body and Blood in the

---

[1] Southern, *The Making of the Middle Ages*, pp. 198–9.

sacrament—was his undoing. He raised against himself an even more astute logician in Lanfranc, and Berengar's propositions were condemned. But in stirring Lanfranc to action, Berengar won a greater victory for logic than he could have won by his own success. Lanfranc had grave misgivings about the use of logic in theology; but he employed it in order to defeat Berengar at his own game, and in doing so fascinated his wide circle of pupils and admirers, and inspired Anselm.

Theology: St Anselm

Anselm was a monk of exemplary life, and his most severely theological works have a devotional element in them.

> Yield room for some little time to God; and rest for a little time in him. Enter the inner chamber of thy mind; shut out all thoughts save that of God, and such as can aid thee in seeking him; close thy door and seek him. Speak now, my whole heart! Speak now to God, saying, I seek thy face; thy face, Lord, will I seek. And come thou now, O Lord my God, teach my heart where and how it may seek thee, where and how it may find thee.

But in his meditations Anselm was not only transported to the human Jesus, or to Augustine writing his *Confessions*; he was also swept away by the love of argument. Argument carefully controlled indeed: 'For I do not seek to understand that I may believe, but I believe in order to understand. For this also I believe—that unless I believed, I should not understand.'[1]

If Aristotle provided the foundation for logic, the dominant influence on early medieval metaphysics was Plato, however little Plato's own works were known. This came out in a variety of ways; most strongly in the widely held belief in the reality of ideas. This was indeed the subject of heated debate in Anselm's day. He himself remained a firm believer in their reality. Yet one idea, the idea of God, he kept firmly distinct from the debate on ideas in general. His famous ontological argument for God's existence depends on the notion that the idea of God is unique. When he was preparing the *Proslogion*, in which he develops this argument,

> his thoughts took away his appetite for food and drink [his biographer, Eadmer, tells us], and—what distressed him more—disturbed the attention which he should have paid to the morning office. When he

[1] *Proslogion*, Chapter I (trans. S. N. Deane, *St Anselm*, Chicago, 1910, pp. 3, 7).

noticed this, and still was unable to grasp what he sought to understand, he began to think that such thoughts must be a temptation of the devil and he tried to put them from him. But the more he tried, the more his thoughts besieged him, until at last one night during Vigils the grace of God shone in his heart, and the thing he sought became clear, and filled his whole being with the greatest joy and exaltation.[1]

The fool has said in his heart, there is no God. But in doing so, Anselm argued, the fool admitted that something like God—something 'than which nothing greater can be conceived'—exists, at least in the understanding. But to exist in reality is greater than to exist merely in the understanding. If, therefore, we can conceive that God exists in reality as well as in the understanding, we conceive something greater than what is merely conceived in the understanding; the greatest thing which exists solely in our understanding, in the nature of things, is out-classed. To say that God does not exist is to postulate something greater than he; but this is to contradict the definition of God, assumed in the fool's utterance. Thus the fool has contradicted himself.

It is no part of my purpose to defend or to contradict this argument, which in its baldness has found little favour, though it has played a part in many more sophisticated constructions. The first defence of the fool was issued by Gaunilo, a monk of Marmoutier, who objected that we conceive all manner of unreal objects in our minds; thus one might conceive a lost island exceeding all others in fertility—would one's understanding of it prove it to exist? The example was unhappily chosen, and Anselm in his reply, offered to make Gaunilo a present of his island; but Anselm's own argument has been shown to imply that the idea of God in the mind must reflect the reality of God outside the mind. It is not an argument which would commend itself to the 'fool', who did not believe in God.

Anselm's most substantial contribution to theology was in his *Cur Deus homo*, his study of the Atonement. Hitherto, theologians had tended to regard the Incarnation as a means whereby—by one method or another—God could ransom or release mankind from enslavement to the Devil. In Anselm's doctrine the essential point was that Jesus was a Man, and only by a Man could man be saved from his sins; yet man as he had been could not accomplish this, and so a new Man was needed; and God solved his problem by becoming Man himself. This

[1] Quoted by Southern, *The Making of the Middle Ages*, p. 190.

317

doctrine was not immediately or widely accepted; but the criticism of Anselm and others did succeed in destroying the old view. The old doctrine had seen mankind as caught in the eternal warfare of God and the devil; in a way it was not unlike the dualist belief that God and the devil were separate powers at war in the world; and the Christian thought of the tenth and eleventh centuries, with its strong ascetic tendencies, had done little to counteract the notion that the world was the devil's creation. The counterblow to the dualists was prepared, at the level of high theology, by Anselm and his successors, who emphasized that the world was God's and had been redeemed by God made man; that the world was therefore basically good, and that God loved it.

Theology and humanism: Abelard

In Anselm logic was applied to theology with great precision, but within a devotional context. In Abelard the devotional context disappeared, and sometimes the precision; but the love of logic was carried a step further.

Peter Abelard was born on the borders of Brittany in or about 1079; he was thus about eleven years older than Bernard of Clairvaux. He started his education in Brittany, then travelled, possibly to Chartres; but it was in Paris that he acquired his training in logic. Soon, however, he turned the weapon against his master, and set up, on the Mont St Geneviève in Paris, as a teacher himself. He quickly acquired a wide reputation for the brilliance of his lectures; but after an illness and a period of meditation he decided to study theology, and set off for Laon, at the age of about thirty-five, to sit at the feet of the leading biblical commentators of the time. Theology at this date meant first and foremost the study of the 'Sacred Page'; and in the school of Laon the deposit of ancient wisdom and new learning were being distilled in the standard gloss (or commentary), the *Glossa ordinaria*, which was to be the companion of thousands of bibles for many centuries to come. The weapons, however, were too blunt for Abelard, who returned to Paris to teach theology himself.

Abelard was evidently a vain man, intensely proud of his own capacity and achievements, scornful and tactless with rivals; self-confident and self-satisfied. In large measure he was the author of his own disasters. Shortly after his return to Paris, he fell in love with and seduced one of his pupils, a clever, intelligent girl much younger than himself, called Heloise. A strange irony has made this incident the cause of Abelard's immense fame in later ages; and it has a deep human and historical interest. They had a child, and Abelard offered to marry Heloise. She knew that marriage would wreck his career in the Church, and tried to refuse; but Heloise's own gifts of character had by now influenced even the egoistical Abelard: he insisted, and they were married. The rest of the tragic story is familiar—the assault on Abelard by her uncle and guardian, his castration, the retreat of both into religious houses, Abelard's restless wandering from monastery to monastery, ending in his return to Paris; how Heloise became a devoted and successful abbess, though she never accepted the religious significance of her position, always regarded herself as first and foremost Abelard's wife; and how Abelard, after incurring Bernard's enmity, appealed from the council of Sens to Rome, was condemned in Rome, retired to Cluny and died (1142); and how, finally, Abelard's searing experience was laid bare in his *History of my Calamities*, and how the relationship of this strange couple was revealed in their letters.

These letters reveal their concern with human and humane values. I have so far avoided the word humanism on account of its ineradicable ambiguity; but we can evade it no longer. Its basic meaning, as it is used by historians of the Middle Ages, is a love of the pagan classics, and in this sense it cuts right across the intellectual world of the eleventh and twelfth centuries. Many men in this age, in Italy, Germany and France especially, loved the pagan classics, but for very few did it oust altogether the primacy of the Christian classics, above all of the Bible. There were exceptions; but the outstanding classical scholars, like John of Salisbury, were commonly men of devotion, Christian humanists. The second significance of humanism is devotion to human values and concern with the expression of human ideas and human emotions; with other modern significations of the term we are not concerned. Devotion to the classics and concern with human values appear in varying degrees in a number of the leading figures of the times.[1] It is helpful, I think, to put aside for a moment the label 'humanism'; and to observe the attributes at work in the differing outlook of the two great opponents, Bernard and Abelard. Bernard, if he had understood the term, would have repudiated the label humanist. Yet in his concern to express human emotion, in his vision of earthly love (in his case, the love of man for man) as in some sense a reflection of the divine, in his love of the past—especially of the fathers—he seems to have more in common with Abelard and Heloise than with many of his contemporaries. Yet in Abelard's identification of himself with Augustine or Heloise's with the pagan Stoics there is a

[1] See Knowles, *The Historian and Character*, Chapter 2.

more complete attempt to live in the past; and the past is attractive, in some measure, for its own sake. It was partly this which made Abelard so daring in his use of logic, and spurred him to go to the lengths he went in trying to find in Greek philosophy anticipations of the doctrine of the Trinity.

Bernard's doctrine of the analogy of divine and human love, and his sponsorship of the cult of the human Jesus and of his human mother, placed him in the van of one of the theological movements of the age— the movement which emphasized God's relationship to man, his divine compassion, instead of the almost exclusive emphasis on God as judge which had been the theme of theology and of art in the immediately preceding centuries. The lovely, and strikingly human, Madonnas of the art of the thirteenth century, and later, were devised outside our period; the concern with Jesus's humanity was only slowly spreading; the striking anticipation of later themes in the famous Weingarten Crucifixion[1]— in which an English artist of the mid eleventh century attempted to portray Christ's human sufferings by a vivid, impressionistic technique —was a rare portent. And to St Bernard's tolerance to new ideas there was a strict limit; he only tolerated them when he failed to realise they were new. Abelard propounded a moral doctrine in which it was the intention not the act which counted, a very salutary reorientation of contemporary teaching; but carried to characteristic excess and expressed with some remarkable inadvertence. 'This most excellent doctor', as Bernard ironically described him, 'prefers free will at the expense of grace.' In his attempt to describe the doctrine of the Trinity Abelard associated each of the persons with an abstract Greek idea, thereby depersonalising God and introducing some rather artificial analogies. 'This most excellent doctor put degrees and grades in[to] the Trinity like Arius . . ., and with Nestorius he divides Christ by denying to the human nature he assumed association with the Trinity.' Worst of all, 'this man, apparently holding God suspect, will not believe anything until he has first examined it with his reason'.[2]

In each case Bernard slightly garbled what Abelard said, or drew on what his pupils were saying as evidence of the master's beliefs. Yet there was more than a spark of truth in Bernard's charges. Abelard never, in principle, reduced faith to the result of human enquiry. But he un-

---

[1] The manuscript, now New York, Pierpont Morgan Library, MS. 709, was bequeathed by the English Judith, widow of Earl Tostig (see pp. 225–6) and wife of Welf IV, duke of Bavaria, to Weingarten abbey in south Germany (see Southern, *The Making of the Middle Ages*, frontispiece and p. vii).

[2] James, no. 249, pp. 329, 328.

doubtedly expressed much greater interest in positions which were capable of rational investigation than in those which were not. Yet what he actually said was this: 'Faith has no merit with God when it is not the testimony of divine authority that leads us to it, but the evidence of human reason.'[1] In intention he was orthodox; but his self-confident skill in logic, his lack of interest in the devotional context which Anselm, like Bernard, had seen as essential to theological enquiry, and the carelessness with which he stated his conclusions, gave serious grounds for disagreement.

If it were our business to sit in judgement at the Council of Sens in 1140, most of us today would no doubt regret that the case had ever been called; if we judged by the standards of the day, we should be bound to admit that Abelard had said things which could easily be construed as heresy; and that his popularity was so great that his carelessness was capable of having wide and serious effect. In fairness to Bernard let us remember that he was driven by his friends to persecute Abelard; that Abelard was considerably the older man and famous for his skill in debate—though the Bernard of 1140 had stood sterner tests than this. In fairness to Abelard let us remember that he was misrepresented, that he felt—not altogether without reason—that he was being harried and persecuted for errors long since repented.

Abelard's real offence in Bernard's eyes was his burning sense of intellectual adventure, when he was approaching the most sacred mysteries of the Christian faith. The inadvertence, the extreme intellectualism—which makes Abelard seem like an agile Greek while Bernard plays the Hebrew Prophet—were no doubt reproduced in many of the ardent logicians of the mid twelfth century, whose work aroused John of Salisbury's suspicion. But these attributes were put on one side by Abelard's most eminent pupils; and the essence of his work, the application of improved logical tools to theology, and a sense of the comprehensive scope of theology, were dominant factors in the schools from the mid twelfth century on. In this the personal influence of Abelard can be exaggerated. Most of his techniques were not new: he came in on the crest of a wave; much of his philosophical work had to be revised as more of Aristotle was recovered by later generations. He gave new meaning to *theologia*, which hitherto had been applied mainly to Christology (or alternatively to the study of pagan Gods), and paved the way for a broader understanding of the science. But it was his pupil Peter the Lombard who first put together authorities and arguments

[1] J. G. Sikes, *Peter Abailard* (Cambridge, 1932), p. 53 (after Gregory the Great).

over the whole theological range, in his *Sentences* (*c.* 1150). Abelard's greatness was as a teacher. His learning was great, but neither his learning nor his techniques were wholly original; what he did was to spread their use, to inspire a whole generation of students; and it is the wide spread of ideas—their influence on a far larger number of students than in the two preceding centuries, and on a more varied range of talent—which made the twelfth century an age of such rapid intellectual development, an age in which the absence of highly organized universities left the human intellect free (in spite of St Bernard) to roam as it had not roamed for many centuries.

Abelard's most famous book was the *Sic et non.* Characteristically, it is a teacher's manual, not a finished treatise. Theologians must base their findings on authority; but what if authorities disagree? Abelard collected a number of discordant authorities, and left his pupils to sort the problem out: a dangerous invitation to disrespect, but that, after all, is the teacher's business.

Canon law

The technique of Abelard's *Sic et non* was very similar to that employed by Ivo of Chartres in dealing with the authorities of canon law at the turn of the eleventh and twelfth centuries. Ivo and the methods of Abelard or of his disciples combined to inspire Master Gratian to his massive and comprehensive attempt to create the *Concord of Discordant Canons* (*c.* 1140). Gratian did for canon law what Peter the Lombard was to do for theology. The publication of Gratian's book was not only a key event in the history of scholarship, it was also a crucial moment in the history of the papal monarchy. In an earlier chapter we spoke of the alliance of the reformed papacy with the intellectual revival. In the case of Abelard we have seen how authority could be used on occasion to stifle intellectual development; in the case of Gratian we have the supreme example of how intellectual development and the papal monarchy could support one another. The papacy owed its authority in the twelfth century and later above all to its position as the supreme appeal court of Christendom; the revival of canon law was an essential element in this. An illustration will serve to underline this fact.

There was a man called William of Sackville, who held a fee (a large, but not particularly important one) in East Anglia and Essex, and also (it seems) some land in France, in the county of Blois; in or about the 1120s he became betrothed to a lady called Albereda, or Aubrey. He never completed the formalities of marriage, and never lived with her. A while later he solemnly married another lady, Adelicia, or Alice, daughter of a local magnate. Aubrey objected, but could not make herself heard in the crowd of wedding guests; and William and Alice were married and had children. But when King Henry I, the lover of peace died, justice was banished from the realm—so Alice's daughter complained—and 'the madness of those who rejoiced in overturning the old order grew ever stronger'. To William de Sackville the old order evidently meant Alice, and so he pressed the local archdeacon to arrange a divorce; that is to say, to declare the marriage null, for divorce in the modern sense was impossible. William raked up his betrothal to Aubrey, claimed that it was a full marriage, and that he could never have been validly married to Alice. The suit did not go undefended. It went before the bishop of Winchester, St Bernard's opponent in the York dispute, Henry of Blois, because Henry was acting as vicar (episcopal caretaker) of the diocese of London during a vacancy in the see. Henry consulted the pope, who said that it depended on what form the betrothal of William and Aubrey had taken: if William had said: 'I promise to take you to wife some time in the future' it was not a binding marriage; if he said: 'I take you to wife here and now', it was binding, William could never have married Alice, and the bishop must celebrate their divorce in due form. And that, accordingly, was what he did. For the rest of their lives the couple lived apart. On William's death in 1158 a new problem arose: he had had children by Alice, and his surviving heiress was Mabel: but as Alice's daughter was she legitimate? If illegitimate, she could not inherit. There was an alternative candidate in William's nephew Richard of Anstey, of whose legitimate relationship to William there could be no question; and Richard promptly sued in the king's court for the inheritance. Meanwhile a continental court presided over by the count of Blois, after consulting a number of ecclesiastical authorities, pronounced that Mabel and her sisters were legitimate, on what ground we do not know.

The case of Richard of Anstey is famous because he left a diary of his expenses in the suit, which gives us an astonishing insight into the difficulties of litigation in a complicated case in the twelfth century. For a year he followed the king's court up and down England, across France, almost to the gate of Toulouse, suing for writs and judgement. The case was then transferred to the church courts, since it turned on whether Mabel was legitimate and therefore on the ecclesiastical law of marriage. In the next year and a half there were no less than eighteen hearings before the archbishop of Canterbury; the delays were caused partly by the obscurity of the case and partly by the frequent absence of one or other of the parties, especially of Mabel, who was married, and often with child. Little wonder that Richard lost confidence in the capacity of the archbishop's court to settle the case. He appealed to Rome; the pope referred the case back to delegates in England; Mabel appealed against the delegates' decision; the pope referred it to a second set of delegates, whose judgement, in Richard's favour, the pope confirmed. At long last, in the summer of 1163, almost five years after Richard of Anstey had opened the case, the king's court decided that the inheritance was his.

What constituted a legally binding marriage?—and under what circumstances, if any, could children born of a marriage which was subsequently dissolved be legitimate? To these questions there was no easy answer. The former question had been asked many times, and answered in many different ways; the latter scarcely seems to have been asked at all before the mid twelfth century. The questions seem comparatively simple to us; and the fact that they involved such complex issues is an indication of the primitive state of canon law at about the time when Gratian's *Decretum* was published, and of the influence of the papal court, in whose jurisdiction lay the answers to such questions.

The story of Richard of Anstey would have astonished Gerbert (Pope Sylvester II) as much as it astonishes us, though for different reasons. The canon law, in his day, had been an impressive pile of ruins, like the city of Rome itself. It had grown to maturity under the wing of Roman Civil Law, in the later days of the Empire, and with Roman Law it had decayed—never entirely forgotten, at some times much studied, but never widely or evenly applied. The papal court, even then, had been in theory the supreme appeal court in spiritual cases in Christendom, or at least in western Christendom. But in practice it was very rare for any appeals to reach it, and it rarely handled any but very portentous or very local cases. Richard of Anstey was neither eminent nor Roman, and the stream of appeals which came to Rome in the mid twelfth century included many of the most trivial character. The ruins of canon law were being rapidly restored, and Gratian provided the materials for the rapid rebuilding of an impressive, effective, legal structure.

To be united and effective, a legal system requires four things at least: a framework of clearly defined laws, a corpus of authorities; a central power to enforce the law, and people or peoples to accept it; a body of trained lawyers to interpret and develop the code and the organization of the system; and a body of judges to act on it. The medieval Church finally acquired all these attributes in the late twelfth and thirteenth centuries, in the pontificates of Alexander III (1159-81) and Innocent III (1198-1216); and it was then that the papal monarchy finally emerged as a state—a spiritual state, it is true, but a state none the less, since it had coercive powers and a defined body of subjects. But if it was a state, it had a curious constitution, for executive and legislature were swallowed up in the judiciary; as if the United States were governed by the Supreme Court, or the Lord Chief Justice was Prime Minister of England.

Before Gratian there was no code or recognized corpus; but that is not to say there was no law. The authorities of canon law consisted of the canons of church councils, the letters of popes—which came to be called decretals—and, since law and theology were so closely inter-twined, the Bible and the fathers. To this one might add Roman Law itself, which had many useful prescriptions in it, though Gratian him-self, and some others, viewed it with suspicion. These authorities were gathered from time to time in a variety of ways in a variety of different collections. In our period, before the advent of Gratian, four came to be of special significance. The supreme collection of material was the Forged Decretals of the pseudo-Isidore, a body of material genuine and spurious put together by a Frankish cleric or atelier of the ninth century. The author or authors were primarily concerned to defend a bishop against his metropolitan, and so did everything they could to diminish the authority of metropolitans (archbishops) and enhance that of bishops —and of the pope. It was known at Rome in the ninth century, then largely forgotten until it was brought back by the reformers in the mid eleventh century; none of its users in our period had any reason to know that its materials were forged. The inconvenience of the Forged Decretals, as of most early collections, was that they were arranged chronologically (or in what was supposed to be chronological order); the first major logical or analytical collection was made by the Emperor Henry II's protégé, Burchard bishop of Worms, in the early eleventh century. This, too, was known to the papal reformers; it was useful, because more or less rationally arranged; but not very popular, because Burchard had no interest in papal authority, though he gave papal supremacy formal acknowledgement. The reformers themselves engaged in a good deal of research. The famous *Dictatus pape* of Gregory VII very probably consists of the headings, or table of contents, of a small collection of canonical authorities on matters essential to the papal position; these authorities can be approximately reconstructed from other collections of the time. But none of these collections was sufficiently lucid or sufficiently comprehensive to have a wide circulation.

The crucial development came in two stages. First, at the turn of the eleventh and twelfth centuries, Ivo, bishop of Chartres—where he was in touch with one of the most active schools of the period, and had the resources of one of the best libraries in Europe—planned a massive collection of all available canons. When this was complete, he had it abbreviated; and the brief *Pannormia*, long enough to cover a good deal of essential ground, short enough to be handled by men who were not trained, professional lawyers, had an immense success in the first half of the twelfth century. Ivo was a blunt and honest administrator, who combined an acute sense of the Church's need with a fluent pen and a magnetic personality; he was able to gather disciples round him to complete the various stages of this large work in the intervals of a busy life.

Gratian, by contrast, was a scholar of original mind, unencumbered by other calls on his time; he too may have had helpers, and it is highly probable that the work as we have it has been revised by other hands than Gratian's; but Gratian's mind informs the whole work. Ivo had pointed out that authorities did not always agree, and suggested the lines on which they could be reconciled, or their value distinguished. In the interval Abelard had taught, and published, the *Sic et non*; and Gratian, living in Bologna, was able to profit more than Ivo by the revival in the study of Roman Law. Gratian regarded Roman Law with suspicion, and tried to avoid using it as an authority. But he used it as a model, and had clearly learned much from the vast, intelligible, coherent massiveness of the most elaborate and sophisticated legal corpus Europe had known; learned much, too, from the work of the scholars who had revived the knowledge of Justinian's *Corpus Iuris Civilis* in the late eleventh and early twelfth centuries at Bologna, Master Irnerius and his successors. Irnerius was both a scholar and a practising jurist: Roman Law was in regular use in the Italian cities. The combination of academic and practical law in Bologna provided an admirable model for the growth to maturity of canon law.

Few works have exercised so immediate, so decisive, and so lasting an influence as Gratian's *Decretum*. Its author has been called the father of the science of canon law, and there can be little doubt that he deserves the title: some grandfathers and great-uncles can be discovered, but no one who could dispute his claim to immediate parenthood.

In the *Decretum* Gratian put together the largest collection of legal texts ever amassed in a collection of canon law; and he also arranged them, harmonized them and inserted a magisterial commentary. It was at once a source book and a textbook. It was not planned as a card index of the law, but as one continuous flowing argument, proceeding like a chain of reasoning from point to point. Since it was a textbook and an argument as well as a collection of texts it could never be an official collection like the *Decretals* of Pope Gregory IX (1234) and the later decretal collections. But Gratian's book was accepted and used at Rome within a very short time after its publication; it was immediately accepted in the schools as the foundation for the study of canon law. It was not officially promulgated; yet everyone treated it as the repository of legal sources before 1140, and the later *Decretals* were intended to be supplements to it; their authors tried to avoid repeating any of its canons.

If two authorities conflict, the lawyer must often decide which is of greater weight, or which is enunciating bad law. This was not Gratian's method. His was a *Concord of Discordant Canons*; with the utmost suavity he compelled them to agree. Adam Smith revolutionized economics by bringing a philosopher's mind to bear on a stale discipline. Gratian combined the new logic of the theologians with the legal subtlety of the Roman jurists; and when his solutions were altogether too subtle and improbable, they roused in his disciples the kind of excitement which Hobbes felt in the presence of the forty-seventh proposition in Euclid: 'By God, this is impossible.' The canons were often wholly discordant, but Gratian was not abashed.

Gratian's work was completed about 1140, and finally revised about 1150; in 1159 his greatest disciple,[1] Master Roland, became pope as Alexander III (1159–81). As pope, he propounded in a long series of decretals the principles of the master converted into a more practical legal frame, and started the work of filling the gaps left by Gratian and his predecessors. This could not have been done before, because before Gratian the gaps were only imperfectly known. From his time on, as the legal prestige and activity of the papal court grew, the number of decisions of disputed points grew also; a large body of decretals (mainly papal letters and decrees of later councils) came to supplement the authorities in the *Decretum*. Gratian supplied the materials for a code of canon law; his disciples and successors provided the body of trained lawyers to develop and interpret it; the rise of the papal monarchy had

[1] It is not known whether Roland was in the strict sense a pupil of Gratian: tradition has it that Gratian was a recluse who had no pupils. But it is hardly likely that this is the whole truth.

greatly strengthened the central authority which could enforce it, and the mid twelfth century saw the machinery of the appeal court becoming firmly established.

Rome's appellate jurisdiction was very old; but the idea that all and sundry should avail themselves of it came in with the twelfth century. Appeals proceeded from the courts of first instance (archdeacon's or bishop's courts), up through the archbishop's court to the pope. Once in Rome, an appeal could be decided on the spot; or, if the pope was dissatisfied with the information available to him, he could refer the case back to men in the country concerned, to judges-delegate, as they were called. A judge-delegate might be a papal legate or a diocesan bishop; as time passed it became normal to appoint two or three delegates for a case; and as appeals became commoner less and less eminent men were appointed. This development lies outside our period. But already in 1150 the idea was spreading that Rome was a court which could actually be used. In the 1140s the flow of appeals first became a steady stream. Rome was not popular with everyone: it was distant, it was expensive. In every European curia a visitor, still more a litigant, had to be liberal in tips and fees to the large number of officials and servants who expected to earn a good living by these means; and the papal court, being one of the grandest in Europe, had the reputation of being particularly expensive. Rome's love for gold and silver was a common theme for satire from the eleventh century on. An early example is the tract on the translation of the relics of St Albinus (the white metal, i.e. silver) and St Rufinus (the red metal, gold), in which among many extravagances, Pope Urban II is made to say 'Albinus is my helper, I shall not fear what man may do to me. It is good to trust in Rufinus, rather than in man.'

Rome was expensive; none the less appeals flowed to it. Partly this was the natural consequence of developing canon law; litigants grew more litigious; many found they could postpone decisions by appeal; frivolous use was often made of the system. But serious use was made too: Rome was comparatively impartial; it could provide answers to otherwise unanswerable questions; it could cut through the tangle of local procedure. To Richard of Anstey it provided a short cut to his inheritance.

Thus the growing prestige of the papal monarchy and the intellectual revival combined to make possible the renewal of canon law, of the hierarchy of the Church's courts; and the position of Rome as the court of highest appeal, to which cases more and more frequently came, was the principal pillar of the papal monarchy in the twelfth century.

XVI

Popular Religion

Religion, art and architecture

When one looks back at the religious experience and outlook of men in the Middle Ages, one tends automatically to contrast the extreme diversity of the modern world with the homogeneous beliefs of the ages of faith. It is clear that the range of opinion and the freedom of choice are very much greater today than they were eight hundred years ago. Choice is comparatively free; alternatives are bewilderingly many; in one society Christians of a dozen denominations may mingle with Jews, Muslims, Buddhists, with men of the most various religious positions and of none. There were Jews in medieval Europe, and occasional Muslim visitors; for the rest, all men were nominally Christians. It was difficult to evade being a member of the Catholic Church. But there were heretics in the eleventh century in various parts of Europe, and by the mid twelfth they were already threatening to outnumber the

BIBLIOGRAPHY. On the layman's religion, see chapters by R. W. Southern and C. N. L. Brooke in *The layman in Christian history*, ed. S. C. Neill and H.-R. Weber (London, 1963). On art and architecture, the classic is E. Mâle, *L'art religieux du XII*e *siècle en France* (4th edn., Paris, 1940); see also K. J. Conant, *Carolingian and Romanesque architecture* (Harmondsworth, 1959); J. Evans, *Art in Medieval France* (Oxford, 1948)—especially on the relation of artists and patrons. On Suger and the origins of Gothic, see E. Panofsky, *Abbot Suger on the Abbey Church of Saint-Denis* (Princeton, 1946); O. von Simson, *The Gothic Cathedral* (New York, 1956); on cathedral building see also J. Gimpel, *The Cathedral Builders* (English trans., London, 1961); on Cistercian architecture, M. Aubert, *L'architecture cistercienne en France* (2 vols., Paris, 1947); H.-P. Eydoux, *L'architecture des églises cisterciennes d'Allemagne* (Paris, 1952); on drawing and illumination, F. Wormald, *English drawings of the tenth and eleventh centuries* (London, 1952); O. Pächt, C. R. Dodwell, F. Wormald, *The St Albans Psalter* (London, 1960); on painting in general, A. Grabar and C. Nordenfalk, *Romanesque Painting* (Geneva, 1958); on sculpture, D. Grivot and G. Zarnecki, *Gislebertus, sculptor of Autun* (London, 1961). For Theophilus, see *De diversis artibus*, ed. and trans. C. R. Dodwell (Nelson's Medieval Texts, orthodox in parts of southern France and northern Italy. Among the orthodox there was more variety of opinion and expression than we easily realize. The bulk of our knowledge comes from the highly educated upper clergy, whose theology was more precise, and by the twelfth century far more sophisticated, than the theology of most men of that age or of this. If we ask what the ordinary man believed we are met by the almost impenetrable barrier of his silence: he was illiterate, and left little memorial of his thoughts for posterity.

In the early thirteenth century, two generations after our period closed, a knight of humble status and without formal education, left us in two great poems his views on many of the problems which engage us now. In his *Parzival* Wolfram von Eschenbach explored the many-mansioned house of chivalry, severely criticized current notions of chivalry and courtly love, but left his own ideals clearly on record. In brief, Parzival loses his faith; yet his constant loyalty, the supreme virtue of true chivalry—loyalty to himself, to his order, to his wife—wins God's approval, and he is guided in the end to recover his faith, to win the Holy Grail, and to be reunited with his wife and family. In *Wille-halm* Wolfram analysed the problem of the good heathen and his place in God's providence. Earlier authors had assumed that the infidel was bound for hell, and popular doctrine permitted the crusaders to hurry them on their way without any sort of qualm. Wolfram subjects this view to penetrating criticism: the heathen are God's handiwork; if they too are true to their order and their faith, God will save them. Such at least is the tendency of *Willehalm*, although the threads are not all brought together.

In part, Wolfram's views reflect the tendency of twelfth-century theology at the highest level; in part they represent personal, and perhaps somewhat eccentric, speculation; their special interest is that they represent a reflective layman's view on his own place in the world and

1961). On pilgrimages, J. Vielliard, *Le guide du pèlerin de Saint-Jacques de Compostelle* (2nd edn., Macon, 1950).

On heretics, see D. Obolensky, *The Bogomils* (Cambridge, 1948); H. Maisonneuve, *Études sur les origines de l'Inquisition* (2nd edn., Paris, 1960); I. da Milano, 'Le eresie popolari del secolo XI nell'Europa occidentale', in *Studi Gregoriani*, ed. G. B. Borino, vol. II (Rome, 1947), pp. 43–89; J. Guiraud, *Histoire de l'Inquisition au moyen âge*, vol. I (Paris, 1935); A. Borst, *Die Katharer* (Stuttgart, 1953); Sir Steven Runciman, *The Medieval Manichee* (Cambridge, 1947). On the subject of the chapter as a whole H. Grundmann, *Religiöse Bewegungen im Mittelalter* (2nd edn., Hildesheim, 1961) is of special importance and value.

on his own life, the religious vocation of the layman. No source from within our period brings these problems so sharply into focus; and Wolfram will serve to remind us what our problems are, and the limit to which a thinking layman, who is yet not a heretic, can reach, very shortly after the close of the period.

In the main, inevitably, the clergy were the leaders of religious thought and devotion; and in their ideas and practices most devout laymen followed the clergy at more or less of a distance. Sometimes the distance was very substantial indeed. Most European peoples had been nominally Christian for centuries; a few, especially the Scandinavian peoples, were converted in this period. In either event the extent of religious instruction which most laymen received is exceedingly obscure. What is clear is that many old superstitions survived, and that it was those elements of Christianity which had most in common with their pagan beliefs and practices which most firmly gripped the illiterate converts in early days. The old Teutonic pantheon, for example, had contained 'high gods', Thor and Woden and the rest, and a host of lesser spirits who were especially attached to physical places and physical objects. Christianity too had its high God, and accommodated devotion to innumerable saints, all of whom had their favourite local habitations, and were closely associated with their physical remains, their relics. Equally alive were the evil spirits, now called devils, whose activities took over many of the activities of the unseen world which could not be attributed to God and his saints.

There is, however, a danger in pursuing this story forwards through paganism to Christianity. Little as we know of the beliefs of ordinary men in the Christian period, we know less still of the paganism which these beliefs replaced; we are in danger of engaging in empty speculation, and we are in danger of forgetting how long Christianity had reigned in most of western Europe even by the tenth century. The cult of relics, for instance, substantially increased in the tenth and eleventh centuries; if we treat it merely as a survival we shall miss much of its historical significance—whatever our personal convictions may be. There is one outstanding point of contact between us and the laymen of this period: they had an increasing tendency to build churches of durable stone; many of these survive; and we can inspect them and observe the standards they wished to attain and deduce something of the ideals which inspired them. Clearly, church-building does not reflect lay attitudes alone, or even, perhaps, mainly. But it represents the point where clerical and lay concerns most obviously met.

331

The period between the tenth century and the twelfth saw an exceptionally high proportion of effort and wealth put into the building of churches. The Carolingian age had seen stately buildings go up in many places, especially in Charlemagne's Aachen. But if we compare Charlemagne's palatine chapel, which still survives, with the churches built by kings and emperors in the tenth or eleventh centuries, we are immediately struck by the growth in scale. Every region has its own history, and we can only give a few selected examples here. In the tenth century cathedrals and abbeys of large dimensions were being built above all in Germany; and they represented the generosity, and concern with the Church, of the Saxon emperors and their leading subjects. They also represented the tastes of the German clergy of the age, and especially of the communities of monks reformed under the inspiration of Gorze in Lorraine. This reminds us that the tenth century was an age of monastic reforms; and across the frontier in France, at a slightly later date, Cluny was also setting an example of increased scale and magnificence. The second church at Cluny, of the early eleventh century, had many imitators; so had the third, of the time of St Hugh (1049–1109). But Cluny stood above all as a symbol of the marriage of magnificent architecture with rich ornament. In the design of large churches, significantly enough, it was the leading pilgrimage churches of France and northern Spain which were most influential—St Martin of Tours (tenth century, largely rebuilt in the eleventh) and St James of Compostella (eleventh century) above all.

Since Carolingian times it had been the convention in the West to build large churches in the shape of a cross, a shape which had practical and came to receive symbolic significance. The proportions of the various limbs of the cross varied very much from time to time and from place to place; as did many other features, such as the shape, size and situation of the tower or towers. But taking the buildings so far mentioned as a group, we can roughly generalize as follows: at the east end they had each an apse, a semi-circular terminus, and here and there a moderate number of other apses, to provide space for additional altars; at the west end they had immense naves, with comparatively plain arcades of round-headed Romanesque arches. Windows were few and small. As time passed they grew larger and more numerous, but originally many of the windows were filled with dark glass, so that the church as a whole tended still to be a dark tunnel. The wall spaces (above the nave arcade, over the crossing arches and above all in the curve of the apse) were adorned by great paintings. Towards the east end of the nave was a screen, which divided the nave, where laymen could freely circulate at this time, from the choir and sanctuary which monks or canons alone might use. But the screen was low; unlike the screens of the later Middle Ages, it did not hide choir and high altar from the nave; over it the altar could be seen, and behind and above the altar, the shrine of the patron saint. In the pilgrimage churches a passage (or ambulatory) ran round behind the high altar and the shrine, so that pilgrims could circulate and worship at the shrine of St Martin or St James without invading the sanctuary itself.

These basic elements, with or without the ambulatory, provided the pattern for church design in many parts of Europe in the eleventh and twelfth centuries; above all in the Norman lands of north France and England, which witnessed an activity in building even more grandiose than elsewhere. They also witnessed technical improvement: the development of improved stone vaulting, to replace the ceiling of wood which had been very susceptible to fire, and the use of the pointed arch, which made a vault in particular stronger and easier to construct; both these innovations were tried out in the nave of Durham cathedral in the early twelfth century. In their other dominion, in the south of Italy and in Sicily, the Normans entered upon and fostered other traditions. In Italy the constant presence of surviving Roman buildings gave frequent inspiration, especially in ages under the spell of Rome, like the age of the twelfth-century renaissance; experts have assigned the baptistery at Florence to every century from the fourth to the eleventh, and the superficial observer would suppose San Clemente at Rome, rebuilt in the eleventh century, to be a Christian basilica of the fourth. Italy, as always, followed its own devices; but here, too, great churches were built; and in the Norman kingdom Roman arches, Greek mosaics, Muslim colour schemes and Norman organization combined to produce the dazzling twelfth-century cathedrals of Sicily.

The first thing these buildings reveal is the generosity of the patrons who provided the bulk of the funds. Many churches were well endowed already; yet it remains broadly true that this great effort would have been impossible without quite sensational contributions from laymen; first of all, from wealthy laymen, kings and great nobles; but also from every sort and condition of man, according to his means. The Saxon emperors and the Norman kings built because they liked large endeavours; because they were fashionable; they built to keep up with the Joneses; they built to pave the road to heaven with stones of well-dressed ashlar; and the Normans and Angevins in particular built out of the sense, which it is difficult not to feel was justifiable, that sensational generosity to God and his saints was needed to expiate their sensational crimes. The motives were mixed. Some of these men hoped not only to win Heaven, but the applause of men; the Normans in England no doubt partly built to display their glory and their power to the defeated English. The religious motives, too, were mixed, according to the simplicity or sophistication of religious thought of the donor. What stands out is that so many were prepared to invest very lavishly in these projects.

If we wish to penetrate beyond the façade of the churches, and to win their aid in showing us into the minds of their builders, we must be as clear as we can about whom they were meant to house. First of all, a church was the house of God: his image looked down in majesty from countless apses, as it still looks down in the mosaic of Monreale; the drama of his Passion was daily re-enacted at all the altars, above all at the high altar, where, in the course of the twelfth century at least, host and chalice came to be elevated so that all the worshippers in the Church could see that God's Body and Blood were present. The Eucharist was the supreme material symbol of the link of earth and heaven. Other material symbols were there; above all in the relics of the saints. The regular reservation of the sacrament in a tabernacle behind the high altar was a practice of a later age; and the patron saint of the church was undoubtedly regarded as its chief regular inhabitant. One must remember that the patron saint was sometimes God himself: Canterbury cathedral had always been dedicated to Christ and the Holy Trinity, although the relics of many saints lived there too and after 1170 its east end was rebuilt as a shrine to St Thomas Becket; the Normans built new cathedrals at Norwich and Chichester and dedicated them to the Trinity. But in most churches a human patron saint was reckoned the chief living presence; and this feeling was enhanced because the saint had a special interest in a particular church, and an overwhelming interest in the Church which held his relics, whereas God's presence and his interest were everywhere. In the popular view the divine monarchy was even more formidable than the earthly monarchies they were used to; one had to find a special friend at court to forward one's interests.

The saint not only lived in his church to receive pilgrims and petitioners, he was reckoned to be its living master, the lord of its property; and the bishop or abbot was his representative, his vicar. This view was widely held: the writings and utterances of Pope Gregory VII are full

334

of the sense of intimacy with St Peter which was the mainstay of his heroism. Collections of miracles are full of stories of how the saint cured the sick who came to his tomb, saved from destruction men who prayed to him, or vowed a present to him, in a crisis, or destroyed those who were rash enough to attack his property or molest his subjects. The more intelligent churchmen would observe that miracles did not make a man holy—a not uncommon theme in the more human lives written in the twelfth century; but miracles were generally regarded as special indications of divine grace, and as such were necessary evidence in the process of canonization, which began to crystallize at the end of our period. Many of these miracle stories are beyond our comprehension now; it is foolish to attempt to rationalize them, especially as most collections, even those mainly derived from the testimony of eye-witnesses, are based on evidence which we should find inadequate. Whatever our view of miracles may be, it is plain that many of these stories would not be called miracles today—stories of coincidence, stories with some evident 'natural' explanation, fantasies pleasant and unpleasant. They witness to the fact that everyone expected the super-natural constantly to impinge on his life. But even in this there was much variety of opinion, as one can see within the pages of a single book in Walter Map's *De nugis curialium* (*c.* 1180–1), in which a learned cleric tells us not only of a miracle he had seen performed by St Peter of Tarentaise, but also (with malicious delight) of an attempted miracle by St Bernard of Clairvaux which had failed.

After the saint the most important occupants of the church were the bishop or abbot and the community of monks and canons. For their use the greater part of the east end, the crossing and often a bay of the nave were reserved. Here they performed the ritual of the mass; and those who were priests said mass daily or as near to that as was convenient. In early days monastic communities had contained few priests, so that the service for blessing an abbot (who early had to be a priest) to this day resembles the form for ordination, which has since the twelfth cen-tury nearly always been superfluous. By the twelfth century most mem-bers of a community would become priests in due course—in a Cistercian community all the 'choir' monks. Hence the increasing need for chapels, which were sometimes placed along the east side of transepts, some-times alongside the choir or abutting the ambulatory and sometimes between pillars in the nave. The monks and canons enjoyed a large nave in which to conduct the long processions which were a feature of the ritual development of these centuries; and, more important, they daily sang the offices in the stalls in their choir. These were commonly surrounded by a low screen to protect them from intruding laymen; the large screens and walls which we see in many great churches today were the product of the later Middle Ages or of modern times—of generations grown sensitive to cold and other distractions, or aware that draughts and laymen were avoidable nuisances. Within limits, laymen were welcomed to abbeys in our period; and kings and important patrons were found seats within the choir. Laymen, in fact, often came in throngs.

Pilgrims came to the saint's shrine in ever growing numbers; and this helps us to understand several points about the churches which housed the relics of the saints. In the tenth century, the church of St Philibert of Tournus (in eastern France, not far from Cluny) was rebuilt for the simple reason that it was too small. It is rare for this reason to be so bluntly stated; but it is likely that it was common enough. This must have been a compelling motive, for instance, with the Normans in England; the old churches represented the fashion of an earlier age, and were often narrow and small by Norman standards. It is Abbot Suger who states the case most plainly. On the great festivals of St Denis in particular, crowds of pilgrims thronged the church, and the crush was fearful and dangerous; ladies wanting to get near to the shrine to see the relics walked on their menfolk's heads as on a pavement. It is clear from stories like these that on great festivals at least the laity were allowed access to the naves even of abbey churches; and it seems probable that the idea of excluding laymen from abbey churches first became widespread with the Carthusians and Cistercians, who built naves solely for their own lay brothers, and was only taken up by the old monastic orders in the later Middle Ages. It was not only the pilgrimage church which had large numbers to deal with; it seems likely that on certain great festivals a high proportion of the population of a diocese would attend its cathedral. From many points of view the scale of church building bears witness to growing popular enthusiasm for religious devotion, of which we have so much evidence, often scattered and elusive, from the late tenth and eleventh centuries. The relics of the patron saint had commonly been housed in the crypt in earlier centuries: this meant greater security and kept the pilgrims out of the main body of the church. For reasons of security the practice was resuscitated in the early thirteenth century when the Basilica at Assisi was designed to hold the relics of St Francis. Fear of theft was a major problem for the relic keeper; theft and chicanery were extremely common; even holy men could be alarmingly unscrupulous. Every church needed to have a collection of relics; every king and every bishop carried a small treasury of relics with him, and expected to have a larger one at home. The demand for relics grew enormously and far outran the supply. The difficulty could be met in three ways: by breaking up old collections, in the sort of way in which St Hugh of Lincoln bit two pieces off a bone of St Mary Magdalene at Fécamp, to the indignation of abbot and monks; or, more decorously, by pious gift, purchase or exchange. Alternatively, new relics could be manufactured. St Benedict had two whole bodies, St Teilo three, in this period; and an ingenious Protestant has estimated that all the fragments of the true Cross in medieval inventories would have built a warship. The third method was to make existing relics more widely available, either by taking them on tour, as was sometimes done by monks and canons appealing for funds, or by displaying them in magnificent shrines behind the high altar so that the maximum number of faithful could see them at one time. The chronicles give us numerous references to the rebuilding of shrines, and to the translation of relics from a crypt to the apse of the main church.

We have talked so far only of the larger churches. But this period also witnessed the building of innumerable parish churches and chapels. The parish system had been established in many parts for centuries; and even in northern Europe it had been growing since the eighth. But many new parishes were formed in the tenth and eleventh centuries and even more parish churches were rebuilt (however modestly) in more durable materials. This is the great age of the stone parish church, and countless parishes in many parts of Europe still rejoice in the possession of a Romanesque church. These are mostly small, though sometimes the parish churches of the mid twelfth century were neither small nor plain. Very often they have rich sculpture over their doors, where Christ still sits in majesty. Very rarely do they have any remnant of the paintings which adorned their walls. In churches large and small these paintings formed a part of the larger designs of their clerical rather than their lay patrons; but they also served to provide instruction in an illiterate age. The contrast already noted between the theology of the eleventh and of the twelfth centuries is noticeable too in the decoration of churches. The familar theme of eleventh- or early twelfth-century art was the Christ in majesty, laying emphasis on Christ's divinity, and the Last Judgement, laying emphasis on man's doom, on the penalties of sin. We may deduce from these and other indications that fear, not love, was the motive of many acts of generosity; and we can feel the pressure of fear in many indications of the presence of the supernatural in this age. But we should be rash to generalize too freely, and there is certainly a change in the late twelfth and thirteenth centuries. By then the emphasis on Christ's humanity, and on the context of that humanity, especially in the person of his earthly mother, has spread down through theologians to folk at large, and the loving cult of the human Jesus can be expressed in St Francis's Christmas crib; painting and sculpture can take increasing interest in Virgin and Child, and in the Virgin's coronation.

Changes in church ornament reflect a much wider movement, which is commonly referred to as the transition from Romanesque to Gothic. In our analysis of some of the motives governing design we have said little so far of that most frequently alleged: the glory of God. This is not because the motive was unknown; indeed it seems to have been a constant and powerful factor in the situation. But as a motive for design it is imprecise. What dictates how men will conceive the glory of God? The answer to this is not simple. In the tenth and eleventh centuries custom and fashion were close together, yet even then designers could change and develop new ideas. In the twelfth century change proceeded more rapidly. It is well known that the pointed arch (originally a Muslim device) replaced the round-headed. Even more striking was the change from wall painting to glass painting as the principal medium of decoration. The dark tunnel came ultimately to be replaced by the glass palaces of the late Middle Ages, in which the stone serves simply as a frame to hold immense windows. This process was gradual; but a crucial stage came in the early twelfth century in the Île de France. There is a danger that the labels 'Romanesque' and 'Gothic' will lead us to make this transition too violent: the change was slow and some aspects of it were hardly perceived at the time. Yet some of its basic principles were already clearly enunciated by the first patron of Gothic art, Abbot Suger himself. Abbot Suger was a practical man: he talks of wood and stone and oxen, and milling crowds; but he talks too of God's glory, of the beauties of rich ornaments, of the symbolism of light. His patron saint was called Denis, and was generally identified in that age with the pseudo-Denis, the author of mystical tracts whose popularity was growing at this time, in which special emphasis had been laid on the divine significance of the symbolism of light. In most Gothic cathedrals today, stripped of their glass, or lit by hideous modern windows, it is hard to recapture the meaning of this. But one can still see it at Chartres, on a sunny day, in the play of light, in the richest blue and red, from the windows to the stone. In origin, the Romanesque cathedral had been a dark tunnel; in the Gothic cathedral, with a quite deliberate and conscious sense of symbolism, 'the light shineth in darkness, and the darkness comprehended it not'.

One characteristic of Suger's work is the close link it reveals between the patron and the artists and craftsmen in this age: there can have been few ages in which it was closer. About the master masons, the technicians, and (in the strict sense) the architects and contractors of this age, we know almost nothing. But it is clear that they worked in close liaison with both lay and ecclesiastical paymasters. The new forms in Saint-Denis are of essentially ecclesiastical inspiration; the unity in Cistercian design in every part of Europe must also be due to close monastic supervision. When we meet a monk who was also an artist in the thirteenth century, like Matthew Paris, we see a rare survival. By the end of the twelfth century, it seems, book-production, painting, and probably architecture were passing into the hands of the lay professionals. The shift was only one of degree: the lay patron or the ecclesiastical clerk of works still had far more influence on design than their modern successor would dare to exert. But the shift was, none the less, significant.

One of the great schools of painting in our period was that known as the 'Winchester school', whose style was dominant in Anglo-Saxon England in the late tenth and early eleventh centuries. Behind this and the other arts of the English monastic reform lay the personal interest and inspiration of Dunstan and Ethelwold, both men of artistic talents; and the Bodleian library contains a famous miniature of Dunstan at the feet of Christ, which is traditionally supposed to have been painted by Dunstan himself. Personal interest in music, painting and sculpture is not infrequently noted by chroniclers as a mark of one or other of the leading abbots of the eleventh and twelfth centuries. To summarize the artistic achievements of an age of flourishing art in a book without illustrations would be futile; but an account of this age which failed to note that it saw great development in the use of stained glass and wall painting, that new styles and traditions grew and flourished, would be woefully misleading.

One of the most flourishing centres of craftsmanship in the late eleventh and twelfth centuries was in north-western Germany. Here, among others, lay the abbey of Helmhausen, an old imperial house, which in the twelfth century became a factory supplying pieces for the leading lay and ecclesiastical patrons of Germany. It was famous as a centre of book-illumination, and, probably, of wall painting and stained glass; and also for metal-work. In Paderborn cathedral one can still see a reliquary of great beauty and elaboration, made by Roger, monk of Helmhausen, in 1100. It is possible, indeed likely, that the same Roger was the German monk who, writing under the pseudonym 'Theophilus', composed in this period the extraordinary treatise *De diversis artibus*, 'On the various arts': extraordinary, because there is scarcely a parallel in the whole Middle Ages for its mixture of humble devotion and precise technical proficiency. This has led to much dispute about its date; but its latest editor, Dr Dodwell, has assigned it on good grounds to the early twelfth century. Theophilus tells us plainly that God has given us talents, and it is our duty to restore them to Him; this is the motive for good craftsmanship. He lives in the world of Suger and in the theological world of the early twelfth century; and also in an age when monks and craftsmen were not uncommonly the same people, when (as at the time of the Italian Renaissance) there was some sense in writing a treatise on craftsmanship and technology in learned Latin.

Even in his own day Theophilus was a phenomenon, and his book was not widely read. We would be wrong to suppose that monks had a monopoly of craftsmanship, or that the advanced techniques described in such detail by Theophilus were mainly pursued in monastic precincts. What he does prove is that the art of this period was produced by collaboration between those in and out of the world; and he reminds us of other significant links in the world of the early twelfth century. About the time when he was writing, a group of English scribes and artists were preparing the splendid St Albans Psalter for the anchoress Christina of Markyate, in Hertfordshire. It contains liturgical texts normal everywhere in Europe in this age, and a French vernacular romance with an ascetic moral suitable for a lady who never ceased to give thanks for having escaped the pains of matrimony. It also contains numerous paintings and miniatures, in which the traditions of many schools mingle, above all the sense of colour of the schools of Germany in which Theophilus taught, and the sense of form and pattern of the Byzantine artists of Norman Sicily. These miniatures represent most forcibly, perhaps, the artistic union of the two Norman empires; but they represent much more than that, the cosmopolitan world of art and religion in what we have learned to call the twelfth-century Renaissance.

The concentration of effort, the excitement, the sense of dedication in the building of the great Gothic cathedrals have sometimes led historians to suppose that everybody was at one in this endeavour. This was not so. The effort, at its highest, was reckoned to be a symbol of man's devotion to God; the rich ornaments, the elaborate liturgy, the gold, silver and precious stones which encrusted the reliquaries were a symbol of the infinite price of the relics and of the saints. Nothing was too good or too rich for God's service. But there were men about who took a different view: gold and silver were also the symbols of riches and pride, of wealth in a society where most men were exceedingly poor; symbols to some that the Church was the Church of the rich and the privileged; to others symbols of pride, the deadliest of the sins; to others again, the images of stone or the pictures on the walls or in the glass savoured of idolatry. We are apt to forget how wide a variety of views could be held on these things even in the central Middle Ages. To remind us of them let us call two more witnesses from France and from the early twelfth century.

The first is the voice of a puritan, but of a man firmly established in the Catholic hierarchy, of unquestioned orthodoxy, and by birth a Burgundian noble—of the class who had patronized the great third church at Cluny, the supreme expression of scale, proportion, decoration, wealth of ornament, richness of liturgy and music, in the Europe of the early twelfth century.

> I put on one side the vast height of their churches, the excessive length, the empty spaces, the rich finish, the curious paintings. We will look rather at the sumptuous ornaments encrusted with gems and gold, put there that money may breed money and pilgrims may give to monks alms that should be bestowed upon the true poor. We will look at their cloisters with their monstrous capitals and arabesques, fit only to distract the idle from their books. Just heaven! Even if they are not choked by their impropriety, they might at least blench at the cost.[1]

Thus St Bernard of Clairvaux, the most famous of the Cistercians, in his *Apologia* against Cluny, written while he was still young and not given to controlling his speech. His puritanism was more extreme than that of many Cistercians; but even if the rules against illuminating manuscripts or adding towers to their churches were only added some time after the foundation of the order, and not very strictly enforced, the Order as a whole retained the artistic simplicity implied in this letter. Their churches (remarkably uniform in design) had large wall

[1] From St Bernard's *Apologia*, as rendered (and somewhat abbreviated) by Dom David Knowles, *The Historian and Character*, p. 63.

surfaces, like Romanesque churches, but unadorned; they had windows similar in scale to those of early Gothic churches, but filled with plain glass. They were light and plain; and intended to emphasize the severely functional character of the whole complex of buildings. Yet to the poor man at the gate, they must have appeared almost as magnificent and expensive as Cluny itself.

Our second witness is Peter of Bruys, a Christian heretic, whose call was to a simpler, more puritanical faith than that of the Catholic church of his day. He held among other things that there should be no ordained clergy and no churches to worship in. It is clear that, at its highest, a sense of the pride and vainglory of the contemporary church, at its lowest, envy of its riches, played an important part in finding Peter his numerous followers among the active and intelligent, but unprivileged members of French society in his day.

Heresies

In the year 1000 heretics were virtually unknown in western Europe. Strange opinions, strange hopes there may have been; we have no means of knowing how garbled a version of orthodox doctrine many ordinary layfolk held; and about 970 a learned grammarian in Ravenna had regarded Virgil, Horace and Juvenal as deities. But there was no organized body of opinion which the Church would find it necessary to repudiate, still less to persecute. By 1150 heresy was common. From the point of view of the layman's religion it is one of the most significant novelties of the period; and heresy became so powerful in the late twelfth century as profoundly to affect the outlook of the orthodox, and, in the end, to call out the terrible machinery of the Inquisition.

Growing population and social change help to account for the large number of folk of active mind in various walks of life who found the teaching of the Church inadequate to their needs. Some were lesser, unprivileged clergy; a few were recruited from the upper clergy themselves; a few from the knightly class; a number from the peasantry; but their strength, both in quality and quantity, lay among artisans and merchants, and it was probably through merchants that their doctrines were disseminated. The first groups of heretics appeared in western Germany, in Flanders, in France and in northern Italy in the first half of the eleventh century. We are not adequately informed about their opinions; but it is clear that there was diversity among them, and it is also clear that most of the groups had been more or less influenced by the doctrines of the Bogomil church in the Balkans and the Byzantine empire. The Bogomils were dualists: they believed that goodness existed in the world of spirit alone, the world of the good God; and that the material world was the creation of an evil spirit. The evil spirit was sometimes regarded as a fallen angel (as in Christian mythology), sometimes as an independent deity. Associated with this was the repudiation of a great part of the Bible; the repudiation also of most earthly pleasures; above all the repudiation of marriage, which led to the creation of more human beings, in whose evil, physical bodies unfortunate spirits were temporarily encased. The dualist doctrine was a gloomy one; none the less, it evidently had great appeal in western Europe at a time when the gloomier aspects of Christianity were definitely to the fore, at least in popular religion.

It is doubtful if all the groups of heretics recorded in the early eleventh century were specifically dualist: some may have been mainly anticlerical and puritanical in aim; but all showed some influence of Bogomil doctrine, all were greeted with violence and dismay by the local population, and a number of the heretics were burnt. Burning was normally the punishment chosen by the local lay power or the mob; it was the traditional treatment for witchcraft. The official Church had no fixed policy for the treatment of heretics, but copious precedents both for leniency and for severity. The papacy did not make up its mind to a policy of repression until the late twelfth century.

The first recorded outbreak of heresy occurred shortly after 1000; from then on outbreaks occurred at intervals of a few years until the Emperor Henry III hanged the last group at Goslar in 1052; then silence falls until the early twelfth century. This silence is mysterious and unexplained. It is unlikely that heresy was entirely dead, because when it reappears, it takes the same form and appears in the same areas as before. On the other hand, it is probable that it had only a shadowy survival through these years; and that the popular interest in some parts of Europe, which had made the soil fertile for heresy, was being satisfied by the Catholic church. This is precisely the period when the papal reform was in the first flush of enthusiasm, and there is much evidence that it won the support of ordinary folk in many places. In Milan the reformed papacy supported and allied itself with the revolt of the Pataria—of the insurgents, mainly humble folk, though led partly by nobles, who attempted to overthrow the established ecclesiastical hierarchy in the 1050s and 1060s (see pp. 274–6). Even before this, popular enthusiasm had as often been ranged against the heretics as for them; and the example of the Pataria suggests the possibility that many would-be heretics were convinced in this period that the reviving Church would canalize their aims and their zeal.

It is clear, furthermore, that in the eleventh and twelfth centuries orthodox and heretical reformers were often recruited from similar milieux. Wandering hermits who gathered round them groups of disciples were a feature of the age. From the disciples of St Romuald of Ravenna came more than one hermit group, who flourished in the early eleventh century, including that which contained St Peter Damian himself, and the order of Camaldoli; later in the century St Bruno organized his followers into the community of La Chartreuse, the nucleus of the Carthusian order; younger contemporaries on the frontiers of Brittany and Normandy collected the nucleus of the congregations of Tiron and Savigny; and Robert of Molesme inspired the reform of Molesme and the foundation of Cîteaux (see pp. 299–300). Peter of Bruys and Henry of Lausanne were men of similar stamp. Like Bernard of Tiron they preached and gathered disciples; they tried to do a work not adequately performed by the official hierarchy. But both Peter and Henry by some means fell under the inspiration of heretical opinions; in due course they met, and Henry accepted much of Peter's teaching. Between them they spread it far and wide over the south of France.

Peter's beliefs had something in common with those of the dualists: he was anti-clerical, puritanical; he had a marked aversion to the cross as a symbol, and his followers burned crosses and sacked churches; he radically altered the Church's sacramental teaching. In some respects his work continued that of the eleventh-century heretics. But we must be careful to distinguish his doctrines both from the dualists and from the orthodox Pataria, for the contrasts are as striking as the similarities. Peter was not a dualist and there is no evidence that he repudiated the world or Christian marriage; he had far more in common with the Waldensians, the sect established by Waldo in the 1170s and 1180s— and more remotely with the Protestant reformers—than with the Bogomils. Waldo began as an orthodox preacher, preaching the blessing of poverty and ministering to the poor; disputes with the clergy drove him to heresy, and to acceptance of many of the 'Petrobrusian' doctrines (as the beliefs of Peter of Bruys are called).

The Petrobrusians made a stir in the south of France in the opening decades of the twelfth century, and Peter the Venerable, abbot of Cluny, was moved to write a book against them. But already there were signs of a revival of the specifically dualist heresy in the same areas; and by the middle of the twelfth century it was flourishing in the Rhineland, in Flanders, in the south of France and in northern Italy; in the last two it organized a substantial hierarchy of its own later in the century. The failure of the Church to keep within its fold the rising energy of which the Milanese Pataria had borne witness is doubtless revealed in this movement; and it may be significant that one of the labels attached to these heretics was that of 'Patarini'—it looks as if they had absorbed the remnant of the Pataria. But we must be careful, once again, not to underestimate the strength of the dualist doctrine itself; and it is clear that Bogomil missionaries had been at work. The influence came partly from missionaries in the west, partly from contact with the Bogomils in the East, especially during the Second Crusade (1147–8). Dualism was on the way to becoming a popular movement over wide areas; and in the second half of the century it challenged the monopoly of the Catholic Church. The extreme asceticism of its doctrines—the prohibition of marriage, for instance, and of the eating of meat (since all animals were thought to have souls)—compelled a division between the strict adherents, the perfect, the pure, and the mass of believers who could not attempt to live the perfect life. From the Greek word for pure (καθαρός) the dualists came to be known as the Cathars; but many other labels were also attached to them, such as 'Albigensians', the men of Albi, because one of their greatest centres of influence lay in the south of France. Meanwhile in two ways the Catholic Church was preparing for the counter-attack which destroyed the Cathar churches in the thirteenth and fourteenth centuries. The papal monarchy was growing increasingly powerful, so that it would in the end be able to inspire the forces of inquisition and repression; and a view of the world and of God more cheerful than that of the early Middle Ages—infinitely more cheerful than that of the Cathars—was being developed among theologians and thinking laymen alike. St Francis in the early thirteenth century preached penitence to all mankind; but he also preached, like Wolfram, that the world was God's, and good, and that the layman was no mere hanger-on in a divine economy principally designed for the celibate and the ascetic.

Life in the world: the layman's religion

In the tenth and eleventh centuries, and in a less pervasive way the twelfth also, the tone and direction of religious reform was dictated by the ideals of monks. The notion was current that the life of renunciation, of personal poverty and celibacy, was superior to that of the layman who married and reared a family. Views on this matter were far from uniform, nor are we well informed upon the limits of the range of opinion. St Paul had made marriage the symbol of the union of Christ and his Church; but he had also said 'it is better to be married than to burn', and stated Christian views of marriage were nicely poised between these two attitudes. Under the conditions of the age a lofty view of marriage was unlikely to be widely held, and we have seen that the entry to marriage, in the upper classes at least, was a matter of bargaining and agreement between families, in which the lady, and even the man, might have little say (pp. 127–8). Doubtless there was much variety in actual practice in different situations; but there is no reason to suppose that most men and women entering marriage had much awareness of the religious significance of the event. The theological movement of the eleventh century made theologians more specific about its sacramental character. But in practice it was entered by a process which we should recognize as betrothal rather than marriage: it was many centuries before the ceremony in Church became an essential or even, perhaps, a common feature of marriage in western society as a whole. There were two essential elements: the exchange of oaths before witnesses, in which rings would normally be exchanged as a token of mutual giving and that the family compact had been completed (this we may call the process of consent); and physical consummation. The comments of leading churchmen in the twelfth century on marriage went little beyond defining its law; but in defining the law they bore witness to a strenuous effort to bring the betrothal ceremony into church, to create, that is, what we should recognize as a marriage service. The theologians discussed sexual intercourse, which was perfectly licit within marriage, so long as carnal passion was avoided, so long as child-bearing was the motive. For the wholehearted acceptance of the joys of marriage as a part of God's purpose we have to wait for Wolfram; though there may well have been lay thinkers who shared his vision in earlier days, and there were undoubtedly plenty of laymen in every century who entered marriage with no sense of shame, with no sense that they were engaging in a vocation which was a second-best. But it took the marriage of Heloise and Abelard to elicit from Peter the Venerable of Cluny the highest expression of the meaning of marriage from this period. After Abelard's death Abbot Peter, who could be gallant and was always a diplomat, wrote to the Abbess Heloise: 'God fosters him, my venerable dear sister in the Lord—him to whom you have been attached, first in carnal union, then in the stronger, higher bond of divine love; under whom you have long served the Lord—God fosters him, I say, in your place, as your other self (*ut te alteram*) in his bosom; and keeps him to be restored to you, by his grace, at God's trumpet call. . . .'[1] A strange irony that it should be the clandestine union of an eminent cleric and his mistress which made a leading church-man thus movingly express the meaning of Christian marriage; but what is significant is that this expression should have been made in the early twelfth century, in the age when the cult of courtly love was making its first appearance on the European scene; and when in matters of theology and ethics a more humane spirit was beginning to be manifest.

Of the general level of morality, of the influence of the Church, that is, in ordinary men's lives, it is almost impossible to say anything coherent. At best one can analyse what was possible; one can show how strong was Christian selfconsciousness in men like the Emperor Henry III or the English King Edgar, men powerfully influenced by a sense of religious vocation; at the other extreme one can show that the full range of human crimes were common in that as in every age. To leave it there would perhaps be unduly agnostic: it is quite clear that the tenth century was an age of extreme violence; that the twelfth century was an age, comparatively, of good order; both, by our standards, were extremely unruly. With an upper class bred to war and a lower class living very near to penury a lofty moral standard was not to be expected; nor was it expected by the churchmen of the day, who were remarkably lenient even to the public offences of kings. Henry I of England could acknow-ledge twenty bastards and be strongly suspected by modern historians of winning his throne by fratricide; yet few chroniclers condemned him, and after his death his reign was remembered as a haven of peace, a reign blessed by God. This was a period which tended to judge a man by his earthly fortunes, to expect God to render him due reward in this world as well as in the next. The full range of Christian moral teaching was accessible to many men; most only knew it in garbled form.

The specific function of the layman in the affairs of the Church was declining. The enhanced significance given to the sacraments drove a wedge between cleric and layman; the papal reform and the conflicts which followed struck heavy blows at the authority of laymen in the churches they had ruled or possessed in earlier days. A layman had never administered the Eucharist, but hitherto he had received com-munion in both kinds. It was during this period that the cup was finally withdrawn from the laity; though in any case communion had long been

[1] Migne, *Patrologia Latina*, vol. CLXXXIX, col. 352.

a comparatively rare event. The days when the mass had represented, in outward activity as well as in symbol, the common act of the whole worshipping community, were long past. Few laymen knew any Latin: language was an insuperable barrier between most men and the liturgy. None the less, they were expected to be regular in attendance: all lay-folk were directed to attend mass on Sunday, as of obligation; and the Church attempted to enforce Sunday observance by prescription of penances for those who worked on the sabbath which were sometimes so savage as to make their ineffectiveness only too clear. The ceremonial of the Mass had been evolved over the centuries to expound the symbolism of the sacrificial drama which was being enacted; and to some extent this ceremonial could replace understanding of the language of the service.

Kings and great lords were expected to be even more assiduous than ordinary folk in attending Mass: they had private chapels, and many attended Mass daily. The few who were literate could follow other devotions too; a shortened version of the monastic office was prepared by Alcuin for Charlemagne, and this was still in circulation in the tenth and eleventh centuries. St Margaret of Scotland (d. 1093), a scion of the English royal family who had been brought up in the court of Hungary—both courts noted for their piety—followed an elaborate round of devotions which included hours of the Holy Trinity, of the Holy Cross and of the Blessed Virgin Mary. The Hours of the Virgin and the Hours of the Dead were to form the nucleus out of which the Primer, or layfolks' book of devotions, was compiled in England in the twelfth century; and in the later twelfth century it was translated into English, and later into French and other languages. But vernacular books of devotion, although they existed, were an extreme rarity in our period. St Margaret was exceptional; more normal was the case of her husband, who could enjoy the sumptuous ornaments of their Gospel Book, but could not read it.

Of the other sacraments baptism could still in an emergency be performed by laymen; but in practice had rarely been so performed for many centuries. Marriage could only be performed by laymen, since it is the parties themselves who administer the sacrament. But as we have seen there was little sacramental in tenth- or eleventh-century marriage, and the efforts to enhance the religious significance of the ceremony in the twelfth century took the form of moving it into church, or at least to the church's door, with a priest to preside. In earlier centuries confession to laymen, in origin public confession, had been common.

Even at the end of the twelfth century an eminent canonist could permit a man to confess to a layman on his death-bed if no cleric was available. But this was a last resort, and the need to receive absolution from a priest was being more and more strongly urged. In countless ways the layman was being shown his place: small wonder that many enterprising spirits were attracted to heresy.

None the less, the churchmen of the eleventh and twelfth centuries were much concerned with the place of the laity in the divine scheme. However strongly influenced by monastic ideals, the papal reformers fully accepted the need for the *ordo laicorum*, and not infrequently discussed its function. Special functions were devised for laymen prepared to renounce a part of their worldly life: as knights in the Orders of Templars and Hospitallers in the early twelfth century, or as peasants among the lay brothers in the Carthusian and Cistercian Orders. Already, in the eleventh century, and even at the end of the tenth, special efforts were being made to civilize the feudal aristocracy, to find a specifically Christian function for warriors in a religion of peace.

The function of the warrior was to protect his vassals and to protect the Church: his special duties to the Church were to ensure that she was not molested, to be generous and to pay his tithe regularly. It is easily said, but this short sentence hides many tensions, a great area of conflict. First of all, the Church had need of protection. In the ninth and tenth centuries the Church had lost a substantial proportion of its wealth; monasteries had been pillaged by the Vikings or the Muslims, their estates taken over by the local nobility. Feudal organization meant that many churches were compelled to alienate large slabs of territory to military vassals; they remained landlords in theory, but had virtually no economic benefit from their lands. To counteract this, it was fashionable among laymen to be generous, to pay handsomely for prayers for themselves and their families; and the late eleventh and early twelfth centuries saw a multitude of new churches founded. Less popular was the Church's insistence on payment of tithes—of one tenth of all the agricultural produce of the land. This obligation had finally been established in the time of Charlemagne and was the subject of much controversy in the ages which followed. It provided churchmen with a tolerably reliable source of income for many centuries to come, and laymen with a constant occasion for grumbling.

In dealing with the layman as warrior, the Church tried first to curb, then to canalize his warlike activities. In the late tenth century Germany was, comparatively speaking, a land of peace; in the south of France feudal anarchy was at its height. About the year 989 a group of south French bishops gathered at Charroux in the presence of the relics of St Junian of Noailles and pronounced anathema on anyone who attacked an unarmed cleric or on anyone who robbed the poor. As time passed more and more of these synods were held; laymen were brought in to take part in them. Private war could not be abolished, so an effort was made to control it by giving it rules. The poor and the churchmen were to be respected; in the more ambitious synods, laymen swore to keep peace for a period of months, and those who failed to keep it were made public enemies. We have the curious spectacle, indeed, of leading ecclesiastics riding to war on peace-breakers. In the early eleventh century the movement spread to the north of France; and in the middle of the century, under the influence of St Odilo of Cluny, a leading supporter of it, the 'Peace of God' was proclaimed from a German pulpit by the Emperor Henry III in person. The effect of these campaigns was limited, but they reflected a growing consciousness that anarchy was not to everyone's advantage. In the end the movement died, or gave way to more developed efforts to enforce peace by the more organized governments of the twelfth century. Meanwhile, the Church had come to supplement its efforts to encourage peace at home by discovering opportunities to canalize warlike activities for sacred, or supposedly sacred, objects outside the boundaries of Christendom.

XVII

The Crusades, Byzantium and Spain

The Byzantine Empire: the reign of Alexius I

Between the death of Basil II in 1025 and the battle of Manzikert in 1071 the tragi-comedy described by Michael Psellus was enacted (see pp. 18–19). The political decadence is evident enough. No doubt Psellus exaggerated it, painted his superiors, colleagues, and victims as more futile and incompetent than they were. No doubt there were compensations: it was an age in which the study of ancient literature and philosophy flourished anew, when the original sources of Greek thought were avidly sought after, and an age of renewal, in certain respects, in theology and in the Greek Church at large. Psellus himself illustrates the paradoxes of Byzantine society. He was the Gerbert of the East, a man of genuine intellectual curiosity which led him to lead a revival in the study of Plato, and a master of political intrigue. As a politician his love of the classics revealed itself in his addiction to a kind of intrigue

BIBLIOGRAPHY. On the Byzantine Empire, see Chapter III. On the Crusades, Sir Steven Runciman, *History of the Crusades* (3 vols., Cambridge, 1951–4), and the collaborative *History of the Crusades*, ed. K. M. Setton (Philadelphia, 1955–   ); N. Daniel, *Islam and the West* (Edinburgh, 1960); R. J. H. Jenkins, *The Byzantine Empire on the eve of the Crusades* (Historical Association, 1953); G. Constable, 'The Second Crusade as seen by contemporaries', *Traditio*, vol. IX (1953), pp. 213–79; R. C. Smail, *Crusading Warfare* (Cambridge, 1956). For the origin of the crusades P. Alphandéry, *La Chrétienté et l'idée de croisade*, ed. A. Dupront, vol. I (Paris, 1954) is interesting and C. Erdmann, *Die Entstehung des Kreuzzugsgedankens* (Stuttgart, 1935) is indispensable; his views have not been adequately reproduced or discussed in English. On the Song of Roland, R. Fawtier, *La chanson de Roland* (Paris, 1933) is a useful introduction.

On Islam and Muslim Spain, see Chapter III. There is a lively account of the Cid and of Spanish history in his time by the great Spanish scholar R. Menéndez Pidal, *The Cid and his Spain* (London, 1934) (cf. *The Epic of the Cid*, trans. J. Markley, New York, 1961); see also C. Petit-Dutaillis and P. Guinard, *L'essor des états d'Occident* (G. Glotz, *Histoire générale: Histoire du moyen âge*, vol. IV, pt. ii); P. David, *Études historiques sur la Galice et le Portugal* (Lisbon-

351

which would have done credit to the Thebes or Mycenae of legend, or to the Rome of Nero and Domitian.

Byzantine politics had been dominated for many years by two powerful groups: the military, quasi-feudal aristocracy and the court officials, the bureaucracy of Constantinople. Basil II had kept both under control. But the danger was checked, not abolished: when he died the warlords proceeded to gather more and more of the empire into their hands. The Byzantine army had in the past contained a substantial nucleus of troops who lived in military small-holdings in the provinces, which were controlled by the imperial governors. In the mid eleventh century these small-holdings were drastically reduced. The emperor could still recruit an army by levying heavier taxation; but it was a wholly mercenary army, the warlords became increasingly independent of imperial control, and those who held high posts in the army acquired dangerous independence. For a number of years it was the court officials who conducted the intrigues and pulled the strings in the capital. In the end, however, it was the most astute of the generals and warlords, Alexius Comnenus, who brought the period of political decadence to a close by weaving an alliance of the most delicate complexity between a powerful military group and a number of the court officials, and so won the throne for himself and his family in 1081.

The political history of Byzantium between 1025 and 1081 appears to the modern eye like a labyrinth of senseless intrigue. Down to 1056 Basil II's nieces, Zoe and Theodora, alternately married would-be emperors and took the veil; and the period between 1042 and 1055 saw a semblance of stability in the strange régime à trois maintained by the elderly roué Constantine IX, who presided at court functions with due pomp attended by his equally elderly empress, Zoe, and his official mistress. But over the empire he did not preside, and it was only good fortune which saved him from being deposed by George Maniaces, the most capable general of the day. At the end of his reign the capital was dominated by the brilliant, ambitious and violent Patriarch Michael Cerularius. Cerularius not unnaturally resisted the attempts of Pope Leo IX to enforce the Roman primacy on him in 1054, and so relations between the churches broke down (see p. 257). Meanwhile political

Paris, 1947); H. J. Chaytor, *History of Aragon and Catalonia* (London, 1933); for recent Spanish scholarship, see L. G. Valdeavellano, *Historia de España*, vol. I (2nd edn., Madrid, 1955); for bibliography, especially of sources, B. Sánchez Alonso, *Fuentes de la historia española e hispano-americana* (3rd edn., 3 vols., Madrid, 1952), which can be kept up to date by reference to the periodical *Indice histórico español*.

events in Italy were preparing another breach between East and West. The rise of the Normans in south Italy spelt the end of Byzantine rule, and in the latter part of the century their raids and conquests carried them ever deeper into Byzantine territory.

In 1071 Bari was captured by Robert Guiscard, and with its fall Byzantine rule in Italy came to an end. In the same year the Byzantine army was overwhelmed at Manzikert by the forces of the Turkish Sultan Alp Arslan. Characteristically, it was partly treachery and court intrigue which led to the defeat. The Emperor Romanus, though defeated and captured, made a tolerable treaty with the Turks. But the court politicians turned defeat into catastrophe. When the patriarch Cerularius had fallen foul of an earlier emperor in 1058, Psellus had accused his old friend, before a synod summoned to depose the patriarch, of nameless heresies; when Cerularius conveniently died before he could be deposed, Psellus turned his pen to a warm panegyric on the patriarch's memory. Manzikert inspired the philosopher to an even more remarkable creation. As the result of an intrigue in which Psellus was deeply involved, Romanus was arrested on his return from captivity, blinded and immured in a monastery. There he received a letter from Psellus expatiating on the blessing the ex-emperor had received: God had found him worthy of heavenly light, and so had taken earthly vision from him. For ten more years the Byzantine leaders squabbled among themselves and made arrangements with the Turks. By these arrangements the cousin of Alp Arslan, Suleiman, was able to build up the Sultanate of Rum—of 'Rome', aptly called since it consisted of the heart of what survived of the Roman Empire, almost the whole of modern Turkey. Thus Byzantium was deprived of what had been one of the main sources of its taxes and native recruits in earlier centuries. Michael IV (1034–41) had started the debasement of the coinage. In the decade after Manzikert the currency collapsed.

Alexius Comnenus succeeded in 1081 because he was a soldier who could outmanœuvre the court officials at their own favourite game of palace intrigue. He held the throne and revived the empire by what can only be called a *tour de force* of diplomatic and military skill—diplomatic first and foremost, because in the early years of his reign his financial and military resources were limited. Yet he was involved in numerous campaigns, because in his early years the vultures were gathering round the carcase of the old Roman Empire. But it refused to die.

In the early 1080s Alexius's most formidable enemy was Robert Guiscard, whose Mediterranean ambitions seemed to have no limit. In alliance with Venice Alexius checked Guiscard; but the danger was still acute when in 1085 the Norman suddenly died. Next, Alexius was threatened by the Patzinaks, the semi-barbarian horde settled to his north-east. Eventually, in 1091, after Constantinople itself had been threatened, the Patzinak armies were annihilated. By the mid 1090s the northern frontier was quiet, the Normans were engrossed in their own affairs and the Muslim rulers were divided among themselves. It was at this juncture that Alexius inadvertently precipitated a new and alarming crisis, so it seems, by appealing to the West for aid.

It is highly probable that Alexius appealed to Urban II for help, and equally probable that it was Alexius's appeal which sparked off the First Crusade. Yet it is most unlikely that Alexius intended to ask for more than a substantial force of mercenaries. He had asked for mercenaries on earlier occasions: western mercenaries, from England and Scandinavia, had long formed the nucleus of his *corps d'élite*, the Varangian guard. The West was the best source of recruits at the time, so long as the recruits could be trained and disciplined within the imperial army. A copy of Alexius's appeal survives but it is a forgery and, even though it may well be based on a genuine document, we cannot tell the precise terms of the original.[1] But we may be reasonably sure that Alexius asked for mercenaries, and that it was the pope's initiative which converted them into the barbarian avalanche whose arrival Anna Comnena and her father witnessed with fascinated horror in 1096.

Perhaps this was merely another of Alexius's series of appeals. Or it may be that he was planning on his own account to take advantage of the divisions in Islam to recover lost territory. In either case an approach to Urban was bound to seem like a challenge to the solidarity of Christendom, and Alexius might have calculated that it would not be interpreted in the West as he had meant it. But he could hardly have foreseen how devastating the western reaction would be.

The launching of the First Crusade

The traditional teaching of the Church had been to condemn war wherever possible. That war was justified where self-defence demanded violent measures few of the fathers had denied; but the consistent effort of responsible churchmen down to the tenth century was to curb the warlike proclivities of the military classes, and, as time passed, to threaten ever direr penalties on those killed in unholy war. Even soldiers acting under orders, who were justified by every code of loyalty of the

[1] See Ostrogorsky, p. 313n., and references there cited.

day, were commonly thought to die unhousselled and unprepared if they died in battle. But as the tenth century was turning into the eleventh we have the first signs of a new outlook. The destruction of the Ealdorman Brihtnoth and his followers by the Danish invaders of England in 991 was the occasion for the poem on the *Battle of Maldon*, which is firmly in the tradition of the German heroic lay: it records and assumes the overriding virtue of loyalty between a lord and his followers. At about the same time the French monk Abbo of Fleury was writing about the death of another English leader who had fallen at the hands of the Danes: Edmund, king of the East Angles, who had been killed in 870. As a Christian and an anointed king Edmund could not (according to the legend) submit to the heathen Dane; he preferred, in the words of the pagan Horace, 'to die for his country'. And so he was killed; and in his death Abbo sees Christian martyrdom. We are coming close to the idea of war, not merely as something justifiable under certain circumstances, but as something capable of being holy.

In the eleventh century this notion made great strides. The founder of the papal reform, Pope Leo IX, had been a warrior as well as a devoted bishop before he became pope, and he led his own troops against the Normans in south Italy. He suffered defeat, and this particular precedent was rarely followed; but the idea that the papacy should find specific tasks for the military did not die with him. Its special protagonist was Pope Gregory VII. Already, as cardinal, he had encouraged Pope Alexander II to give his blessing to the Norman invasion of England. Duke William could claim that he was going to oust a perjured usurper and also to remove from the see of Canterbury an archbishop not recognized in Rome. So the pope sent him a banner which gave the campaign of Hastings, at least in some eyes, the aura of a crusade. A similar blessing (more obviously defensible) was given to the Normans who invaded Sicily in order to recover it from Islam; and the idea gained currency that the reconquest of Spain from Islam was a holy war. This idea inspired knights from France to flock to the assistance of the struggling Christian kingdoms in northern Spain; but there was clearly a nice distinction between the attitude of men north of the Pyrenees, who regarded the Muslim as the wicked infidel, as cattle for the slaughter, and the Christians who had lived among them in Spain and who regarded them as misguided fellow-humans. The distinction is underlined in the career of the Spanish nobleman commonly known as the Cid (see pp. 377–8). Historically, this engaging adventurer carved out a career on the frontiers of Christendom and Islam without troubling himself much about religious differences: he was happy to ally himself with Muslims when it suited him. Later legend, however, made him out a Christian hero in a relentless (though not unchivalrous) religious war.

To Gregory VII a crusade could be fought against any of God's enemies, whether infidel or Christian. But war against the Muslim was his dream; and in 1075 he devised a remarkable scheme by which he himself was to lead a crusade to the east, to restore Byzantium after the disaster of Manzikert and to recover Jerusalem. He outlined his scheme in a letter to Henry IV of Germany, whom he fondly imagined would look after the interests of the papacy in his absence. But within a year Gregory and Henry were at war, and Gregory had to divert his 'crusade' to deal with enemies nearer home. His readiness to pronounce Holy War in what many men thought most unpropitious circumstances did a good deal to bring both Gregory and the idea of a crusade into disrepute. From this it was rescued by the skill and inspiration of Pope Urban II (1088–99).

In 1095 Pope Urban received an embassy from the Emperor Alexius Comnenus, asking for help in recruiting mercenaries. At first sight it might seem that Urban was hardly in a position to provide it; he was without military resources of his own, and depended on such allies as he had to defend him against the Emperor Henry IV, who still refused to recognize him as pope. By a bold and imaginative decision, Urban not only answered Alexius's call—though hardly in the way he had intended—but roused the enthusiasm of Christendom, restored the credit of the papacy and ruined the prestige of the emperor. He presided at the councils of Piacenza and Clermont (1095), and preached with fervour war against the infidel, for the defence of Christendom and the recovery of the holy places.

The popular view of the Crusades

It is not to be supposed that Urban's call at Clermont in 1095 would have been answered if it had come without preparation; nor must we confuse his doctrine of the crusade with that which stirred the enthusiasm of knights and burghers and peasants all over western Europe. To Urban it was a defensive war, however much he might welcome the opportunity to canalize the military activities of European knighthood in adventure outside the frontiers of Europe; however much he might distinguish the crusade from secular defensive war by providing a free pardon in heaven—a plenary indulgence—to those who fought and died in a state of grace. But in preaching it he met another doctrine, the popular doctrine of the crusade: its origin is obscure, and we must beware of rationalizing its nature unduly; but of its power and wide influence there can be little doubt. Before we analyse it, it is necessary to look rather more widely at the background to the crusades.

For centuries Christendom had been on the defensive, watching itself being encircled by higher civilizations, by wealthier races, by stronger political units. Now the tide was turning; and some leaders of feudal bands, as conditions grew more settled inside Europe, began to look beyond the frontiers for scenes of new adventure. This was one reason for the growing interest in the wider world; and it was singularly fortunate for western Europe that a wider world existed, into which its wilder spirits could be drained.

The other reason for the widening horizons of folk in western Christendom was the growing popularity of the pilgrimage. The pilgrimage, as we have seen, did not necessarily lead men far afield. Wherever lay the shrine, the tomb, the relics of a saint, there the pilgrims could gather. But in the eleventh century three pilgrimages had a special prestige: that to Rome, to the tombs of the apostles and the innumerable Roman martyrs; that to the tomb of St James at Compostella in the north of Spain; and that to the Holy Sepulchre at Jerusalem, a long and dangerous exploration—but for those who liked exploring, and for those who wished, as many did, to find the road to heaven on their travels, a supremely rewarding one. Its growing popularity was revealed in the early eleventh century when two of the leading feudatories of France, the count of Anjou and the duke of Normandy, went to Jerusalem. Duke Robert was known to later tradition as Robert the Devil and, although pious Norman historians have urged us to remember his other soubriquet, the Magnificent, Robert was certainly not a man of peace; Count Fulk the Black was one of the most formidable of the formidable line of the counts of Anjou, noted for their violence, strength and cruelty, and also, on occasion, for attempting to make their peace with the Church by dramatic acts of piety like the foundation of monasteries and this remarkable pilgrimage.

It was the pilgrimage which acquainted men with the distribution of spiritual treasure in the world; and especially with the notion of the special value and sacredness of Jerusalem. It used to be said that it was the attempt by the Seljuks to prevent Christians from reaching Jerusalem which led to the First Crusade. This cannot be sustained: it had always been difficult and there is no evidence that the Seljuks made it conspicuously worse. The appeal of the crusade was manifold and thoroughly mixed. There were political motives: some wished (like Pope Urban) to save the Eastern Empire; others wished to disembody the Eastern Empire and carve out principalities for themselves—contradictory motives, perhaps, but both leading to similar activity. Others, again, wished to defend Europe against Islam; the dukes of Normandy and Lower Lorraine may have been fleeing from their incapacity to rule their duchies. There were economic motives, for the crusades owed much to the commercial enterprise of the Italian cities. Most complicated and difficult to analyse were the religious motives, ranging from a direct yearning to follow in the footsteps of Christ to an opportunity to escape the pains of hell. 'Some hoped to be saved by going; others didn't care if they were damned so long as they found new fields for profit and adventure. There was something in the Crusade to appeal to everyone.'[1]

The crusade was more than the great pilgrimage launched by Pope Urban in 1095; it was part of a larger movement, the expansion of Europe, against Islam and paganism in Spain, all though the Mediterranean, in Syria and the Holy Land, and in the Slavonic countries bordering on East Germany. In part this was a purely secular expansion, and the usual causes—rising population and prosperity, the plethora of younger sons, and the rest—may be found for it. But it was also a religious movement: the invasion by Christian knighthood of the infidel world; it aroused the savagery for which war in the name of religion has so often been the excuse.

The religious outlook of the crusaders was more complex and more elusive than Pope Urban's. Above all, it was ambivalent; and a brief inspection of the obverse and reverse of the coin will help to give us an insight into its meaning.

By great good fortune we are able to inspect the stage which had been reached on the eve of the First Crusade in the pages of the *Song of Roland*. The *Song of Roland* is based, very remotely, on fact: a Breton count of that name was killed by a Basque ambush when Charlemagne was retreating after his quite unsuccessful Spanish campaign of 778. The details of the legend's growth are obscure, but it is now known that it was developing steadily in northern Spain and southern France in the centuries between the eighth and the eleventh. By the late eleventh century it was the common possession of the French-speaking world. A version of it heartened the Normans in 1066; and it is even possible that the earliest surviving version was composed in Normandy.

[1] Southern, *Making of the Middle Ages*, p. 54.

However this may be, it is both the climax of a long tradition of minstrelsy and in part, perhaps in large part, the work of a poet of considerable accomplishment.

In form the *Song of Roland* is like a succession of vivid, jerky photographs, like an early motion picture; it is as though the author had set out to describe something similar to the Bayeux Tapestry, depicting the tragedy, not of Harold, but of Roland.[1]

> The tenth column is of barons of France,
> Five score thousand of our best capitans;
> Lusty of limb, and proud of countenance,
> Snowy their heads are, and their beards are blanched,
> In doubled sarks, and in hauberks they're clad,
> Girt on their sides Frankish and Spanish brands
> And noble shields of divers cognisance.
> Soon as they mount, the battle they demand,
> 'Monjoie' they cry. With them goes Charlemagne.
> Gefreid d'Anjou carries that oriflamme;
> Saint Peter's 'twas . . .[2]

—that is, it came from Rome, a papal banner.

There is a great deal of this kind of description in the *Song of Roland*, and a great deal more: action, speech and sentiment.

Charlemagne has been fighting for years in Spain, and has almost completed its conquest from the Saracens. The Spanish king sues for peace, offering to accept Charlemagne's suzerainty. Two of Charlemagne's leading magnates, Roland and Guenelon (or Ganelon), have fallen out, and Roland suggests that Guenelon should go to the Saracen court to discuss terms with the Muslims; treachery is suspected, and the embassy is regarded as very dangerous. Guenelon bears a grudge in his heart, which eventually blossoms into a scheme for revenge. He makes a secret compact to betray the rearguard of Charlemagne's army as it passes the Pyrenees, and then returns to Charlemagne's court and arranges for Roland to lead the rearguard. The army sets out on its way to France, and Roland is duly posted to lead the rear, together with the

[1] A direct link with the Bayeux Tapestry—as with almost everything else of the period—has been suggested. This version of the *Song of Roland* is undoubtedly of the late eleventh or early twelfth century, but the experts are divided whether it belongs to the years immediately before or immediately after the First Crusade.

[2] *Song of Roland*, trans. C. S. Scott-Moncrieff (London, 1919), lines 3083-93 (this translation reproduces the metre of the original).

flower of Charlemagne's feudatories, the twelve peers of France. When the main army is far ahead, and the rearguard is entering the pass of Roncesvalles, it is suddenly attacked by an immensely superior force of Saracens. Roland's close friend and companion, Oliver, begs him to blow his great horn (the oliphant) and summon Charlemagne back to the scene of battle. Roland refuses, and the rearguard, knowing it is doomed, prepares to fight. Wave after wave of attackers is routed, and Roland alone kills many hundred. But eventually the French are reduced to a small band, and Roland realizes that he did wrong to send his faithful followers to death by his proud refusal to blow the oliphant. And so, when it is too late, he blows it, and Charlemagne returns; but the blast on the horn, coupled with the fatigue of fighting, is too great an effort for Roland's strength; he bursts a blood vessel or two, and from then on is a dying man. In this way the author (somewhat naïvely) avoids the anti-climax of making Roland fall victim to a Saracen sword. Roland lives long enough to see all his followers die, and also to see the last remnants of the Saracen army void the field in confused rout, and then he dies. The emperor returns and chases the Muslim host to the gates of Saragossa; defeats them in another battle. Then, without warning, the Muslims are reinforced by the emir of Babylon (i.e. Cairo), who comes with an immense array from all the states of Islam. In a final battle Charlemagne is again victorious, and the emir is killed. The emperor returns to Aachen, and the poem closes with the trial of Guenelon and his death.

> When the Emperour his justice hath achieved,
> His mighty wrath's abated from its heat,
> And Bramimunde has christening received;
> Passes the day, the darkness is grown deep,
> And now that King in 's vaulted chamber sleeps.
> Saint Gabriel is come from God, and speaks:
> 'Summon the hosts, Charlès, of thine Empire,
> Go thou by force into the land of Bire,
> King Vivien thou'lt succour there, at Imphe,
> In the city which pagans have besieged.
> The Christians there implore thee and beseech.'
> Right loth to go, that Emperour was he:
> 'God!' said the King: 'My life is hard indeed!'
> Tears filled his eyes, he tore his snowy beard.[1]

[1] *Song of Roland*, lines 3988–4001.

'My life is hard indeed'—the life of the leader of a feudal host, whose business it was to defend and protect his followers; the ruler of fair France, *la douce France*, whose business it was to protect and govern his country; the emperor of Christendom, whose business it was to maintain the fortress of Christian Europe and to expand its borders. From these tasks there was no respite for the Christian emperor, the faithful feudal overlord. The aspirations of the knightly class at its best and the sense that Christendom must go over to the offensive against Islam are nowhere more succinctly expressed than in this poem, written when the Christian reconquest of Spain was well under way, but when the crusades had only just begun, shortly before or shortly after the launching of the First Crusade.

The *Song of Roland* was the work of a Christian cleric, and his picture of feudal knighthood is idealistic. Even so, his vision of Christianity is fairly primitive. It is a fighting religion, which sends its enemies to death and hell; only in the figure of the queen of Spain is there a hint of conversion, of a chance of salvation for the heathen. The author was not interested in Islam as a religion; he gives a grotesque caricature of it. The theme was always the Christian attack. Nor is his picture of the clergy a particularly spiritual one: those who pray and those who work are never mentioned, but the cleric who was also a warrior has his place, and after Roland perhaps the most heroic figure of all is the leading ecclesiastic of France, the archbishop of Rheims. In the Bayeux Tapestry, the Conqueror's half-brother, the warrior bishop of Bayeux, is represented in full armour; but out of respect for his office he carries, not a sword, but a mace. Archbishop Turpin, however, had no use for blunt instruments: he wields lance and sword like the rest and the only hint of his ecclesiastical status is his dying blessing on Roland and the fallen. Turpin is no monk, but he is a Christian bishop: not only is he, as a feudal lord, a part of the military hierarchy of Charlemagne's realm, but he represents the unity of all segments of Christendom in the fight against the infidel. It is the angel Gabriel who comes to Charlemagne at the end of the poem, just as Gabriel and Michael—the fighting archangel, whose cult was flourishing anew in the tenth and eleventh centuries—come to Roland to carry his soul to heaven; the poem is definitely Christian, and an attempt to set a religious seal on knightly glory; but the knightly glory has in its turn captured the Church, and harnessed it, in the person of the archbishop of Rheims, to the Holy War against the infidel.

Charlemagne represents the universal theme of the poem, and the centre of the loyalties of its characters; and Turpin the place of the Church in its rather crude scheme of Christian idealism; but the central figure is undoubtedly Roland. In his failure to sound the horn in time there is tragedy, but it is not of a very complicated kind. The tragedy must rest solely on the simple problem of the relation between his intense loyalty to his followers and to his lord, and his own pride as the supreme warrior. The directness of the theme as compared with earlier heroic lays or with the later romances is perhaps indicated by the absence of ladies from the scene. Roland is betrothed, and the lady Alde, on hearing the news of his death, instantly collapses and dies. This is a trivial incident in the poem, a fact which is made very clear when we compare it with the description of Roland's death: he thinks of his followers and of his lord, of *la douce France*, which he will never see again, but never for a moment thinks of the unfortunate lady. There is much pathos, but no romance in Roland.

On a hill looking down towards Spain Roland meets his end; and, although his death is not the end of the poem, it is its climax, and it enshrines almost all that is really great in it. It is a long passage, and a summary can do it no justice. Roland is fearful that his sword Durendal will fall into unworthy hands, and tries, unsuccessfully, to break it; and as he strikes it against a stone he laments over it:

'Ah! Durendal, white art thou, clear of stain!
Beneath the sun reflecting back his rays!
In Moriane was Charlès, in the vale,
When from heaven God by His angel bade
Him give thee to a count and capitain;
Girt thee on me that noble King and great.
I won for him with thee Anjou, Bretaigne [Brittany],
And won for him with thee Peitou, the Maine,
And Normandy the free for him I gained,
Also with thee Provence and Equitaigne,
And Lumbardie and all the whole Romaigne,
I won Baivere, all Flanders in the plain,
Also Burguigne and all the whole Puillane,
Costentinnople, that homage to him pays;
In Saisonie [Saxony] all is as he ordains;
With thee I won him Scotland, Ireland, Wales,
England also, where he his chamber makes;
Won I with thee so many countries strange

That Charlès holds, whose beard is white with age!
For this sword's sake sorrow upon me weighs,
Rather I'ld die, than it mid pagans stay.
Lord God Father, never let France be shamed!'[1]

He lists the relics in its golden hilt—the tooth of St Peter, the blood of
St Basil, some hairs of his lord St Denis (the patron saint of France)
and a piece of St Mary's dress. And so he turns aside under a pine tree,
lays his sword and oliphant under him and lies down to die: he makes
his confession, holds up his right glove to God and angels come and
carry his soul to Paradise.

Rollant is dead; his soul to heav'n God bare.
That Emperour to Rencesvals doth fare.
There was no path nor passage anywhere
Nor of waste ground no ell nor foot to spare
Without a Frank or pagan lying there.
Charles cries aloud: 'Where are you, nephew fair?
Where's the Archbishop and that count Oliviers?
Where is Gerins and his comrade Gerers?
Otès the Duke, and the count Berengiers
And Ivorie, and Ive, so dear they were?
What is become of Gascon Engelier,
Sansun the Duke and Anséis the fierce?
Where's old Gerard of Russillun; oh, where
The dozen peers I left behind me here?'
But what avail, since none can answer bear? . . .
No chevalier nor baron is there, who
Pitifully weeps not for grief and dule;
They mourn their sons, their brothers, their nephews,
And their liege lords, and trusty friends and true . . .
Thereon Duke Neimes doth act with wisdom proof,
First before all he's said to the Emperour:
'See beforehand, a league from us or two,
From the highways dust rising in our view;
Pagans are there . . .'[2]

Thus was God's blessing, fortified by relics and talismans and the
flowering of legends, promised to those who pursued the pagans down

[1] *Song of Roland*, lines 2312–35. The poem, with deliberate bravado, makes
Charlemagne lord of the whole of Christendom.
[2] *Ibid.*, lines 2397–2411, 2418–21, 2423–7.

the dusty road into Spain, or the still dustier tracks of Syria. But we must not be misled by the atmosphere of religious exaltation: the pagans are, by implication, cattle for the slaughter; the call is not to missionary work, nor even to humane conquest, if such a thing exists, but to slaughter. In the German version of the poem, written some two generations or so later, this is quite explicit. We may be sure that many people even in the eleventh century had doubts about this doctrine; just as St Anselm was convinced that the road to Jerusalem which could be pursued within the walls of a monastery was safer and holier than that to Jerusalem itself. If the heroism of Roland is the obverse of a coin, the reverse is the doctrine of holy war as it impinged on the cruder minds of thousands of contemporaries. That it impinged as a call to slaughter first and foremost seems only too clear; for the first result of the preaching of the crusade was a fearful massacre of the one species of 'infidel' within easy reach. The lot of the Jews had been an uneasy one for many centuries; now, for the first time, they were massacred in western Europe. There were, no doubt, special reasons for this. Those who preached the crusade dwelt on the significance of Jerusalem and on the death of Jesus, and so roused men to fervour against the Jews who had killed him as well as against the Muslims who had captured his tomb; and apocalyptic notions of the time associated the conversion or elimination of the Jews with the liberation of Jerusalem, as a necessary prelude to the end of the world. But the outcome only serves to emphasize the sadistic element in the popular doctrine of the crusade. In the eyes of ordinary folk, the crusade was a holy war for the sake of war. By a curious irony the Muslim doctrine of Holy War was turned against Islam.

The crusades were preached by the official Church; but the enthusiasm with which the preaching was greeted was due to a wide variety of emotions, of which zeal for a different doctrine from the pope's was one of the most powerful. The crusade was inspired by many motives, of which one can surely say that the lowest—and perhaps, with less conviction, the highest too—were religious. Yet the crusading movement in many ways helped to civilize Europe. It compelled the Church to come to terms with lay society; to find an accommodation between its own ideals and those of the warrior aristocracy; and so, in the end, to civilize that society, as well as, in some respects, to lower its own ideals. One of the last of the *Chansons de Geste* was the *Willehalm* of Wolfram von Eschenbach. Wolfram may never have seen a Muslim; but he preaches, with outspoken conviction, the common humanity, the common place in God's purpose, of Christian and heathen —'spare God's handiwork'. Behind the famous outcry of the converted Muslim princess in his poem lay a century in which theologians had humanized Christian teaching, and Christian and Muslim had met and mingled on all the frontiers of southern and south-eastern Christendom.

The First Crusade: its course

When that time had already come, of which the Lord Jesus warns his faithful people every day, especially in the Gospel where he says, 'If any man will come after me, let him deny himself, and take up his cross, and follow me,' there was a great stirring of heart throughout all the Frankish lands, so that if any man, with all his heart and all his mind, really wanted to follow God and faithfully to bear the cross after him, he could make no delay in taking the road to the Holy Sepulchre as quickly as possible.

Thus opens the *Gesta Francorum*, of all the early crusading chronicles that which gets us nearest to the rank and file of the army. This anonymous Norman knight was quite clear that the Crusade was not caused by the Emperor Alexius, nor even, except incidentally, by the pope. The hour had come. This view was widespread; the response exceeded Urban's expectation; it far exceeded Alexius's.

Before he had enjoyed even a short rest [writes Alexius's daughter], he heard a report of the approach of innumerable Frankish armies. . . . And indeed the actual facts were far greater and more terrible than rumour made them. For the whole of the West and all the barbarian tribes which dwell between the further side of the Adriatic and the pillars of Heracles, had all migrated in a body and were marching into Asia through the intervening Europe, and were making the journey with all their household.[1]

There is a notable contrast between the history of the first and later crusades. The leaders of the first were great nobles and minor prophets; those of the second and third were kings. Henry IV of Germany was excommunicated in 1095; so was the king of France; William of England was uncertain in his allegiance to Urban. So it was lesser men who answered the call: some, like Godfrey of Lower Lorraine or Robert of Normandy or Raymond of Toulouse, owing to a nice combination of enthusiasm for the cause and incapacity for their job at home; others,

[1] *Gesta Francorum*, trans. R. Hill, p. 1; *Alexiad*, trans. E. A. S. Dawes, p. 248.

like Godfrey's brother Baldwin and most of all the Norman Bohemond, who were landless, hoping to carve out principalities for themselves in the East. The second contrast is that the First Crusade was essentially a land operation; ships took part only at a late stage. The navies of Byzantium and the Italian cities played a somewhat larger part in the Second Crusade; sea power was an essential part of the Third. And thirdly, the First Crusade set off a wave of religious enthusiasm which swept through every stratum of society. Later crusades were mainly organized military campaigns, though there were notable exceptions, such as the tragic children's crusades. The fervent, apocalyptic preaching of men like Peter the Hermit brought on the First Crusade a horde of unarmed or half-armed men from every walk of life. Anna Comnena's vision of the barbarians on the move was not fanciful. Peter's throng behaved like a mob of rioters, without discipline and without restraint. Fortunately for Alexius, Peter arrived first; and the judicious emperor allowed his rabble to be ferried across the Bosphorus, and then left it to be massacred by the Turks. The remnant, including their leader, were ferried back into Europe; and Alexius was much relieved to have escaped the barbarian avalanche so lightly.

The emperor had meanwhile had good intelligence of the approach of the armies of knights, which had gathered as a result of Pope Urban's summons. The emperor formed his plans with care. There could be no question of treating the crusaders as mercenaries; but they might still be used to further his ends. If they reconquered Asia Minor and Syria for him, well and good. But they must conquer as his vassals. He could not be expected to trust an army which included his old enemy Bohemond, Robert Guiscard's son and one-time lieutenant, and it was only natural that Alexius should do everything he could to ensure that he did not exchange a quiescent sultanate on his eastern frontier for an actively hostile Frankish principality. Asia Minor and Antioch, furthermore, had been among the oldest and most valued possessions of his predecessors. Alexius was determined to recover them for himself or, failing that, to extract some measure of allegiance from his unexpected and unwelcome allies.

Each band was met as it approached the empire and carefully escorted to the capital. Alexius wished to make the knights' rendezvous in Asia Minor, but they insisted on gathering outside Constantinople; and one by one, in the winter of 1096-7 and the spring of 1097, the armies collected. As they came in, Alexius took an oath of allegiance from the leader of every group, which almost all gave, and which most subsequently broke. His precautions were only too necessary; even the armies of knights were far from well-disciplined, and on one occasion they attacked Constantinople itself on hearing a rumour that Alexius had imprisoned some of their leaders. A co-operative venture on this scale was something quite new for these western counts. They were under the nominal direction of a papal legate; but on the march and in action their cohesion depended on relations with and between their leaders. Necessity made the leaders act together for much of the time; but the alliance was always somewhat uneasy. Godfrey of Bouillon, duke of Lower Lorraine, Robert of Normandy and the count of Flanders, among others, were tolerably conscientious men, seriously anxious to reach Jerusalem; and Bohemond and Baldwin were too intelligent to cause a rift in the army before their designs had been achieved.

Bohemond was well known to the Greeks from his share in his father's piratical expeditions to Greece in earlier years; and he was also leader of the army in which the author of the *Gesta* fought. He is thus the principal figure in the *Gesta* and the chief villain of the *Alexiad*. He 'took after his father in all things,' says Anna Comnena, 'in audacity, bodily strength, bravery, and untamable temper'; and she gives a famous description of him, the most precise we have of any great figure of the period. 'Let me describe the barbarian's appearance more particularly', she says; and tells us that he was extremely tall,

> narrow in the waist . . . with broad shoulders and a deep chest and powerful arms [and with a slight stoop]. His skin . . . was very white, and in his face the white was tempered with red. His hair was yellowish, but did not hang down to his waist like that of the other barbarians; for the man was not inordinately vain of his hair, but had it cut short to the ears. Whether his beard was reddish, or any other colour I cannot say, for the razor had passed over it very closely. . . . A certain charm hung about this man but was partly marred by a general air of the horrible.

Blue eyes, a savage glance, laughter which sounded like snorting, complete her picture of the strong and cunning barbarian who fascinated as well as horrified her.[1]

The interest of Anna and the *Gesta*, from very different points of view, have given Bohemond a special place in the story of the First Crusade; but the other sources do not contradict the notion that he was

[1] *Alexiad*, pp. 37, 347.

the most forceful and effective of the western generals, and that he was in effective command until the capture of Antioch.

The crusaders' task was formidable. Their army was large, but had little cohesion; it carried numbers of non-combatants; it was quite unused to the climate and terrain of Asia Minor and Syria; and even its leaders had no experience of fighting the Seljuk Turks. It was very likely Bohemond who adapted the military techniques of the West to local conditions. Even so, it is doubtful if the crusading armies would have survived but for a great stroke of good fortune: at the time of the First Crusade the Turkish leaders were at loggerheads among themselves. Their nominal leader was the Sultan Barkyaruq; he had ruled in Baghdad since the death of his father Malik Shah, Alp Arslan's son, in 1092, and in Syria and Asia Minor since he had defeated and killed his brother Tutush in 1095. As he had previously dealt the same way with Suleiman of Rum, Rum was very cool in its allegiance, and Damascus and Aleppo, whose emirs were sons of Tutush, were even more so; nor were Damascus and Aleppo of one mind. Thus the crusaders had to deal with a series of isolated Turkish enemies, instead of facing the united strength of the sultan.

Even so, their enemies were powerful. At Dorylaeum in central Asia Minor their vanguard was ambushed by the lord of Rum. The Turks showered arrows on the crusaders, but had not closed with them when the rest of the army came up and frightened the Turks off the field. The men of Rum offered no further resistance; but the crusaders were nearly baffled by nature. Most of the army crossed the Anti-Taurus range of mountains in September and October, which was no mean feat; after much suffering they came to Antioch. Baldwin of Boulogne, meanwhile, had shown his hand; after taking a different route through Armenia, he turned east, and established himself at Edessa: he had founded his own principality and his crusade, for the moment, was at an end.

Antioch was the most substantial city and fortress in the crusaders' march to Jerusalem. The crusaders had no regular naval support, although western flotillas from time to time gave them assistance. They may therefore have had some reasonable qualms about leaving Antioch in hostile hands in their rear. But it is difficult not to suspect that they could have by-passed it, as they later by-passed Damascus, but for the ambition of Bohemond. It was Bohemond's intention to win Antioch, one of the largest and most prosperous cities in the Middle East, as a centre for his own principality. He therefore insisted on its being taken,

and convinced his colleagues that this was necessary. The siege of
Antioch nearly destroyed the crusade, but in the end Bohemond's skill
in generalship and intrigue converted disaster into a major and decisive
victory.

Late in 1097 and early in 1098 relieving forces sent from Damascus
and Aleppo were beaten off; and a sortie from Antioch was also checked.
But Antioch was large and very strong; and the crusaders soon found
themselves caught between the city and the most formidable army they
ever had to face, that of Karbuqa, emir of Mosul, one of the sultan's

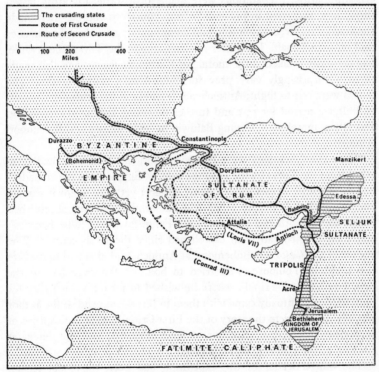

7. THE CRUSADES

most powerful generals. The Christian army was saved by two rather
different interventions. Bohemond took the opportunity of this crisis to
win a concession from his colleagues: they would let him keep Antioch
if he could capture it. Meanwhile he had made an arrangement with
one of the defenders to betray a tower at one corner of the walls, and a
scaling party was able to enter the city: the author of the *Gesta* was in

this party and gives a vivid description of the excitement and the mishaps of the night assault, the confusion as day broke, the ensuing panic and massacre. And so the crusaders ceased to be besiegers and became the besieged; and soon their plight was very serious. It was at this point that a group from Provence, in response to a vision, unearthed a lance in St Peter's church. The lance was supposed to be that which had pierced Christ's side in the Crucifixion. The papal legate thought it spurious, but its discovery and the comforting nature of the visions which accompanied it had a miraculous effect on the morale of the crusading army. Preparations were made for a sortie; the army fasted three days, and went in procession from church to church; then made confession, received absolution and communion; gave alms; had masses said on their behalf. The bitter rivalries among the Turks, meanwhile, had seriously weakened the morale of Karbuqa's forces; and this made them a surprisingly easy prey for Bohemond's skilful tactics. The Turks were put to flight; Antioch was securely in the crusaders' hands; and after a period for rest and further bickering they could march on Jerusalem unmolested, leaving Baldwin to enjoy Edessa and Bohemond Antioch.

While the Christians were besieging Antioch, Jerusalem had been taken from the Turks by the Fatimite ruler of Egypt. Thus the crusaders had yet another considerable enemy to face; yet once again it was an enemy divided from the other Muslim armies, by long established differences of faith and tradition—the Fatimites were Shiite 'heretics', and their empire had been established since the tenth century. The author of the *Gesta* left Bohemond at Antioch, and attached himself to the count of Toulouse, who tried to hold up the crusaders in the neighbourhood of Tripoli, where he wished to form a principality for himself, but eventually came with them to Jerusalem. And so the author was able to complete the story of the First Crusade with the capture of Jerusalem (1099), the slaughter of its inhabitants, and the defeat at Ascalon of the relieving Egyptian army.

The official leader of the expedition had been the papal legate, Ademar of Le Puy. But he did not live to see Jerusalem. Some months after the capture of the city, his successor, Daimbert archbishop of Pisa, a vigorous, but ambitious and somewhat unscrupulous man, arrived to take his place. With him came Bohemond, on pilgrimage from Antioch; and in Jerusalem they found Godfrey of Lorraine, who had been chosen by the other crusading leaders, in command. Godfrey refused to take the title king: he was Advocate of the Holy Sepulchre—

advocate by analogy with the advocates of German monasteries, ruler of the domain, protector of the church, but essentially subordinate to the church's authority. When Daimbert arrived he was, on Bohemond's initiative, elected patriarch of Jerusalem, and both Bohemond and Godfrey acknowledged his suzerainty: he invested them with Antioch and Jerusalem. Godfrey's act symbolized the genuine piety of this weak, but energetic and conscientious feudal noble; Bohemond was more concerned to provide himself with an excuse for ignoring the claims of Byzantium to be his overlord, if not to supplant him; Jerusalem was far enough away from Antioch not to trouble him when he was not in need of help.

Godfrey's advocacy was shortlived. In 1100 he died, and after a bitter dispute, his brother Baldwin was chosen to succeed him. Baldwin came from Edessa and soon made peace with those who had opposed his election, especially with the patriarch Daimbert, who abandoned the ambition to be a theocrat. Baldwin I, in contrast to his brother, was exceedingly capable and not over-scrupulous. By one means and another he succeeded in preserving his kingdom (for he insisted on being a king not an advocate) and extending its frontiers. He was the first of a succession of notable kings who held their own under peculiarly difficult circumstances well into the second half of the century. The kingdom had its vicissitudes. In 1123 Baldwin II, Baldwin I's nephew and successor, was imprisoned in a Turkish gaol. But in 1125 he had his revenge, and it was an apparently secure kingdom that he handed over to his son-in-law Fulk of Anjou (father of Count Geoffrey, grand-father of Henry II of England); nor were Fulk's two sons and successors, Baldwin III and Amalric, weak or incompetent. But the difficulties of their position were mounting.

The feudal barons who garrisoned the kingdom of Jerusalem were always in the position of lords of an occupied country. Palestine had been in Muslim hands for centuries, and the population mainly consisted of Muslims or Christians of the Greek obedience. Farther north, especially in the principality of Antioch, the traditional allegiance was not to Islam but to Byzantium. The Christian states were surrounded by a ring of enemies: orthodox Christians in Byzantium, orthodox Muslims in the Turkish states, Shiite Muslims in Egypt. These enemies happily never agreed among themselves; but neither did the kingdom's allies, and it was hard work for the kings even to keep their feudal vassals in control. The kingdom could not live on its own strength. In the later stages of the First Crusade it had received much help from the ships of Pisa and Genoa; later even more from those of Venice; but the fleets were rivals of each other, not allies, in this work. The climate of Syria and Palestine and the continuous and strenuous warfare took its toll of the crusaders, and they needed constant recruits. The Church constantly encouraged western pilgrims to help in its defence, and also encouraged the organization of the Orders of Knights, the Hospitallers and Templars, formed to recruit soldiers dedicated to the defence of Jerusalem.

Byzantium and the Latin kingdoms

The Latin kingdom of Jerusalem relied considerably on its Latin Christian allies, Antioch, Edessa and Tripoli. Although Muslim states were intertwined with the Christian, these three formed a substantial buffer to the north and north-east; from the south, from Fatimite Egypt, which was in decline, the kingdom had less to fear. But beyond Antioch lay Byzantium, and the relations of the new states with the old Roman Empire were crucial to them.

After his return from Jerusalem to Antioch in 1100, Bohemond's good fortune deserted him. In the same year he was captured by a Turkish emir, and after his release he was defeated again in 1104 by another Turkish army. Alexius took the opportunity to lay hands on a number of towns and fortresses along the coast of Cilicia and Syria, and Bohemond determined to resume his father's plan to attack the Byzantine Empire itself. To this end he travelled in the West, spreading propaganda against Alexius—the forged appeal of Alexius attributed to 1095 was probably one of his weapons—and gathering support. In 1107 he landed in Greece once again. But the emperor was ready for him, and well prepared. After a brief campaign Bohemond was en-circled and compelled to surrender. He was allowed to retain Antioch as a Byzantine vassal. But he gave up hope of realizing his ambitions soon after and retired to the West, leaving his nephew Tancred as lord of Antioch, and to his uncle's treaty Tancred paid no attention. Nor could Alexius enforce it, since his last years were fully occupied in campaigns against the Turks and in resisting the intrigues of his family. In both he was successful, and his son John, the most attractive of the Comneni, was left in possession of the empire on Alexius's death in 1118.

Looking back after 800 years it is easy to simplify the picture and to be astonished that Alexius and Bohemond did not sink their differences and realize their common interests and their common religion, and make an alliance against the Turks. Yet the issues between them were not so easily soluble; and great as was the fervour of many of the crusaders, the division between Christianity and Islam was never wholly decisive in the alignment of the powers of the Near East in the age of the crusades. Alliances between Muslim and Christian were common, and quarrels between Christian and Christian even commoner. Bohemond and Alexius were both by origin adventurers who aspired to rule some substantial fragment of the old Roman Empire. As emperor, Alexius fought with limited means for limited ends. He never forgot how precarious was his own position, nor how weak was his empire. He did little to improve internal administration; the system of taxation seems to have been both oppressive and inefficient. In a way still not entirely clear, he made a substantial improvement in the coinage, which recovered some of its former prestige and value. He attempted to replace the old small-holdings with larger, quasi-feudal tenures. The *pronoia*, a grant of land for a limited term, had been used by his predecessors to reward good service. By attaching specifically military duties to its holders, Alexius converted it into a kind of feudal holding, thus reviving the native element in the Byzantine army. The effects of his comparatively stable, comparatively enlightened government took time to ripen. His successors gathered the harvest.

John II was able to embark on a scheme of expansion more ambitious than his father could envisage. He revived Byzantine power in the Balkans and beyond; he reconquered much of Asia Minor. He had little success in reviving Byzantine naval power in the Mediterranean or in his efforts to weaken the grip of the Venetian fleets on the sea or of Venice's merchants in the markets of his capital. He had no opportunity to involve himself seriously in western affairs. But at the end of his life, in the early 1140s, he prepared to reconquer Syria. In 1143 he was planning the conquest of Antioch, and casting his eyes on Palestine, so it seems. But Antioch was saved by his death in a hunting accident, and from then on the danger to the crusaders came once more mainly from the Turks.

John II was succeeded by his youngest son, Manuel I (1143–80), the most imaginative and daring of the Comneni. He had inherited the love of the Greeks for theological speculation and a strong sense of Byzantine autocracy and imperial ambition. Yet his heart lay in the Mediterranean world; he was deeply interested in the West; both his wives were western princesses, and his court became the centre of western gaiety and chivalry. Although he seems to have had a streak of recklessness in his nature, and the later years of his reign were to witness disastrous defeats, it is far from clear that his involvement in western politics was a mistake. The Turks were once more on the move, and he had little to hope for in the East. He had inherited from his predecessors a bitter feud with the Norman kingdom of Sicily and a strong respect for western mercenaries. His chief western alliance, with Conrad III of Germany, whose sister-in-law became Manuel's first wife, had already been planned by John II. Manuel's unsuccessful efforts to play the part of a second Justinian in the West lie beyond the scope of this volume. But the orientation of his concerns towards the West was already in progress in the brief interval before his plans were interrupted by the outbreak of the Second Crusade.

In 1143 Antioch had been saved by the death of John II. In 1144 Edessa fell to the formidable Turks, and Christian rule in the Middle East was seriously threatened. An emir of Mosul had arisen more powerful and successful than Karbuqa, called Zangi. He was able to unite the Turkish armies of Mesopotamia and of much of Syria, and he set to work to gather all Syria under his rule. In 1144 he captured Edessa, and both Antioch and Jerusalem lay open to attack. In 1146 he was murdered, but his successor, Nur al-Din, was even more formidable. In the West, meanwhile, the shock of Edessa's fall had led to the launching of a new crusade.

The Second Crusade

It had not escaped the notice of Europe's kings that their predecessors had suffered severely in prestige by their failure to join the First Crusade. Stephen of England was in no position to leave his troubled kingdom; but Conrad of Germany and Louis of France determined to go east in person. A grand parade of Europe's chivalry led by two of her most considerable kings might sound a more orderly affair than the barbarian avalanche described by Anna Comnena. But the Second Crusade was little more disciplined than the First, nor was it even in the eyes of contemporaries sanctified by success. Pope Eugenius III launched the crusade, as had Pope Urban, for the protection of Christendom against the infidel—in this case of existing Christian states and especially Jerusalem against the threat of destruction by the Muslims. He set St Bernard himself to preach it; and Bernard, though reluctant to engage in such an activity, had no hesitation about the rightness of the cause; his eloquence created a fervour comparable to that of 1095–6; once again a rabble filled with apocalyptic hopes and sadistic dreams joined the procession to the east—though nothing like so large a rabble as that of Peter the Hermit. One can hardly hold Bernard responsible for the notions of the crusaders; but the exalted violence which he and the pope unleashed prevented there being any semblance of good order in the crusaders' march.

Conrad and Louis, it seems, were too well informed about the First Crusade: they set out to follow its route through Greece and Asia Minor, step by step. Once again the Byzantine emperor had a mob on his hands, once again he was at his wits' end to prevent his subjects being mercilessly pillaged. Conrad and the Germans followed the old route as far as Dorylaeum, where Bohemond had triumphed over the ruler of Rum; and there the army was severely defeated. The Germans, for the most part, abandoned the crusade; Conrad attached himself to Louis. The French more prudently followed the coast road; but even this was not easy, and in the south of Asia Minor they decided at last to take to the sea. The Greeks hired them ships, and Louis was able to sail to Antioch with a small company of his *élite* troops. Louis had made an arrangement with the Greeks for the safety of the rest of his army; but the Greeks felt it more prudent to leave them at the mercy of the Turks, who cut them to pieces. It is little wonder that the Emperor Manuel (1143–80) acquired a reputation for perfidy in the West; but the Latin Christians were not there by his invitation; he had little advantage to hope for from them; and in view of what Alexius I had suffered and of the behaviour of the crusaders in his own territory, Manuel had every reason to wish to be rid of them. The crusaders paid the penalty of their own violence and the perjury of the leaders of the First Crusade.

If the rulers at Antioch and Jerusalem had been of one mind in 1148, they might still have led Germany and France to a combined operation of some use. But the prince of Antioch was concerned to organize a campaign against Nur al-Din and for the recovery of Edessa, while the king of Jerusalem felt that the first objective should be to round off his own territory by the capture of Damascus. A decision was taken in favour of the siege of Damascus; the first steps were entirely successful; but just as the crusaders were preparing for the final assault, they fell out among themselves so violently that the siege had to be abandoned. 'It is notorious', says John of Salisbury, 'that. . . the most Christian king [Louis VII] had been betrayed and deceived.' Just how, we do not know; but the disputes were sufficiently serious to wreck the crusade. Conrad saw no profit in remaining but only a chance of winning an alliance with

Manuel, which would be of use to him in Italy, if he travelled back through Constantinople. The French leaders melted away 'until the king of the Franks remained almost alone'. Nur al-Din was left to continue his career of conquest; Antioch soon ceased to be a military power to be reckoned with; and the kingdom of Jerusalem was left increasingly to its own devices. That it survived till 1187 is a measure of the skill and courage of King Baldwin III (1143–63) and King Amalric (1163–74).

In 1154 Damascus fell to Nur al-Din; in the same year Louis VII's queen, Eleanor of Aquitaine, became queen of England. Her behaviour at Antioch had given Louis VII seriously to think of divorce and, although their marriage was patched up for a time by the pope, it was finally annulled in 1152, and Eleanor married Henry, who became king of England two years later. The two events of 1154 were the most notable political consequences of the Second Crusade.

And yet, for all its failure, for all the disgrace this entailed, anyway for a time, for Pope Eugenius and Abbot Bernard, the Second Crusade, like the First, had shown that Christendom would answer such a call to arms, would accept papal leadership in such a case; and Urban and Eugenius had succeeded, perhaps more effectively than any amount of royal justice could have done, in clearing the most violent and disreputable elements out of western Christendom.

Christianity and Islam in the Spanish peninsula

The most substantial gain to Christendom produced by the Second Crusade was the capture of Lisbon. In Spain and Portugal the Christian kingdoms had been advancing with some reverses for a century before 1147. Their relations with the Muslim powers were calmer, and their offensives less spectacular, than those of the crusaders in the Near East. But in the eyes of the popes, the conquest of Muslim Spain qualified as a crusading effort: it earned the same indulgences. The Spanish 'crusade' began long before the First Crusade to Jerusalem, and was concluded finally, in the late fifteenth century, when the idea of a crusade in the East was all but forgotten. It must not therefore be regarded merely as a subsidiary episode in the history of the crusades; yet it is fitting that it should be considered in this context. Histories of the crusades have often lacked a proper perspective because they concentrated too exclusively on Syria and Palestine.

After the collapse of the Caliphate of Cordova, Muslim Spain broke up into a number of petty emirates, the *taifas*, each centring in a cultivated city and court. The Christian empire in the north, meanwhile, was similarly inclined to break up into fragments, which were, however, poorer, less cultured and more militant than the Muslim (see pp. 38–41). There were two centres of Christian power, in León-Castile and in Aragon. León was the ancient home of the northern 'emperors', but in the late eleventh and twelfth centuries Castile came to surpass it in importance; to León-Castile were attached, when political circumstances allowed, Galicia, and such parts of central Spain as the Christians reconquered. To Aragon the counts of Barcelona and the kings of Navarre owed an uncertain and fluctuating allegiance.

The political history of Christian Spain can only be given any semblance of unity in this period by following the fortunes of the dynasty of Ferdinand I of León-Castile (1037–65). He was the first of the emperors seriously to undertake the conquest of the *taifas*. He conquered a substantial area in the west—much of what later came to be Portugal—and the emirs of Seville and Toledo paid him tribute. Loot and tribute provided the Christians with much wealth; and contact with the Muslims taught them the value of literacy, a little of the arts of peace and of architecture. But it taught them nothing of how to achieve political unity and stability, a lesson the Muslims themselves were far from wishing to learn. When Ferdinand died in 1065, his empire, as was the custom of his house, was divided between his sons. Castile fell to Sancho, León to Alfonso and Galicia to Garcia. By the end of 1072 Alfonso VI was established, after several vicissitudes, as sole ruler. In 1071 he and Sancho had conspired to remove Garcia; early in 1072 Alfonso himself was sent into exile to Muslim Toledo; later in the same year Sancho was murdered, and Alfonso was able to return. In the following year he took the precaution of capturing Garcia by a trick and imprisoning him for life in the castle of Luna in León.

Alfonso ruled in León-Castile from 1072 till his death in 1109. He was never an embittered enemy of the Muslims, and partly for that reason seemed in his early years to stand a reasonable chance of bringing the whole peninsula under his sway. For this he needed four things: a long life, a brilliant general, reinforcements from outside his kingdom, and freedom from interference. The first was granted to him; and if a tithe of the stories told of the eminent Castilian warrior, Rodrigo Diaz, el Cid, are true, Alfonso had among his subjects the most talented soldier in Europe. Of the Cid's prowess and skill, and astonishing luck, there can be little doubt. But Alfonso never trusted him. In part, no doubt, he was jealous; and at the opening of his reign the Castilian nobles, led by Rodrigo, had insisted on extracting a highly circumstantial oath from Alfonso that he was innocent of his brother's murder. The oath protests a great deal, which suggests at least that strong suspicion had attached to Alfonso; and the pressure brought on him at this time may well have made the king hate the Cid as well as fear him. Again, if the tales are true, the Cid's loyalty was complete; it outlived the king's enmity and years of exile. As for foreign reinforcements, they came from time to time, but were more nuisance than they were worth. Warfare in Spain in the eleventh century was (comparatively speaking) friendly and fraternal; when the pope launched a crusade in 1063 Alfonso's father had been almost as embarrassed as the Byzantine emperor by the First Crusade and, although it provided him with some assistance, he was on the whole relieved when the great army of fanatical crusaders was safely out of Spain. In spite of Alfonso's quarrel with the Cid and the necessity, in the main, to rely on his own resources, he came near at least to suzerainty over the whole of central and southern Spain, and might well have come even nearer but for a Muslim revival.

In his early days Alfonso fought in the centre of the peninsula, and the Cid, partly by judicious arrangements with Muslim friends, carved out a principality for himself at Valencia, which he preserved by a grandiose mixture of intrigue, violence, chivalry and heroic prowess which makes the Cid of history as fantastic a figure as the Cid of fiction. When Valencia was conquered he heaped coals of fire on Alfonso's head by immediately acknowledging himself Alfonso's vassal. But the king did not trust him, and he remained in semi-independence at Valencia till his death in 1099. Attempts at Muslim reconquest foundered either on his military skill or on the glamour of his name; but when he was dead Valencia had to be abandoned by the Christians.

In 1085 Alfonso scored his most notable success, and captured Toledo. The capital of the ancient Visigothic kingdom was a substantial prize, and the settlement of more Christians in central Spain, combined (at first) with tolerably liberal treatment of the Muslims, rapidly made Toledo a Christian centre once again; the pope revived the old archbishopric, and Toledo's new archbishop was declared primate of Spain. Alfonso had a shrewd sense of the value of the papal alliance. Earlier in his reign the Spanish church had renounced its ancient ritual, and conformed to the Roman rite; and Gregory VII had tried to claim that Alfonso was a papal vassal. This was too much for the king, but his relations with Rome remained friendly, and the pope gave him moral support and encouraged recruits to go to his assistance.

Meanwhile a great Muslim power was rising in North Africa. In 1086 the emir of Seville, fearful of suffering the same fate as Toledo, called in the Almoravid prophet-general Yusuf. Yusuf came, checked Alfonso in the battle of Zalaca, and returned to his meditations in the desert. In 1090 he came again, and the Muslim emirs found that Islam was more formidable than Christendom. Alfonso's troops occasionally engaged in atrocities, but he himself was comparatively easy-going. Yusuf was a fanatic who had no use for cultivated courts. The *taifas* were swept away and Muslim Spain once more united. Toledo remained in Christian hands, but Seville and Cordoba (brief interludes apart) remained out of their reach until the thirteenth century, and Valencia was lost after the death of the Cid. The check to Alfonso was confirmed in a major defeat at Ucles in 1108, in which Alfonso lost his son and heir, and by the disorder into which his kingdom fell after his death in 1109.

After Alphonso's death power and initiative passed from Castile to Aragon, and its neighbour the county of Barcelona. Alfonso I of Aragon indeed tried to forestall the union of Ferdinand and Isabella three and a half centuries later by marrying the queen of Castile, Urraca (1109–26), daughter and heiress of Alfonso VI. But the marriage was a failure and was presently annulled on grounds of consanguinity; Alfonso of Aragon's intrigues continued, however, unabated. The old king of Castile had left the legitimate daughter who succeeded him and an illegitimate daughter, Theresa, who with her husband held a substantial county in what is now Portugal as vassals of Queen Urraca. Theresa and Urraca each had a son; Urraca's (by her first husband, who had died before her father) was to be the future Alfonso VII of Castile (1126–57), Theresa's, Alfonso Henriques, was to be the first king of Portugal. The half-sisters were not on the best of terms. Theresa hatched a plot to replace Urraca by her son. The plot failed, but it gave Alfonso an idea which was put into execution after Urraca's death, when he, with the aid of Alfonso VII, sent Theresa into exile, and became count of Portugal in his own right. After some vicissitudes, he felt strong enough in 1139 to assume the title of king, which was eventually recognized by Castile in 1143. In 1147 he rounded off his dominions by diverting a contingent on its way to the Second Crusade to conquer Lisbon for him; and although his later years were not free from difficulty, it was a securely established kingdom which he left to his heir when he died in 1185.

For a brief space in the 1140s it looked as if Alfonso VII might revive the ambitions of his grandfather. The power of the Almoravides collapsed after the death of Yusuf's son in 1143. The *taifas* were revived, and Alfonso broke into Andalusia, capturing Cordoba, advancing to the sea. Meanwhile a new Muslim sect, the Almohades, had arisen in north Africa, and rapidly revived the empire of the Almoravides. In 1146 they invaded Spain, and set to work to reunite the Muslim princi-palities under their own rule. Alfonso's new conquests were lost. His own kingdom was not threatened, but further advance could no longer be undertaken.

Alfonso VII was never the unquestioned leader of the Spanish Christians that his grandfather had been, even though for a time Aragon acknowledged his overlordship, and he assumed the title 'emperor' traditional in his family. But he was compelled to recog-nize the independence of Portugal, and his influence in Aragon was ephemeral. That kingdom, long insignificant, had acquired new influence in the days of Alfonso I, who had married and bullied Urraca of Castile, at the same time that he was himself absorbing the emirate of Saragossa, and his neighbour of Barcelona was advancing on Valencia. When Alfonso of Aragon died, the king of Castile coolly asserted that he was heir of Aragon on account of his mother's marriage. The nobles of Aragon countered by producing an heir in Gilbertian fashion. Alfonso of Aragon had had a brother, who was a monk; he was given dispensation, unfrocked, married, had a daughter, abdicated and returned to his monastery, all in the space of two years. The baby girl was declared queen of Aragon and betrothed to Count Raymond-Berengar of Barcelona, who was also lord of Provence. In 1151 Queen Petronilla consummated her marriage to Raymond-Berengar; in 1162 her husband died; in 1164 she abdicated, now an ageing widow of about twenty-eight; and her son, Alfonso II, joined Barcelona, that is, the whole of Catalonia, and Provence, to the kingdom of Aragon. The two halves of this kingdom have never been closely knit from that day to this; but the appearance of unity was preserved owing to the dominance of Catalonia, with its Mediterranean outlook and its com-mercial wealth, in the union from which the medieval kingdom of Aragon was formed. Thus the mid-1150s saw three kingdoms firmly established in Christian Spain, with an Alfonso growing old in Castile, an Alfonso in the prime of life in Portugal, and a small Alfonso[1] growing up to be heir of Aragon, all dedicated to spread moderate confusion among the Muslims of their own day, and extreme confusion among historians until the end of the world.

[1] Who was, however, called Raymond (Ramon) until his accession.

XVIII

Epilogue

In 1151 died Geoffrey, count of Anjou, in 1152 Conrad III; in 1153 Pope Eugenius and St Bernard, King David of Scotland and Count Eustace, King Stephen's elder son; in 1154 King Stephen himself and Roger the Great. The stage was cleared for the rise of Count Geoffrey's son and Eustace's rival, Henry II of England, Normandy, Anjou and Aquitaine. It was cleared for Frederick Barbarossa and the Indian summer of German monarchy. The church found new leaders. With Bernard's passing the storm of Cistercian success began to abate a little, and the theologians of Paris could breathe, perhaps, a little more freely. The age of monastic dominance in literature and scholarship was also passing. In some ways the most characteristic figure in this gallery was King David. Many aspects of the twelfth century were summarized in the career of this cultivated and attractive man, son of the learned Margaret, patron and friend of St Ailred, founder and benefactor of over half the monasteries in Scotland, and patron of the bloodless Norman conquest of Lothian, the man who girt the sword of knighthood on the young Henry of Normandy and Anjou. But it was an age of great variety, and in its variety lies its interest; it would be false to give it unreal unity by laying too much emphasis on any single man as its epitome. If we wish to understand it and to enjoy our study of it, we must not make a pilgrimage to a single shrine. We shall find the twelfth century as much in the splendour of Vézelay as in the austerity of Fountains, in the sophistication of the troubadours as in the simple pathos of the *Song of Roland*, in the sadism of the crusades as in Anselm's Bec or Ailred's Rievaulx. It was an age which saw an intellectual, artistic and spiritual vision such as Europe had not seen for many centuries; but an age in which most of mankind lived in constant fear of famine and disease, and a very high proportion of Europeans were serfs or slaves.

Appendix I

BIBLIOGRAPHICAL NOTE

Most suggestions for further reading are given in the bibliographies and notes to each chapter: special attention is called to the list of sources in Chapter II and the historical atlases in Chapter III. For an interpretation of the period, selective but extremely penetrating, see R. W. Southern, *Making of the Middle Ages* (London, 1953). For a general account, with a fuller narrative than is attempted in this book, see Z. N. Brooke, *A History of Europe, 911–1198* (London, 1938). For reference, the *Cambridge Medieval History* is still valuable, especially vol. v; see also C. W. Previté-Orton, *The Shorter Cambridge Medieval History* (2 vols., Cambridge, 1952), A. Fliche and V. Martin (edd.), *Histoire de l'Église*, vols. VII–XIII.

For a full bibliography: the standard work of L. J. Paetow, *Guide to the Study of Medieval History* (revised edn., New York, 1931) is being brought up to date by G. C. Boyce. There are useful bibliographies in J. Calmette, *Le monde féodal* (nouv. edn. by C. Higounet, Paris, 1951).

Appendix II

CHRONOLOGICAL LISTS

Political Events (including popes, emperors and kings mentioned in the text)

THE PAPACY AND ITALY

962	Coronation of Otto the Great by Pope John XII
963–5	Leo VIII
965–72	John XIII
985–96	John XV
996–9	Gregory V (Otto III's cousin)
999–1003	Sylvester II (Gerbert)
1012–24	Benedict VIII
1016	First Normans arrive in South Italy
1024–32	John XIX
1032–45	Benedict IX
1045–6	(anti-pope) Sylvester 'III'
1045–6	Gregory VI
1046	Synod of Sutri; deposition of Benedict, Sylvester and Gregory
1046–7	Clement II
1048	Damasus II
1049–54	Leo IX (Bruno, bishop of Toul)
1049	Council of Rheims
1057–8	Stephen IX (Frederick of Lorraine)
1059–61	Nicholas II
1059	Papal election decree
1059–85	Robert Guiscard duke of Apulia and Calabria
1061	Roger I invades Sicily
1061–73	Alexander II (Anselm, bishop of Lucca)
1073–85	Gregory VII (Hildebrand)
1075	First decree against Lay Investiture
1080 (crowned 1084)–1100	(anti-pope) Clement 'III'
1088–99	Urban II

383

1095–9	First Crusade
1099–1118	Paschal II
1101	Death of Roger I count of Sicily
1103–54	Roger II count (later king) of Sicily
1119–24	Calixtus II
1122	Concordat of Worms
1123	First Lateran Council
1130	Papal schism
1130–43	Innocent II
1130–8	(anti-pope) Anacletus 'II'
1139	Second Lateran Council
1139	Recognition of Roger the Great as king of Sicily
1145–53	Eugenius III
1147–8	The Second Crusade
1154	Death of Roger the Great, king of Sicily

GERMANY AND THE EMPIRE

936–73	Otto I, the Great
962	Imperial coronation of Otto I
973–83	Otto II
982	Otto II defeated by the Muslims in south Italy
983–1002	Otto III
992–1025	Boleslav the Mighty, duke of Poland
1000	Otto III's pilgrimage to Gnesen and Aachen
1001	St Stephen crowned king of Hungary
1002–24	Henry II
1014	Imperial coronation of Henry II
1024–39	Conrad II
1027	Imperial coronation
1039–56	Henry III
1046	Henry III presides over reform of papacy; imperial coronation
1056–1106	Henry IV
1066	Beginning of Henry's effective rule (minority formally ended 1065)
1073–5	Saxon revolt
1076	Outbreak of conflict with Gregory VII: excommunication of Henry

1077	Meeting of Henry and Gregory at Canossa
	Election of anti-king Rudolf at Forcheim
1080	Excommunication and deposition of Henry confirmed
1081	Death of Rudolf
1084	Henry IV captures Rome: imperial coronation by anti-pope
1091	Rebellion of King Conrad (Henry IV's son) and his allies
1104	Rebellion of Henry (the future Henry V)
1106–25	Henry V
1110–11	Henry V in Italy: imprisonment of pope and imperial coronation
1114	Marriage of Henry V and Matilda, daughter of Henry I of England
1125–37	Lothar III
1127	Conrad (the future Conrad III) proclaims himself (anti-) king
1133	Imperial coronation of Lothar
1136–7	Lothar drives Roger the Great out of Italy
1138–52	Conrad III (never crowned emperor)
1139	Henry the Lion succeeds to Saxony
1152–90	Frederick I, Barbarossa
1155	Imperial coronation of Frederick I

FRANCE

954–86	Lothar
966–96	Richard I, duke of Normandy
986–7	Louis V
987–96	Hugh Capet, the first Capetian king
987–1040	Fulk the Black, count of Anjou
996–1031	Robert II, the 'pious'
996–1026	Richard II, duke of Normandy
1027–35	Robert I, duke of Normandy
1031–60	Henry I
1034–67	Baldwin V, count of Flanders
1035–87	William the Conqueror, duke of Normandy
1040–60	Geoffrey Martel, count of Anjou
1044	Capture of Tours by Geoffrey Martel
1054	Battle of Mortemer
1060–1108	Philip I

1086–1127 William IX, duke of Aquitaine
1092   Marriage of Philip I and Bertrada
1107   Resignation by French king of right of investiture
1108–37 Louis VI
1122–51 Suger, abbot of Saint-Denis
1137–80 Louis VII

ENGLAND, BRITAIN, AND SCANDINAVIA
(Names without titles are of English kings)

959–75   Edgar
973   Coronation of Edgar
975–8   Edward the 'Martyr'
978–1016 Ethelred II
995–1000 Olaf Tryggvason king of Norway
1014   Death of Swein king of Denmark
1015–28 St Olaf king of Norway
1016–35 Cnut (king of Denmark, 1019–35; of Norway from 1028)
1027   Cnut's pilgrimage to Rome
1034–40 Duncan I, king of Scotland
1035–40 Harold I
1040–2   Harthacnut, king of England and Denmark
1042–66 Edward the Confessor
1057   Death of Macbeth, king of Scotland
1058–93 Malcolm III, Canmore, king of Scotland
1063   Defeat and death of Gruffydd ap Llywelyn
1066   Harold II
          Battle of Stamford Bridge: death of Harold Hardrada, king of Norway
          Battle of Hastings
1066–87 William I, the Conqueror
1070–87 Lanfranc, archbishop of Canterbury
1081–1137 Gruffydd ap Cynan, king of Gwynedd
1086   Domesday Book
1087–1100 William II, Rufus
1093–1109 St Anselm archbishop of Canterbury
1100–35 Henry I
1107   Settlement of investiture dispute in England

1115–48   Bernard bishop of St Davids
1124–53   David I, king of Scotland
1135–54   Stephen
1137–70   Owain Gwynedd king of Gwynedd
1139–48   Empress Matilda in England
1154–89   Henry II

SPAIN
(Names without titles are of rulers of León-Castile)

1002   Death of Almanzor, vizier of the caliph of Cordoba
1037–65   Ferdinand I
1072–1109 Alfonso VI
1085   Capture of Toledo
1099   Death of Rodrigo Diaz, the Cid
1104–34   Alfonso I, king of Aragon
1109–26   Queen Urraca
1126–57   Alfonso VII
1137–62   Petronilla queen of Aragon
1139–85   Alfonso Henriques, king of Portugal
1147   Capture of Lisbon
1152   Birth of Ramon, later Alfonso II, king of Aragon

THE BYZANTINE EMPIRE

963–1025   Basil II (effective ruler from 976)
1028–50   Empress Zoe
1034–41   Michael IV
1042–55   Constantine IX
1055–6   Theodora
1057–9   Isaac I Comnenus
1059–67   Constantine X Ducas
1071   Battle of Manzikert
1081–1118 Alexius I Comnenus
1118–43   John II
1143–80   Manuel I

AUTHORS AND BOOKS

c. 920–72	Liudprand of Cremona
c. 945–1003	Gerbert (Pope Sylvester II, 999–1003)
c. 1007–72	St Peter Damian
c. 1010	Decretum of Burchard, bishop of Worms
c. 1010–89	Lanfranc (archbishop of Canterbury, 1070–89)
c. 1033–1109	St Anselm (archbishop of Canterbury, 1093–1109)
c. 1059–78	*Chronographia* of Michael Psellus
c. 1040–1116	Ivo, bishop of Chartres
1077	Close of *Annales* of Lampert of Hersfeld
c. 1079–1142	Peter Abelard
c. 1090–1153	St Bernard of Clairvaux
c. 1090–*c.* 1143	William of Malmesbury
c. 1115–1180	John of Salisbury
c. 1120	*Alexiad* of Anna Comnena
c. 1138	*History of the Kings of Britain* of Geoffrey of Monmouth
c. 1140	Completion of Gratian's *Concordia discordantium canonum*
1141	Close of *Historia ecclesiastica* of Orderic Vitalis
1146	Close of *The two cities* of Otto of Freising

Index

Henry II, king of Germany, emperor, prev. duke of Bavaria, 52, 144, 149, 173–5, 175–80 *pass.*, 202, 220, 248–9, 325; his education, 177; illnesses, 180; and the bishops, 144, 173, 183; his widow, 175

Henry III, king of Germany, emperor, 144, 178–9, 183, 186, 193, 196, 200, 221, 255, 261–2, 272, 275–6, 284, 347, 350; and heretics, 343; and Italy and the papacy, 179, 251–2

Henry IV, king of Germany, emperor, 133–4, 155, 178–88 *pass.*, *esp.* 180ff., 221, 356, 365; and the papacy, 154, 268–9, 272–87, 290, at Canossa, 56, 279–83; and towns, 114–15; coinage, 77; sources for, 11, 23, 187–8

Henry V, king of Germany, emperor, 126–7, 133, 155, 182, 187–91, 197, 205–6; and the papacy, 287–9; his marriage, 92, 206, 233

Henry VI, king of Germany, emperor (1190–7), 190

Henry, count of Champagne, king of Jerusalem, 92

Henry, of Blois, bishop of Winchester (1129–71), 17, 311–13, 323

Henry I, duke of Bavaria, 159, 166

Henry II, the Wrangler, duke of Bavaria, 166–9, 173

Henry IX, the Black, duke of Bavaria, 189, 191

Henry X, the Proud, duke of Bavaria and Saxony, 191–2

Henry XII, the Lion, duke of Bavaria and Saxony, 158, 189, 191–2

Henry of Lausanne, 344

Heresy, heretics, 1, 329–30, 342–5

Herman, bishop of Bamberg, 277

Herman, bishop of Metz, 272

Herman of Salm, Count, anti-king of Germany, 185

Hermits, 170, 260, 294–5, 299, 344

Hersfeld abbey, 11, 244

Hezekiah, king, 144

Hildebrand, *see* Gregory VII

Hildegarde of Bingen, St, 123

Hirsau abbey, 290

Hoel, bishop of Le Mans, 12–13

Hohen-Mölsen, battle of, 185

Hohenstaufen, 189, 190ff., 195

Holland, 87

Holstein, 87–8

Horace, 310, 342, 355

Hospitallers, Knights, 304, 349, 372

Households, royal, 138–41

Hugh, St, abbot of Cluny, 180, 244, 247, 281, 332

Hugh, St, bishop of Lincoln (1186–1200), 337

Hugh the Great, duke of the Franks, 159, 200

Hugh Capet, duke of the Franks, king of France, 59–60, 159, 166, 169, 195–7, 201

Hugh Candidus, Cardinal, 285

Hugh de Champfleuri, bishop of Soissons, chancellor of France, 140

Hugh of Avranches, earl of Chester, 102

Hugh of Die, archbishop of Lyons, 203, 262, 287

Hugh of St Victor, 296

Humanism, 5, 16, 21, 23, 314–15, 319–20

Humbert, cardinal bishop of Silva Candida (d. 1061), 257, 260–1, 263

Hungary, Hungarians, Magyars, 36, 46, 51–4, 57, 63, 65, 130, 143, 162, 172, 175, 179, 210, 284; court of, 155, 348

Hywel the Good (Dda), Welsh prince (d. 949 or 950), 214

Iceland, 46, 48–9, 101, 118; Icelandic, 30

Ignatius Loyola, St, 267

Imphe, 360

Ingelric, 139

Ingulph of Crowland, 231

Innocent II, Pope (Gregory Papareschi), 193, 205, 223, 271, 291–2

Innocent III, Pope (1198–1216), 325

Inquisition, 342

Investiture, lay, 2, 204, 248, 269, 276, 285–91

Ireland, Irish, 48, 55, 61, 210–11, 215, 228–9, 362; languages in, 64; Irish Sea, 215

Irnerius, Master, 326

Isidore, Pseudo- (Forged Decretals), 27, 271, 325

Islam, 1, 36–41, 49–51, 56–7, 60, 361; Muslim armies, 129; art and architecture, 333, 338; castles, 129; coinage, 77–8; fleets, 80; marriage, 122; pirates and trade, 81, 329, 349; and the Crusades, 354, 364–5; and Italy, 167; and Otto I, 164; and Sicily, 220–3, 355; and Spain, 60–1, 80, 145, 228, 355–6, 376–80

Israel, 154

Italy, Italians, 54, 56–7, 60, 106, 112; cities and states of, 41, 60, 81–2, 112, 114, 115ff., 134, 137, 148, 222,

INDEX

Simony, 254 ff.
Slaves, 39–40, 79–81, 105–9, 116–17, 215, 381
Slavonic, 62–3, 65, 162
Slavs, Slavonic countries, 39–40, 50–1, 54, 80, 87, 162, 164, 358
Soissons, St Medard abbey, 28
Solomon, King, 144, 155
Spain, Spaniards, 54, 56, 60–1, 64, 106, 215, 304, 376–80; Christian Spain: and *Song of Roland*, 358 ff.; churches in, 332; coinage, 77; languages in, 63–5; monasteries in, 245, Cistercian, 301; scholars in, 308; Muslim Spain: 31, 36, 38–41; courts in, 228; queen of, *see* Bramimunde; slaves in, 80
Spinning wheel, 83
Stamford Bridge (Yorks.), battle of, 127, 226
Stavanger, 82
Stephen IX, Pope (Frederick of Lorraine), formerly abbot of Monte Cassino, 260, 262–3
Stephen, of Blois, count of Mortain, king of England, 13, 76, 127, 207–8, 233–4, 374, 381; and monasteries, 299
Stephen, St, king of Hungary, 52–3, 172, 175
Stephen, count of Blois, 200
Stephen Harding, St, abbot of Cîteaux, 300
Strathclyde, kingdom of, 210–11
Suetonius, 20
Suger, abbot of Saint-Denis, 22–3, 73–4, 86–7, 126–7, 140, 197, 204–5, 207, 336, 338–40
Suleiman, Sultan of Rum, 353, 368
Sutri, synod of, 179, 251, 255, 266
Swabia, Swabians, 9, 56, 59, 146, 159, 166, 176, 179, 187, 189–91
Sweden, 46–8, 217
Swein, king of Denmark and England (d. 1014), 48, 61, 216–17
Switzerland, 56, 64, 187; monasteries in, 244–5
Sylvester II, Pope, *see* Gerbert
Sylvester III, anti-pope, 251
Syria, 99, 129, 358, 364, 366–8, 372–4, 376; monks in, 239

Tagus, river, 41
Tancred, prince of Antioch, 372
Tancred de Hauteville, 219–20
Technical improvements, 70, 83–4, 89, 130
Teilo, St, 337
Templars, order of Knights, 41, 180, 304, 349, 372

Theobald, abbot of Bec, archbishop of Canterbury (1139–61), 234, 324
Theobald III, count of Blois (d. 1089), 200
Theobald IV, count of Blois and Champagne (d. 1152), 70, 127, 206–7
Theodora, Byzantine empress, 42, 352
Theophanu, queen of Germany, empress, 123, 159, 163, 166, 169
Theophilus, *De diversis artibus*, 82, 340
Theresa, countess of Portugal, 379
Thetford (Norfolk), 110
Thietmar, bishop of Merseburg, 164, 172, 174, 248–9
Thomas, *see* Becket
Thomas Aquinas, St, 296
Thor, 47, 49, 331
Tinchebrai, battle of, 127, 131, 233
Tintern abbey (Monmouthshire), 301
Tirol, 64
Tiron abbey, 118, 299, 344
Tithes, 84, 349
Titian, 117
Toledo, 41, 377–9; emir of, 377
Tostig, earl of Northumbria, 225–6, 320 n.
Toulouse, 208, 323; counts of, 196, 370
Touraine, 198, 200
Tournus, St Philibert's church, 336
Tours, 77, 197–8, 202; church of St Martin, 332–3; council of (1163), 258
Towns, 1, 78–80, 94, 109–18, 187; townsmen and city patriciates, 109–18
Trade, 49–50, 69, 79–82, 111 ff., 211
Transport, 74–5, 110, 112
Trebuchet, 83, 130
Tribur, 154, 184, 279
Trier, archbishop of, 159
Trimalchio, 224, 310
Tripoli, 370, 372
Troubadours, 30–1
Troyes, council of, 287
Tulketh abbey (Lancs.), 299
Turkey, 353
Turks, *see* Seljuk
Turpin, archbishop of Rheims, 361–3
Tuscany, counts of, 60; duke of, 167
Tusculani, 175, 177, 251
Tusculum, counts of, 251
Tweed, river, 214

Ucles, battle of, 379
Ukraine, 50
Urban II, Pope, 182, 204, 285–7, 328, 354, 356, 358, 365–6, 374, 376

402

DATE DUE
